MEDIATING SPORTS DISPUTES:
NATIONAL AND INTERNATIONAL PERSPECTIVES

This publication was realised with the cooperation of

FBO - Nederlandse Federatie van Betaald Voetbal Organisaties
(Netherlands Organisation of Professional Football Clubs)

and

≡⫼ ERNST & YOUNG   and   **HOLLAND VAN GIJZEN**
ADVOCATEN EN NOTARISSEN

Ernst & Young and Holland Van Gijzen
Attorneys at Law and Civil Law Notaries

T.M.C. ASSER INSTITUUT
The Hague

MEDIATING SPORTS DISPUTES:

National and International Perspectives

Ian S. Blackshaw

With a Foreword by

Judge Keba Mbaye

T·M·C·ASSER PRESS

Published by T.M.C.ASSER PRESS
P.O.Box 16163, 2500 BD The Hague, The Netherlands

Sold and distributed in North, Central and South America
by Kluwer Law International,
101, Philip Drive, Norwell MA 02061

In all other countries, sold and distributed
by Kluwer Law International, Distribution Centre,
P.O.Box 322, 3300 AH Dordrecht, The Netherlands

ISBN 90-6704-146-7

T.M.C. Asser Instituut - Institute for Private and Public International Law, International Commercial Arbitration and European Law
Institute Address: R.J. Schimmelpennincklaan 20-22, The Hague, The Netherlands; P.O. Box 30461, 2500 GL The Hague, The Netherlands; Tel.: (31-70)3420300; Fax: (31-70)3420359
Over thirty years, the T.M.C. Asser Institute has developed into a leading scientific research institute in the field of international law. It covers private international law, public international law, including international humanitarian law, the law of the European Union, the law of international commercial arbitration and increasingly, also, international economic law, the law of international commerce and international sports law. Conducting scientific research either fundamental or applied, in the aforementioned domains, is the main activity of the Institute. In addition, the Institute organizes congresses and postgraduate courses, undertakes contract-research and operates its own publishing house. Because of its inter-university background, the Institute often cooperates with Dutch law faculties as well as with various national and foreign institutions. The Institute organizes Asser College Europe, a project in co-operation with East and Central European countries whereby research and educational projects are organized and implemented.

FOREWORD

I am very pleased to welcome this book by Ian Blackshaw, a widely experienced and recognised International Sports Lawyer, on the extra-judicial settlement of sports disputes through mediation.

This process is proving to be an effective alternative form of settling disputes in general and those related to sport in particular. Its growing importance in the sporting arena has been recognised and reflected by the introduction in 1999 of a Mediation Service by the Court of Arbitration for Sport.

As the author points out, mediation can be used successfully in a wide range of sports disputes, including an increasing number of commercial and financial ones. But its effectiveness depends on the willingness of the parties in dispute to compromise and reach creative and amicable solutions in their own interests and also those of sport.

This book will, I am sure, quickly establish itself and prove to be a useful tool for all those wishing to learn about and take full advantage of this modern, flexible and effective way of resolving sports disputes, at the national and international levels, as sport continues to develop and expand globally.

Lausanne, Switzerland
May 2002

Judge Keba Mbaye
President of the International Council of Arbitration for Sport and the Court of Arbitration for Sport

PREFACE

This book is believed to be the first of its kind in its particular field. It reflects the growing interest in and importance of alternative dispute resolution methods for settling sports-related disputes, at the national and international levels, as sport continues to develop significantly as a global social phenomenon and business activity. The use of the term 'mediating' in its title is interpreted in both a strict sense of mediation as a discrete process and technique with its defined aims and special dynamics, as well as in a broader, loser sense of settling disputes in other non-traditional and informal ways, that is, extra-judicially. So, for example, we will also look, *inter alia*, at the process of conciliation, the use of Advisory Opinions and the possibilities of employing a dedicated Sports Ombudsman to resolve sports disputes. We also include the so-called 'Protest Rules' of the International Paralympic Committee.

The international business community has been experimenting with and using for very many years alternative ways of settling amicably and quickly a variety of commercial disputes, not least in the fields of shipping and insurance, with a view to saving precious management resources of time and money and also facilitating the continuity of commercial intercourse and trade with the minimum of interruption and disruption. Over the centuries, the customs and practices of merchants consistently applied and followed around the world have crystallised into a settled and discrete body of Law, which has come to be known as the '*Lex Mercatoria*' (the Law Merchant).

As sport has developed in recent years into a global business, the number of disputes has risen exponentially and the need for alternative forms of dispute resolution has grown significantly too. Sport has also developed its own special characteristics and structures, as well as a distinctive ethos. This, in no small measure, has been a consequence of the revival of the Modern Olympic Games by Baron Pierre de Coubertin in 1896 and the subsequent development, promotion and marketing of them in the last thirty years or so into what has justly been described as 'the greatest sporting show on earth'.

It is perhaps not surprising, therefore, that the recently retired President of the International Olympic Committee, Juan Antonio Samaranch, early on in his presidency saw the need to provide an alternative forum to the courts in which sports related disputes could be fairly, effectively, quickly and relatively inexpensively settled within 'the Olympic Family'. Thus, the Court of Arbitration for Sport (CAS) was born in 1983, with the specific purpose of fulfilling this particular role. Originally, purely an arbitration body, in May1999, a mediation service was added to reflect the growing popularity and success of this form of dispute resolution.

In this book, we will, of course, look at the work of the CAS in general and its mediation service in particular. But we will also look at other international and national bodies B sporting and non-sporting alike B offering mediation and similar sports disputes resolution mechanisms, including the UK Sports Dispute Resolution Panel, the Australian National Sports Dispute Centre and the new FIFA Football Arbitration Tribunal and the UK ADR and CEDR Groups and the US CPR Group respectively.

The book adopts an essentially practical approach to what, in fact, quintessentially, is a practical subject with an end game, but also provides an explanation of the theoretical background to the subject. It also fits in well with the series of books on the Basic Documents of International Sports Organisations published in the last few years by the T.M.C. Asser Instituut, The Hague, The Netherlands, details of which appear in the Select Bibliography. As such, the book also collects together in the Appendices a wide-ranging set of relevant and useful texts and documentation.

Whilst all reasonable care has been taken in the preparation of this book, the author wishes to make it clear that the book is intended to provide a general guide only and should not be taken or relied on as providing any specific or general legal advice on any of the matters discussed, for which the reader should seek specific professional advice. The Law and Practice are stated as of 31 March, 2002 according to the sources available at that date.

As previously mentioned, the settlement of international sports disputes by mediation is an evolving one and is expected to develop still further in the foreseeable future. The emergence of a 'Lex Sportiva' (Sports Law) or, at the least, a 'Lex Specialis' (a Specialised Body of Law) is an exciting prospect too for jurists and practitioners alike.

For all those concerned with the effective and amicable resolution of sports disputes of whatever kind or nature, including sports governing bodies and administrators, marketers, event managers, sponsors, merchandisers, hospitality providers, sports marketing, public relations and advertising agencies, broadcasters, in-house and outside legal advisers, students and researchers, it is the sincere aim and wish of the Author and the Publishers that this book will quickly become their 'Vade Mecum'.

May 2002   Ian Blackshaw
Weybridge, Surrey, United Kingdom

ACKNOWLEDGEMENTS

The author gratefully acknowledges the assistance of a number of people and sports and other organisations in the preparation and production of this book and for their kind permission to reproduce various materials and publications. In particular, my sincere thanks go to Rob Siekmann and Janwillem Soek, International Sports Law Centre at the T.M.C. Asser Institute, The Hague, The Netherlands, for all their enthusiasm, encouragement and support, and Simon Gardiner for his helpful suggestions. Also to Philip van Tongeren and Marjolijn Bastiaans of T.M.C. Asser Press and Dick Blom of the Asser Institute library for all their particular help. My special thanks also go to Judge Keba Mbaye, President of the International Council of Arbitration for Sport and the Court of Arbitration for Sport, and Matthieu Reeb, Acting Secretary General of the Court of Arbitration for Sport (CAS) for respectively writing the Foreword and providing useful research material and information on the CAS. I would also express my sincere thanks to all those who have kindly given permission for the reproduction of articles and other materials. Lastly and by no means least, I would also like to thank my wife, Christine, for acting as an unofficial and unpaid moderator and critic of the book!

Whilst acknowledging all of this assistance, to use the time-honoured phrase, any errors or shortcomings in the book that may remain are, of course, my responsibility alone.

Ian Blackshaw

TABLE OF CONTENTS

LIST OF ACRONYMS

AAA	American Arbitration Association
ACAS	UK Arbitration and Conciliation Advisory Service
ADR	Alternative Dispute Resolution
AFL	Australian Football League
ANZSLA	Australian and New Zealand Sports Law Association
AOC	Australian Olympic Committee
ASA	UK Amateur Swimming Association
ASA	Swiss Arbitration Association
ASC	Australian Sports Commission
ASF	Swiss Football Association
ATF	Arbitration Tribunal for Football
ATF	Swiss Supreme Court Decisions
BAS	Belgian Arbitration Commission for Sport
BBBC	British Boxing Board of Control
BOA	British Olympic Association
BWLA	British Weightlifters Association
CAS	Court of Arbitration for Sport
CCAS	Italian Court of Conciliation and Arbitration for Sport
CCPR	UK Central Council of Physical Recreation
CEDR	Centre for Effective Dispute Resolution
CGCE	Commonwealth Games Council of England
CONI	Italian Olympic Committee
CPR	Center for Public Resources
ECHR	European Convention on Human Rights
EU	European Union
FA	Football Association of England and Wales
FAI	Football Association of Ireland
FEI	International Equestrian Federation
FFV	French Sailing Federation
FIA	International Motor Sport Federation
FIFA	International Federation of Football Associations
FIFPro	International Football Players Union
FILA	International Federation of Associated Wrestling Styles
FIM	International Motorcycling Federation
FINA	International Amateur Swimming Federation
FISA	International Rowing Federation
FPJ	Portuguese Judo Federation
FRBSE	Royal Belgian Equestrian Federation

GNP	Gross National Product
IAAF	International Association of Athletic Federations
IBF	International Badminton Federation
ICAAN	International Corporation for Assigned Names and Numbers
ICAS	International Council of Arbitration for Sport
ICC	International Chamber of Commerce
ICFA	International Court for Football Arbitration
IFs	International Federations
IFCAI	International Federation of Commercial Arbitration Institutions
IIHF	International Ice Hockey Federation
IOC	International Olympic Committee
IPC	International Paralympic Committee
ISFs	International Sports Federations
LCIA	London Court of International Arbitration
LDIP	Swiss Federal Law on Private International Law
LEN	European Swimming League
NAA	National Athletics Association
NBA	National Basketball Association
NGBs	National Governing Bodies
NOCs	National Olympic Committees
NRL	Australian National Rugby League
NSDC	National Sports Dispute Centre
OC	Olympic Charter
OCOG	Olympic Games Organizing Committee
QC	Queen's Counsel
RFU	Rugby Football Union
SDRP	Sports Dispute Resolution Panel
SOCOG	Sydney Organizing Committee for the Olympic Games
TAS	Tribunal Arbitral du Sport (CAS)
UCI	International Cycling Union
UEFA	Union of European Football Associations
UIAA	International Mountaineering and Climbing Federation
UN	United Nations (Organization)
USAW	United States of America Wrestling Association
USOC	United States Olympic Committee
WBC	World Boxing Council
WBO	World Boxing Organization
WIPO	World Intellectual Property Organization

CHAPTER I
GENERAL INTRODUCTION

The Business of Sport

Sport is now big business.

It has developed into a global industry and represents more than 3% of world trade. And it is worth more than 1% of the GNP of the European Union (EU). In the EU alone, two million new jobs have been created directly or indirectly by the Sports Industry.

This phenomenal growth in the value of the Sports Industry is largely due to the increase in the broadcast coverage of sports events and the exponential rise in the fees paid by broadcasters for the corresponding rights. A quarter of the world's population watched the television coverage of the 1998 World Cup Final in Paris and an audience of 3.7 billion watched the opening ceremony of the Millennium Olympic Games in Sydney on 15 September 2000. The broadcast rights to the Sydney Games were sold for a record US$1.3 billion – five times more than those for the 1984 Los Angeles' Games. Whilst, earlier in the summer of 2000, the TV rights to The Premier League in England for the next three seasons were sold by auction for a staggering £1.65 billion.

Increased television coverage has also led to a spectacular rise in the value of sports sponsorship, by national and multinational companies wishing to associate themselves and their products and services with major national and international sports events, such as the Olympic Games. An exclusive global sponsorship package of the Games now costs some US$50 million. It is not surprising, therefore, that the world-wide market for sports sponsorship grew in 1999 by 14% to US$22 billion, whilst spending in Europe alone increased by 16% to US$6.5 billion. And furthermore, the cost of an exclusive sponsorship for three seasons of the English Premier League has increased by more than 40% to £48 million.

The increase in leisure time in the developed world has also played a significant part in the meteoric rise of the Sports Industry with more people participating in and watching sport than ever before. This, in turn, has seen the rise of sports men and women as sports personalities with salaries, especially footballers – we are fast approaching, according to a recent Report on Football Finance by Deloitte & Touche, the age of £100,000 per week footballers – sponsorship and endorsement deals akin to the fabulous incomes of Hollywood 'stars'. In fact, sport is now part of the world-wide entertainment industry.

All of this, combined with the development of the Internet and other new forms of media, including mobile phones, to deliver sports programming, content and information (e.g., the latest cricket score), the value of the Sports Industry is set to grow even further in the future.

The Need for Alternative Dispute Resolution Mechanisms in Sport

With all this money and wealth circulating in sport, winning is now everything – the privilege and satisfaction alone of taking part is passé. And, with the increasing use of performance enhancing drugs by sports persons, it seems to be a case of winning at all costs! For top sports persons, winning means money and riches. So, in line with the old adage, where there is money to be fought over there are likely to be disputes, it is not surprising that sports litigation is also on the increase.

This raises the question, given the special characteristics and structures of sport, well recognised around the world and not least by the EU Commission in Brussels in its evolving Policy on Sport, how best to resolve sports disputes.

In this work, we will examine the possibilities of using, instead of the traditional forms of litigation and arbitration, one of a growing number of alternative forms of dispute resolution, namely, mediation, as a means of settling sports disputes. To put the subject in context and by way of background, we will first take a brief look at the attitude of the courts generally to being involved in sports disputes.

CHAPTER II
THE COURTS AND SPORTS DISPUTES

Generally

Generally speaking, the use of alternative methods of resolving disputes, including arbitration, conciliation and mediation, is not opposed by the Courts.

Indeed, in many jurisdictions around the world, the Courts are very sympathetic and often actively encourage the amicable extra-judicial settlement of disputes of various kinds, not least in the sporting field.

The Position in England

For example, in England, there is a long tradition that the Courts do not generally intervene in sports disputes. They tend to leave matters to be settled by the sports bodies themselves regarding them as being, as Megarry, a former Vice Chancellor of the Chancery Division of the High Court of Justice, put it in the case of McInnes v. Onslow-Fane [1978] 3 All ER 211: 'far better fitted to judge than the courts'.

In similar vein, Lord Denning, the famous English Judge of the last century, expressed the point in the following succinct and typical way in the case of Enderby Town Football Club Ltd v. Football Association Ltd [1971] 1 All ER 215:

'... justice can often be done in domestic tribunals better by a good layman than by a bad lawyer'.

In England, there are also new rules requiring the parties to disputes to attempt to settle their disputes by mediation at an early stage in the litigation process (see next section).

However, the English Courts will intervene, where there has been a breach of the rules of natural justice (Revie v. Football Association [1979] The Times, 19 December 1979) and also in cases of restraint of trade, where livelihoods are at stake (Greig v. Insole [1978] 3 All ER 449).

The position is the same in North America. Let us first take a look at the US and then Canada.

The Position in the US

In the US, sports disputes are regarded as private matters. The attitude of the Courts is well summarised by the Federal District Court in Oregon in the Tonya Harding case in 1994[1] as follows:

> 'The courts should rightly hesitate before intervening in disciplinary hearings held by private associations … Intervention is appropriate only in the most extraordinary circumstances, where the association has clearly breached its own rules, that breach will imminently result in serious and irreparable harm to the plaintiff, and the plaintiff has exhausted all internal remedies. Even then, injunctive relief is limited to correcting the breach of the rules. The court should not intervene in the merits of the underlying dispute'.

Again, on purely sporting issues, such as eligibility to compete in sports events, according to Judge Richard Prosser of the Seventh Circuit in the case of Michels v. United States Olympic Committee:[2]

> '… there can be few less suitable bodies than federal courts for determining the eligibility, or the procedure for determining the eligibility, of athletes …'

US Courts are willing to hear sports disputes only between Sports Bodies in accordance with Federal Law, and in due process and breach of contract cases.

The Position in Canada

In Canada, the Legal System is, in general, based on the English Common Law and the attitude of the Courts to sports disputes is well illustrated by the 1996 case of McCaig v. Canadian Yachting Ass'n & Canadian Olympic Ass'n.[3]

There, the Judge refused to order the Canadian Yachting Association to hold a second regatta for selecting the 'mistral class' sailing team to compete in the 1996 Olympics remarking:

> 'the bodies which heard the appeals were experienced and knowledgeable in the sport of sailing, and fully aware of the selection process. The appeals bodies determined that the selection criteria had been met … [and] *as persons knowledgeable in the sport … I would*

---

[1] *Harding* v. *United States Figure Skating Association* [1994] 851 FSupp 1476 741 F.2d 155, at p 159 (7th Circ. 1994).

[2] *Michels* v. *United States Olympic Committee,* 16 August 1984 Seventh Circuit 741 F.2d 155; 1984 U.S. App. LEXIS 19507.

[3] Case 90-01-96624 [1996] (QB Winnipeg Centre).

be reluctant to substitute my opinion for those who know the sport and knew the nature of the problem' (italics added).

The Position in the European Civil Law Countries

GENERALLY

In the European Civil Law Countries too, the Courts are generally amenable to the parties trying to settle their disputes by arbitration and other extra-judicial methods, and will adjourn proceedings in cases where there is an express contractual requirement to refer disputes to, say, arbitration, to allow this process to be pursued. Only in the event of failure to reach an extra-judicial solution, and in some other very limited cases, will the Courts be prepared to entertain a suit and adjudicate on the dispute.

Also, generally speaking, the Courts will not intervene in sporting disputes, which concern the 'rules of the game' of the sport concerned.

The position in Switzerland provides a good example of these general principles.

SWITZERLAND

Under article 190(2) of the Swiss Federal Code on Private International Law of 18 December 1987 a decision of the CAS, which is treated as an arbitral award under Swiss Law, can only be challenged in the following circumstances:

'a) if a sole arbitrator was designated irregularly or the arbitral tribunal was constituted irregularly;
b) if the arbitral tribunal erroneously held that it had or did not have jurisdiction;
c) if the arbitral tribunal ruled on matters beyond the claims submitted to it or if it failed to rule on one of the claims;
d) if the equality of the parties or their right to be heard in an adversarial proceeding was not respected;
e) if the award is incompatible with Swiss public policy'.

Also, the Swiss Federal Tribunal (the highest Court) has held, as part of a seminal ruling of 15 March 1993 on the juridical nature of awards made by the Court of Arbitration for Sport (CAS), that any judgement, that has as its sole object the application of games rules, is '... in principle, outside a juridical control'. We will return to this important case later in the section on the CAS.

SPAIN

In some jurisdictions, for example, Spain, there is a legal requirement for the parties in dispute to attempt a resolution through conciliation proceedings conducted before a Judge ('acto de conciliacion') before being permitted to proceed with an ordinary legal action before the Courts. In such proceedings, the Judge explores with the parties in dispute the possibilities of their settling their dispute amicably.

ITALY

There is a similar situation in Italy in relation to sports disputes.

CHAPTER III
ALTERNATIVE DISPUTE RESOLUTION (ADR)

Before looking at the pros and cons of using Mediation to settle sports disputes, it would be useful to put the subject of ADR into context and look at what it is and the reasons for its growth and popularity in general.

What is ADR?

GENERALLY

Like many other innovative business practices, ADR originated in the States and has quickly spread around the world. For example, a number of US organisations, including one appropriately called 'JAMS/ENDISPUTE'[4] has been providing an ADR service to individuals and companies for more than 20 years, claiming a settlement rate of 90%.

ADR has been defined by the ADR Group[5], which is based in Bristol and claims to be the UK's first and largest private commercial dispute resolution service, as follows:

'Any process that leads to the resolution of a dispute through the agreement of the parties without the use of a judge or arbitrator'.

The ADR Group was established in 1989 by a group of lawyers, businessmen and professional mediators to provide a 'quick and inexpensive means of resolving disputes without the need to resort to the courts'.

The ADR Group has affiliated offices in the USA, Canada and throughout the EU, and mediates in more than 12,000 cases annually, claiming a 94% settlement rate. The Group offers services in dispute prevention and management and training courses in negotiation and mediation.

The other body providing ADR services in the UK is the 'Centre for Effective Dispute Resolution' (CEDR), which is based in the City of London. CEDR[6] was established one year after the ADR Group in 1990. CEDR also offers training programmes and its members include leading lawyers and law firms and many 'blue chip' companies. CEDR claims an 85% settlement rate.

---

[4] Further information on 'www.jamsadr.com'.
[5] Further information on 'www.adrgroup.co.uk'.
[6] Further information on 'www.cedr.co.uk'.

ADR has grown out of the need to provide parties to a dispute with an alternative to litigation as a means of settling their disputes. Over the years, litigation has come to be regarded, especially by businessmen, as an expensive, inflexible and dilatory method of dispute resolution. Arbitration, originally seen and embraced by the commercial community, as a quicker and less expensive way of settling disputes, is also now regarded as suffering from similar defects.

THE 'WOOLF REFORMS' IN ENGLAND

The English Courts have responded to these complaints by promoting attempts to settle cases in the early stages of the litigation process as part of new reforms of the Rules of Civil Procedure introduced on 26 April 1999 by Lord Woolf. Writing in 'The Times' on 4 April 2000, Frances Gibb, the newspaper's legal editor, noted:

> 'Gladiatorial-style litigation is losing its appeal. In its place, mediation – a conciliatory way to tackle disputes outside the courtroom – is finally taking off. These are the findings of a survey [by "MORI"] into Lord Woolf's shake-up of civil justice. The message one year on is that the reforms have promoted a "cultural shift" towards mediation.'

In fact, to encourage attempts at mediation, the Courts may impose an adverse order for costs on a party refusing to mediate who is considered to have acted unreasonably.

As the Lord Chancellor, Lord Irvine of Lairg, told the CEDR Civil Justice Audit Conference, held in London on 7 April 2000:

> 'There is no doubt that ADR can provide quicker, cheaper and more satisfactory outcomes than traditional litigation. I want to see ADR achieve its full potential'.

It is interesting to note, *en passant*, that, in the 1995 unreported case of Lennox Lewis v. The World Boxing Council and Frank Bruno, the High Court ordered Lewis to try to settle the dispute with Bruno and the WBC over a fight with Mike Tyson, as required by the WBC Rules, by compulsory mediation, which the Judge considered would be 'a perfectly proper independent process of mediation'.

Advantages of ADR

As CEDR, the Centre for Effective Dispute Resolution, another UK provider of ADR services, puts it:

> 'All disputes, whether in difficult business negotiations or full-scale litigation, can become a drain on resources, sapping money, time and management focus, and destroying important commercial relationships'.

ADR addresses these particular issues and, again, according to CEDR, offers the following advantages:
- Speed – ADR processes can be set up quickly and usually last only one or two days.
- Cost Savings – ADR costs a fraction of litigation.
- Confidentiality – ADR is confidential, thus avoiding any unwanted publicity.
- Control and Flexibility – Unlike a court hearing, the parties themselves remain in full control of the ADR process and any settlement agreed. If no settlement is reached, the parties retain their rights to sue. In other words, the ADR process is conducted on a 'without prejudice' basis.
- Commercial focus – The parties' commercial and/or personal interests influence the outcome, thereby making more creative settlements possible.
- Business relations – ADR processes, being closer to business negotiations than adversarial courtroom procedures, can be better preserved or restored.
- Independence – Parties can benefit from rigorous and confidential analysis of their position by a genuinely independent mediator.

ADR can be used in conjunction with litigation and arbitration and in national and international disputes. It can also be used in almost any area of law or business (see later).

But, as the Lord Chancellor, Lord Irvine of Lairg, has also pointed out in the Inaugural Lecture to the Faculty of Mediation and ADR in London on 27 January 1999:

'ADR is not a panacea, nor is it cost-free'.

Indeed, it is worth setting out the text of the complete Lecture, which the reader will, I think, find interesting and informative:

Lord Irvine of Lairg
The UK Lord Chancellor

Inaugural Lecture to the Faculty of Mediation and ADR
Wednesday, 27 January 1999 London

Let me begin with a quotation for everyone who still thinks that the concept of alternatives to combative, court-based, Olympian dispute resolution is today's modishness. It is from *The Charitable Arbitrator*, written in 1688, by the so-called 'Prior of St Pierre', who was evidently no fan of litigation. If you are minded to satirise lawyers in print, a pseudonym may have been then, as now, a shrewd move! He wrote:

'... to be a good mediator you need more than anything patience, common sense, an appropriate manner, and goodwill. You must make yourself liked by both parties, and gain credibility in their minds. To do that, begin by explaining that you are unhappy about the bother, the trouble and the expense that their litigation is causing them. After that, listen patiently to all their complaints. They will not be short, *particularly the first time around.*'

The Academy of Experts has worked hard in recent years to improve the standards of dispute resolution in this country. I am delighted to be here today, to deliver the inaugural lecture of this Faculty of Mediation and ADR. I hope that this lecture – like the Faculty itself – will continue to take forward the essential public debate about ADR.

The modern development of ADR has its origins in the United States of America in the 1970s as a reaction against the high cost and long delays of litigating business disputes. ADR has now come to be recognised internationally as an effective alternative to highly expensive and rigid adversarial systems.

ADR has spread primarily through the influence of the institutions. These include the international arbitration organisations, national and regional arbitration and conciliation centres, national arbitration institutions, professional institutions and national courts. Whilst not dependent on government endorsement, this can provide additional impetus. The International Chamber of Commerce, recognising that the conduct of formal arbitration or litigation may be costly, time consuming, and entail considerable disruption for the parties involved, has always had a procedure for conciliation and two thirds of all ICC arbitration cases are resolved through negotiation before the imposition of an award. Other major international arbitration organisations to offer conciliation services include the American Arbitration Association, the London Court of International Arbitration, the World Intellectual Property Organisation and the International Centre for the Settlement of Investment Disputes. Building on this international framework, most national arbitration centres and organisations now actively promote the use of ADR.

In the UK the Centre for Dispute Resolution (CEDR) was launched with the support of the Confederation of British Industry in 1990 to promote ADR in dispute handling. CEDR promotes ADR, trains and accredits mediators and arranges mediations and they claim a 95 per cent success rate in resolving disputes. The Academy of Experts, although its main purpose is to promote the better use of experts, is also at the forefront in the development of ADR processes and was the first UK body to establish a register of qualified mediators. The British Association of Lawyer Mediators was set up in 1995 with the aim of promoting mediation in the UK and of the role of lawyers in mediation and the maintenance of high professional standards. The City Disputes Panel, was founded in 1994 to settle financial disputes in the financial services industry. Its panellists are dedicated to the resolution of financial disputes through mediation, evaluation, determination and arbitration. Also the use of ADR has been established in the UK in resolving family and divorce disputes, employment disputes, environmental disputes, and community or neighbour-hood disputes.

The Government freely recognises that ADR has a significant part to play in the delivery of civil justice. In Opposition, we advocated the development of alternatives to litigation, including the use of legal aid to fund access to mediation, arbitration and tribunals. Almost four years ago, at the Labour Party Annual Conference of 1995, we drew attention in our Policy Statement to what we considered to be: 'an imbalance between public provision for traditional litigation on the one hand and mediation services on the other'.

We also made it plain that we proposed to use the existing legal aid budget 'to expand access to alternative forms of dispute resolution such as mediation, arbitration and tribunals'. Last year, I approved the LAB's decision to make legal aid available for mediation.

And in Government we have continued to encourage the use of mediation, most notably in the area of family law, where it is a central tenet of divorce law reform. The importance of mediation and ADR in family law cases can scarcely be understated, given the high incidence of family breakdown and the appalling social consequences which result.

Those of you here who heard me deliver the CEDR conference Keynote Address last November will know that I have no doubt whatsoever of the considerable potential benefits which ADR can deliver, for the system of civil justice, and for the individuals and parties who seek redress through that system. I spoke then of cost-effectiveness; of high approval ratings from those who have used mediation or other alternatives; of the wide endorsement and support that so many experienced judges and senior lawyers have for ADR processes. I wholeheartedly share their enthusiasm, and their desire to develop this potential to its fullest extent.

Equally, I recognise that ADR is not dependent on Government endorsement. It is a thriving, autonomous, profitable industry. In his address to the CEDR Conference, Professor Karl Mackie referred to 'a recognition that ADR is a serious market opportunity for professional firms, a significant management tool for companies'.

Private sector companies and individuals are increasingly choosing to investigate alternatives to the courts and arbitration. Institutions such as CEDR itself, and the City Disputes Panel, are reporting rapidly increasing caseloads. It is also significant that much of this new work is international – an affirmation of London's position as the leading centre for international commercial dispute resolution.

The courts have taken their own steps to ensure that the potential benefits of ADR are, at the very least, given ready consideration by the parties before them. A pilot mediation scheme at the Central London County Courts was set up in 1996. Mediations continue to take place regularly. Those who have participated in them generally express a high degree of satisfaction with the process. I wish to pay tribute tonight to the mediators themselves – some of whom have been provided by the Academy of Experts – for their enthusiasm and support for this pioneering scheme.

I am also pleased to commend the introduction of a mediation initiative in the Technology and Construction Court – a new court which I opened last October. It is well recognised that heavy construction cases in particular are suitable for mediation, and we know from experience both in this country – but particularly in other jurisdictions such as Hong Kong, the United States and Australia – that mediation can be a, if not the , most effective way of resolving such disputes, often within the life time of the contract, and at very considerable cost savings to the parties.

The Court of Appeal continues to support ADR actively. Specialist panels of senior, widely experienced lawyers have been set up, to assist in mediating pending appeals. At the setting down stage, the Master of the Rolls now writes to both parties, urging them to consider ADR. Should they decide not to, they are invited to indicate why. This protocol helps, not only to impress upon appellant and respondent that the Court sees ADR as a serious option, but to gather direct empirical information why it is not entertained by some.

The Commercial Court issued a Practice Direction in 1993, stating that judges of the court wished to encourage parties to consider ADR. This was strengthened in a further direction, in 1996, allowing judges to consider whether a case is suitable for ADR at the interlocutory stage, to invite the parties to try it if appropriate, and to arrange early neutral evaluation.

The active support and participation of the judiciary sends a clear message to litigants and their legal representatives. ADR is not some fashionable quirk – it is a valid avenue of settlement, recognised and even promoted by the courts.

Further a discretionary power for judges will come from the new Rule 26.4, which I have approved, part of that tranche of the civil justice reforms which are due to come into effect this April. The new Rule will enable judges, at their own volition, or if requested by both parties, to stay cases they consider may be amenable to some other, more satisfactory form of resolution, such as mediation. Now, within a process driven by the imperative to keep adjournments and delays to a minimum, this Rule is remarkable in recognising that there may actually be a time benefit in delaying full proceedings, to see if quicker, more satisfactory resolution can be brought about by mediation.

This Government's increased focus on the potential benefit of ADR is, to some extent, a recognition of what the market-place is demonstrating. ADR clearly can succeed – it *can* deliver great benefits to parties in dispute. Individuals and companies are increasingly willing to pay for the services of mediators and arbitrators because they believe that they can achieve a more satisfactory resolution to their dispute than they are likely to secure through the full process of the court.

And for parties who have, or want to leave, 'ongoing' commercial relationships, mediation is of particular value.

Let me make this point clearly. I have no doubt whatsoever that ADR has a role – an expanding role – within the civil justice system. But my Government and my Department's support is neither unconditional, nor is it absolute. There are serious and searching questions to be answered about the use of ADR. I believe that anybody who is genuinely committed to the better development of ADR is not only aware of these concerns, but shares my determination to see them addressed fully. It is in the interests of those who provide ADR to try to ensure that their services are professional, governed by universally-recognised competencies; and, above all, to ensure that they provide a service that people do need.

Professor Mackie referred in his speech to a 'gravy boat' trailing in the wake of current ADR opportunities. It is perhaps an expression that lawyers should avoid. Nobody wants to be accused of lapping at that trough. There may indeed be profits to be made from the provision of alternatives to court-based dispute resolution. But I can assure you that this Government will not be suborned into swelling them.

I want to set out my key concerns to you this evening – because I want you – the practitioners, the interested academics and experts, the experienced lawyers – to help us to find the answers. It is particularly appropriate to use the forum of this inaugural address to put these questions unequivocally on record. And I would ask anyone with views on these questions – based on comparative studies, or with the unique insights borne of experience – to pass your thoughts on to me. Your help in this will be of the greatest value.

The central objective of ADR is to encourage and promote the settlement of disputes without the need to start litigation. If that cannot be achieved, ADR still aims to assist in achieving a negotiated settlement before the trial itself starts. To succeed, ADR settlements must be fair and just, to the satisfaction of both parties in dispute. A settlement achieved without trial must be a sound and valid outcome in itself, not a compromised measure deemed by one or the other party to have short-changed them of something a trial would have achieved.

Some unstinting admirers of ADR assert that all disputes are suitable for ADR, and can benefit from it. I doubt that such unlimited enthusiasm does much to help promote wider use of ADR in the long run. Courts have a vital – indispensable – part to play in the resolution of many categories of dispute. It is, at best, naïve to claim that mediation and its alternatives can adequately equate to this role. An obvious example is the establishment of significant judicial precedent – this can arise in any category of case in dispute. Or consider the issues of cases which set the rights of the individual against those of the State. The experience of the United States suggests this is an extremely sensitive area, which must be approached with extreme care.

I think the use of ADR in administrative cases is of necessity limited. There may be more to be gained from the development of the ombudsman system, though I appreciate that ombudsmen are more concerned with the resolution of grievances, than with the resolution of disputes over conflicting rights.

But this is our current position: we do not have sufficient analytical information about ADR to claim, with certainty, that it can be useful in every category of case. We must undertake a comprehensive process of research and consideration, to answer with certainty the question: what kinds of case are suitable for ADR.

Another key area to be addressed in the development of ADR is, who are the beneficiaries? And how do they benefit? In the broadest sense, our civil and criminal reforms are driven by the need to improve access to justice. Widening the means by which everyone can gain a degree of redress for wrongs done, which lives up to expectations. Providing alternatives to the court-based resolution process must clearly be a step in the right direction.

But each step must be taken with an eye to its effect on all players in the system. Improved access to the courts will inevitably increase the burden of the workload in the courts. The introduction of the small claims arbitration scheme in 1985 was hugely popular and successful. Yet the very success of this measure imposed an unexpectedly significant burden on the county courts and the District Judges charged with administering it.

Consider, for example, the impact on the courts of ADR becoming a significantly more active part of proceedings. We would have to be sure that the Court Service actually had the capacity to deliver this substantive new function. And not at the expense of existing procedures, or other reforms – either in funding or time. Advocates of tangible Government support for ADR have argued that the Court Service will eventually benefit, through a reduction in procedural delays, or a saving of judicial time in court. This may prove to be true. But they, and we, must be able to demonstrate that the wider use of ADR in the courts is economically viable. We will need to measure and evaluate these schemes through widespread monitoring, and through pilots. And those who are active in campaigning for an expansion of ADR will need to co-operate fully in this process of assessment.

The principal argument commonly advanced in support of ADR is the potential for cost savings to the parties themselves. But again, this assumption is not straightforward. When cases do settle through ADR – particularly if this is at an early stage of litigation – very substantial cost savings can be realised. But every case which takes the option of attempting some alternative form of dispute resolution incurs an additional element of cost which does not arise if the conventional route is followed. In doing so, both parties are, in essence, taking a speculative gamble – that the investment of additional money in ADR will be rewarded by a successful pre-trial resolution, or at least a shorter case.

And the simple fact is, that some parties will lose the gamble. And ex port facto, they will have wasted time and money on testing the possibility of an alternate resolution – waste which would have been avoided had they chosen to stick to the conventional process of settling their dispute through the courts. The cost of gambling on successful ADR is not borne by the mediators and arbitrators, but by the parties themselves, and by civil justice itself.

Now this is not a matter of trifling costs, or a few days' delay. Those of you with professional or personal experience of ADR will acknowledge that it is often a demanding, skilled and sophisticated process. Proponents of mediation will readily cite statistics relating to saved court time and costs in some of the most complex business disputes. They are perhaps less ready to collate information on the costs arising from failed arbitrations. To ignore these elements – to make no determined attempt to weigh them up against the well-promoted benefits of ADR – is, at best, not balanced.

I don't wish to minimise the less measurable benefits which ADR can bring to parties in dispute. Those who have used it successfully report notably high levels of satisfaction with the actual outcomes achieved, and with the route taken to achieve settlement. ADR can reduce acrimony and aggression which is, regrettably, a common factor in court-based disputes. The benefit of this in mediated family disputes is, I think, very generally accepted.

Last October, speaking at the closing session of the fourth European conference on family law, in Strasbourg, I was pleased to acknowledge the wide international appreciation of the potential of mediation in family cases. I drew attention to the many positive benefits of the family mediation process. In reducing conflict; in encouraging a constructive and forward-looking perspective to the plans and aims of both parties. In securing agreements with a better chance of being adhered to, because they are based on step-by-step decisions reached and accepted by the individuals themselves. In the basic potential for financial savings.

So, we should not ignore the benefit of empowering the parties in less personal, emotional contexts. They too can appreciate a process of settlement which actually leaves them with the conviction that they have received a more truly satisfactory outcome, than that which follows months of stressful, fraught litigation. There is a convincing argument that parties feel more genuine satisfaction from an outcome achieved through a mediated solution.

By definition, practitioners of ADR have the most opportunity to benefit. Those who are able to offer competent and successful ADR and mediation services will find they are part of a burgeoning – and a profitable – new profession.

Lawyers in particular have a great opportunity to increase the range of services they can offer to their clients. That announcement last year from the Legal Aid Board that I referred to – that franchise legal aid will be available for mediation – should also cultivate the interest of many in the legal profession – including perhaps some who have remained sceptical to date.

It is clear that there is much greater awareness and interest in ADR amongst professionals from various disciplines and within the business community than was the case only five years ago or so. One good measure of ADR's growing importance is the number of mediators undergoing institutional training courses, and the fact that the Law Society and other professional bodies are devoting considerable attention to drafting appropriate ethical standards and guidelines for mediators.

New business opportunities will present the legal profession – indeed, all professions whose members are working to develop these alternatives – with considerable challenges. Certainly, compared to the majority of relevant professional organisations, ADR is not governed by any commonly agreed codes of practice, guidelines for training or professional conduct. The degree to which the public – and this Government – will put its faith in ADR, will depend greatly on the level of responsibility which those who wish to practise it can demonstrate.

So I hope that my comments, this evening and elsewhere, have demonstrated my unequivocal support for the better development of ADR. It has already begun to have a significant effect on the overall approach to civil justice. This will continue, and it will expand. My Department has taken active steps in the last year to forge links with leading providers of ADR and mediation services. Their willingness to co-operate with my officials, to offer advice, and to participate in pilot studies in the courts, is greatly appreciated, and augurs well for the future.

It is in our common interest to go forward – but festina lente – we must proceed slowly, on the basis of sound analysis and evaluation. This is a lesson which other jurisdictions have learned at a price. America, which often takes the lead in innovative legal practices, is raising serious questions over the claims made for the efficacy of ADR in the courts there. Professor Hazel Genn's thorough scrutiny of the pilot mediation work carried out in the Central London County Court, suggests that much the same challenges may be levelled at ADR in this country.

Perhaps one of the most alarming findings from Professor Genn's Report was that, throughout the time of the pilot exercise, only five per cent of the parties who might have elected to try mediation, actually did so. Only 5%. This was in spite of concerted efforts to encourage take-up.

In part, of course, this can be attributed to a lack of understanding – both of what mediation is, and of how successful and satisfying it can be for those in dispute. In part, it stemmed from concerns over cost. But we must be careful, and certain, that we are promoting and developing a service which meets a genuine – if undiscovered – need. Providers must take particular care that it is not the other way round.

So I want to emphasise this. We need more, detailed, analytical information, answering the specific concerns which I have touched upon tonight, and others.

Do people know and understand enough about ADR? Can it really be of benefit to a majority of cases? Under what circumstances is it not the right avenue? Can its benefit be had at a reasonable cost to the system as a whole, and the individual parties? What consideration should we give to an element of compulsion?

This last question is particularly difficult. Many supporters of ADR argue strongly that the current low take-up of pilot schemes comes from lack of knowledge of its potential, and a general resistance to change and the unknown. Only with an element of compulsion, they claim, will those whose reluctance is through ignorance be able to make an informed choice. But to some extent, evidence from America suggests that compulsion does not improve settlement rates. Moreover, there are fundamental constitutional issues about the right of the individual to access of justice in the courts. I have no ready answer for you this evening – the only rational answer at this time is that we must scrutinise, consider and take great care before we act.

Very difficult too is the question of costs sanctions if mediation fails. I suggested earlier that ADR adds an extra layer of costs to the litigation process. How should these costs be dealt with by the trial Judge where mediating has failed? Is it right for the Judge simply to award costs, without making an investigation of what actually happened in the mediation? That would involve the breach of a cardinal principle of ADR, its confidentiality. Is it sufficient – as some have suggested   simply to invite the Judge to exercise his own judgement as to whether this is a case in which ADR ought to have been tried? And if he thinks it should have been but it was not, should he express that opinion in his costs award? Should we ask the mediators, when mediation has failed, to indicate how they think the Judge should exercise his discretion with respect to costs? These questions are increasingly being asked – and they need answers.

I also referred earlier to the responsibility of the professional organisations who want to see greater use of ADR in this country. It is not the habit of the Government to constrain the activities of professional bodies. But if we are to support the expenditure of the justice budget on ADR, we will need to be sure that this industry does not become monopolistic or covert. Practitioners must demonstrate a united approach to developing standards of competence and effective training. A regime of self-regulation measurable by the Government, and by the people whom you will be looking to as clients.

ADR is, I believe, entirely consistent with the principle of the better delivery of justice.

I am optimistic about ADR's future place in the system – but I am required to be a sceptic. As Lord Chancellor, I am charged with the responsibility to ensure that what I endorse can deliver – can make a positive contribution to the justice system in total. It is therefore my duty to ask the difficult questions, and to test the answers to the limit.

ADR has many supporters. But they too have a responsibility to proceed with care. ADR is not a panacea, nor is it cost-free. But I do believe that it can play a vital part in the opening of access to justice. But to do so, it must be properly implemented, properly developed and properly regulated. So let us proceed together, with caution, and in the clear light of experience and consideration. For, if ADR can live up to the hopes of its most passionate advocates, we may together bring about one of the most far-reaching, significant – and universally appreciated – reforms to civil justice.

Now let me end on a more lyric note. It is from *The Lover Arbitrator*, written in 1799. Volnay, a lawyer, is asked to arbitrate a separation between husband and wife. He agrees, with this morally uplifting sentiment:

> 'Neither accused nor arbitrator, I'll always be a conciliator, Although a lawyer by profession To reconcile is my obsession. And so my business always ends With no more clients, just more friends'.[7]

What forms of ADR are available?

Forms of ADR

ADR takes various forms and these have been defined, again by the ADR Group, as follows:

Conciliation – The intervention of an independent third party in order to bring the disputing parties together to talk.

Mediation – A voluntary private dispute resolution process in which a neutral person helps the parties to reach a negotiated settlement. The neutral third party would ordinarily play a more pro-active role than in conciliation. The mediator has no power to make any decision or award.

The Mini-Trial – A voluntary non-binding procedure allowing both parties to present their case before senior executives from each party. They would normally do so in the presence of a neutral 'expert' who would assist the parties to settle and who may if necessary give a legal or technical view of the merits of the case or likely litigation outcome. This procedure has been described as being 'structured to reconvert a legal dispute back into a business dispute'. The neutral 'expert' could also be a mediator.

---

[7] The text of this lecture can be found on 'http://www.open.gov.uk/lcd/speeches/1999/27-1-99.htm'.

Neutral Evaluation – The use of a neutral to evaluate the facts and offer an opinion designed to help the parties reach a settlement.

Expert Determination – The last two forms of ADR are, in essence, species of Expert Determination. This is particularly valuable and useful dispute mechanism in cases involving technical issues that need to be resolved. For example, in the sports field, an overrun on the quoted costs in the building or refurbishing of a sports stadium or arena could be quickly settled with the intervention of an independent and suitably qualified expert, whose decision the parties agree to accept as binding on them.

Med-Arb – A blend of mediation and arbitration in which the issues in dispute are identified – but not settled – by the mediator and subsequently determined by an arbitrator in an arbitration proceeding.

Although a popular form of ADR, Michael F. Hoellering, in an interesting overview of Med-Arb, entitled 'Mediation & Arbitration – A Growing Interaction'[8], came to the general conclusion that, although there is an expanding culture that favours combining arbitration with conciliation, each operates best when functioning separately. He also pointed out that:

'... throughout the general business community, appreciation of mediation has now reached the point that it is standard [American Arbitration Association] policy to inform disputants of its availability at the beginning of every arbitration, and to provide a mediation "window" which the parties can take advantage of at any stage of the arbitration process'.

And added by way of example:

'in ... [an] ... arbitrated case, in which liability was determined in a series of interim awards, the chairman of the arbitral tribunal was asked to mediate the damge issue. He did so, successfully, after resigning as chairman of the tribunal'.

---

[8] Dispute Resolution Journal, Spring 1997, at pp. 23-25.

CHAPTER IV
MEDIATION IN GENERAL

Introductory

According to the ADR Group, CEDR, JAMS and other ADR service providers, the most popular form of ADR is Mediation with high success rates.

Mediation is also taking off in the rest of Europe, which, according to Jane Player, head of litigation at the London Law Firm of DLA, 'is more receptive to mediation because on the whole the continent is less adversarial [with] fewer large law firms with strictly litigation departments [and] lawyers [who] do both corporate and litigation'.

Why is Mediation so popular and successful? The ADR Group claims a settlement rate of 94% of the mediation cases it handles; whilst CEDR and JAMS/ENDISPUTE claim success rates of 85% and 90% respectively.

Advantages of Mediation

Mediation enjoys the following main advantages:

Mediation is quick – it can be arranged within days or weeks rather than months or years as in the case of litigation and can also be conducted in a very short time.

It is less expensive – quick settlements save management time and legal costs.

It is confidential – adverse publicity is avoided and unwanted parties, such as competitors or journalists, are not present.

It covers wider issues, interests and needs – underlying issues and hidden agendas are exposed making creative solutions possible to satisfy the needs of all the parties.

It is informal – a common sense and straightforward negotiation results.

It allows the parties to retain control – the parties make the decisions rather than control being handed over to a judge or an arbitrator.

It is entirely 'without prejudice' – the parties have nothing to lose, their rights are not affected by the mediation, thus litigation can be commenced or continued if the mediation fails to produce an agreed settlement.

As Sam Passow, head of research at CEDR, has put it in an a report, entitled, 'Hands across the table', by Kelly Parsons in 'The European Lawyer' in July 2000:

> 'Mediation differs from other alternative dispute resolution methods, such as arbitration, because the outcome or solution is not imposed. It has to be concluded voluntarily by the parties on either side. The mediator facilitates by evaluating the dispute and proposing solutions, but does not make a judgment as happens in an arbitration or independent expert determination. This means the parties own the outcome, it is their problem but also their solution, Therefore they are more likely to get an outcome that they can live with'.

So, what is Mediation?

The Concept of Mediation

Mediation is not a new thing. People have been mediating – that is, trying to reconcile differences between individuals and groups – for thousands of years. The Bible and other ancient texts are full of examples. Indeed, the Roman Catholic Church emerged during the Middle Ages as an effective arbitrator (for which read 'mediator') between Christian sovereigns. As Henry T. King Jr. and Marc A. Le Forestier point out in a fascinating article, entitled 'Papal Arbitration – How the Early Roman Catholic Church Influenced Modern Dispute Resolution':[9]

> 'To avoid war between Christian sovereigns, an arbitrator with inherent authority and a divine commission to do justice was made available … Papal sovereignty permitted secular kings to submit to papal arbitration … Within the framework of the divine right of kings, the pope was a proper arbitrator because he too derived his position from divine right'.

However, in the last twenty years or so, mediation, as a method of settling commercial disputes, has grown in popularity in the business community and has taken on certain features and characteristics.

Many learned books have been written and seminars given on the theory of mediation and the underlying principles of negotiation, as well as manuals published on its practical application to a range of disputes and issues (some of these publications are mentioned in the Select Bibliography).

It is beyond the scope of this work to go into the theory of mediation and the part played by psychology and its practical application in a dispute situation and context. Suffice to say, that mediation, if not a science, is certainly an art, and there is need for mediators to be properly trained in it. Many professional training and accreditation courses are available, and many litigators have taken or are taking

---

[9] Dispute Resolution Journal, Summer 1997, at pp. 74-80.

advantage of them. Mediation is growing as a new legal practice area to satisfy a developing need amongst a wide range of clients.

What is Mediation?

Mediation is a voluntary, non-binding, 'without prejudice' process that uses a neutral third party (mediator) to assist the parties in dispute to reach a mutually agreed settlement without having to resort to a Court. It differs from litigation and arbitration in that a binding decision is not imposed on the parties by a judge or an arbitrator. The main advantage of the mediation process is to permit the parties to work out their own solution to their dispute with the assistance of the mediator.

Mediation is a natural extension of the most common method of resolving disputes, namely, negotiation. However, negotiations either break down or cannot be commenced for a variety of reasons. Mediation gives the parties in dispute the option to start or continue negotiations in a controlled setting. If the mediation is not successful, the parties are still free to go to court or arbitration, so nothing has been lost.

Common Concerns about Mediation Answered

Many people regard agreeing to mediation as an admission of failure. This is not the case. As previously mentioned, negotiations break down for various reasons, and so mediation gives the parties the chance of keeping the negotiations going. The negotiations have not failed until mediation has been attempted.

Putting the dispute in the hands of a mediator does not involve any loss of control by the parties. On the contrary, the control remains with the parties, as the mediator has no authority to render any decision or force any settlement. A settlement is only reached if and when the parties consider that the settlement proposed is fair and reasonable.

Mediation does not create extra work for the parties in dispute. In fact, in the long run, mediation saves time. The parties do have to invest some time and effort in the mediation, but most cases submitted to mediation settle, saving further time. Even in the minority of cases in which mediation does not lead to a settlement, the time spent on the mediation reduces the time needed for preparing for a trial.

Neither does mediation create extra costs. Mediation reduces costs related to litigation through the early settlement of the dispute. It also, as already mentioned, reduces the trial preparation time required in those cases, which do not settle.

Many people shy away from mediation because they think that an opponent will use the mediation to gain more information about their case. In the mediation process, each party is completely in control of the information disclosed. If a party does not wish the other side to know something, they can keep it to themselves or disclose it to the mediator in confidence. However, if the information is something that might persuade the other party to accept a settlement, or is something they will find out about later on through the civil procedural legal process of '*discovery*', there is little, in those particular circumstances, to be lost by freely disclosing that information.

The parties are entirely free to choose the mediator. In fact, they must agree on his or her appointment. Organisations, such as CEDR, that offer mediation services, have a list of trained mediators with details of their qualifications and experience.

Most mediations are quick, lasting a few hours or a few days, but the mediator will continue to work with the parties as long as they wish to continue with the mediation.

It is often said that arbitration rather than replacing litigation tends to lead to litigation. On the other hand, mediation is not just an extra step in the dispute resolution process; it is usually the final step as most cases settle.

As already mentioned, nothing is lost if the mediation is not successful. Because the mediation process is conducted on a '*without prejudice*' basis, the parties are free to go to court or arbitration. It is as if the mediation did not take place. Nothing revealed in the mediation can be used by either party and neither can the mediator be required to give evidence on behalf of either party in any subsequent court or arbitration proceedings.

When is Mediation Appropriate?

Mediation is not suitable for all kinds of disputes and in all circumstances.

Mediation will never work unless the parties are genuinely willing to reach an amicable settlement of their dispute and ready to make compromises in the process.

Equally, not all types of dispute are suitable for mediation (more on this later when we look at the use of mediation for settling sports disputes).

Mediation should be seriously considered by parties in a dispute in the following circumstances:

– When they wish to control the outcome of the dispute rather than leave the decision to a judge or arbitrator.
– When they wish to preserve or restore a business relationship.
– When they wish to settle if they can get acceptable terms from the other side.
– When they wish to save the costs of preparing for a trial which may never take place.
– When they wish to avoid or limit the risks of going to trial.
– When they wish to have a quick settlement, including preferring to settle for less now than perhaps more later.
– When they consider that the legal and/or technical complexities of the case are in danger of eclipsing the economic and commercial realities.
– When they prefer to settle a dispute in private.

- When they feel that an injection of common sense or communication is needed to reach a settlement.
- When they believe that a few hours of concentrated effort is likely to produce an acceptable settlement.

When should a Dispute be referred to Mediation?

A dispute can be referred to mediation at any time, but certain times have been identified by experience as being opportune.

According to the ADR Group, there are four 'windows of opportunity' for referring a dispute to mediation. They may be summarised as follows:

- When each party to a dispute has taken legal advice and before the dispute escalates. A process called a mediated Pre-Litigation Review can be helpful at this stage. The parties meet to decide whether they really wish to litigate and what information they need in order to make an informed decision
- When a writ has been served. Until then the defendant may not recognise the seriousness of the dispute to warrant mediation.
- When discovery has taken place and the parties have a clear idea of the situation.
- When the case is ready for trial and before the parties have incurred the heavy costs of a trial.

However, it is possible to mediate at any stage of a dispute and, if the mediation proposal is refused, there is no reason why it cannot be proposed again at a later stage.

Dispute Management

In deciding whether mediation is suitable in any given dispute, the ADR Group, based on their experience of successful mediation, have developed for the use of lawyers, accountants, claims personnel and business people alike a helpful 'flow diagram', see page 26.

Case analysis

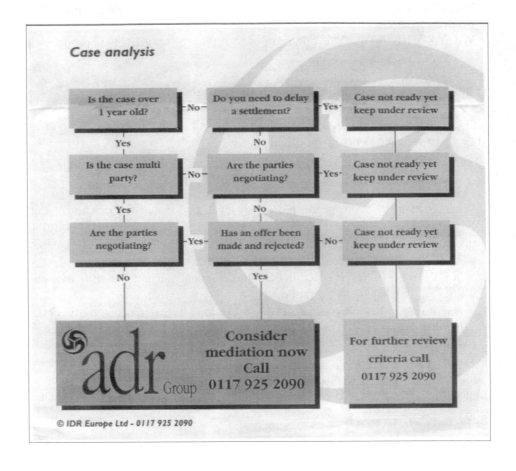

CHAPTER V
MEDIATION IN PRACTICE

Having decided to try to settle a dispute by mediation, how does one go about doing it? Obviously, the first thing is to begin the process.

How to Start a Mediation

In practice, the party interested in mediation contacts one of the mediation service providers, such as the ADR Group or CEDR, and discusses, in complete confidence the nature of the dispute and its suitability for mediation. If the case is considered to be suitable, the next step is to discuss the possibility of mediation with the other side. This is often done through solicitors or the mediation service provider. According to the ADR Group, an indirect suggestion to mediate is often more effective than a direct approach by one of the parties.

If the other side agrees to mediate, the parties need to choose a mediator who is acceptable to them. The mediation service providers maintain lists of qualified mediators with details of their qualifications and experience to help the parties to decide on the most suitable mediator for their particular dispute.

The next stage is to set a date, time and place for the mediation to commence, which is mutually convenient to the parties. This date should be as far ahead as necessary to give the parties the time they need to prepare fully for the mediation.

The parties are asked to sign an Agreement to Mediate (the terms of this Agreement are discussed later) and also provided with notes on how to prepare for the mediation. They are also required to confirm that they have authority to settle the case at the mediation if agreement is reached.

About a week before the date on which the mediation is scheduled to commence, the mediator will call the parties to introduce him/herself and to answer any preliminary questions the parties may have on the mediation.

The next step is to actually mediate.

Before describing how mediation works in practice, it would be useful to identify the sort of qualities that a mediator should possess, also describe the Agreement to Mediate the parties will have to sign before the mediation begins and how to prepare for the mediation.

Qualities required by a Mediator

GENERALLY

Much has been discussed and written on what makes a good and effective mediator. For example, writing as long ago as 1688 – mediation is not, in fact, that new! – the Prior of St. Pierre had this say:

'... to be a good mediator you need more than anything patience, common sense, an appropriate manner, and goodwill. You must make yourself liked by both parties, and gain credibility in their minds. To do that, begin by explaining that you are unhappy about the bother, the trouble and the expense that their litigation is causing them. After that, listen patiently to all their complaints'.

Although, as in the above quotation, a number of general qualities and attributes have been identified, much depends on the nature of the dispute and the context in which it has arisen. In the final analysis, to use a sporting metaphor: it is a question of 'horses for courses'!

PARTICULAR QUALITIES

However, in an insightful article, entitled 'Strategic Considerations in Choosing a Mediator', published by JAMS/ENDISPUTE, an appropriately named Washington DC based provider of mediation and arbitration services, who describe themselves as 'The Resolution Experts', Dr. David S. Ross, an attorney and mediator with 10 years' experience, sets out some of the main considerations in selecting a mediator.

In this article, he points out upfront that 'Because the mediation process is only as effective as the mediator who manages it, choosing the right mediator is critical'.

According to Ross, the most important qualities needed in a mediator are the following:

– Mediation experience;
– Mediation process skills;
– Substantive expertise;
– Reputation for neutrality;
– Creativity;
– Strong inter personal skills; and
– The ability to help parties reach agreements.

He strongly advocates obtaining references on any mediator proposed, pointing out that most mediators provide references on request. He goes further than this, however, and advises that parties should take the time to speak directly to individuals who have used the mediator proposed and obtain their feedback on the mediator's abilities and competence, especially strengths and weaknesses and mediation style.

He also underscores the need for the mediator to have 'substantive expertise' that is, specialist knowledge in the particular field in which the dispute arises. He notes that, as more mediators are specialising in specific substantive areas, parties are able to choose a mediator with both 'substantive expertise' and 'mediation process skills', regarding both as essential qualities.

He also stresses the importance of mediator 'empathy' and defines the ability to 'empathize' as the capacity to 'demonstrate an understanding of the feelings and needs of another person'. And he adds:

'Empathic mediators can build strong, trusting relationships with parties, leading to more open and effective communication ... [which] drives the mediation process, creating opportunities for joint problem solving ...'.

Finally, he addresses the tantalising gender issue: do female mediators have particular advantages over male mediators. Although he ducks the issue, he does seem to imply that, again, it depends on the nature of the dispute and the gender of the parties themselves. But what he does say with more certainty is that if a party is 'highly emotional, then a mediator with strong interpersonal skills should be a priority.' He also adds for good measure that the parties have a common interest in choosing a mediator who makes them 'feel comfortable and confident'. We will return to this and other qualitative issues when we take a look at mediating sports disputes later.

In a fascinating new Book, entitled 'Mediating Dangerously: The Frontiers of Conflict Resolution'[10], Ken Cloke, Director of the Dispute Resolution Center in Santa Monica, California, USA, looks at what it takes to be what he calls a 'dangerously good mediator'. Amongst many pertinent issues, he raises the question: 'do you want to be professional or effective?' And suggest that, on occasions, mediators must let their hair down to gain attention, trust and honest involvement of the disputants. 'The goal here' he says 'is to be authentic, which can only happen if you are seen as truly mediating from the heart'. And poses the question: 'When appropriate, will/can you wear your heart on your sleeve?'

Professor Karl Mackie, the Chief Executive of CEDR, a leading authority on ADR in the UK (he is Professor of ADR at Birmingham University), has also opined on the essential qualities of a good mediator. In an article in the Maritime Review of 1997, he wrote:

'Mediation is the ADR technique which enables the parties to resume, or sometimes to begin, negotiations. The very presence of a mediator changes the underlying dynamic of

---

[10] Published by Jossey-Bass (www.josseybass.com) 2001.

the negotiating process. The mediator brings negotiating, problem-solving and communication skills to the process, deployed from a position of independence and neutrality,
making real progress possible where direct negotiations have stalled'.

So, a good mediator needs to be a skilled negotiator, trouble-shooter and communi-
cator as well.

PROFESSIONALITY OF MEDIATOR

On the subject generally of the qualities required of a mediator, one further
important matter needs to be addressed. That is, the professionality of the mediator.
Mediation is still a relatively new method of dispute resolution and many parties
may be reluctant to try it because they are not sure of the professional status of the
mediator.

To what extent, for example, can the parties rely on the mediator acting impartially and avoiding any conflicts of interest? If the mediator is a lawyer, he will
presumably be bound by the Rules of the Law Society or The Bar Council in
discharging his duties as a mediator. In such a case, if the mediator contravenes
those rules, he or she can be disciplined. But mediators are drawn from a variety of
professions and none. So, to protect the public from an unscrupulous mediator and
ensure high standards amongst mediators, many of the organisations providing
mediation services have anticipated this and issued their own Codes of Conduct.

CODES OF CONDUCT

As a sample, the text of the 'Professional Code of Practice for Solicitors' of the
ADR Group, drawn from the Society of Professionals in Dispute Resolution, is set
out in Appendix I.

As you will see, the ADR Group Professional Code of Practice for Solicitors is
designed to operate in conjunction with any other Professional Code of Conduct
that may be applicable in the circumstances. As all the mediators appointed by the
ADR Group are English Solicitors, they are also subject to The Law Society of
England and Wales' Code of Practice for Civil/Commercial Mediation. In particular, it may be noted that, under article 8 of the ADR Group Code of Practice for
Solicitors, solicitor mediators are required to have Professional Indemnity Cover in
respect of their acting as mediators.

The ADR Group Code of Practice for Solicitors covers such matters as impartiality, confidentiality, conflicts of interest, disclosure of fees and advertising and
promotion. In practice, the rules dealing with potential and actual conflicts of
interest (article 3) are of particular importance.

It is not clear what is the legal status of this Code. It seems to fall into the
category of other self-regulating Codes of Practice. However, if the mediator
contravenes any part of the Code, this will provide support in any claims for 'wilful

misconduct' or 'gross negligence' brought by a party against the mediator under the terms of the 'Mediation Agreement' (see next section).

Standards in mediation have also caught the attention of the European Commission, who are working on a 'Green Paper' (consultation document), which will lay down minimum standards for mediation throughout the European Union. The Paper is expected to be formally published later this year (2002).

ADR Group Mediations are conducted in accordance with a prescribed 'Mediation Procedure' which parties pursuing Mediations under the auspices of the ADR Group are taken to have accepted. The ADR Group Mediation Procedure Rules are reproduced in Appendix II.

Once the parties have agreed to mediate, they need to start the process by signing a Mediation Agreement.

The Agreement to Mediate

Before looking at how to prepare for a mediation and how a typical mediation is conducted and proceeds in practice, we will look at the terms and conditions to be found in the normal standard Agreement to Mediate, often referred to as a 'Model Mediation Agreement', that the parties to a mediation are required to sign before commencing the mediation.

CPR EUROPEAN MODEL MEDIATION AGREEMENT

For the purposes of our review, we will use the Model Mediation Agreement ('Agreement') used in Europe by the CPR Institute for Dispute Resolution ("CPR")[11], based in New York. The full text of this document is set out in Appendix III.

As will be seen, in the clause defining the parties to the Agreement, the mediator is joined by a trainee. This is normal practice, so that future mediators can obtain 'on the job' training, which is now becoming more commonplace in most professions. However, according to the 'Procedure', as mentioned and defined in the following paragraph, the trainee does not take any active part in the mediation process, neither does he charge any fee and may only observe the process if the parties agree.

After defining the nature of the 'Dispute' that has arisen between the parties, the Agreement confirms that the parties have agreed to mediate following the CPR Model Procedure for Mediation of Business Disputes in Europe ('Procedure'), the text of which is set out in Appendix IV, and appoint the mediator. The Procedure is, therefore, incorporated in the Agreement by reference and is fully binding on all the

---

[11] Further information on 'www.cpradr.org'.

parties to the Agreement.

The Agreement then goes on to define the duties and obligations of the parties and the mediator, including the trainee. In particular, all the parties to the Agreement expressly agree to be bound by the Procedure, including the 'without prejudice' and confidentiality provisions set out in para. 9. In these days of litigation management, there is a specific relaxation of the obligation of secrecy to allow the parties to inform the court of 'the schedule and overall status of the mediation for purposes of litigation management'.

As with all confidentiality obligations, the parties are free to disclose things if they all agree to do so, and also are not bound by the confidentiality provisions if required by law or the court to make any disclosures.

To reinforce the 'without prejudice' status of the mediation process, there is a specific obligation on the parties to the dispute not 'to require the mediator to give evidence in any subsequent litigation about the dispute except in the case of an allegation of misconduct during the mediation proceedings'.

The Agreement expressly provides that the mediator, which also includes the trainee, shall not be liable for any act or omission in the mediation, except where such is the result of the mediator's 'own wilful misconduct or gross negligence'.

As time is of the essence in a mediation, there is a declaration by the mediator and the trainee that they do not have any previous commitments which would "significantly" delay the 'expeditious' conduct of the mediation process and neither will they make any such commitments.

Again, consonant with the crucial need for the mediator and the trainee to be entirely neutral (actually referred to as 'neutrals' by JAMS/ENDISPUTE), there are express obligations on the part of the mediator and the trainee to disclose, inter alia, any prior business or professional relationships or 'any other circumstances' which may affect their impartiality

These obligations are supplemented by other ones regarding future relationships, requiring the mediator and the trainee, as well as any other person assisting them in the mediation, not to 'personally' work on any matter for or against any party, regardless of specific subject matter, for six months after the cessation of their services in the mediation. The mediator and the trainee and anyone else affected by this restriction can be released from it with the consent of all the parties. It may be noted, *en passant*, that this restriction amounts to a 'restraint of trade' clause and, as such, must be reasonable in all respects if it is to be legally enforceable.

The Agreement is completed by remuneration and governing law and jurisdiction clauses. The fees and expenses of the mediator are to be shared equally by the parties and no part of them shall accrue to CPR – this provision is designed to protect the independence and integrity of CPR. Again, *en passant*, I would note that the governing law and jurisdiction clause is vague and needs more precision and substance to avoid it being legally unenforceable for uncertainty.

'GROUND RULES OF PROCEEDING'

For the sake of completeness, as the Procedure is also made part of the Model Mediation Agreement, as explained above, one or two comments on its provisions should be made. Perhaps the most important of these provisions are those contained in para. 3, which lay down the so-called 'Ground Rules of Proceeding'.

In particular, the mediation is a voluntary process, depending on the co-operation of the parties, and the mediator does not issue a binding decision.

The Procedure also deals with other practical matters, including what happens in the event that the parties to the dispute fail to agree. In such a case, the mediator is required to discuss with the parties the possibility of their agreeing on another form of ADR to settle their dispute.

In any case, each of the parties is free to withdraw from the mediation at any time on giving written notice to the mediator and the other party or parties.

If the dispute goes to arbitration, the mediator may not be an arbitrator.

How to Prepare for Mediation

The key to success in mediation or, indeed, in any other form of negotiation is to follow the Boy Scouts' Motto and 'Be Prepared!'

In a helpful practical booklet, entitled, 'Making the Most of Mediation', the ADR Group devote a section on how to prepare for mediation. They point out that a common reason for mediation not producing a settlement agreement is that one side or the other has failed to prepare sufficiently for the mediation.

Although preparing for a mediation is less time consuming and expensive than for a court trial or arbitration, mainly because there is no formal presentation of evidence or cross-examination of witnesses, the parties need to be clear about what they wish to achieve and be ready to evaluate settlement offers from the other side.

The ADR Group offers a preparation strategy, which, they claim, will enable parties to go into a mediation with 'confidence'.

This strategy may be summarised as follows:

– Check that you have all the information needed to value your case (e.g., expert reports, counsel's opinion, and medical evidence).
– Make sure that you have authority to settle the case.
– Make sure you know all the facts and what witnesses you can call on if the case goes to trial.
– Determine the particular questions you wish the mediator to ask the other side (mediators only have the power the parties give them)
– Identify and analyse the legal issues.
– Consider what you wish the mediator to have in advance – ideally a two-page summary of the facts and the arguments.

- Decide on your tactics – what you wish to disclose to the other side. If you are not sure of its relevance or value, discuss in confidence with the mediator.
- Consider how best you can use the mediator – not only is the mediator a channel of communication, but also can play devil's advocate, be a problem solver and source of new ideas and approaches.
- Work out a mediation plan and how best you can persuade the other side to your point of view and position.
- Be realistic about what you want and how best to persuade the other side that you are being realistic.
- With this in mind, prepare your opening statement, which should be designed to impress the other side with your grasp of the facts and the strength of your arguments.
- Decide who is to do what, especially if you are represented by a solicitor, but be ready to participate actively in the private meetings.

In other words, as in any kind of negotiation – and mediation essentially is an assisted negotiation – careful preparation, planning and structuring of the process pays dividends.

How Mediation Works in Practice

GETTING STARTED

Most mediations start rather formally.

In the early stages, the parties, who may act alone or with their legal representatives (if one party is legally represented and the other not, the mediator normally encourages the unrepresented party to obtain independent legal advice), tend to argue about the facts of the dispute and state their respective legal positions.

Later on, in the private sessions with the mediator, the mediation usually becomes more informal with the parties discussing settlement options and trading settlement positions back and forth.

THE ROLE OF THE MEDIATOR

The mediator acts as a facilitator to get the parties to open up and discuss matters and try to reach a settlement of their dispute. As one satisfied client of a CEDR organised mediation put it:

'The mediator did a first class job – facilitating the discussion rather than trying to take charge'.

And added for good measure:

'I think we would have regarded the mediation process as productive even if it had not culminated in a settlement'.

The mediator controls the procedural aspects of the mediation, but there are no formal rules of procedure or evidence. In international mediations, the mediator decides on the language in which the mediation is conducted and whether and what documents should be translated.

The mediator holds individual meetings (known in mediation speak as 'caucuses') and joint meetings with the parties and, in consultation with them, fixes the time and place of each session and the agenda. The mediation is to be conducted expeditiously. Only if authorised by the party concerned to do so, does the mediator disclose to the other side anything that is discussed or revealed to the mediator by that party.

Like any kind of negotiation, the mediation is a developing and evolving process and its success depends on the skills of the mediator to bring the parties closer together to try to reach a settlement. As a satisfied client of the ADR Group put it:

'The mediation was principally to discuss quantum and try and resolve the enormous gap between the two sides ... We must say, before it took place we were a little sceptical but we were impressed by the way the negotiations were handled by the mediator ... We feel that we secured a very reasonable settlement when balancing the risks for costs and damages ... We therefore feel that in the sort of case where the parties have reached an impasse and their valuations are poles apart, mediation is worth trying before the last resort of trial'.

However, the mediator does not impose any solution on the parties. But, if they are unable to reach a settlement and, if all the parties and the mediator agree, the mediator will produce for the parties a non-binding written recommendation on settlement terms. The mediator will not attempt to anticipate what a court might decide, but, based on all the circumstances of the particular case, will set out what the mediator would suggest could be appropriate terms on which to settle the dispute.

No formal record or transcript of the mediation proceedings is made – the mediation is conducted on an entirely confidential basis. Only the parties can agree to disclose or publish anything.

Any settlement reached, as a result of the mediation, will not be legally binding on the parties until it has been incorporated in a Settlement Agreement signed by or on behalf of the parties.

GENERAL STEPS IN THE MEDIATION PROCESS

Although each mediation is unique and follows its own particular course, most mediations tend to follow a certain broad general framework, which Professor Karl

Mackie of CEDR has usefully identified as follows:

'1. Preliminary contact between the parties and the mediation organisation (or mediator)
to:
– agree to mediation;
– agree terms of mediation including
    dates, duration, location, representation, legal framework,
    costs documentation;
– agree on a named mediator.

2. Limited, brief written summaries of the case submitted by the parties in advance to:
– inform the mediator;
– focus the parties on the real issues.

3. Initial joint meeting at which:
– the mediator clarifies the process and establishes the ground rules;
– the parties present a summary of their case to each other;
– the issues are clarified.

4. Private, confidential meetings between the mediator and each party separately to:
– examine important issues and needs of each party;
– encourage openness about weaknesses as well as strengths;
– discuss options for settlement.'

THE ROLE OF THE PARTIES IN THE MEDIATION

Although the success or failure of the mediation process largely depends upon the
skills of the mediator, the attitude, co-operation and preparedness of the parties also
play an important part. With this in mind, the ADR Group has issued some guidelines to help parties get the most out of a mediation. They throw further light on the
nature of the mediation process and are worth summarising as follows:

– Ensure that whoever attends the mediation is totally prepared, has authority to
  make decisions, and all who need to attend are present.
– Allocate sufficient time for the mediation: start early and stay as long as it takes.
– Be punctual at sessions: being late may give a wrong impression.
– Your opening statement should deal with the facts of the case and, if the other
  side has gone first, indicate where you agree or disagree with them.
– Stay calm and be realistic.
– Only use emotive language, if you feel genuinely aggrieved about something and
  wish the other side to know it.
– Avoid making your opening demands too specific. For example, if you say 'I will
  only settle for x amount', the other side will stop listening and start thinking why
  you should not get it.

- Keep an open mind throughout. Mediation is a creative process and often reveals possibilities for agreement of which the parties may not be aware.
- Be persistent. Every mediation has a 'low point' when agreement seems unlikely. This is normal and most cases go on to settle. A break for reflection by the parties often helps in such cases.

As previously mentioned, mediation is essentially a negotiation and its success will often depend upon following the so-called '*golden rule of negotiation*', namely:

'Do not go for the last penny – in a good negotiation everybody wins something!'

The Costs of Mediation

One of the attractions of mediation as a dispute resolution method is that, compared with litigation and arbitration, it is cheaper.

In general, the parties to the mediation pay their own mediation costs and expenses (including the costs of any legal representative) and share equally the fees and expenses of the mediator and those of the mediation service provider. The mediation fees are usually in accordance with an 'ad valorem' scale of fees. This is the case of mediations conducted under the auspices of CEDR and SDRP.

However, in some cases the costs may be paid by one party as part of the settlement and, on certain occasions, the party proposing mediation may offer to fund the entire cost of the mediation.

The ADR Group operates a different – more flexible – system of charging for its mediation services as follows. But in all cases, charges by the ADR Group for mediations are always agreed in advance.

For the 'average' case, which takes between 5 and 7 hours, the mediation costs are based on a per party per hour basis. For cases, which may take less time, the ADR Group offers a half-day (3-hour) mediation for a fixed fee.

For relatively low value cases (under £25,000), the ADR Group recommends a 90 minute mediation on what they call a 'Mediated Settlement Day' for a fixed fee.

The ADR Group also – quite enterprisingly – offers telephone mediations for smaller or less complex cases at a lower rate.

The ADR Group also offers a mediated 'Pre-Litigation Review' ('PLR') process, which is designed to help the parties to a dispute to decide whether or not to proceed with litigation. The cost of a PLR is negotiated on a case by case basis.

Finally, the ADR Group can also provide mediations on a daily consultancy basis to resolve disputes within organisations or advise on dispute prevention.

Irrespective of who pays for the mediation, the mediator is always paid by the ADR Group to avoid any suggestion of bias that might arise if the parties or party (as the case may be) pays the mediator direct.

The UK Sports Dispute Resolution Panel, whose activities are described below at p. 94 et seq., has yet to draw up a standard Fee Schedule and Terms and Condi-

tions of Business, operating on an *ad hoc* basis for the time being. Jon Siddall, its
Director, has expressed the current operating position as follows:

> 'In terms of fees, we currently issue a bespoke schedule of fees for each mediation that
> we undertake. It is possible/probable that we may publish an agreed schedule following a
> review by the SDRP Board, although this would not be until May 2002 at the earliest'.

CHAPTER VI
MEDIATION 'ON LINE'

The Rise of the Internet

With the rise and increasing use of the Internet, it is not surprising that mediation 'on line', using video conferencing, is now being offered to parties in dispute. Where? In the States, of course! It will be interesting to see how this method of mediating develops. It would certainly seem to be attractive in international commercial disputes and, with access to the 'world wide web' becoming more widespread and the cost of going 'on line' becoming cheaper and quicker, it must save time and money, both of which are precious commodities as far as business people are concerned.

For further information on the potential of 'Online dispute resolution' (ODR) for settling a wide range of commercial and other disputes, includes sports-related ones, please refer to a recent Book with the intriguing title 'Online Dispute Resolution: Resolving Conflicts in Cyberspace by E. Katsh & J. Rifkin published 2001 by Jossey-Bass London.

In his address to the 2001 Annual Conference of the International Federation of Commercial Arbitration Institutions (IFCAI), William K. Slate II, President and Chief Executive Officer of the American Arbitration Association, focused on the role of 'on line' dispute resolution in the burgeoning field of 'e-commerce'. In his view, 'on line' dispute resolution is to the arbitration field what the ATM card was to the banking and financial industry, and over time more conflicts will migrate to 'on line' methodologies. The following article, entitled 'Online Dispute Resolution: Click here to Settle Your Dispute'[12] is based on Slate's remarks to the IFCAI Conference, which was held in Prague in the Czech Republic:

William K. Slate II
Online Dispute Resolution: Click Here to Settle Your Dispute

The focus of this article is online dispute prevention and resolution in e-commerce. But before looking discretely at arbitration and the world of technology, I think it important to first step back and see 'technology' as a great deal more than just a tool or modern gadget, but as the larger force that is driving the new globalization system-where the world has become increasingly an interwoven place.

---

[12] Dispute Resolution Journal, Nov. 2001/Jan. 2002, at pp. 10-14.

This globalization system is characterized by a single word: the Web! In the words of Thomas Friedman, the author of a compelling book on this subject entitled, *The Lexus and the Olive Tree,* '... *in* the globalization system we reach for the Internet, which is a symbol that we are all increasingly connected and nobody is quite in charge'.

So what then is the essence of globalization driven by technology? James Surowicki, a business columnist, has said: 'It is the notion that innovation replaces tradition. The present – or perhaps the future – replaces the past. Nothing matters so much as what will come *next,* and what will come *next* can only arrive if what is here now gets overturned!'

While this makes the globalization system a terrific place for innovation, it clearly makes it a difficult place to live, since most people prefer some measure of security about the future, as compared to a life lived in almost constant uncertainty.

So, you may well ask, does this globalized economy driven by ever newer and newer technologies have implications, indeed impacts on arbitral institutions and dispute resolution processes? And, the answer is of course – yes – and very much so!

E-Commerce Market

The e-commerce market, in terms of two generic groups, consists of sales between businesses, or B2B, and also sales between businesses and consumers, known as B2C. While the expected growth for both areas is astronomical, I do have some figures on the expected growth in the business-to-business area.

B2B e-commerce transactions worldwide will grow from $145 billion in 1999 to $7.9 trillion in 2004. Over $1.2 trillion of B2B e-commerce sales were made in the year 2000. Over $6.3 trillion of B2B e-commerce sales will occur by 2005. Thus, analysts are predicting that 2B2 e-commerce sales will grow six fold over the next five years. At the same time it is expected that access to the Internet will grow by over 100 million users in the next four years, bringing the total to over 3 50 million users by 2005.

Online Dispute Resolution

In the short span of a couple of years the proliferation and varied uses for online dispute resolution services has exploded. The World Intellectual Property Organization and a handful of other institutional providers are daily resolving Internet domain name disputes through an online arbitration process.

At last count, over 3,000 such cases have been filed. When a party registers a domain name they agree to submit any disputes to the online arbitration process. The fees are kept low for consumers and the process is simple and quick.

In the United States we see parties also using online dispute resolution services, and in the past year no fewer than 12 new entities have emerged providing online dispute resolution options.

And so, for example, there are online business services available today with names such as Cyber-Settle, and Click 'N Settle, where if you have a simple dispute about a number, as in dollars and cents numbers, you can submit it to one of these services which operates on an algorithm based computer program. The parties get up to three opportunities for a 'match' (a meeting of the minds) with the party on the other side. In this exercise each party is offering a figure to the computer. The entire process is technology driven with no human-being involved in the decisional process.

You may ask, who would do that? Well, one of the providers boasts 5,000 cases handled last year and the prediction of at least 10,000 cases in the current year. It is true that the referenced cases are primarily automobile insurance matters where fault or liability is clear and the parties needed simply to agree on a dollar figure. Nonetheless, parties' willingness to use these processes opens the door, and warms up the business community for more possibilities.

On a larger volume scale, SquareTrade, a San Francisco-based online dispute resolution provider (largely for B2C transactions for eBay, an online auction site), reports handling over 40,000 cases involving buyers and sellers worldwide since their launching in February 2000.

The underlying point here is that online dispute resolution is already very much with us. This holds out the specter of 24/7 (24 hours a day, 7 days a week) of online dispute resolution possibilities. I have come to believe that online dispute resolution is to the arbitration field what the ATM card was to the banking and financial industry; a breakthrough in technology that led to around-the-clock, service, accessible from anywhere in the world.

On the arbitration side, the traditional paradigm of a neutral replicating a courtroom has already given way to the resolution of disputes where only a dollar figure is involved and no neutral and no hearing room exist. Interestingly, the providers of algorithmic services have turned anonymity in the decisional process into an advantage-just a computer program that matches numbers.

The business-to-consumer sector of e-commerce is an area in which policymakers in Europe, the U.S., and the rest of the world will look very closely out of an interest in protecting the consumer from the strength and the will of big business.

Commissions in Europe, the U.S., and Japan, including the European Commission, are actively studying the business-to-consumer online area and attempting to establish cross-border standards. The European Commission estimates that annually some 15% of thousands of business-to-consumer online transactions will require some form of alternative dispute resolution methods and the Commission, of course, wants to insure that it is a fair process.

E-Commerce in the B2B Environment

On a much larger business scale, and more consistent with the traditional work of arbitral institutions, is the need to provide services for e-commerce business-tobusiness transactions. In, this context one should consider a variety of business transactions where the Internet is utilized as the medium for exchange.

At a very simplistic level this involves a corporation that offers its goods and services for sale over the Internet and a buyer enters into a contract for the sale and delivery of goods or services on the Web.

Another model involves the growth of so-called B2B vertical, digital market-places, where companies move all of their supply chain operations onto the Internet. In so doing, they join competitors to create an exchange where they buy all of their supplies together online.

One of the first of these so-called vertical exchanges is composed of General Motors, Daimler-Chrysler, and Ford, and is known as Covisint. This joining with other competitors and suppliers uses computers and Web sites to buy and sell goods, trade market information, and run back-office operations, such as inventory control. In the end they predict they will save billions of dollars by moving all these shared purchases onto the Internet.

At last count there were over 300 vertical business-to-business marketplaces buying everything from energy to paper goods to airline parts. The number of business transactions for just one of these B2B marketplace exchanges is in the hundreds of thousands of individual transactions annually. And of course, these online transactions will incur traditional problems, such as late delivery, the condition of goods, and standard breach of contract.

The pertinent question is this: will parties to e-commerce transactions, particularly those involving B2B online markets, want to resolve their problems in court or even by traditional alternative dispute resolution methods such as offline arbitration? The answer is probably no to both questions.

They will want to resolve matters online, have their complaint filed online, their documents *considered* online, their hearing *held* online, their decision *rendered* online, and be serviced by institutional providers.

The speed and volume of transactions of business-to-business online vertical markets will not tolerate inordinate time bumps in the process. It is simply economically too inefficient. Hence, online dispute resolution will be deemed not only highly desirable, but by many, required.

Of course, in the near term complex matters will continue to go offline to the traditional route, but over time more conflicts will migrate to online methodologies.

B2B E-Commerce Survey

We, at the American Arbitration Association, knew from the information just provided that B2B e-commerce is growing rapidly, and that as business relationships change, the nature of disputes might change as well. As a consequence, we determined to ascertain whether or not this shift to e-commerce and the use of e-commerce exchanges is as prevalent as forecasted and, if so, what the impact might be on disputes and how organizations might move to address them. Thus, the AAA conducted a survey by contracting with an independent research firm.

The study was based on 100 interviews with senior executives and corporate counsel of Fortune 1,000 or similar large firms. In total, interviews were conducted with 40 general counsel, 45 CEOs, CFOs and COOS; and 15 CIOs and CTOs. In response to questions regarding the impact of a dispute on their business; two out of three (68%) said that they would be concerned about a B2B dispute with a major supplier. Forty-six percent of the respondents said an e-commerce dispute with a major trading partner would have an impact on their business. While 57% say that managing supply chains online will create new and different types of disputes.

In response to questions concerning their involvement in business-to-business e-commerce most of the respondents or 91% said that they are already involved in B2B e-commerce. Ninety-five percent said that they expect their involvement with B2B e-commerce to grow in the next year and 35 % of those responding said they expected that involvement to grow significantly.

When asked what they saw as major challenges in the B2B e-commerce environment, 91% said they had concerns about issues of integrity and security. Eighty-six percent said they had concerns about the effectiveness of technology and 9% were concerned about cost issues.

In regard to B2B e-commerce dispute management, 51% of those responding say their company incorporates dispute clauses into all contracts. Frankly, I would have thought the number would have been higher. Forty percent say they assigned staff other than the general counsel to manage disputes. Forty-one percent have set guidelines for conducting B2B e-commerce relationships. And finally, 27% assign general counsel to manage these disputes.

When asked what additional business-to-business guidelines were needed, the respondents coalesced around four answers. The one receiving the most answers was 'how to resolve disputes quickly'. This harkens back to my earlier observation that once companies have committed to e-commerce relationships they do not want to have to resort, except where necessary, to traditional conflict management modalities.

Other areas in which survey respondents said additional guidelines are needed were in the area of pricing/billing, confidentiality, and delivery and shipments. The latter item has to do with keeping delivery and shipments going while disputes are promptly resolved.

Is it expected that new types of disputes will emerge' as a result of increased e-commerce? The majority of executives and general counsel say that moving their supply chain online will create new or different types of disputes. They believe that those 'new classes of disputes' would include information-related issues, security/privacy issues, and ordering.

So, in summary with regard to the E-Commerce Readiness Survey, three major points emerged: 1) 95% of those responding expect their company's involvement in B2B e-commerce to increase; 2) however, 64% of those responding said their company does not yet have a plan in place to deal with B2B e-commerce disputes; and 3) almost 70% expressed a felt need for additional guidelines, for e-commerce rules to assist in managing disputes.

E-Commerce Protocol

Related to the felt need for guidelines, the American Arbitration Association with the involvement of a number of major global corporations earlier this year developed an E-Commerce Protocol for the management of online disputes. Ultimately 20 global corporations signed the Protocol as charter signatories.

It is in large measure an e-commerce dispute management 'wake-up call'. The basic idea was to have a vehicle for encouraging businesses to think about the management of disputes in the e-commerce context. The principal components of the Protocol are fairness, continuity of business, clear dispute management policies, a range of options for the parties to avail, and a commitment to the use of technology.

The E-Commerce Protocol was the first step to address fairness and confidence in the integrity of transacting business in the electronic environment. Trust for all parties in this new business medium is critical to its use and success. The Protocol has now been joined by new online rules, which support the Protocol and are specific processes to be followed in conducting dispute resolution online.

And, as every institutional provider would appreciate, it is important to have a specifically trained e-commerce panel of neutrals available, competent in the use of technology to receive, send, and consider legal and business issues online. The AAA has developed a training curriculum and identified a cadre of individuals from our global panel to be a part of a discrete roster of e-commerce arbitrators and mediators.

New Services for e-commerce

Along with rules and processes for handling disputes in B2B e-commerce, new technologies have evolved to help improve the efficiency of dispute resolution and provide information that all participants in the conflict management process can use to help prevent disputes. Some of the most notable new approaches are:

Online Claims Submission – This terminology refers to the capability to permit a claimant to submit claims' directly through the Internet for one type or multiple types of claims, including claims that may still be processed largely offline.

- *Online Algorithmic ADR* – This dispute resolution method utilizes the Internet and an automated set of rules to assist parties in simple disputes to be able to reach agreement without the involvement of mediators or arbitrators.

- *Online Assisted ADR* – This process contemplates combining Internet access and online applications to dispute resolution services such as document sharing, postings, case status, and mediator or arbitrator selection, and instructional exchanges instantly, anytime, anywhere and *in support* of offline, traditional meetings or hearings.

- *Online ADR* – Today this means dispute resolution services that are accomplished completely online, including documents only arbitrations, algorithmic methods, and limited subject matter mediations. All interactions are accomplished through the Internet, through chat rooms, posting boards, and, if necessary, conference calls, and Web-based meetings. This is not an effective method today to do complex cases or full arbitration solutions.

- *Online DRM (Dispute Risk Management)* – This process extends the continuum of dispute resolution (negotiation to litigation) to that of dispute risk management, focusing on: risk assessment, prevention, and containment in addition to dispute resolution. These online services allow all participants in the B2B e-commerce process to actively find and share ways to prevent missed expectations entirely or contain disagreements before they expand into a dispute.

As we continue to build dispute information into conflict management databases, it is inevitable that information will accumulate to assist like parties in avoiding disputes when certain conditions or actions emerge. This knowledge will lead to increased opportunities to engage in dispute avoidance mechanisms, and provide new opportunities to assist organizations in reducing disputes; as well as improve the fairness and integrity in B2B e-commerce.

The Future
As I summarize a few points and look over the horizon to the days ahead, I will attempt to avoid the result that a well-known U.S. law professor noted when he said that 'people who live by crystal balls are destined to eat glass'.

First, for those of us who would like things to remain just the way they are right now-which is all of us – the question must be asked – will there still be traditional arbitrations – only modestly affected by technology? The answer is yes, of course, but I strongly believe there will be a fewer number of those cases with each passing year. Therefore, if one aspires to a long life, you will have to get online.

As business-to-business e-commerce grows there is a significant opportunity for institutions (particularly as contrasted to ad hoc neutrals) to engage B 2B online markets and provide a range of services from the low-tech online claims submission to online assisted methodologies all the way to dispute risk management.

A challenge here for traditional thinkers is to begin to ponder a new paradigm where arbitration and related services are not offline with parties coming to institutions in the traditional way, but where institutions are an integral part of the very technology systems which are enabling the operation of B2B e-commerce to flourish. Here institutions must move quickly in order to remain relevant!

I also believe the growth of arbitration and resolution of international commercial transactions will produce straight-line upward growth in the use of online modalities as the world business communities become more homogeneous in their practices, and interdependent in their dealings across national borders.

The e-commerce world has clearly signaled that national borders, with each ensuing year, will mean less and less in the global marketplace. Indeed, it is my belief that the use of online technology to resolve disputes will grow very quickly to the extent that one year from now we will all be amazed at the exponential use of online options.

Finally, we expect to see in the coming days greater movement in the direction of 'dispute avoidance' before parties ever reach the stage of requiring mediation and arbitration. This is already taking place in the construction field, both domestically and internationally, through the use of 'partnering facilitation' dispute review boards and other holistic approaches to anticipating disputes.

Once again, I think that this will be further facilitated by the use of online competencies where the collection of data about disputes, including the frequency and the nature and circumstances in which they arise, will enable parties to *anticipate* with a greater degree of accuracy pressure points where disputes might arise.

Think about it, with all of the pertinent information online and readily available, parties will be able to resolve more disputes or address potential disputes among themselves. To the extent a third party is needed, this will require a new kind of dispute resolution facilitator who will work with parties in an anticipatory way to avoid disputes and hence utilize well-developed negotiation skills.

Telephone Mediation

Mediation by telephone is also now becoming popular and more use of this medium is being made. As mentioned above, the ADR Group offers a telephone mediation service.

However, face to face discussions are, in my view, more preferable as personal interaction and 'body language' are fundamental elements in the success of any mediation.

Incidentally, it is not unknown for 'hearings' before the CAS to be held by telephone – using conference calls and other 'hook-ups' – where the parties and their representatives (especially their lawyers) are spread across more than one continent or in different hemispheres.

Internet Disputes Mediation

The phenomenal rise in the popularity and use of the internet – not least in relation to sports content – has spawned its own peculiar kinds of disputes and produced a particular kind of mediation for settling them. For example, 'Cybersquatting', which is abusive registration of 'domain names', is subject to a particular form of adjudication process under the auspices of the World Intellectual Property Organisation (WIPO), a specialised agency of the UN, headquartered in Geneva, Switzerland.

Abusive registration of a domain name occurs where:
– a domain name complained of is identical or confusingly similar to a trade mark of another;
– is registered by a party who has no rights or legitimate interest in that domain name;
– and the domain name in question is registered and used in bad faith.

All three conditions must be satisfied for the complainant to succeed.

As to the bad faith requirement, the ICAAN (Internet Corporation for Assigned Names and Numbers) Uniform Domain Name Dispute Resolution Policy provides examples of acts, which prima facie constitute evidence of bad faith.

They are as follows:
– offering to sell the domain name to the trade mark owner or its competitor;
– an attempt to attract for financial gain internet users by creating confusion with the trade mark of another;
– registration of a domain name in order to prevent the trade mark owner from reflecting his trade mark in a corresponding domain name; and
– registration of the domain name in order to disrupt the business of the competitor.

Using the WIPO adjudication procedure, a number of sports disputes have been quickly and effectively settled – not surprisingly over the internet itself!

For example, FIFA successfully challenged the use of its trade mark 'world cup' in 13 domain names by another party, who had used some of the domain names in the address of his website, which not only related to the FIFA event, but also included copyrighted content from FIFA's official website.[13]

---

[13] ISL Marketing AG and The Federation Internationale de Football Association v. J.Y. Chung, Case no: D2000-0034, 3 April 2000.

In addition, the other party contacted FIFA with an offer to sell some of the domain names concerned prior to FIFA filing the complaint. WIPO found bad faith ordered the other party to transfer those domain names to FIFA. However, in the same proceeding, WIPO refused to order the transfer of two competing domain names consisting of the letters 'wc', holding that these would not be unequivocally seen as an abbreviation of the name 'world cup' and were not sufficiently distinctive to constitute a trade mark.

In line with this decision, WIPO disallowed a complaint made by a group of companies involved in the organisation of the Formula One Grand Prix Motor Racing Championship against the use of the domain name 'f1.com', on the grounds that 'f1' was its famous trade mark and an abbreviation of the mark 'Formula 1'. WIPO held that, because the trade mark 'F1' consists of merely of a single letter and a numeral, it was not sufficiently distinctive. In order to claim a monopoly right over the use of the abbreviation 'F1', proof of considerable use of this mark would need to be adduced. Although the complainants were able to establish some reputation in this mark, they were not able to show that its use was so widespread as to be able to claim that any commercial use of it implied a connection with their activities.

On the other hand, a complaint by Jordan, owner of the Formula One motor racing team and proprietor of the registered trade mark 'JORDAN GRAND PRIX', as well as the domain name 'jordangp.com', against the use of the domain name 'jordanf1.com', was upheld by WIPO.[14]

They considered that there was a real danger of confusion in this case, bearing in mind that the name Jordan is well known as being associated with Formula One and both the expressions 'Grand Prix', which forms part of its trade mark, and 'F1' will be associated with motor racing and therefore with Jordan. There was also other evidence of bad faith, including the fact that the other party had offered to sell the offending domain name to Jordan.

Complaints against other sporting domain names, 'uefachampionsleague.com' and 'niketown.com', by UEFA and NIKE Inc. respectively were also successfully and quickly resolved using the WIPO adjudication process.[15]

However, as the above cases illustrate, all claims of 'cybersquatting' on the Net are decided on their own particular facts and merits, in line with the above bad faith criteria.

---

[14] Jordan Grand Prix Ltd. v. Sweeney, Case no: D2000-0233, 11 May 2000.
[15] Union des Associations Europeennes de Football v. Alliance International Media, Case no: D2000-0153, 25 April 2000; NIKE Inc. v. Granger & Associates, Case no: D2000-0108, 2 May 2000.

CHAPTER VII
MEDIATION BY SPORTS BODIES

Introductory

A number of Sports Bodies offer mediation as a means of settling sports disputes – or more correctly 'sports-related' disputes.

We will take a look at the Court of Arbitration for Sport (CAS); the UK Sports Dispute Resolution Panel (SDRP); and the Australian National Sports Dispute Centre (NSDC).

Although not in stricto sensu a mediation body, but in a number of respects close to being one, we will also examine the new Arbitration Tribunal for Football (ATF) being set up by FIFA, the World Governing Body, particularly with reference to the settling of compensation disputes under the new International Transfer Rules.

Again, *en passant*, although not strictly a form of mediation, it is worth mentioning that the International Association of Amateur Athletic Federations (IAAF) offers parties in dispute so-called 'Paper Only' Arbitrations, which are more flexible and designed to speed up the dispute settlement process. They are also cheaper avoiding the costs associated with a hearing. Paras. 9 & 10 of Rule 23 of the IAAF Handbook (Division II Constitution) provide as follows:

'9. Where a matter has been referred to the Arbitrators under Rule 21.3 then, in place of an oral hearing, an athlete may request that the Arbitrators reach their decision solely on the basis of written submissions. Details of the applicable procedures are to be found in the "IAAF Arbitration Guidelines".

10. The Arbitrators shall have the power to decide all matters of fact and law, as well as the powers specified in the IAAF Arbitration Guidelines'.

The IAAF Arbitration Guidelines contain the following provisions on 'Paper Only' Arbitrations:

'1. Where a "paper only" arbitration has been requested, the following additional procedures will apply:

a) Within 28 days of the reference, the athlete shall prepare a full statement of his case, attaching any necessary documentation in support.

b) Within 21 days of the receipt by the IAAF of the athlete's statement, the IAAF shall prepare a statement in response, a copy of which shall be delivered to the athlete's Member federation.

c) The athlete shall have the opportunity to submit a reply to the IAAF's statement of response. Such reply shall be delivered to the IAAF within 10 days of the delivery of the statement in response. If it so chooses, the IAAF may submit a reply.

d) The IAAF may request that any member federation or Area Group Association submits a statement for consideration by the arbitrators. This statement shall be submitted within 21 days of the request of the General Secretary. A copy of the statement shall be given to the athlete by his member federation. The athlete shall be given the opportunity to reply. The reply shall be submitted within 10 days of the receipt of the statement by the athlete.

e) The general secretary may, in his absolute discretion, lengthen or shorten the time available for the service of any of these documents.

f) Once all statements and replies have been received by the IAAF, they shall be dispatched to the arbitrators forthwith. The arbitrators shall consider the evidence and may request any further information necessary from the athlete, the IAAF, the Area Group Association or member federation involved.

g) The arbitrators shall reach their decision within 28 days. On any given issue, the decision of a majority of the arbitrators shall be regarded as the decision of the Arbitration Panel. No minority opinion shall be delivered. The decision shall be communicated to the General Secretary who shall inform all relevant parties forthwith.

h) The decision shall be final and binding on all parties and upon all IAAF Members. The arbitrators shall not be obliged to give any reason for their decision.

i) The decision shall have immediate effect. The fact of referral and the arbitrators shall be reported in the next notice being sent by the General Secretary to all members of the IAAF'.

The Court of Arbitration for Sport (CAS)

GENERAL INTRODUCTION

The CAS is an arbitration body created by the International Olympic Committee (IOC) in 1983. Also known by its French acronym 'TAS' (Tribunal Arbitral du Sport), it is based in Lausanne, Switzerland, and has two permanent outposts in Sydney, Australia, and New York, USA.[16] During the Olympic Games, it operates an AD Hoc Division, which was set up on 28 September 1995.[17]

The CAS has a minimum of 150 arbitrators from 37 countries, who are specialists in arbitration and sports law.[18] They are appointed for 4-year renewable terms and must sign a 'letter of independence'. The CAS also has a permanent President,

---

[16] Further information from the CAS website: 'www.cas-tas.org'.

[17] See 'Why does sport need its own jurisdiction?', by Professor Heiko T. van Staveren at pp. 229-232 in 'International Law and The Hague's 750ᵗʰ Anniversary' (1999) published by T.M.C. Asser Instituut, The Hague, The Netherlands; 'The Role of the Court of Arbitration for Sport' by Matthieu Reeb, ibid., at pp. 233-238; and 'The Court of Arbitration for Sport and the General Process of International Sports Law', by Professor James A.R. Nafziger, ibid., at pp. 239-250. See also, M. Reeb, 'The Court of Arbitration for Sport' (2000) 3(4) Sports Law Bulletin at p. 10.

[18] At the time of writing, there are 186.

who is Judge Keba Mbaye of Senegal, a former member of the International Court of Justice at The Hague. And he has written the Foreword to this book.

CAS arbitrators are not generally obliged to follow earlier decisions or obey the sacred Common Law principle of '*stare decisis*' (binding precedent).[19] However, in the interests of comity and legal certainty they are usually prepared to do so.

The CAS is dedicated to hearing and settling any disputes directly or indirectly relating to sport, including commercial issues, for example, a dispute over a sponsorship contract. Any natural person, for example, an athlete, or legal person, for example, a sports association or a company, may bring a case before the CAS. The parties must agree to do so in writing.

It should also be mentioned that the working languages of the CAS are French and English and, in the absence of agreement between the parties, the CAS shall select one of the two languages as the language of the proceedings. The parties can choose another language provided the Court agrees, in which case the CAS may order the parties to pay all or part of the translation costs (Rule 29 of the CAS Procedural Rules).

The CAS also offers non-binding Advisory Opinions on potential disputes similar to the concept of 'expert determination' in the commercial world. The CAS Code of Sports-related Arbitration including the Rules governing these Advisory Opinions, the latter which, in a number of respects, are akin to Mediation, are set out in Appendix V.

Also, by way of example, we reproduce the following article entitled '*You don't win silver – you miss the gold*' by Janwillem Soek[20] on the CAS Advisory Opinion delivered by Professor Richard H. McLaren of Canada prior to the 2000 Sydney Summer Games in the case of the controversial FINA 'full body' swimsuits:

Janwillem Soek
You don't win silver – you miss the gold

Introduction
After the Olympic Games of Atlanta in 1996 swimwear manufacturer Speedo started the development of a fibre for a new generation of swimsuits. Scientists had discovered that the miniscule ridges in the skins of sharks greatly reduced turbulence in the water caused by the shark's movements. In order to attain the same effect at swimming competitions the fibre of the new swimsuits had to bear a strong resemblance to sharkskin. Developing the fibre took two years. Not only was a swimsuit designed, made of the new fibre, but the suit was also divided into different panels connecting the muscle groups used in swimming. The

---

[19] See case of UCI v. J. 7 NCB, CAS 97/176 Award of 28 August 1998, p 14.
[20] September 2000 issue of *The International Sports Law Journal* at pp. 15-18.

seams between the panels acted like tendons. The fabric was highly elastic and felt like a second skin. It was a revolutionary swimsuit with which, according to the manufacturer, the top times in swimming could be set at even sharper levels. Not only would the new suit enable the swimmer to develop more speed, increase his endurance, reduce his resistance in the water, but the new suit would moreover give the swimmer more buoyancy. Competitor Adidas had, meanwhile, also developed a swimsuit bearing a strong resemblance to Speedo's. On 8 October 1999 the FINA Bureau in Kuwait dedicated a long meeting to the new swimsuits.

Representatives of both manufacturers submitted reports of their research, design and other aspects of the 'full body' swimsuits to FINA and they supplied background information concerning the technology behind the design of the 'full body' swimsuits, accompanied by video animations. The Bureaus arrived at the conclusion that the use of the 'long john' swimsuits would not be in violation of existing FINA rules and approved the suits. It was left up to the swimmers whether they would actually use them.

On 16 March 2000 the new Speedo suit was introduced in Athens. The President of Speedo International told reporters of the British newspaper 'The Independent' at that occasion: 'independent testing shows this to be the fastest suit ever made. Some of our team swimmers have shown time savings enough to make a difference between winning and losing a race'. The shark suit was not only revolutionary, it was controversial right from the time of its introduction. British swimmers in March assumed that they would not be able to appear in shark suits at the Olympics, because the team was sponsored by Adidas. This manufacturer insisted that the swimmers would use its suits. Adidas had not yet launched its new swimsuit onto the market in mid-March. Various Australian top swimmers, among who Ian Thorpe, were under contract with Adidas and could not dispose of a 'long john'. John Coates, chairman of the Australian Olympic Committee (AOC) and member of the organizing committee SOCOG feared not only unfair competition, as the suit could not be worn by everybody, but also that a possible world record would not be recognized if it had been set using a banned swimsuit. Coates' fear was based on his judgement that the FINA had misinterpreted its own rules. The AOC had to select the Australian swimmers for participation in the Olympic Games on the basis of the results during the Open Australian championships from 13 to 20 May. It was of great interest to the AOC to know whether the use of the bodysuits really fell within the rules of the FINA. Could the AOC nominate swimmers, who would wear the bodysuits at the selection rounds, for the Olympics? In the background the question whether the results of the Australian swimmers at the Olympics, achieved by using the new swimsuits, might not become the subject of legal claims at a later stage also played a part.

Barely a week after the introduction of the Speedo suit the Australian swimmers O'Neil, Dunn and Klim said they considered not using the suits, because they feared that wearing them could perhaps cost them medals. The AOC requested an advisory opinion from the CAS in this controversial matter and submitted five questions to it for answering:

1. is wearing the new swimsuit not a violation of FINA rules because it helps swimmers with their speed, buoyancy and endurance during competitions?
2. is the FINA competent to approve the use of any device which could be in violation of FINA Swimming Rules (SW) 10.7?
3. if the FINA is so competent, what then is the effect of such approval?
4. if the FINA is not so competent, what then is the effect of the results achieved by swimmers in the new swimsuits?
5. did the FINA actually validly consent to the wearing of the new suits?

The advisory opinion
The President of the CAS, Judge Keba Mbaye, appointed Canadian Professor and solicitor Richard H. McLaren arbitrator. According to R61 of the CAS Procedural Rules it is at the discretion of the CAS President to decide whether a request for an advisory opinion will be granted. The Article also stipulates that the President has the right 'to formulate, in his own discretion, the questions submitted to the Panel ...'. Mbaye deemed it necessary to rephrase the AOC's questions. McLaren was presented with the following question:

1. may the swimsuits at issue be considered a 'device' in the sense of SW 10.7?
2. did the FINA approve the use of the swimsuits?
3. is the FINA competent to approve the use of swimsuits that are possibly in violation of SW 10.7?
4. if so, what is the effect of such approval?
5. if not, what is the effect on the results achieved by swimmers in the new swimsuits?

The AOC did not entirely agree with this rephrasal and requested the President of the CAS to include a question 1A: in case the answer to question 1 is in the affirmative, do the bodysuits contribute to the speed, the buoyancy and the endurance of the swimmer during a competition? The President denied the request, being of the opinion that question 1A was already included in his phrasing of question 1.

May the swimsuits at issue be considered a 'device' in the sense of SW 10.7?
This rule states:
'No swimmer shall be permitted to use or wear any device that may aid his

speed, buoyancy or endurance during a competition (such as webbed gloves, flippers, fins, etc.) …'

McLaren was of the opinion that this question was not for the CAS to be answered. Pursuant to Constitution C 14.11.2 and C 14.11.3[21] it was the task of the FINA Bureau to interpret the rule. The FINA had declared to the CAS that SW 10.7 'has never been interpreted as being applicable to swimming suits and certainly not to their dimensions and material. It had always been interpreted as concerning other elements ('devices') which are supplemental'. The question remained unanswered for reasons, which would be entered into in the answer to question 3.

Did the FINA approve the use of the swimsuits?
The Bureau had reviewed the shark suit within the framework of rules concerning the 'costume' of General Rules GR6[22] and not in the framework of the competition rules of SW 10.7. The Bureau _ as the only institution entitled thereto under the FINA Constitution _ had declared on the basis of the information submitted to it that using the suit would not be in violation of FINA rules. C 14.11.3 endowed the Bureau with the competence to review the swimsuits within the framework of the FINA rules. 'Once again under rule C14.11.3, the effect of reviewing the full bodysuits and determining them to be compliant with the Rules has caused FINA *in effect* to have granted its approval to the full bodysuit', McLaren found. The Bureau had the wide-ranging competence on the basis of C 14.11.3 to promulgate a rule with regard to the swimsuits but has chosen not to make use of this competence. Now that the Bureau failed to make us of its legislative competence the review of the swimsuits did not need to be submitted to the next congress for confirmation. The arbitrator found that the answer to question 2 should be in the affirmative.

---

[21] C 14 - Bureau
C 14.11 - Rights & Duties of the Bureau shall include the following:
C 14.11.2 - to interpret and enforce the Rules of FINA, subject to confirmation at the next meeting of the Congress,
C 14.11.3 - to decide and take action on any matter pertaining to the affairs of FINA, subject to confirmation at the next meeting of the Congress.
[22] GR 6- Costumes
GR 6.1- The costumes of all competitors shall be in good rnoral taste and suitable for the individual sports discipline.
GR 6.2 - All costumes shall be non-transparent.
GR 6.3 - The referee of a competition has the authority to exclude any competitor whose costume does not comply with this Rule.

Is the FINA competent to approve the use of swimsuits that are possibly in violation of SW 10.7?

The AOC wished for the CAS to give an advisory opinion concerning the proper interpretation of SW 10.7 and the application of that provision to the swimsuits. This should not be considered odd, given the provisions of R60 of the CAS Procedural Rules. Pursuant to that provision an OCOG, such as, in the present case, the AOC, may 'request an advisory opinion from the CAS about any legal issue with respect to the practice or development of sports or any activity related to sports'. So what did McLaren find? He found that 'this question (question 3) presupposes an issue as to the scope of the review to be made by CAS as the quasi-judicial authority overseeing disputes'. This is where the advisory opinion starts going astray. McLaren unjustifiably speaks of 'the scope of the review' and 'disputes'. There was no dispute in the case at hand. Once having arrived at the wrong station, the next few cannot be right either. McLaren treats the request for an advisory opinion as if it concerns a dispute between the AOC and the FINA. He peruses the FINA rules for the mandate the FINA extends to the CAS in the case of disputes. He stumbles on rules C 10.8.3 and C 21 of the FINA Constitution, both concerning 'disputes'[23] and stipulating under which circumstances the CAS may be called in as arbitrator. For proper understanding it should be mentioned that C 10.8.3 is part of C 10, the subject of which is 'Sanctions'. According to C 10.8.3 judgments of, among others, the Bureau, which contain sanctions, may be appealed before the CAS. The AOC's request is hard to reconcile with the wording of C 10.8.3. Even harder is the link McLaren finds between C 21 and the AOC's request. Not only does that provision make mention of 'disputes', which are not at issue in the present case, it also speaks of 'disputes' between the FINA and its members and between the members themselves. The AOC cannot be considered a member of the FINA. Although he is playing his part supported by the wrong props, McLaren refuses to acknowledge it; he considers: 'for the purposes of this opinion it is presumed that the scope of the review discussed is in connection with a dispute arising under these two constitutional provisions, which dispute is before CAS for consideration'. Even though R60 of the CAS Procedural Rules gives the arbitrator every freedom to

---

[23] C 10.8.3 An appeal against a decision by the Bureau or the FINA Doping Panel shall be referred to the Court of Arbitration for Sports ('CAS'), Lausanne, Switzerland, within the same terms as in C 10.8.2. The only appeal from a decision of the Doping Panel shall be to the CAS. The CAS shall also have exclusive jurisdiction over interlocutory orders and no other court or tribunal shall have authority to issue interlocutory orders relating to matters before the CAS. Decisions by the CAS shall be final and binding, subject only to the provisions of the Swiss Private International Law Act, section 190.
C 21 - Disputes between FINA and any of its Members or individual members of its Members or between Members of FINA which are not resolved by a FINA Bureau decision may be referred for arbitration by either of the involved parties to the Court of Arbitration for Sports (CAS), Lausanne. Any decision made by the Arbitration Court shall be final and binding on the parties concerned.

advise on every possible legal issue concerning the practice or development of sports, McLaren stubbornly maintains that the case at hand concerns a 'dispute', which is being appealed. 'CAS is the international adjudication body to whose jurisdiction FINA has attorned its disputes if they remain unresolved following exhaustion of FINA's procedures. The CAS conducts its appeals proceedings under the Code.' R58 of the CAS Procedural Rules,[24] forming part of Section C 'Special provisions applicable to the appeal arbitration proceedings', is pointed at.

The arbitrator worked from the assumption that the CAS 'had discrete and limited review of IF decisions on certain specific grounds'. He went on to formulate the respective 'specific grounds' and proceeded to evaluate whether these had been met in the present case. The CAS can be petitioned to adjudge disputes concerning the interpretation of the Constitution, but this is not what is at stake in the present proceedings.

'The request for this opinion does not deal with the constitution of FINA. Therefore, there is no reason for a review of the decision of the Bureau by the CAS on the grounds that it would be interpreting the constating (*sic!*) instrument, the constitution.'

When an athlete violates the rules adopted or promulgated by a sports organization, the CAS may be petitioned when an institution has given a final judgment about such violation in disciplinary appellate proceedings. Such disciplinary proceedings have not taken place prior to the present request.

'The request for this opinion does not deal with the review of powers exercised over a particular individual pursuant to an IF's contractual arrangements which affect their (*sic!*) personality or property. Therefore, there is no basis for CAS to review the bodysuit decision of the Bureau on this jurisprudential theory.'

The grounds McLaren reviews that could enable the CAS to exercise jurisdiction are already placed in the incorrect framework of review of decisions of international federations. Now he finds that this situation does not occur in the present case. This conclusion should have put him on the right track; i.e. that the whole investigation into the grounds for 'discrete and limited review of IF decisions' should not have taken place.

SW 10.7 is a provision in Part III of the 'Swimming Rules'. The provisions of Part III describe how swimming competitions should be run, as opposed to the 'General Rules', which are applicable to all types of swimming sports, including diving, water polo, synchronized swimming, etc. General Rule GR6 is of the

---

[24] R58 The Panel shall decide the dispute according to the applicable regulations and the rules of law chosen by the panties or, in the absence of such a choice, according to the law of the country in which the federation, association or sports body is domiciled.

same character. The decision of the FINA Bureau concerning the shark suits was based on competition rules.

'Therefore, this Advisory Opinion is in connection with the rules of the sport as it is to be played; or, the basis upon which the swimming competition is to be held. Such rules are established by contract. They do not have the effect of defining the constitution, or, being used to affect directly individual rights of personality or property. They are the rules of the game sometimes referred to as the 'game rule'. There does not appear to be a consistent practice throughout the world in dealing with the review by judges of the 'game rule'.

Had the decision of the Bureau violated the 'general principles of law or natural justice', the CAS would have had grounds for review of the decision, but in the present request such a claim was never presented. Therefore, the CAS is also unable to take any action on the basis of this third 'threshold value'. Nor has the CAS looked into this option of its own accord.

'While this would be a basis for a review by the CAS of the Bureau decision there is no indication that the Bureau acted without good faith in making its decision or otherwise acted contrary to general principles of contract law.'

According to McLaren, the CAS may also review the case if lack of procedural reasonableness and fairness may be shown. In this case, however, there is no indication whatsoever to suspect that the Bureau has acted in violation of the procedures when it took its decision of 8 October 1999.

'There would be no basis for reviewing the Bureau decision on this ground.'

There is another reason for review of a decision. If the decision of an IF is so unreasonable that no institution competent to take decisions could reasonably have arrived at it, the decision may be reviewed. But this was not the case here either.

'The Bureau in this matter is the appropriate body of the FINA who is in the best position to decide on the interpretation of the game rules and the application of them to the development of the bodysuit. In the Bureau's decision there are no sanctions arising from the application of the rules. Applying the above principles, it can be said that the Bureau in making its decision on the bodysuit, acted within the limits (i.e. did not act unreasonably) of the rules, which have been laid down by taking into consideration only those matters to which the rules applied. Consequently, CAS has no basis for a review of the FINA bureau decision on these grounds.'

The CAS was unable to answer the question whether the FINA, in approving the use of the new swimsuits, had acted in violation of SW 10.7.

'There is no review by CAS of a game rule in these circumstances. Therefore, it is not for CAS in the circumstances of this Advisory Opinion to offer an opinion on whether the bodysuit may contravene Rule SW 10.7. The Bureau decision had the effect of approving the bodysuit since in its view the suit did not contravene any rule.'

The arbitrator found question 4 to be no longer relevant and given the analysis he delivered in his answer to question 3, it has become unnecessary, in his opinion, to answer question 5.

The reaction to the advisory opinion

The advisory opinion of the CAS received worldwide attention. Headlines appeared in the papers reading 'Court supports FINA ruling', 'Court accepts FINA ruling on full-length bodysuits', 'Sportgericht erlaubt "Haihaut"'. Not everybody was convinced, however. 'Far from clarifying the legality of the Fastskin neck-to-ankle swimsuits, a Court of Arbitration for Sports ruling has further muddled the issue', The Independent cited John Coates on 2 May. In this the chairman of the AOC was absolutely right; the arbitrator had been unable to enter into the content of the decision of the FINA Bureau, because that decision concerned the interpretation of a competition rule and the interpretation of such rules is not subject to CAS judgment. The FINA Bureau could approve the 'long john' completely legitimately, because in doing so it stayed within the bounds of existing FINA rules. Even if the Bureau would have had to draft a new rule as basis for its approval, such approval would still have been legitimate, at least until the next congress would have given its verdict on that new rule. Given the fact that a swimsuit is not a 'device' in the sense of SW 10.7 and another rule does not prohibit it, a swimsuit may possess qualities, which have a positive effect on the speed, the endurance and the buoyancy of the swimmer wearing it.

The scope of the advisory opinion of the CAS

Pursuant to S12 sub c of the CAS Statutes it is part of the 'mission' of the CAS 'to give non-binding advisory opinions at the request of the IOC, the IFs, the NOCs, the associations recognized by the IOC and the Olympic Games Organizing Committees (OCOGs)'. Paragraph 3 of R27 stipulates that the Procedural Rules of the CAS also apply where the CAS is called upon to give an advisory opinion (consulting proceedings)'. In the *Digest of CAS Awards 1986-1998* Reeb remarked at the beginning of the part in which several advisory opinions are printed that 'of the requests for advisory opinions received, many have been for the interpretations of statutes or regulations'. Unfortunately, no examples of advisory opinions holding such interpretations are included in the Digest. Polvino[25] was of the opinion that the advisory opinions, 'which pertain to the relatively undeveloped area of international sports law, provide a cost-free benefit to those parties seeking to avail themselves of this institution of legal

---

[25] Anthony T. Polvino, Arbitration as preventative medicine for olympic ailments: the International Olympic Committee's Court of Arbitration for Sport and the future for the settlement of international sporting disputes, in Emory International Law Review, Vol. 8 1994, p. 370.

expertise. These advisory opinions are analogous to the submission of a dispute to an expert; a cheap non-jurisdictional form of conflict resolution found ... in the commercial world.' Simma,[26] too, is very positive about the possibility of seeking advisory opinions. The relevant provisions of the Procedural Rules 'would allow the CAS to pronounce upon a far wider range of questions in its advisory function than in its arbitral role. Therefore, if its advisory potential actually came alive, the CAS could develop into an instrument of 'constitutional' review and standard-setting in the realm of international sports law'. The advisory opinion is therefore an instrument for the interpretation of statutes and regulations (Reeb), it cheaply provides legal expertise (Polvino) and a far wider range of questions may be dealt with through it than is the case with arbitration (Simma). According to R60 of the Procedural Rules an advisory opinion may concern 'any legal issue with respect to the practice or development of sports or any activity related to sports'. All these advantages have not been brought to fruition in the present advisory opinion. The cause should not only be sought in the way in which the arbitrator interpreted his task (namely appeal of an IF decision); the way the AOC phrased its questions is also to blame. The Independent of 3 May reported the views of the head swimming coach of Australia, Don Talbot, who said: 'The Australian Olympic Committee was well meaning but has taken the wrong strategy by challenging the legality of full-length body-suits'.

R61 of the CAS Procedural Rules accords a prominent role to the President of the CAS in requests for advisory opinions. Not only does he decide whether the request will be dealt with and does he appoint – if he so decides – the arbitrators from the list to act on the panel, but he is moreover competent to rephrase the questions posed. His freedom to decide whether the panel shall consist of one or three arbitrators may have consequences for the outcome of the advisory opinion. His discretionary power to submit the questions asked to the panel in a different form than the one in which they were originally submitted might also bear a strong influence on the outcome of the advisory opinion. Even a change in the order of the questions asked might influence the outcome. The Procedural Rules set no limits within which the President must exercise his discretionary powers. The requesting party cannot object to the changes the President makes to the questions; he can only ask the President to change the rephrasal, but again, the decision lies with the President. In 'normal' arbitrations the President's powers are not nearly as extensive. The question is why so much power rests with the President in the field of advisory opinions and what end this serves. The

---

[26] Bruno Simma, *The Court of Arbitration for Sport*, in: Völkerrecht – Recht der Internationalen Organisationen – Weltwirtschaftsrecht / Law of Nations – Law of International Organizations – World's Economic Law, Festschrift für Ignaz Seidl-Hohenveldern, p. 579.

IOC's influence in the advisory practice is considerable, given the position accorded to the CAS President. Pursuant to S6 of the CAS Statutes the ICAS appoints a President from among its members, who shall also be President of the CAS (S9), but who is 'proposed by the IOC'.

As an aside it should be mentioned here that Mbaye[27] wrote in 1984: 'par ailleurs, l'ensemble du contentieux relatif au sport peut être divisé en de rubriques: les 'questions techniques' et les 'questions non techniques' (du point de vue du sport, bien entendu). Les 'questions techniques' relèvent des organes du sport'. He could have rejected the request for an advisory opinion as the questions of the AOC focused on the interpretation of FINA SW 10.7 and thus were 'questions techniques'.

Communication

Coates feared that the FINA's decision would result in an unfair balance during the qualifications between the swimmers who did and those who did not dispose of a shark suit. He feared even more that the lesser-endowed swimmers would at a certain moment legally challenge the results of the swimmers in shark suits. The reason why Coates did not take the principle of fair play as point of departure in phrasing his questions to the CAS may well be found in an aspect of the FINA decision that has not been dealt with yet. This aspect was left aside by the FINA itself in its publicity about the approval. The brief paragraph in the advisory opinion that makes mention of the approval of the swimsuits during the meeting of the FINA Bureau on 8 October in Kuwait is concluded by the arbitrator with the words 'that approval was based upon the provision that it would be available to every competitor'. This sentence, which plays no role of further importance in the advisory opinion, may be read thus that during competitions a 'long john suit' was not allowed to be worn by any participant, if not all participants could dispose of one. Whether the participants would actually use the suit would be irrelevant; what would matter is that they could dispose of one. We may well suspect that the AOC did not know of this condition.

From the previous issue of *Sportzaken Magazine,* in which Berry Bertels dedicated a few sentences to this advisory opinion on page 61, it appears that the CAS did not give permission to publish the advisory opinion *in extenso.* From the headlines quoted above it likewise appears that the press, too, has had to content itself with the announcements of the CAS concerning the advisory opinion. Pursuant to R62 of the Procedural Rules the advisory opinion can 'be published with the consent of the party who requested it'. We must therefore

---

[27] Keba Mbaye: *Une nouvelle institution d'arbitrage: le Tribunal Arbitral du Sport (T.A.S.),* in: Annuaire Français de Droit International XXX (1984), p. 411.

conclude that the AOC did not consent to the publishing of the advisory opinion. Stricter conditions apply to the publishing of advisory opinions than of arbitral awards of the CAS. With regard to arbitral awards, R59 paragraph 5 states that these 'shall be made public by the CAS, unless both parties agree that they should remain confidential'.

In conclusion

Since the approval of the 'long johns' by the FINA several new world records have been set by swimmers wearing the new swimsuits. It is impossible to decide whether the swimsuits have had any influence on these results. In the meantime, the swimwear manufacturers have taken care that all top swimmers have access to the new suits. With this, the fear of unfair competition has subsided. The CAS decision has in no way contributed towards the question whether these suits may be used in future competitions. The FINA allows it and the national federations, too, have given their approval. There will be swimmers who will not be using them, but there will also be those who wish to swim in as little fabric as possible. After a while, we will know whether the shark suits are really as revolutionary as the manufacturers claimed or whether this has been just another hype. Research at the faculty of motion studies of the *Vrije Universiteit* has shown that some swimmers in Speedo suits actually experienced more resistance in the water than without those suits. The Russian Alexander Popov, who set the world record for the 100 metres free stroke without a shark suit, said in an interview: 'You don't win the silver – you miss the gold'. Of the CAS advisory opinion, neither can be said.

CAS MEDIATION SERVICE

In May, 1999, the CAS introduced a mediation service. Article 1, para. 1 of the CAS Mediation Rules provides as follows:

> 'CAS Mediation is a non-binding and informal procedure, based on a mediation agreement in which each party undertakes to attempt in good faith to negotiate with the other party, and with the assistance of a CAS mediator, with a view to settling a sports-related dispute'.

The second paragraph of this article goes on to limit mediation to disputes under what is called the 'CAS ordinary procedure', and to exclude mediation in relation to any decision passed by a sports organisation and also disputes related to disciplinary matters and doping issues. The CAS ordinary procedure applies to cases brought in the CAS Ordinary Division, which is dedicated to resolving commercial disputes.

CAS MEDIATION RULES

The CAS Mediation Rules ('the Rules') are set out in Appendix VI and a few comments on them follow.

Article 2 of the Rules defines a 'mediation agreement' as one whereby the parties agree to submit existing or future sports-related disputes to mediation, and further provides that it may take the form of a separate agreement or a mediation clause in a contract.

Such a clause may be along the lines, *mutatis mutandis*, of the following standard so-called 'comprehensive clause' of the ADR Group:

> 'In the event of any dispute arising between the parties in connection with this [agreement] [contract] the parties will in good faith seek to resolve that dispute through mediation under the auspices of the [ADR Group]. The mediator shall be agreed upon within [15] days of one party requesting mediation, failing which the mediator shall be appointed by the then President of The Law Society. Unless otherwise agreed the parties shall share equally the costs of the mediation. If the dispute is not resolved within [30] days, or one of the parties refuses to participate in mediation, the dispute shall be referred to [arbitration in accordance with the rules of the Chartered Institute of Arbitrators, whose rules are deemed to be incorporated by reference into this clause] or [litigation]. Nothing in this clause shall prevent either party seeking a preliminary injunction or other judicial relief at any time if in its judgement such action is necessary to prevent irreparable damage'.

For agreements involving one or more non-UK parties, it is suggested that the London Court of International Arbitration be substituted for the Chartered Institute of Arbitrators as the arbitral body. Likewise, in relation to international mediations, the mediation clause should also include provisions on the language to be used in the mediation and who is responsible for providing necessary translations and who pays for them.

Once again, *en passant*, I would note that the reference to the President of The Law Society may be considered to be vague and held to be invalid for uncertainty under English contract law, because there is more than one Law Society in the UK. To avoid this result, the correct reference should be to 'The Law Society of England and Wales'.

Under article 3 of the Rules, except where the parties agree otherwise, the version of the Rules in force at the time the written request for mediation (pursuant to article 4) is filed at the CAS shall apply. Apparently, the parties may agree to apply other rules of procedure.

Pursuant to article 6 of the Rules, the President of the CAS chooses the mediator from the list of CAS mediators, who, in turn, are chosen from the list of CAS arbitrators or from outside, where the parties themselves cannot agree on the mediator. The mediator appointed must be and remain independent of the parties.

The parties may be represented or assisted in their meetings with the mediator (article 7). In line with the procedures of the CAS generally, the person representing the parties need not be a lawyer or legally qualified.

Under article 8 of the Rules, the procedure to be followed in the mediation shall either be agreed by the parties themselves or determined by the mediator. This is a slight deviation from the general principle, noted above, that the mediator is the one who controls the procedural aspects of the mediation.

The role of the mediator is laid down in article 9 of the Rules.

Article 10 of the Rules makes provision for the confidentiality of the mediation process and also lays down and spells out the 'without prejudice' principle on which the mediation shall be conducted.

Article 11 of the Rules deals with the questions of when and how the mediation may be terminated.

Article 12 of the Rules requires that any settlement of the mediation must be in writing and signed by the mediator and the parties.

Article 13 of the Rules deals with the question of failure to settle.

CAS MEDIATION COSTS

Article 14 of the Rules deals with the important matter of costs of the mediation.

In typical Swiss style, until the CAS fee is paid, the mediation proceedings cannot be started, and the CAS Court Office may require the parties to deposit an equal amount as an advance towards the mediation costs. The parties are required to pay their own mediation costs and share equally the other costs, which include the CAS fee, the mediator's fees, a contribution towards the costs of the CAS, and the fees of the witnesses, experts and interpreters.

CAS MEDIATION SYMPOSIUM

Since its introduction in 1999, the CAS has received only one request for mediation, which did not proceed as the dispute was settled without the intervention of the mediator. The case concerned a sale of images between a company and a sports organising body and the amount in dispute was significant.

To promote its mediation service, the CAS held a symposium in Lausanne on 4 November 2000. Three Papers were presented by Bernard Foucher, President of the French Institute of Mediators; Christopher Newmark, a Partner in the London Office of the Baker & Mckenzie Law Firm and a CEDR Registered Mediator; and William K. Slate II, President and CEO of the American Arbitration Association. For ease of reference, we set out below the texts of these Papers. The one by Bernard Foucher on 'Mediation as a Method of Settling Sports Disputes under French Law' was given in French.

Bernard Foucher[28]
Conciliation as a way of resolving sports related disputes in France

LA CONCILIATION COMME MODE DE RÈGLEMENT DES CONFLITS
SPORTIFS EN DROIT FRANÇAIS

Le système de la conciliation a été introduit par la loi no 92-652 du 13 juillet
1992 relative à l'organisation et à la promotion des activités physiques et
sportives (article 19), à partir d'un amendement parlementaire.
Il aménage dans le domaine du sport, un mode de règlement des conflits tout à
fait original, qui emprunte à la fois à l'arbitrage et à la médiation, sans être
juridiquement ni l'un, ni l'autre, et qui a pour objectif de limiter l'intervention du
juge étatique dans les contentieux sportifs.
Depuis maintenant sept ans, le système de 'la conciliation à la française' a fait
ses preuves. La loi du 6 juillet vient de le confirmer et de le renforcer.
Quel est ce mécanisme original? (I); Comment a-t-il fonctionné? (II).

I- LE MÉCANISME DE LA CONCILIATION

A- L'organisation de la conciliation.

Qui est chargé d'assurer la conciliation?

Dans sa dernière version, c'est-à-dire celle du 6 juillet 2000, la loi attribue au
CNOSF *'une mission de conciliation dans les conflits opposant les licenciés, les
groupements sportifs et les fédérations agréées, à l'exception des conflits
mettant en cause des faits de dopage'*.

Ce n'est pas une nouveauté. Déjà la loi du 25 octobre 1975, dite loi 'Mazeaud'
avait prévu à l'article 14 que: *'Le CNOSF arbitre à leur demande, les litiges
opposant les licenciés, groupements et fédérations. Un décret en Conseil d'Etat
détermine les conditions d'application du présent décret'*. Mais faute de décret
d'application à l'époque, cette mission n'avait jamais été exercée.
La loi de 1984 avait elle aussi confié une mission de conciliation au CNOSF,
mais cette mission restait facultative.

La loi de 1992 lui confiera une mission de conciliation obligatoire dans certains
cas, mais sans autre précision quant à l'organisation de cette mission.

---

[28] Président de la Conférence des Conciliateurs, Secrétaire général des tribunaux administratifs et
des cours administratives d'appel.

Le CNOSF s'est donc dans un premier temps organisé lui-même en établissant une liste de conciliateurs et en regroupant ces conciliateurs en une 'conférence des conciliateurs' ayant, à sa tête un président.

La liste des conciliateurs a été arretée par le Conseil d'administration du CNOSF, sur proposition du bureau et après agrément des candidatures par la commission juridique.

L'idée a été de retenir des candidatures qui présentaient un double profil: des compétences juridiques et une connaissance approfondie des institutions sportives.

Actuellement cette liste comporte 14 noms et comprend:
– des professeurs de droit (4)
– des magistrats de l'ordre administratifs (2)
– des magistrats de l'ordre judiciaire (3)
– des avocats (4)
– une expert comptable (1)

Quant au président de la conférence des conciliateurs, un certain nombre de pouvoirs d'organisation des audiences de conciliation et d'instruction des dossiers lui avaient été reconnus par un 'règlement de concillation' adopté là encore, par le Conseil d'administration du CNOSF.

Enfin, pour gérer les demandes de conciliation, le CNOSF a mis en place un service de la conciliation comprenant notamment 3 assistants de conciliation qui assurent la gestion des dossiers, et a mis à disposition des locaux pour permettre la tenue des audiences de conciliation.

Pour donner plus de rigueur juridique à toute cette organisation, la loi du 6 juillet 2000 est venue officialiser l'existence de la 'Conférence des conciliateurs', ainsi que celle du président de la conférence des conciliateurs qui se trouve investi, de par la loi cette fois-ci, d'un certain nombre de prérogatives.

De même, la loi vient renforcer sérieusement l'obligation de confidentialité des conciliateurs qui en cas de violation de cette obligation s'exposent à des sanctions pénales.

B- Le champ d'application de la conciliation.

Sur quels litiges porte la conciliation?

A l'exception de ceux mettant en cause des faits de dopage, tous les litiges opposant les licenciés, les groupements sportifs et les fédérations peuvent être soumis à la conciliation. Mais il convient de faire une distinction entre les conflits qui relèvent d'une procédure de conciliation facultative et ceux qui relèvent d'une procédure de conciliation obligatoire.

Les conflits qui relèvent d'une procédure obligatoire demeurent les plus nombreux.

Selon la définition retenue sur le nouvel article 19 issu de la loi du 6 juillet 2000, il s'agit des conflits qui résultent *'d'une décision susceptible ou non de recours interne, prise par une fédération dans l'exercice de prérogatives de puissance publique ou en application de ses statuts'*.

La condition posée par la loi de 1992 qui exigeait que le conflit concerne une fédération titulaire de la délégation du ministre chargé des sports, n'est donc pas reprise et il suffit que le conflit concerne une fédération seulement agréée.

La plupart des décisions réglementaires ou individuelles concernant l'organisation et le fonctionnement de la discipline sportive, dont la fédération a la gestion, relèvent donc de la conciliation obligatoire. Il en est de même des décisions de la fédération qui concernent le fonctionnement interne de l'association et mettent en cause l'application des statuts.

Le conflit relevant d'une procédure de conciliation obligatoire ne pourra alors être directement soumis au juge. La saisine du juge sera en effet sanctionnée par une irrecevabilité.

Un certain nombre de conflits sont exclus de la procédure de conciliation obligatoire mais ils pourront toujours faire l'objet d'une procédure de conciliation facultative, si les parties l'acceptent.

Il en est ainsi des litiges concernant des contrats de travail ou des contrats commerciaux (sponsoring – droits de télévision ...).

C- La procédure de la conciliation.

Comment fonctionne la conciliation?

La procédure de conciliation comporte un certain nombre de mesures contraignantes destinées à assurer l'efficacité du système.

Toutefois, ces règles de procédures, insuffisamment détaillées dans la loi de 1992 ont dû être complétées en pratique, et sont améliorées et définies par la loi du 6 juillet 2000.

1- La saisine du conciliateur.

Elle est faite par toute partie au litige au moyen d'une demande adressée au président de la conférence des conciliateurs. C'est celui-ci:

- qui est chargé de désigner un ou plusieurs concillateurs en fonction de la difficulté de l'affaire;
- qui est chargé de procéder à une instruction sommaire de la recevabilité de chaque affaire et de rejeter directement les demandes qui ne concernent pas des litiges rele-

vant de la procédure de conciliation obligatere ou des demandes qui lui paraissent manifestement infondées ou irrecevables.

La loi du 6 juillet 2000 confirme l'attribution de ces pouvoirs du président de la conférence des conciliateurs, pouvoirs qu'il détenait au préalable de manière un peu sommaire du 'règlement de la conciliation'.

Elle peut intervenir avant l'épuisement des voies de recours internes devant les instances fédérales.
Cette disposition, qui n'est pas remise en cause par la loi du 6 juillet 2000, est motivée par le souci de ne pas bloquer le litige dans des délais d'examen trop longs par les organes de recours de la fédération.

Elle entraîne l'interruption des délais de recours juridictionnels éventuels.

Elle entraîne la suspension de la décision contestée.

On perçoit l'intérêt de cette mesure. Si la décision est déjà exécutée, quel est en effet l'intérêt de rechercher une conciliation? Cette mesure constitue donc un moyen incitatif pour engager le plus rapidement la discussion et parvenir à un compromis.
Mais on s'est interrogé sur son application. D'une part le texte n'était pas très clair sur la durée précise de la suspention. D'autre part, les fédérations manifestaient à son égard quelques critiques lorsque la saisine du conciliateur avait essentiellement pour but de pouvoir bénéficier de l'effet suspensif et revêtait alors un caractère dilatoire.

> Ex: Alors qu'un joueur de football a commis sur le terrain une faute grave et indiscutable entraînant une sanction de suspension de plusieurs matches, la simple saisine du conciliateur entraîne la suspension de la sanction et 'l'autoriserait' à participer au match suivant.

C'est pourquoi un aménagement avait été apporté par 'le règlement de conciliation'. Il consistait à considérer que ce n'était pas la saisine du conciliateur qui entraînait la suspension de la décision contestée, mais la décision du président de la conférence des conciliateurs se prononçant sur la recevabilité de la demande. Une marge de manoeuvre était ainsi laissée au président de la conférence des conciliateurs qui en différant sa décision sur la recevabilité de la demande et sur la désignation d'un conciliateur différait aussi 'l'effet suspensif'.
La loi du 6 juillet 2000 vient donner une base légale et compléter cet aménagement: '*lorsque le conflit résulte de l'intervention d'une decision individuelle, l'exécution de cette décision est suspendue à compter de la notification à l'auteur de la décision de l'acte désignant un conciliateur*'. L'effet

suspensif ne trouvera donc plus à s'appliquer que pour les actes individuels. La loi accorde même un pouvoir supplémentaire au président de la conférence des conciliateurs: celui-ci *'peut lever ladite suspension dans le cas où la décision contestée est motivée par des actes de violence caractérisée'.*

2- L'intervention du conciliateur.

Le conciliateur doit se prononcer dans le délai d'un mois à compter de sa saisine.

À l'issue d'une 'audience de conciliation' le conciliateur doit formuler des propositions de conciliation aux parties.

Les propositions doivent être acceptées par les parties, mais il existe, un système d'approbation tacite.
En effet, la proposition est présumée acceptée, sauf opposition notifiée au conciliateur et aux parties dans le délai d'un mois à compter de la notification de la proposition du conciliateur.

II- LA PRATIQUE DE LA CONCILIATION

A- Le nombre d'affaires traitées.

La conciliation a fait ses premiers pas en 1993. Sept ans plus tard, elle a examiné son millième dossier.
Le tableau suivant permet de retracer son activité au 1er septembre 2000.

1141 dossiers enregistrés			
913 dossiers soumis à une procédure de concillation			228 dossiers directment rejetés pour irrecevabilité
239 dossiers ont fat l'objet d'un accord entre les parties lors de l'audience de conciliation	674 dossiers ont donné lieu à des propositions de conciliation		
	421 dossiers où les propositions de coniciliation ont été acceptées	253 dossiers où les propositions de coniciliation ont été refusées	
660 dossiers où le litige a été résolu (soit un taux de 73%)		70 dossiers où le litige a été porté devant les tribunaux	

Ce tableau appelle les brefs commentaires suivants:

– Le mécanisme de la conciliation a démarré lentement les deux ou trois premières années. Il est aujourd'hui bien connu des acteurs du monde sportif, et le nombre de dossiers enregistrés se situe aux alentours de 160 par an.
– Un nombre significatif de ces dossiers (1/5 environ) a été rejeté pour irrecevabilité, soit parce que la demande était manifestement infondée ou tardive, soit parce que le litige ne relevait pas du champ d'application de la procédure de conciliation obligatoire. Mais dans ce dernier cas, une procédure de conciliation facultative, où le conciliateur intervient alors à titre de bons offices peut-être engagée si les parties l'acceptent explicitement.
– Une situation n'a pas d'explication précise. C'est celle qui résulte de l'écart entre, le nombre de litiges non résolus (253) et le nombre de litiges portés devant les tribunaux (70). Il s'agit de cas où très généralement, la proposition faite par le conciliateur a été refusée par la fédération, et où l'autre partie ne 'poursuit' pas. Il est probable que celle-ci ne souhaite pas faire de procédure juridictionnelle ... à moins que la proposition du conciliateur, même non suivie d'effet, ait permis de lui donner une satisfaction 'suffisante'.

B- Le type d'affaires traités.

Il n'est pas possible de donner une liste exhaustive des litiges soumis à la conciliation, ni de les identifier, au risque d'ailleurs d'enfreindre le principe de la confidentialité. Les questions soumises au conciliateur sont très variées et concernent toutes les disciplines sportives, ou presque.
Le nombre d'affaires traitées permet surtout de repérer les litiges qui reviennent le plus souvent devant le conciliateur, et de dresser ainsi une typologie du contentieux sportif en portant un diagnostic sur ce contentieux. Ce diagnostic n'est pas inutile car il permet de renseigner les fédérations notamment, sur les points faibles de leurs réglementations ou de leurs décisions.
Cinq types de litiges peuvent cependant être plus clairement distingués.

1 - Les litiges relatifs à l'application des réglementations fédérales.

Ce sont les plus nombreux. Ils concernent essentiellement:

a) les licenciés.

– *Litiges concernant la délivrance les licences mais aussi la régularité des licences.*

Beaucoup de litiges ont, un temps concerné, par exemple, les manquements aux mentions obligatoires que doit comporter une licence (attestation de certificat médical, mentions incomplètes ou erronées ...).

Ces problèmes entraînent des réactions en chaîne, puisque la participation d'un joueur 'non' licencié ou "non régulièrement" licencié à une compétition peut remettre en cause les résultats de la compétition.

– Litiges concernant les mutations de licenciés.

Certaines fédérations encadrent ces mutations par des règles tellement contraignantes que le conciliateur en arrive à se demander si ces règles ne constituent pas une entrave illicite à la liberté d'association et au respect du droit à la pratique sportive affirmé par l'article 1er de la loi sur le sport.

b) Les groupements sportifs.

– Litiges concernant des refus d'affiliation souvent fondés sur de circonstances de fait étrangers à la réglementation sportive.

– Litiges liés d'une manière générale à l'application de la réglementation sportive.

Ce domaine est très vaste et très varié. Pour cibler quelques litiges importants, nous pouvons relenir:

– D'une part, les problèmes résultant de l'organisation et du fonctionnement des compétitions.

À *titre d'exemples*:
le droit de participer à une compétition sous réserve
d'inscrire plusieurs équipes, ou un nombre de joueurs minimum

le problème de la participation aux compétitions, de sportifs étrangers.

(NB: s'agissant du sport professionnel l'application de l'arrêt BOSMAN ne pose plus, aujourd'hui de difficultés, mais s'agissant du sport non professionnel, la parti-cipation de sportifs étrangers pose toujours des difficultés).

le problème de report de matches pour terrains impraticables.

le problème des décisions d'arbitrage.

(NB: il existe sur ce point une irrecevabilité de principe, sauf s'il est constaté une erreur dans l'application du règlement: l'arbitre prend une décision que le règlement

sportif ne lui permettrait pas de prendre (pas faute technique d'arbitrage mais faute 'juridique' d'arbitrage)).

– D'autre part, les problèmes résultant de décisions d'accession au professionnalisme.

– Litiges liés à des modifications de règlements sportifs (modification en cours de saison ou de compétition par exemple).

À partir de ce premier type de litiges, plusieurs constatations s'imposent:

– Celle tout d'abord d'une inflation de réglementation de la part des fédérations qui en arrivent à mettre en place des 'usines à gaz'. Plus la réglementation est dense, détaillée, pointilliste, plus elle risque d'être confuse et donc source d'interprétation et de litiges.

– Celle ensuite d'une confusion entre les décisions de nature 'administrative' et de nature 'disciplinaire'(les procédures applicables seront pourtant différentes).

Par exemple: le refus de mutation d'un joueur, qui ne remplit pas les conditions réglementaires n'est pas une sanction. Il ne résulte pas d'une faute, mais du non respect des conditions posées.

– Celle enfin de dispositions réglementaires souvent imprécises voire lacunaires:

Exemple:
– la suspension de terrain, s'applique t-elle à toutes les compétitions ou à certaines d'entre elles?
– la suspension de joueurs est -elle prononcée pour une durée ou pour un nombre de matches défini?

2 - Les litiges relatifs aux sanctions disciplinaires.

Ces litiges représentent environ 30% des demandes de conciliation.
C'est un domaine très sensible, d'autant que l'effet suspensif de la saisine du conciliateur revêt ici toute son importance et son particularisme, ainsi qu'il a déjà été indiqué.
Dans ces litiges, le conciliateur suit la même démarche que le juge, et en particulier le juge adininistratif.
Il examine la régularité de la décision (c'est-à-dire la légalité externe) en

s'appuyant notamment sur le décret de 1993. Celui-ci prévoit en effet un certain nombre de règles de procédure que certaines fédérations ignorent encore, ou n'appliquent pas (double degré de 'juridiction'; composition des instances disciplinaires de 5 membres au moins, et majorité d'entre eux n'appartenant pas au comité directeur; respect du droit de la défense; motivation de la décision, qui ne doit pas être stéréotypée).

Il examine le contenu de la décision (c'est-à-dire la légalité interne) en s'appuyant notamment sur deux principes: la sanction doit être prévue par un texte (principe de la légalité des peines); la sanction doit être proportionnée à la faute.

À partir de ce type de litiges, plusieurs remarques doivent être faites:

– Souvent la décision disciplinaire est entachée d'une procédure irrigulière qui l'exposerait à une annulation irrémédiable par le juge.

– L'appréciation du principe de proportionnalité est généralement mal comprise. Certaines fédérations se dotent d'un barème de sanctions extrêmement détaillé, au point de ne plus laisser aux organes disciplinaires une marge d'appréciation, et donc une possibilité de respecter le principe de proportionnalité.

– Ce type de litiges peut exposer le système de la conciliation à une difficulté d'application résultant de la nécessité de faire 'valider' en principe, la proposition de conciliation par l'organe disciplinaire (à priori indépendant de l'autorité fédérale présente à la conciliation).

3 - Les litiges relatifs aux sélections et notamment aux sélections nationales.

Ce sont des litiges résultant généralement du refus de sélectionner un athlète, ils sont difficiles à gérer par le conciliateur. En effet, ces litiges portent en réalité sur des appréciations subjectives des qualités des athlètes, et procèdent souvent d'un climat de défiance entre l'athlète et la fédération.

Dans ces litiges, l'athlète n'attend ni plus ni moins du conciliateur, qu'il lui donne son 'billet' de sélection à la sortie de l'audience.

De plus, ces litiges doivent souvent être réglés 'en urgence'.

Dans ces litiges, le conciliateur ne peut certainement pas se substituer à l'appréciation qui a pu être faite par les spécialites (sélectionneur – directeur technique national) sur les capacités d'ensemble de l'athlète à participer à une compétition, et imposer la sélection de l'athlète. Il s'agit en effet d'une appréciation paticulièrement discrétionnaire.

Cependant, le concillateur peut d'une part, vérifier s'il existe des règles pré-établies de sélection et dans ce cas exiger leur respect. Certaines fédérations encadrent en effet la procédure de sélection en retenant des critères objectifs, tels que la réalisation de résultats sportifs ou de minima exigibles (seront sélectionnés les 2 premiers, par exemple ...). D'autres, au contraire, laissent une totale liberté au selectionneur pour faire ses choix. Dans le premier cas, si la fédération a entendu se lier par des critères précis, le conciliateur veillera au respect de l'application de ces critères. Dans le second cas, le conciliateur ne discutera même pas du choix du sélectionneur, sauf à considerer que celui-ci s'est fondé sur des considérations totalement étrangères à la valeur sportive de l'athlète (il s'agirait presque d'une selection déguisée ou d'un détournement de pouvoir).

Le conciliateur peut d'autre part, obtenir la meilleure transparence possible des motifs de refus de sélection. Il est vrai que le droit, la jurisprudence n'obligent pas les fédérations de motiver un refus de sélection. Mais de nombreux litiges révèlent que les athlètes ont saisi le conciliateur parce qu'ils s'estimaient écartés de la sélection sans en connaître les raisons. Une simple explication réduira les tensions et mettra un terme au litige.

4 - Les litiges concernant le contrôle de la gestion des clubs professionnels.

Ce n'est pas un domaine quantitativement important. Mais c'est un domaine délicat.

Il touche en effet à la situation financière des clubs et à leur devenir.

Certaines disciplines sportives ont mis en place une branche 'professionnelle' avec des organismes spécifiques (les ligues nationales). La nécessité d'avoir un secteur professionnel viable a conduit à assurer un contrôle de la gestion des clubs professionnels, et à confier à des organes de contrôle de gestion le soin d'apprécier la situation financière de ces clubs. Des décisions peuvent alors être prises pour refuser une accession ou un maintien en professionnalisme en raison d'une situation financière insuffisante ou dégradée.

Or ce domaine touche à une conception un peu nouvelle du sport. En effet il ne suffit pas d'être le meilleur sportivement, et de se prévaloir de résultats sportifs pour accéder à un championnat professionnel, il faut aussi se prévaloir de critères extra-sportifs (bonne situation financière, et même, autres critères matériels). Le conciliateur se trouve donc saisi de décisions de refus d'accession ou de maintien en professionnalisme pour des raisons tenant à la gestion et la situation financière d'un club examinées par des organes de contrôle de gestion.

Le conciliateur ne peut certainement pas refaire l'expertise financière. Il n'en a ni les moyens matériels, ni les compétences techniques. Mais il peut vérifier si la procédure prévue à bien été respectée (délais pour présenter les documents comptables – nature des pièces produites – double examen parfois prévu, par un organisme d'appel), et si la décision repose sur des faits exacts, n'est pas entachée d'un détournement de pouvoir ou ne comporte pas une erreur manifeste d'appréciation.

Quel constat faire de ce type de litiges?

Il est double. D'une part, la réglementation est souvent imprécise en la matière (que veut dire 'une situation financière saine'? à quel moment précis apprécier la situation financière du club?). D'autre part, ce type de litiges aboutit à une véritable dérive contentieuse, où l'éthique sportive est balayée.

Que penser du contentieux généré par le club classé dernier de sa division et relégué sportivement, qui va mettre en cause la montée du club arrivé en tête de la division inférieure et acquise sportivement, en se bornant à contester l'examen qui a été fait de la situation financière de ce dernier?

5 - Les litiges relatifs à l'application des statuts fédéraux.

Ces litiges sont distincts de ceux précédemment évoqués dans la mesure où ils ne résultent pas de la mise en oeuvre de prérogatives de puissance publique, mais de l'application des statuts fédéraux réglementant la vie associative de la fédération, et dans la mesure aussi, où ils relèvent ensuite généralement à la competence du juge judiciaire.

Les litiges concernent surtout:

– Le contentieux résultant de l'application des statuts de la fédération.

Le conciliateur va s'attacher à ce que ces statuts soient respectés et que les décisions internes à la vie de l'association soient conformes à ces statuts.

Le problème intéressant s'est posé de savoir s'il fallait avant de veiller à l'application des statuts, vérifier si ces statuts étaient conformes aux statut types annexés au décret n° 85-236 du 13 février 1985 modifié, conformité permettant et validant en principe, l'agrément ministériel.

L'option a plutôt été de s'en tenir à la stricte application des statuts qui tiennent lieu de loi à l'association (la non conformité aux statuts-types pose alors le problème de la légalité de l'agrément accordé par le ministre, mais reste étrangère au seul litige concernant l'application des statuts).

– Le contentieux électif qui couvre à la fois la régularité des candidatures et la régularité des votes.

– Le contentieux résultant de la tenue des assemblées générales (convocations irrégulières – débats irriguliers – tenues d'assemblées ordinaires ou extraordinaires).

– Le contentieux résultant des relations entre fédération et organes déconcentrés.

Trois remarques s'imposent à partir de ce type de litiges:

– Ils se doublent la plupart du temps de considérations personnelles.

– Ils résultent souvent d'un manque de rigueur, notamment dans la tenue des assemblées générales. Ce manque de rigueur est 'acceptable' lorsque la vie de l'association est 'paisible'. Il devient source de litiges lorsque la vie de l'association est conflictuelle.

– Ces litiges n'offrent que peu de solutions au conciliateur qui ne peut se limiter qu'à proposer par exemple, de refaire l'assemblée générale ou les élections.

C - Le mode de traitement des affaires.

1 - La tenue d'une audience de conciliation.

Chaque affaire qui a été déclarée recevable est examinée 'lors d'une audience de conciliation' qui réunit le conciliateur désigné et les parties concernées par le litige. Ces parties sont généralement le demandeur et le défendeur qui est le plus souvent une fédération sportive. Mais dans certains cas, une partie tierce, intéressée par la résolution du litige peut être invitée à participer à l'audience.
L'audience ne saurait être empreinte de formalisme, mais elle doit se dérouler dans le respect du principe du contradictoire et du débat équitable,
Il importe surtout que les parties présentes à l'audience, qui par ailleurs doivent veiller à garder une confidentialité des débats, soient suffisamment représentatives, et capables de s'engager efficacement pour accepter les solutions éventuellment proposées. Cette remarque concerne essentiellement les représentants des fédérations qui ne sauraient venir 'assister' à une audience de conciliation sans avoir la capacité de décider au nom de la fédération et de s'engager dans la conciliation. Il y va bien sûr de l'intérêt de l'audience de conciliation et de ses chances de succès.

2 - L'acquisition d'une 'culture de la conciliation'.

L'expérience acquise au fil des dossiers et des audiences de conciliation permet de considérer qu'il existe bien une "culture de la conciliation" qui doit être bien comprise de l'ensemble des participants.

Le conciliateur tout d'abord, doit faire preuve d'une capacité d'écoute (il doit permettre aux parties de s'exprimer et de 'se parler'), de patience (il faut désamorcer des situations conflictuelles générant parfois une certaine agressivité entre les parties) de conviction et de persuasion (il faut essayer de convaincre et non d'imposer).

Les parties ensuite, doivent être capables d'admettre l'idée du compromis. À la différence d'un procès devant le juge qui se termine par un 'vainqueur' et un 'veincu', la conciliation doit permettre de dégager une solution consensuelle où il n'y a ni vainqueur, ni vaincu. Mais pour y parvenir, chaque partie doit souvent admettre d'abandonner une partie des ses prétentions et accepter le compromis.

Il n'est pas rare enfin que les parties soient représentées par un avocat. Là aussi, l'attitude de l'avocat en conciliation ne doit pas être tout à fait la même que celle de l'avocat en procès. Devant le juge il doit défendre son client avec pour but essentiel d'imposer sa solution. Devant le conciliateur il doit développer une capacité de facilitation du litige et non de blocage du litige, même parfois au prix d'un recul dans la ligne de défense de son client.

3 - La recherche d'une solution équilibrée.

L'intérêt essentiel du mécanisme de la conciliation est de faciliter l'adoption d'une solution équilibrée à la résolution d'un litige sportif.

L'intrusion du droit dans le domaine du sport ne s'est pas faite sans heurts et la résolution de litiges sportifs par le juge étatique n'est pas toujours adaptée (délais de réponse trop longs, inefficacité de solutions juridiques à des situations spécifiques de l'activité sportive).

La conciliation permet précisément de régler différemment les conflits en tenant compte de la spécificité sportive et en recherchant des solutions qui essaient de préserver un équilibre entre les intérêts des parties et un équilibre entre l'ordre sportif et l'ordre juridique.

Le mode de traitement des affaires pourra alors, en conciliation, être à géométrie variable. Soit une conciliation entre les parties est envisageable et la solution proposée sera plus pragmatique que juridique, soit une conciliation n'est pas envisageable et la solution proposée restera essentiellement juridique.

En conclusion, le bilan de la 'conciliation à la française' mérite d'être défendu.

Certes le mécanisme de la conciliation n'est pas exempt de toute critique. Le juriste pourra y trouver matière à interrogations. Les dispositions de l'article 19 sont-elles suffisamment précises? Quelle est la valeur juridique de la proposition de conciliation? Comment assurer juridiquement son exécution?

La fédération, placée le plus souvent en position de défendeur, pourra y trouver matière à critiques. L'effet suspensif est-il opportun? La saisine du conciliateur avant l'épuisement des voies de recours internes est-elle souhaitable? Comment mettre en application certaines propositions du conciliateur? *(par exemple pour les propositions concernant les mesures disciplinaires, faut-il revenir à l'organe disciplinaire?)*. La conciliation obligatoire n'est-elle pas tout simplement une atteinte intolérable à l'autorité fédérale?

Le requérant pourra y trouver matière à insuffisance. L'encadrement procédural n'est-il pas trop contraignant? Pourquoi le mécanisme de la conciliation obligatoire est-il limité à certains litiges? Pourquoi le conciliateur n'a-t-il pas le pouvoir de faire ou de décider?

Mais au delà de toutes ces questions, le mécanisme de la conciliation apparaît pour les litiges sportifs comme un système original, efficace et adapté.

Il est original dans la mesure où il se distingue:

– du recours au juge, où le mode de règlement du conflit est imposé et où la solution retenue a force exécutoire;
– du recours à l'arbitrage, où le mode de règlement du conflit est librement accepté et où la solution retenue a force exécutoire;
– du recours à la médiation où le mode de règlement du conflit est librement accepté et où la solution retenue n'a pas force exécutoire.

Dans la conciliation à la française, le mode de règlement du conflit est en effet imposé, mais la solution retenue n'a pas force exécutoire.

Il est efficace et adapté dans la mesure où:

– Il évite le recours au juge qui n'est pas le censeur naturel de l'activité sportive;
– Il permet de résoudre les litiges dans 'la famille du sport';
– Il permet de disposer d'une expertise juridique à partir de l'analyse faite par le conciliateur et de ses propositions;
– Il permet de disposer d'une solution rapide, gratuite, pragmatique qui peut concilier sport et droit.

C'est en ce sens que la conciliation est bien une procédure au service du sport.

Christopher Newmark[29]
Is Mediation Effective for Resolving Sports Disputes?

A. Introduction

This paper gives an overview of the use of mediation for resolving sports disputes. As a preliminary matter it is perhaps helpful to make it clear where we are in the evolution of mediation in sports disputes, at least in Europe. To use an American sporting metaphor, we have barely got off first base. The Court of Arbitration for Sport ('CAS'), which introduced its mediation rules in May 1999, has not carried out any sports mediations yet. Nor has the LCIA, the other lead organiser of this conference. This does not mean that these institutions do not have sensible mediation rules. They do. it is just that mediation in this specialist area is in its infancy, especially in the international arena.

In the UK, where the use of mediation for general commercial disputes has grown exponentially over the last 18 months, the Centre for Dispute Resolution ('CEDR'), which is the leading commercial mediation provider, has assisted in about 10 sports mediations in total. I will be referring to one of these which hit the sporting headlines later. A new body, the Sport Dispute Resolution Panel ('SDRP'), is about to undertake its first sports mediation.

These statistics suggest that, as in all areas of ADR, the US is still well ahead of the game in the use of mediation for resolving sports disputes. We will hear from William Slate from the AAA about the use of mediation in the US for sports related disputes, and we can probably learn most by examining the US experience. But we can also learn by going back to basics, by looking at what the process of mediation actually is and what it offers, and by then looking at some of the types of dispute that arise in the sporting world. This process, which is the focus of the next two sections of this paper (Sections B and C below), should show us where there are matches and where mediation is likely to have a role. In Section D, the paper then examines some of the practical issues that users and providers – of mediation should give careful consideration to as they develop mediation services and insert mediation clauses in their contracts.

B. What does mediation offer?

This is not the place to embark on a complete A-Z of the mediation process. I will however remind us all of some of the key features of mediation which always need to be borne in mind when considering its application for a dispute:

---

[29] Christopher Newmark is a partner in the London office of Baker & McKenzie and a CEDR registered mediator. Andrea Dahlberg and David Green of Baker & McKenzie assisted with the research for this paper.

- **Mediation is nothing more than 'supercharged' settlement negotiation.** The process can be misunderstood to be more complex than it is. It is certainly powerful, it certainly has many subtleties and dynamics which give it advantages over direct negotiation, but, fundamentally, it is a process which involves negotiation with a view to arriving at a compromise agreement. As a basic rule, where a dispute is capable of resolution by means of a negotiated settlement agreement, mediation is viable.

- **Mediation is *usually* consensual – i.e. the parties attend the mediation by agreement.** The word usually is italicised because we will need to come back to this in the context of 'mandatory' mediation imposed by the rules of governing bodies.

- **The mediator does not give a decision, but acts as a facilitator to assist the parties in achieving a settlement.** Styles of mediation differ. Some mediators are more evaluative than others. Parties sometimes request mediators to propose solutions. But the key distinction between mediation and adjudicative dispute resolution processes remains.

Mediation can be (and usually is) very fast.

- **Mediation is always private and confidential (provided that confidentiality is upheld by the courts).** In the common law countries, the confidentiality of the mediation process is a given. In civil law countries, the attitude of the courts is less clear.

- **A successful mediation invariably requires some compromise on the part of all parties.** Mediated agreements where one party effectively capitulates are not unknown, but they are rare. Compromise of some sort is invariably involved, but this does not mean that the result always 'splits the baby'.

- **The outcome of a mediation cannot bind third parties who did not participate in the mediated settlement.** This is fundamental and of particular relevance in the sporting context. Where the interests of third parties need to be taken into account, then those parties need to buy into the mediation process so they can be bound by its outcome.

- **A settlement achieved in a mediation is only enforceable as a contract (unless it is subsequently embodied in an arbitration award or court order).** This is sometimes raised as a weakness of the process. However, this feature of mediation goes back to the underlying nature of the process – it is just a negotiation hopefully leading to a contractual agreement.

– **The terms of the settlement agreement are in the hands of the parties and
are not limited to the normal remedies associated with courts or
tribunals.** This is of course a feature of direct negotiations as well. But the
intervention of the mediator creates an environment in which creative
solutions are more likely to be explored.

C. Sports disputes in all their different shapes and sizes

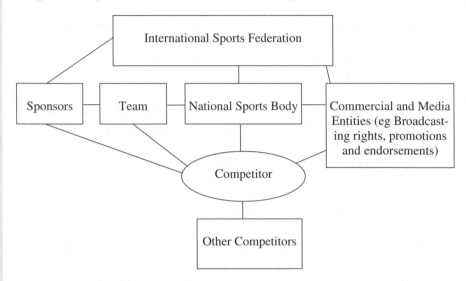

This diagram does not purport to depict all relationships in the sporting world –
but it does pick out some of the key relationships. And wherever there is a relationship there is potential for a dispute. The disputes differ in nature. In the introduction to this paper, reference is made to 'sports disputes' as if that is a term of
art or describes a clearly defined set of disputes. In fact the term is imprecise and
is used to refer to the miscellany of disputes arising out of the world of sport.
Some such disputes are purely commercial contractual disputes (e.g., those
between a competitor and a sponsor). Others are regulatory (e.g., a dispute
between a competitor and a governing body over eligibility) or quasi criminal
(e.g., disciplinary or doping disputes). A selection of characteristic disputes
(which can be illustrated with real examples) and their suitability for mediation
are described below. As will be seen, whilst mediation clearly has something to
offer for some, it is inappropriate for others.

Disputes arising when a national sporting body bans an athlete for a doping offence and the athlete appeals the decision.

The case of the German long distance runner, Dieter Baumann, illustrates this type of dispute. Baumann was found to have an excessive amount of the steroid nandrolone in his blood and was therefore automatically suspended from participating in any sport by the National Athletics Association ('NAA') in Germany. Baumann then claimed that his toothpaste was contaminated by the drug and that he was the victim of a conspiracy. The NAA refused to lift the suspension as, according to its rules, if an athlete tests positive, the burden is on the athlete to prove his innocence. Baumann filed for injunctive relief in two German courts but both courts upheld the NAA's ruling. Baumann then appealed to the NAA's own tribunal which, perhaps surprisingly, stated that a conspiracy was a viable possibility and lifted the ban. This allowed Baumann to become a member of the German Olympic team and he flew to Sydney this summer to compete. Unfortunately for Baumann, the International Athletics Association then barred him from participating.

Instinctively it is easy to conclude that this type of dispute is not suitable for mediation. The reason is that a doping offence is a quasi-criminal matter. It is not a matter capable of being settled by negotiation. A ruling of innocence or guilt is required. The rights of other competitors are also affected. Those that do not take drugs need to see that sanctions which are known and understood are imposed against drug takers. The sporting bodies need to send a clear deterrent message to other drug users. A private dispute resolution process aimed at compromise is therefore wholly inappropriate.

The CAS mediation rules recognise this and so expressly exclude such disputes from mediation with these words:

> 'CAS mediation is provided solely for the resolution of disputes related to the CAS ordinary procedure. A decision passed by the organ of a sports organization cannot be the subject of mediation proceedings before the CAS. All disputes related to disciplinary matters, as well as doping issues, are expressly excluded from CAS mediation'.
> (CAS Mediation Rules, Art 1)

What about the disputes which may *result* from the imposition of a ban?

The US runner Harry 'Butch' Reynolds tested positive for the steroid nandrolone and was banned by the IAAF. He was banned for two years and, having failed to have the ruling set aside, brought a battery of legal proceedings against the IAAF and the Athletics Congress seeking monetary compensation. His claims included breach of contract, defamation, denial of due process and tortious interference with business relations. This resulted in the IAAF banning

Reynolds from the 1992 Olympics. Subsequently Reynolds succeeded in obtaining a default judgment for more than $27 million including treble punitive damages and attempted to enforce the judgment against four of the IAAF's creditors. A further four years of appeals followed and resulted in Reynolds' case finally being dismissed for lack of jurisdiction – a matter that the IAAF had always contested.

Claims for compensation like this one are capable of compromise – especially where complex legal and jurisdictional issues arise. They raise questions such as: Where can the governing body which imposed the ban be sued (if anywhere)? Which law applies to the suit against actions of the governing body? These complexities and uncertainties make litigation even more hazardous and costly and, in such circumstances, mediation may become significantly more attractive. In England, part of the reason for the growth in the use of mediation a couple of years ago was not because lawyers and their clients thought it was a fantastic process. It was because they felt that they had to find an alternative to the cost, delays and uncertainties of the litigation process.

Disputes arising after disciplinary proceedings (other than those relating to doping).

The Football Association of England and Wales ("FA") banned the Arsenal manager, Arsene Wenger, from the touchline for twelve matches and fined him four weeks wages on 10 October this year for an alleged confrontation with an official. Wenger was found guilty by the FA of 'threatening behaviour and physical intimidation'. He pleaded not guilty at a disciplinary commission hearing and has said he will appeal the FA's decision. He was the first person to be charged under the FA's new hard-hitting disciplinary code of conduct. The fine alone amounts to about £100,000 and the ban, set to begin on 30 October this year, will affect his ability to work effectively for a considerable period.

Is this dispute concerning the severity of a punishment a matter capable of settlement? It is certainly a closer call than the Baumann case. One can perhaps envisage a negotiation where the competitor pledges better behaviour in return for a lighter sentence. But ultimately it remains a disciplinary matter where a point of principle is concerned and the governing body cannot be seen to compromise its own rules. Mediation is also typically considered inappropriate where one party needs to make a public example of a case in order to deter others. This would appear to be such a situation.

Disputes between a competitor and a governing body arising from the selection process for a representative event.

An interesting example of this type of dispute is the litigation and arbitration which arose in the last few weeks from a dispute as to which of two wrestlers should represent the US on the Greco-Roman US Wrestling Team at the Olympic Games in Sydney. Our Chicago office acted for the United States of America Wrestling Association ('USAW'), which is the national governing body for amateur wrestling, runs the Olympic trials and nominates wrestlers to the US Olympic Committee which rules on which athletes are on the team.

What happened was this: Keith Sieracki defeated Matt Lindland 2-1 in the deciding bout of the Olympic trials. USAW accordingly nominated Sieracki for the Olympic team. Lindland protested but two levels of protest committees agreed with the referee's decision on the mat. Lindland then took his case to arbitration under the rules of the USAW arguing not that the referee's judgment had been wrong, but that the referee had misapplied the rules. This, argued Lindland, made the decision one which was capable of appeal. Surprisingly, the arbitrator ordered a re-match. Sieracki protested and referred the matter to a second arbitration which was to operate effectively as an appeal of the first decision. In the meantime, Lindland won the re-match, but the USAW declined to change its nomination.

The day before the final hearing in Sieracki's arbitration, Lindland filed an action to enforce the first arbitration award (which had resulted in the re-match that Lindland had won). The Federal Court denied enforcement and Lindland appealed to the 7th Circuit Court of Appeals. Within 24 hours, after no oral argument, the 7th Circuit reversed the District Court and enforced the arbitration award and required USAW to nominate Lindland.

At about the same time that day, the second arbitration (filed by Sieracki) was concluded and the arbitrator ordered USAW to nominate Sieracki. In compliance with both the court order and the second arbitration award, USAW nominated both wrestlers. The US Olympic Committee ('USOC') delayed its selection beyond the stated deadline and Lindland brought a contempt motion against USAW (at midnight on a Friday) to compel it to name only Lindland. On Saturday, the USAW was compelled to nominate Lindland.

The USOC ignored this nomination and selected Sieracki. Lindland then sought to compel the USOC, who was not a party to the first arbitration, to accept the USAW nomination and name Lindland to the US Olympic Team. USOC appealed to the 7th Circuit.

Meanwhile Sieracki filed his own motion to enforce the second arbitration award in the Colorado Federal Court and the application was transferred to the Chicago Federal Court. The Chicago Federal Court denied enforcement of the second award simply because Lindland had enforced his award first. Sieracki then appealed this decision to the 7th Circuit. Again after no oral argument, the same appellate panel of the 7th Circuit upheld both decisions, compelling USOC to name Lindland and denying Sieracki's motion to enforce the second arbitration award. USOC sought a stay of enforcement from the United States Supreme Court and this was denied.

Lindland then went to the Olympic Games in Sydney and won a silver medal.

This case was unprecedented in the 7th Circuit. There were three separate appeals, plus additional motions in a period of 2 weeks. The 7th Circuit had not had this level of activity on such an urgent basis, even in death penalty cases.

With this level of procedural complexity and uncertainty, and with the need for a speedy solution, one might think that the ingredients were ideal for mediation. However, although this was not a disciplinary dispute, a final, non-negotiated decision was required all the same. The mediator could hardly have proposed a compromise 'Lindland, you can go to Sydney, but Sieracki, don't worry, you can go to Athens in 2004'.

Even though mediation may not seem appropriate in such cases, the English court has, on, at least one occasion, been prepared to send parties off to mediation where the rules of the governing body require this. In *Lennox Lewis v. The World Boxing Council and Frank Bruno* (unreported transcript, 3 November 1995), Lewis brought an action against the World Boxing Council ('WBC') based in Mexico and against Bruno who lived in England. Lewis wanted to stop both these parties from acting so as to allow Bruno to fight Mike Tyson for the WBC title instead of Lewis. Lewis, having served the proceedings on Bruno in England, obtained leave ex parte to serve the WBC in both Mexico and Puerto Rico. The English court subsequently ruled that the action against Bruno was just a ploy so as to enable Lewis to found jurisdiction in England against the WBC, the real defendant in the case. The court refused the relief sought and sent Lewis off to the US to conduct compulsory mediation under the WBC rules. This is interesting for a number of reasons:

– The WBC's rules provide for compulsory mediation for all claims against the WBC without distinguishing between disputes which may be suitable for mediation and those which may not.

– It is an indication of the English court's willingness to support the dispute resolution procedures of a sports governing body where those procedures provide for mediation.

– The Judge even rejected Lewis' claim that because any mediation would be under the auspices of the WBC itself, it would not be impartial. In this regard the Judge appeared to be influenced by the fact that the WBC rules did not deny Lewis access to a court if the mediation did not resolve the matter. The Judge stated:

'I see no reason to assume that such compulsory mediation process which will be carried out in Dallas pursuant to the clause will not be a perfectly proper independent process of mediation. But in any event, I see no reason to take the view that whatever the defects of the mediation process the plaintiff will be bound to accent its consequences, because in my judgment the effect, so far as I can understand it, of the exclusive jurisdiction clause, bearing in mind as I do that it is not a provision governed by English law, is that there is a backstop of litigation in the courts of Dallas as the final means of resolving any dispute between (in this case) the plaintiff and the WBC.'

Transfer disputes involving players, their clubs and, on occasions, their governing bodies.

In 1999, in a case in which our Zurich office was involved, a Canadian ice hockey player was in dispute with his former Swiss club and the International Ice Hockey Federation (IIHF) in connection with the player's intended transfer to a team in Canada. Because the player had an ongoing contract with the Swiss team, the IIHF objected to the transfer and refused to give the player the necessary release. A settlement with the club was reached so that the player could join the Canadian club. Prior to that, the Swiss team managed to have all other Swiss teams (which were members of Switzerland's premier league) sign a 'gentlemen's agreement' according to which they would not contact the player for at least two years. Two months later the player wanted to come back to Switzerland and was offered a job by one of the Swiss teams (despite the agreement). His former club intervened and requested that the Swiss National Hockey League not allow the player to play for this new club. The case was then referred to the Hockey League's (internal) judicial body (a single judge) who after a short procedure decided in favour of the hockey player.

In retrospect, mediation might have been a very useful tool to settle the dispute. These kinds of disputes are basically commercial disputes involving contractual relations between players and teams. Where, as in this case, the governing body (the IIHF) was involved, there may be issues of principle which need to be adhered to in order to protect the interests of other players and teams and the integrity of the governing bodies' rules. It would by dangerous to mandate mediation in every such case, but it may certainly have a role when used appropriately on a case by case basis.

Contractual disputes between competitors and managers, promoters etc.

In 1999 the boxer, Richie Woodhall, a WBC super middle weight champion and

Frank Warren, Woodhall's boxing promoter, were engaged in an entrenched contractual dispute. Woodhall was angry about a contract he had signed with Warren, claiming that it meant that a third party received money every time he fought (and that he had not previously been made aware of that fact). Woodhall was also unhappy about delays in payment for his fights. In the press, Warren vigorously defended his position and denied the claims. Litigation commenced before the English courts and both parties stated publicly that they were heading for court.

As a last ditch attempt to achieve a settlement, the parties agreed to mediate and they approached CEDR. CEDR appointed a mediator, found a venue and, working with the parties, had all the documentation ready within two days. After a further two days the mediation was concluded and accorded in a binding contract. The press and sports commentators were amazed at the speed of the process and its successful outcome. Before the parties entered mediation they were engaged in a war of words on television and in the press. Their relationship appeared to be very acrimonious. The mediation resulted in new contracts being drawn up which were acceptable to both parties. Both parties' lawyers and the parties themselves were full of praise for the mediation process. Frank Warren said '*It was important to all to bring this matter to a speedy conclusion. We have shaken hands and look forward to resuming our successful partnership*'. ('How to settle disputes – without a legal punch up', by Francis Gibb, The Times, 3 August 1999).

The benefits to the parties were speed, confidentiality and the ability to get on quickly with their business. Relationships can of course be very important in sport, and mediation, because of its non-adversarial nature, can assist in preserving these relationships. In this case speed was essential to the resolution of this dispute. Both parties also stood to gain by continuing their successful relationship after the resolution of the problem.

The rugby league coach, Ellery Hanley, found himself subject to an indefinite suspension after he made some unflattering comments about his club's directors. Both sides called in legal advisers (Hanley using the same firm that had represented Woodhall). Hanley received the backing of over 1,000 supporters who staged a sit-in protest. The support Hanley received showed that sacking him would be an unwise option for the club. However, his comments had been made publicly and the directors wanted an apology. The situation seemed to be deadlocked. However, after a full day of discussions a compromise was reached which was acceptable to both parties. Ellery Hanley publicly apologised and returned to his position after just 10 days suspension. Like the Woodhall and Warren case, the dispute was one which was capable of settlement through negotiation, and in both cases, mediation was the most effective way of structuring the negotiations.

Disputes between teams as to the organisation of their sport.

As this paper is being written the Rugby Football Union ('RFU') is attempting to resolve a major dispute over automatic promotion and relegation between the top two divisions in English rugby union involving 26 professional football clubs. The RFU has failed to resolve the dispute and is now proposing to the clubs that they mediate the dispute, although the clubs themselves appear less than enthusiastic with the idea. While the Chairman of the RFU has been reported as saying that he hopes the clubs will recognise that appointing an independent third party with specialist skills in resolving major and difficult issues is the right way forward, the Head of English First Division Rugby has been quoted to say: '*It wouldn't make any difference if they brought the Queen in to arbitrate*' (The Guardian, 20 October 2000).

This example illustrates the importance of the consensual nature of mediation. It is very difficult to force it on people. The RFU may think mediation is a good idea, but if the teams who are in dispute don't, it is unlikely to work. Watch this space.

D. Some important practical issues concerning the use of mediation

In England, reluctance to embrace mediation for general commercial disputes has given way to unbridled enthusiasm. Mediation clauses are being inserted into contracts and institutions are building mediation into their dispute resolution procedures. All the signs are that this heady enthusiasm for mediation may soon break out in continental Europe. Whilst those who have experienced the benefits that mediation can offer will approve of these developments, some care needs to be taken. There are few horror stories to tell (it is early days), but it is already clear that there are some trip wires ready to catch the unwary. This section addresses a few of these.

Getting to mediation

How parties arrive at mediation has a significant bearing on the mediation itself. The usual routes to me on are:

– By an agreement between the parties reached before any dispute has arisen and typically recorded in the dispute resolution provisions of a contract. As in the *Lewis v. Bruno and WBC* case described above, that contract might take the form of the rules of a governing body to which the individual or team is said to be bound.

–   By an agreement between the parties reached after a dispute arises but before litigation or arbitration have been commenced.

–   By an agreement between the parties reached in the course of either litigation or arbitration.

–   By reason of a court order which either compels or 'recommends' that the parties should use mediation before proceeding with litigation.

Before drafting a mediation clause, either in a contract or in the rules of a governing body, consider the following issues:

Clauses compelling the use of mediation

A clause which simply provides that the parties to a dispute will consider the use of mediation, but which does not compel its use, is straightforward and harmless. It overcomes the hesitancy to recommend mediation that parties often feel, but it does not require the use of mediation in cases where it is not appropriate for any reason. The perceived problem with such clauses is that they are likely to be ignored because they have no teeth. As a result, there is an increasing tendency for lawyers to draft 'binding' mediation clauses, often as part of a tiered dispute resolution procedure starting with negotiation, moving on to mediation and ending in either arbitration or litigation. These binding clauses may seem attractive, but they are, in the author's experience, fraught with danger for the following reasons:

–   The jury is still out in the court rooms of most jurisdictions as to whether such clauses are actually enforceable. Where one party refuses to mediate even where there is a clause requiring him to do so, should courts or arbitrators decline to entertain proceedings until the mediation phase has been completed? This is not a straightforward question, particularly where, in the context of the rules of sporting bodies which are based in another jurisdiction, there may also be uncertainty as to which law governs the issue.

–   One party may successfully argue that its conduct prior to mediation is covered by the same confidentiality as would have been applicable in the mediation itself if such confidentiality is upheld, it may make it difficult, if not impossible, for a court or tribunal to attribute fault where a mediation has failed to happen.

–   The development of a fundamental right of access to a court has been marked in recent years. In Europe this development has come under Article 6 of the

European Court of Human Rights (ECHR). Whilst the ECHR has been around since 1950, the powerful right of access to justice has been developed substantially in recent cases, most notably in *Osman v. UK*. Any attempt to restrict the ability of a party to 'have their day in court' is now potentially under attack. However, at least under the ECHR, rights under Article 6 are not absolute. They can be waived. Also the rights protect parties in regard to the 'determination' of the dispute as a whole, not merely one, informal stage. Provided that parties have recourse to courts or arbitrators if the mediation fails, it is unlikely that Article 6 will be successfully invoked.

– Although good drafting can probably get around the difficulty in most countries, the need for one party to commence litigation urgently either to get injunctive relief or to prevent a limitation period from expiring, can run counter to the requirement to spend time mediating before litigating.

– In order to succeed in mediation, the parties need enough information about the strengths and weaknesses of their position in order to take an informed view on settlement. In some cases, parties do not have that information until after a formal dispute resolution process has been commenced and they have had the opportunity to set out claims clearly and exchange information.

– Once the dispute arises, it may be patently unsuitable for mediation.

– Where the mediation clause is contained in the rules of a governing body, there may be a dispute as to whether such rules actually bind the other party. Lennox Lewis argued that he was not bound by the dispute resolution rules of the WBC because he was not a member of the WBC. The English court rejected this argument at the hearing on jurisdiction, but it remained a live issue. Such debates can complicate, not simplify the dispute resolution process.

Who is to act as mediator?

It is imperative that all parties in the mediation have confidence in the skills of the mediator and, even more importantly, the mediator's independence and impartiality. Where disputes arise in specialist areas, the protagonists usually want a mediator who is steeped in that specialist area. For example, in the sporting context, rugby teams arguing about the system of relegation and promotion between the divisions of their league, instinctively want a mediator who knows rugby inside out. The problem is that such individuals, by virtue of being steeped in the sport, are often not perceived as being wholly independent or impartial. Somewhere in their history, they are likely to have expressed views that could make them seem biased.

The problem is likely to be exacerbated if a sports governing body uses a fixed panel of mediators. Those mediators may, over time, become tainted with association with the governing body, and become distrusted by parties who are in dispute with the governing body. This will be all the more so if the mediations are administered by the governing body itself.

Both these factors suggest that the mediation services offered by bodies such as the CAS and SDRP, which have access to a large number of mediators who have experience in sports disputes generally, but do not have direct affiliations with any of the parties, will prove to be the most successful.

Mediation used in combination with arbitration

Parties may start an arbitration, trust their arbitrator, and decide to ask him or her to mediate. Should he accept the invitation? In the course of a mediation, the parties may realise that they are not going to be able to reach agreement, but that they would like to take advantage of the knowledge gained by the mediator and ask him or her to switch roles and become an arbitrator. Can he accept that invitation?

On the face of it these are simple requests and the neutral arbitrator or mediator should be able to do what the parties want, provided he or she feels suitably qualified to do so. However, the combination of mediation and arbitration where the same neutral is involved can give rise to real difficulties, which one needs to be wary of.

– If the parties know before the mediation phase that the mediator may become arbitrator if no settlement is reached, they may be disinclined to be frank with the mediator during the mediation phase. This may prevent the mediation from being effective.

– If a mediator has become an arbitrator, what information gleaned during the mediation phase of the case can the arbitrator use in arriving at an award? Will the use of information obtained in confidence from one party render the award vulnerable to attack or render it unenforceable?

These are not insurmountable problems. An increasing number of institutions which have traditionally offered arbitration services are now offering mediation services. CAS, the LCIA, the AAA, and, shortly the ICC are notable examples. These institutions have an important role to play in developing systems and safeguards that enable users of their services get the best out both mediation and arbitration.

Conclusion

Mediation has an important role to play in settling certain types of sports disputes. We are bound to see its use grow. The mere fact that more sports dispute resolution bodies establishing their own mediation rules and promoting its benefits will ensure this. But for mediation to succeed it should not be made mandatory. It will be most successful when used because it is suitable in the particular circumstances of each case. When it retains this flexibility – particularly in relation to use and timing – it will greatly assist the sporting world in the effective management and resolution of disputes.

William K. Slate II
The Growth of Mediation and Mediation in Sports Disputes in the US.

Good morning. As the program suggests my remarks to you are bifurcated somewhat to the extent that I first address the growth of mediation and thereafter discuss mediation in sports disputes in the U.S. Suffice it to say there is a great deal more to say about the former (i.e. growth generally) than can be said at the present time regarding mediation in sports disputes in the U.S. or to my knowledge any place else for that matter.

As to the growth of mediation in the U.S. and the world, it is certainly enjoying a heyday. At the American Arbitration Association, we see mediation, as a percentage of cases growing at a faster rate than arbitration. To be clear here, however, we are doing considerably more arbitrations day-to-day than mediations, but the growth factor of mediations is still quite evident. And, while mediation has reached a state of maturity in the states such as California, where private mediation and court-referenced mediation involve thousands of cases a year, we also see significant growth in other parts of the world. In Latin America, both Columbia and Argentina have statutes which contribute in significant ways to the utilization of mediation in a broad range of cases from civil cases to small claims to family matters. At a conference just held in Washington, DC last week, co-sponsored by the Inter-American Development Bank and the American Arbitration Association, a representative from the Columbian government stated that mediation has potentiated the availability of quasi-judicial processes to women in a way that the traditional court system has failed to deliver.

In the UK, CEDR (Centre for Dispute Resolution) advises that mediators are successful in about 85% of the cases involving business problems. Apparently one of the reasons for the tremendous increase in mediation in the UK is the new Civil Procedure Rules devised by Lord Harry Woolf, which replaced the old High Court and County Court rules on 26 April 1999. The growth of mediation is reported in other parts of Europe including Germany and France, where in Paris this past summer a program devoted to mediation was held at the House of the Paris Bar and co-sponsored by the Paris Bar and the Dispute Resolution Section of the American Bar Association. Reports were given in that meeting to suggest that mediation is taking a strong foothold now in Paris.

In returning to the U.S., a recent survey of 530 of the largest corporations in the U.S. reveal that 88% say they use mediation to resolve disputes while 79% use arbitration. Also in the U.S., a number of entities have emerged on the Internet, which provide online mediation services. The process of course necessitates high levels of security and a protected 'chat room' where a technology proficient mediator and the parties come together for a discussion and a mediated result. I have not seen any case numbers to date, but that is a capacity which all institutions will have very shortly if they do not already offer such a service. And, in speaking of online capabilities as related to mediation, it is very clear to us that the online disposition of business-to-business (B2B) conflicts which will arise out of vertical integrated marketplaces will further encourage the use of online mediation disposition when one realizes that the tens of thousands of online transactions, which will take place in vertical marketplaces cannot tolerate the inefficiency of going off-line to resolve traditional business disputes. Thus, a range of technology methodologies which incorporate mediation will clearly insight the growth of mediation as an alternative.

At the American Arbitration Association, we see contractual clauses increasingly employing mediation backed up by final and binding arbitration. As an institutional practice, we offer mediation to all parties who file arbitrations as an alternative. Thus, throughout the course of a given calendar year we have a significant number of cases which come to us with arbitration clauses which are 'converted' to mediations. Indeed this is occurring to a modest degree in our International Center where parties coming to the Center from different countries, different cultures, and different languages are willing to attempt mediation in somewhere between 7-10% of our international cases. However, in the international context the question does arise as to the effectiveness of the enforcement of foreign awards outside of the context of the United Nations Convention on the recognition and enforcement of foreign arbitral awards. There are 111 countries who are parties to the New York Convention, and of course parties may also seek enforcement, if appropriate, under the Inter-American Convention, popularly known as the Panama Convention. While an agreement signed after a mediation would have the same effect as a binding commercial contract, at least one writer, James D. Wangelin, who both writes and practices actively in international commercial arbitration, has observed that some parties have avoided the court system or mediation for reasons that include concern that a judgment or mediation award will not be recognized or enforced in a foreign jurisdiction, while arbitration awards, on the other hand, are widely recognized and enforced. So, will mediation be used increasingly in the resolution of complex, multinational commercial disputes – undoubtedly. However, I do not believe, for the reasons just articulated, that it will be an overnight success story internationally. Arbitration, after all, has taken about 75 years to reach this point of international maturity and global acceptance.

Well, how does all of this growth of mediation across every conceivable field, from employment to environmental to international relate to the use of mediation to resolve sports disputes? Apparently, precious little, if at all, if one confines sports disputes to the area of 'individual athlete participation issues.' Our research to date suggests that as to disputes involving athletes (drug use, eligibility, identity, selection to participate by an NGB), no cases have been found as ICAS (which has a new set of mediation rules, of course), at the USOC or at the American Arbitration Association where we are by federal statute the place where NGB or USOC disputes end up – no cases received.

As to athletes, the reasons for reliance on arbitration are fairly obvious. A decision on drugs/no drugs – participate or non-participation in an event, are the kinds of issues about which there is (a) very little if any middle ground; and (b) acceptance of a non-participation result is totally unacceptable to the athlete. Does this mean that mediation has no place in disputes involving athletes? I think the answer is no, but it would appear to me that its applications are limited. Might an athlete for a minor infraction agree to limited non-participation in lieu of a more extended ban? Perhaps, but then the question might arise as to whether such a result (if it involved drugs for example) is in the best interest of the governing body or the sport. And, while it needn't be the 'tail wagging the dog' the time required to reach a mediated result – even one backed up by final and binding arbitration – would very likely take too long in the midst of a major sporting event such as the Olympic Games. In such a setting, a focused, time-limited arbitration can and does produce the required timely result. So, at the end of the day, in what I am labeling as 'individual athlete participation issues' I find little incentive on the part of either side to pursue mediation.

That having been said, a host of other sports related disputes do lend themselves quite suitably to mediations. Here I have in mind a range of controversies surrounding licensing, trademark, and logo usage. I also believe that greater use of mediation might be employed as to relationships among sports entities including vying federations. Likewise there are a number of typical business issues surrounding organized sports for which mediation is appropriate including contractual disputes, sponsorship disputes, and commercial/advertisement disputes. Indeed, a number of disputes in the categories just referenced have resulted in negotiated settlements which if not mediations were clearly the first cousin to mediations.

There is one interesting development in the United States which perhaps holds out the specter of some application to athletes and sports. I have in mind here the development of a Uniform Mediation Act (UMA) which is in draft form and is the product of the National Conference of Commissioners on Uniform State Laws. Before 1980, not a single state in the U.S. had legislation requiring ADR. Today each state has multiple statutes, and in 1998 the United States Congress reinforced the use of ADR by adopting the Alternative Dispute Resolution Act of 1998. While leaving broad discretion to the courts to select the particular forms of ADR to be included in their own local programs, the Act requires all federal district courts to adopt some form of ADR and this generally means some form of mediation. Well, the Uniform Mediation Act, which would have implications principally for the states in its draft form is being discussed as a vehicle, not only for the range of civil disputes, but also to be utilized as an alternative in addressing criminal misdemeanor matters. I mention this only as a parenthetical reference since the draft is still in circulation and the debate about it continues as we speak. Nonetheless, since arguably some of the issues surrounding individual athletes, such as drugs and identity cases, have quasi-misdemeanor elements associated with them, then I ponder whether a Uniform Mediation Act that encourages experiences in the misdemeanor realm might in due course offer examples and experience that would be applicable to individual athlete disputes.

In closing I would note the disaffection which the speaker has with his own remarks since it is infinitely more interesting to offer positive ideas and suggestions in a form such as this as contrasted with concluding that the principal subject seems to have limited application to the issue at hand. Having said that I do believe mediation will continue to flourish and a host of issues, particularly the business related ones, which are so much a part of amateur and professional sports today. I do, however, conclude for the present that mediation's role will be a quite limited one, at least for the near term in the resolution of disputes involving individual athletes and their understandable desire to be allowed to participate in the events to which they have devoted themselves. Thank you very much for your kind attention.

The UK Sports Dispute Resolution Panel (SDRP)

BACKGROUND

The SDRP[30] is largely the 'brain child' of an English Lawyer, Charles Woodhouse, CVO, a former Legal Adviser to the Commonwealth Games Foundation. It was

---

[30] Further information on 'www.sportsdisputes.co.uk'.

established on 1 January 2000 and is headquartered in London. It was set up to provide sports governing bodies, commercial organisations and individuals throughout the UK with 'a simple, independent and effective mechanism ... to resolve their differences fairly, speedily and cost effectively'. It is modelled on the CAS.

In addition to offering binding arbitration and providing non-binding advisory opinions, the SDRP also offers mediation. The mediation service has been set up with advice and assistance from CEDR and exhibits many of the features characteristic of the mediation process offered by CEDR, but adapted to a sporting context.

A number of Sports Bodies in the UK have now incorporated into their Rules and also their Contracts referral of disputes to the SDRP. For example, the British Olympic Association now includes in its Commercial Contracts a standard dispute resolution clause, which provides firstly for mediation and, if that fails, then arbitration. This clause is in the following terms:

'In the event of a dispute arising out of or in relation to this Agreement including any question regarding its existence, validity or termination, the parties shall first seek amicable settlement of the dispute by mediation in accordance with the Mediation Procedure of the Sports Dispute Resolution Panel ("SDRP") in London in force at the date the dispute is referred to mediation.

If the dispute is not settled by mediation within 60 days of the appointment of the mediator, or such further period as the parties agree in writing, the dispute shall be referred to and finally resolved by arbitration under the SDRP Rules for Arbitration, which Rules are deemed incorporated by reference in this Clause.

The number of arbitrators shall be one.

The seat of the arbitration shall be London.

The Agreement is governed and shall be construed in accordance with English Law'.

Likewise, several commercial companies and firms engaged in sports marketing and promotion in the UK are also now using a similar dispute resolution clause in their Agreements.

SDRP MEDIATION RULES

The Rules of the SDRP Mediation Procedure ('the SDRP Rules') are set out in Appendix VII. Again, a few comments on them follow.

The parties to the mediation must enter into a Mediation Agreement based on the SDRP Model Mediation Agreement (based on the CEDR Model Mediation Agreement), the text of which is set out in Appendix VIII.

The mediator is chosen by the parties from a list maintained by the SDRP and, in case they are not able to agree on the mediator, the SDRP Chairman will appoint the mediator (rule 1.3). The SDRP published its first list of approved mediators in September 2000.

Rule 3.2 lays down the legal status of the mediator as an 'independent contractor'. In other words, the mediator is not acting as an agent or employee of the SDRP and so no legal liability attaches to the SDRP for any wrongful or unlawful act or omission of the mediator.

The SDRP Rules provide for the mediation to be on a *'without prejudice'* basis. These principles are reinforced by the detailed provisions of rules 11.3 and 11.2 respectively. Rule 11.3 provides as follows:

> 'None of the parties to the Mediation Agreement will call the mediator or the SDRP (or any employee, consultant, officer or representative of the SDRP) as a witness, consultant, arbitrator or expert in any litigation or arbitration in relation to the dispute and the mediator and the SDRP will not voluntarily act in any such capacity without the written agreement of all the parties'.

Rule 11.2 provides as follows:

> 'All documents (which include anything upon which evidence is recorded including tapes and computer discs) or other information produced for, or arising in relation to, the mediation will be privileged and not admissible as evidence or discoverable in any litigation or arbitration connected with the dispute except any documents or other information which would in any event have been admissible or discoverable in any such litigation or arbitration'.

As with all mediations, the SDRP Rule also state that the mediation shall be confidential (rule 11), including, it may be noted, the fact that the mediation is to take place or has in fact taken place (rule 11.1 (a)) except, of course, to the extent it may be necessary to implement or enforce any Settlement Agreement (see later).

Rule 10 provides for a stay of any court or arbitration proceedings pending the mediation, and rule 7.1 provides that no formal record or transcript of the mediation shall be made.

Any settlement reached in the mediation will only be legally effective if incorporated into a Settlement Agreement, signed by or on behalf of the parties (rule 8).

If the parties arc not able to reach a settlement, again, the parties may request the mediator, if the mediator agrees, to issue a 'non-binding written recommendation on terms of settlement' (rule 7.2).

Rule 13 of the SDRP Rules excludes liability of the SDRP and the mediator for acts or omissions in the mediation except in cases of fraudulent or wilful misconduct. Quaere: claims for negligence? Under well established general principles of tort (*Donoghue* v. *Stevenson* [1932] AC 562 and subsequent line of cases), I would consider that the SDRP and the mediator owe the parties a legal duty of care and, in the event of its breach and resulting damage, a legal action would lie despite this 'waiver of liability'.

The usual rules apply in relation to the payment by the parties of fees, expenses and costs of the mediation (rule12).

The SDRP has not yet issued a Mediators' Code of Conduct, but intends to do so and this will follow the CEDR version. The text of the CEDR Code of Conduct for Mediators and Other Third Party Neutrals is attached as Appendix IX. As will be seen, there are several provisions on the impartiality of the mediator and the avoidance of any conflicts of interest.

SDRP ADVISORY OPINIONS

Like the CAS, the SDRP issues non-binding Advisory Opinions, which, as previously mentioned, are of practical importance in assisting the parties to identify the legal issues arising in connection with their dispute.

The SDRP Advisory Opinion Rules are set out in Appendix X.

SDRP FIRST TWO YEARS' REPORT

At the time of writing, the SDRP has been in operation for two years and its Director, Jon Siddall, from whom general information on the SDRP can be obtained,[31] has issued the following Report:

The UK Sports Dispute Resolution Panel – Report on the First Two Years

In the United Kingdom, Sport's answer to the growing trend towards disputes and litigation has been to establish its own dedicated independent dispute resolution service, the Sports Dispute Resolution Panel ('SDRP').

Established by the key representative bodies of sport as a not for profit company limited by guarantee, and with support and funding from UK Sport, which has recently been renewed for a further three years, SDRP works independently on Sport's behalf in providing a comprehensive range of dispute resolution (and prevention) services, designed to meet the needs of the sports market in the UK at all levels and in all forms of dispute resolution, including those of arbitration and mediation.

It is a unique and forward-thinking initiative that brings together all sides of sport in jointly tackling the major threat that disputes represent to Sport, whether by acting as a drain on resources, tarnishing its image, straining the relationships that are key to its success, or simply detracting from the enjoyment that an

---

[31] 'jsiddall@sportsdisputes.co.uk'.

involvement in sport offers to its participants. The current members of the company are the British Olympic Association (including the BOA Athletes Commission), the Central Council of Physical Recreation, the Institute of Professional Sport, the Institute of Sports Sponsorship, the Northern Ireland Sports Forum, the Scottish Sports Association, and the Welsh Sports Association.

At the end of SDRP's second full year of operation, it is a good time to reflect on the progress that SDRP has made towards delivering its goal of 'Just Sport' – just sport in the sense of creating a sporting environment that is free from the unwelcome and costly distraction of unresolved disputes and litigation, and just sport in the sense of achieving fairness in sport through the availability of an independent mechanism to resolve and prevent disputes.

In statistical terms, SDRP has already received nearly fifty case referrals of one sort or another and a further fifty enquiries where SDRP's involvement has often assisted the process of resolving the dispute or identifying an appropriate mechanism to do so.

One of the interesting features has been the wide range of issues covered by the disputes, including discipline, selection, doping, expulsion from membership, funding, contractual rights, commercial rights, and alleged emotional abuse.

Referrals have also covered more than fifteen sports to date, both professional and amateur, and have come from a number of sources, including governing bodies of sport, individual athletes, and those advising them.

This represents an encouraging return, given SDRP's recent arrival on the scene and particularly bearing in mind that the service has as yet not been fully promoted. This reflects, in turn, a deliberate intention on SDRP's part to ensure that it operates effectively and within the resources available to it.

A key objective has been to first gain the confidence and trust of those who might use the service. Furthermore, SDRP sees its role as promoting dispute resolution arrangements that are in the best interests of Sport rather than simply persuading sports organisations to refer all disputes as a matter of course to SDRP. Some situations will merit this; others will not.

Not surprisingly, the vast majority of referrals to date have arisen on an individual case basis, although it is expected that the position will change as more and more organisations make provision within their regulations and contracts to refer disputes (involving both commercial and non-commercial matters) to SDRP where this is appropriate.

In that context, SDRP is now actively seeking arrangements with individual sports bodies to provide agreed dispute resolution services to meet their specific needs. By way of illustration, SDRP is in the second year of an agreement with The Football Association to appoint an independent chairman to all FA Appeal Boards. More recently SDRP has been appointed by the Commonwealth Games Council for England to appoint and administer the CGCE Independent Appeals Panel that considers applications for reinstatement of eligibility for Team England by individuals found guilty of a doping offence.

A good deal of SDRP's work to date has been in the appointment of independent chairpersons or panels on behalf of governing bodies thus demonstrating SDRP's flexibility and ability to provide a range of services that extends beyond simply acting as a last point of referral prior to a dispute ending up in court.

SDRP recognises the importance and value of adapting its service to meet requirements. Increasingly, this may involve an active role for SDRP in the early mediation or facilitation of disputes.

Certainly, SDRP's own experience confirms the generally held view that mediation has much to offer in a sporting context. SDRP's role in providing mediation services and in encouraging the use of mediation is an obvious one, as is its role in providing training opportunities in dispute resolution, including the art of mediation, in conjunction with other agencies such as the Sports Councils.

A sample of some of the cases dealt with to date by the SDRP illustrates the considerable and diverse potential of the service offered:

– The parties had been in dispute for a period of nine months over an alleged infringement of intellectual property rights with no immediate prospect of a resolution, and with the major sports event at the centre of the dispute imminent. A framework was agreed and a specialist QC appointed as arbitrator. The dispute was then dealt with by 'written arbitration', thereby keeping costs to a minimum, and a decision issued within four weeks of initial referral.

– A dispute involving three complaints against a coach, his club, and the governing body regarding its handling of the matter complained of. The dispute had been running for almost 18 months with little sign of agreement even as to the process. The referral to SDRP gave the complainants the confidence to abandon their complaints in favour of an independent review by a leading QC into the governing body's handling of the matter. His subsequent report identified some 'best practice' lessons of general application to sport and led to a review of the governing body's dispute resolution procedures.

– A disagreement arose over the correct interpretation of the selection regulations for a World Cup race. A single arbitrator dealt with the matter by way of written procedure and an acceptable resolution of the dispute was achieved within 10 days.

– An athlete appealed against the selection procedures applied for the World Championships, which were due to take place within two weeks. A full hearing was arranged before a panel of three arbitrators leading to an agreed outcome within seven days.

– A dispute that had been running for two years between two football clubs over the payment of a transfer fee was successfully resolved through a one-day mediation.

– A dispute between a football manager and his club following the termination of his contract was successfully resolved through a one-day mediation.

– A former official of a governing body was charged with bringing the sport into disrepute. The governing body recognised the importance of there being clear independence in the appointment of a Disciplinary Panel chairman from outside the sport. SDRP undertook this appointment and the matter was concluded satisfactorily without the need for any appeal.

The scope and success of the SDRP service is, of course, largely dependent on the involvement of the SDRP Panels of Arbitrators and Mediators.

Much progress has been made in recruiting leading experts in the arbitration and mediation fields, and SDRP is now able to call on the services of some 125 members of the Panel of Arbitrators and 50 members of the Panel of Mediators. The opportunity is being taken gradually to build on the existing levels of expertise to ensure that all areas of specialisation and experience are available.

Two years on, there is good reason to be positive about SDRP and the role it can play in delivering a best practice and modernisation agenda within dispute resolution, thereby resulting in savings for Sport, which may be measured in hundreds of thousands of pounds.

With the continued backing and support of Sport, the UK SDRP will be looking to consolidate the initial progress that has been made in establishing a service that offers a truly independent, speedy and expert dispute resolution framework at an affordable cost.

FINAL COMMENT

It is interesting to add that Kate Hoey, the former UK Sports Minister, is quoted in an article by John Goodbody, published on 12 July 2000 in 'The Times', entitled, 'Hoey aims to give Britain sporting chance' as saying that she favours 'resolving drugs cases through the new independent Sports Dispute Resolution Panel, and not through the disciplinary systems of individual sports' governing bodies'.

A nice idea perhaps, and certainly a vote of official confidence in the SDRP, but not, in my view, either a realistic or advisable one. Sports Governing Bodies jealously guard their rights and powers over disciplinary matters in their sports and doping cases are not a suitable subject for mediation (see above under 'The CAS' at page 49 et seq. and later in the section on 'Sports Mediation Limitations' at page 184 et seq.).

The Australian National Sports Dispute Centre (NSDC)

Let us now take a look at how they handle sports disputes extra-judicially 'down under'.

BACKGROUND

According to the NSDC:[32]

> 'Sporting disputes have become an epidemic in Australia in the last five years. No longer are sports disputes settled by a friendly argument between mates over a beer. Sport is big business. Even amateur sports cannot escape the potential for a dispute. Faced with potential high costs, time delay and pressure associated with Court proceedings, sports organisations have been crying out for an alternative.'

So, the NSDC, based in Sydney, Australia, was established in January 1996, to provide 'an inexpensive, fast and effective means of resolving sports disputes'.

The background to the setting up of the NSDC is described in the following extract from an article by Brian Doyle, a leading Australian Sports Lawyer and former President of the Australian and New Zealand Sports Law Association, who was involved in the setting up of the NSDC:[33]

---

[32] Further information from Kathy Tessier on 'anzsla@bigpond.com'.
[33] Sports dispute resolution in Australia (2000) vol. 3 no. 4 Sports Law Bulletin at p. 13.

'In 1992 the Australian and New Zealand Sports Law Association (ANZSLA) at its annual conference held a session specifically directed towards dispute resolution. At that time there were no facilities available in Australia that could effectively avoid the civil court system with all its disadvantages of expense, delay and the fracturing of sporting relationships.

The meeting urged the establishment of a registry of the Court of Arbitration for Sport to cover the Oceania region, and the Executor Director of the Confederation of Australian Sport (the umbrella organisation that lobbies on behalf of most Australian sports) called for the establishment of an independent disputes resolution to be established for all sports when he said:

The reality is that there are going to be severe disputes in sport which inevitably end up in the courts. Sports is emotional, it involves complicated commercial arrangements, it is often about personal and organisational power. It is multi-faceted and involves a veritable kaleidoscope of opinions – nearly all of them "expert". Ask an athlete, a coach, an administrator and a neutral observer about a sporting issue and receive four different perspectives.

Shortly after that Conference ANZSLA prepared an issues paper on the role of alternative dispute resolution in sport, and that eventually led to the establishment of the ANZSLA Dispute Resolution Scheme which was launched at the Auckland annual conference in 1995.

The service had a number of arms:
– mediation
– arbitration
– providing assistance to sporting judiciaries/tribunals and
– providing suitable people to carry out expert investigations

The proposal for a separate mediation service was to overcome what we saw as a problem within the Court of Arbitration for Sport where the arbitrators were firstly to try to settle the dispute. Most people involved in mediation or arbitration accept that to try to settle a dispute, and in doing so hear the issues and the arguments, can cause a difficulty in then sitting as an arbitrator.

Perhaps the CAS arbitrators got over this by paying lip service to the requirement to mediate. There was an overwhelming response from qualified arbitrators and mediators with that special interest in sport that we required, and panels were formed throughout the States of Australia and in New Zealand. The value of having qualified people available to conduct independent inquiries was seen in the appointment of the then President of ANZSLA Hayden Opie to investigate problems within the gymnastics section of the Australian Institute of Sport. Allegations had been raised by (mostly) parents of some of the younger girls attending the Institute as to the conduct of some of the staff. Mr. Opie conducted a long and very searching inquiry that required him to travel throughout Australia before presenting a very thorough report to the Australian Sports Commission.

The service suffered from lack of resources and funds but was nevertheless able to provide assistance to a number of sports in dispute.

In 1996 the establishment of an Oceania Registry of the Court of Arbitration for Sport in Sydney was announced. With the Olympic Games of 2000 being conducted in that city it was considered a priority to have a court up and running in the lead in to the Games.

At the same time the Australian Olympic Committee, the Confederation of Australian Sport, the Australian Sports Commission (ASC – the arm of the Federal Government that administers sport in Australia) and ANZSLA reached agreement on the establishment of a National Sports Dispute Centre Pty Limited (NSDC). Each of these organisations jointly owns an equal share in and operates the Centre, with a Director from each organisation and an appointed Registrar who is assisted in carrying out his duties by funding from the ASC.

The NSDC essentially took over the ANZSLA Dispute Resolution Service ... To some degree there may be competition between the NSDC and CAS ... The value of the NSDC has been proved. It future success will depend upon financing from the Australian Sports commission, its ability to continue to publicise itself and the enthusiasm of the lawyers who sit as mediators, arbitrators or investigators'.

LEGAL STATUS OF THE NSDC

The NSDC is a non-profit organisation and offers arbitration and mediation in 'sporting disputes', which it defines as 'including any dispute involving a person or organisation which has a connection with sport' (para. 2 of the NSDC 'Mediation Process'). It defines mediation as 'a process designed to assist parties resolve their dispute by agreement' and describes the mediator as 'an independent neutral third party who does not make a decision for the parties but facilitates honest and open discussions between them on all the matters raised' (para. 3, ibid.).

The NSDC is an independent organisation jointly operated by the Australian Olympic Committee, the Australian Sports Commission, the Australian and New Zealand Sports Law Association and the Confederation of Australian Sport. It is managed by a Board comprising four experienced sports lawyers and administrators appointed by each of these four constituent bodies.

NSDC MEDIATION SERVICES

Its mediation services are available to any individual, company or organisation whose activities are sports related, including athletes, sports governing bodies, organising committees, sponsors and companies involved in sports broadcasting, print and electronic media.

Use of the services of the NSDC are purely voluntary: the NSDC can only act if the parties to a sports dispute agree, either at the time the dispute arises, or previously if agreed in the relevant rules or contract. The NSDC offers the following standard mediation clause for inclusion in sports contracts and sports governing bodies constitutions or rules:

'In the event of a dispute arising in connection with [this Agreement/this constitution /these rules/these regulations], the dispute will be submitted by the parties for mediation to be conducted by a person agreed to by the parties, or (failing agreement) to a person appointed by the Registrar for the time being of the National Sports Dispute Centre Pty Limited (NSDC) and such mediation will be carried out in accordance with the Mediation Process of NSDC as published from time to time.'

NSDC DISPUTE RESOLUTION CLAUSES

As the use of sports mediation becomes better known and used, more Sports Bodies are including in their Rules and Regulations and parties to sports commercial deals, ventures and transactions are including in their Contracts and Agreements a Dispute Resolution Clause providing for mediation.

The NSDC has drawn up useful practical Clauses for referring sports disputes to either mediation or the process of 'med-arb' (mediation and arbitration), which we have already mentioned a useful form of alternative dispute resolution (see page 19).

The texts of these Dispute Resolution Clauses are as follows:

Mediation

'In the event of a dispute arising in connection with [this Agreement*/this Constitution*/these Rules*/these Regulations], the dispute will be submitted by the parties for mediation to be conducted by a person agreed to by the parties, or (failing agreement) to a person appointed by the Registrar for the time being of the National Sports Dispute Centre Pty Limited (NSDC) and such mediation will be carried out in accordance with the Mediation Process of NSDC as published from time to time'.

(* delete as appropriate)

Mediation and Arbitration

'(a) In the event of a dispute arising in connection with [this Agreement*/this Constitution*/these Rules*/these Regulations], the dispute will be submitted by the parties for mediation to be conducted by a person agreed to by the parties, or (failing agreement) to a person appointed by the Registrar for the time being of the National Sports Dispute Centre Pty Limited (NSDC) and such mediation will be carried out in accordance with the Mediation Process of NSDC as published from time to time; and

(b) If, after the period of 30 days from the date of appointment in accordance with (a) above, there is a continuing dispute connection with [this Agreement*/this Constitution*/these Rules*/these Regulations], either party may submit that dispute to Arbitration by written Notice to the other party. The Arbitrator will be agreed by the parties, or (if no agreement has been reached within 7 days of the Notice), the Arbitrator shall be appointed by the Registrar for the time being of NSDC. The Arbitration will be conducted in accordance with the Commercial Arbitration Act and any Arbitration Guidelines of the NSDC as published from time to time'.

(* delete as appropriate)

Let us now turn to the NSDC mediation procedure.

NSDC MEDIATION AGREEMENT AND PROCEDURE

The parties are required (described as a 'condition precedent') to sign a Mediation Agreement, in a form approved by the NSDC, before the mediation can begin (para. 11, ibid.). The form of the Standard NSDC Mediation Agreement will be found in Appendix XI.

The parties appoint the mediator, whose functions are set out in clause 2 of the Agreement as follows:

'2.1. The mediator will assist the Parties to explore options for and, if possible, to achieve the expeditious resolution of the Disputes [as defined in Schedule 1] by agreement between them.

2.2. The mediator will not make decisions for a Party or impose a solution on the Parties.

2.3. The mediator will not, unless the Parties agree in writing to the contrary, obtain from any independent person advice or an opinion as to any aspect of the Disputes, if the parties do so agree then only from such persons or persons as may be agreed by the Parties in writing.'

As will be seen, the Mediation Agreement contains provisions on other matters relevant to the proper and efficient functioning of the mediation and its success. Interestingly, these include express obligations on the part of the parties to 'co-operate in good faith with the mediator and one another...and use [their] best endeavours...to promote the efficient and expeditious resolution of the Disputes'(clause 4), and also specific rights to enforce any settlement reached in the mediation by judicial proceedings and 'adduce evidence of and incidental to the settlement agreement including [evidence] from the Mediator and any other person engaged in the mediation' (clause 14).

Returning now to the mediation procedure, this is determined by the mediator appointed by the parties. If they cannot agree on the appointment within a prescribed time limit of 7 days, then the Registrar, acting on behalf of the NSDC, is deputed to make the appointment from the panel of mediators maintained by the

NSDC. Under paragraph 5 of the Mediation Process, in choosing the Mediator, the Registrar must have regard to the following considerations:

'(a) the geographical location of the parties and the mediator;
(b) the nature of the dispute and the sport involved;
(c) the parties to the dispute;
(d) the fees that are proposed to be charged by the mediator and the ability of the parties to pay those fees; and
(e) any other matter that in the opinion of the Registrar is relevant.'

To ensure that its mediators are qualified and competent and, in order to facilitate quick and effective solutions, by having qualified people in each capital city and principal regional centre throughout Australia, the NSDC operates a strict 'Accreditation Policy'.

Under this Policy, persons wishing to become accredited arbitrators or mediators must complete a detailed Application Form and provide two referees. The texts of the NSDC Accreditation Policy and Accreditation Application Form are set out in Appendix XII.

Once accredited, they are required to pay an accreditation fee of AU$50 to NSDC towards administrative costs, refundable, incidentally, to any accredited person acting in a NSDC matter on a 'pro bono' basis.

In deciding whether or not to grant accreditation to mediators, the NSDC will take into account:

'... the overall qualifications and experience of the applicant including, without limitation;
whether the applicant has undertaken a course in mediation of a length and quality approved by the Board or Registrar;
the number of mediations that the applicant has conducted;
references of parties who have used the applicant as a mediator;
the professional experience and qualifications of the applicant;
whether the applicant has a good knowledge and understanding of the Australian Sports Industry; and
whether the applicant currently has, or is prepared to take out, a policy of professional indemnity insurance and keep current whilst the applicant remains accredited.'

Whilst all of these matters are relevant and important, in the opinion of the writer and also other sports mediation bodies consulted, knowledge and appreciation of the sports industry is of crucial importance, given the peculiarities, characteristics, structures and ethos of sport generally and the sports business, in particular (all of these matters being recognised by the EU in its Policy on Sport). It is not sufficient to be a good and experienced mediator without this specialised knowledge and understanding of what the sports industry is and what makes it tick!

Returning once again to procedural matters, as usual, the mediation is entirely confidential and conducted on a 'without prejudice' basis (paras. 18 and 19 respectively of the Mediation Process).

Any settlement (referred to as a 'resolution') of the dispute by the mediation must be incorporated in a Settlement Agreement signed by the parties (para. 15, ibid.).

Under paragraph 21 of the Mediation Process, there is also a waiver, release and indemnity in favour of the NSDC and the mediator from all liability in respect of any act or omission by them in the mediation, except in the case of fraud. As with all 'exclusion clauses', their legal validity is always questionable – this, in the final analysis, being a matter for the Courts to decide in the particular circumstances of the particular case – and this fact is recognised by the inclusion in this clause of the qualifying words: 'to the extent permitted by law'.

ROLE OF NSDC REGISTRAR

The role of the Registrar of the NSDC is set out in various paragraphs of the Mediation Process and, in particular, under paragraph 17:

> 'The Registrar shall keep a Register of all disputes referred for mediation and shall include in the Register:
>
> – the date of the appointment of the mediator;
> – the date and venue of the mediation;
> – the name of the parties;
> – the name of the mediator;
> – a brief outline of the dispute; and
> – the result of the mediation.'

NSDC MEDIATION COSTS

Now, what about the costs of a NSDC Mediation?

As previously mentioned, the aim of the NSDC is to provide an 'inexpensive' service. As a not for profit organisation, there is no charge for general enquiries and the NSDC referral service.

But for using the NSDC facilities for mediation, the parties pay a fee of Aus$250 each on execution of the Mediation Agreement (clause 10.2 of this Agreement). In addition, in the absence of agreement to the contrary, they are jointly and severally responsible for paying, in equal shares, the costs of the mediation, including the costs of the venue and the mediator's fees, and any other related costs (e.g., translation fees in mediations involving a foreign element)(clause 10.1 of the Mediation Agreement).

These fees vary according to the complexity of the matter, and the time and resources involved (equivalent to an English Solicitors' 'Schedule II Charge') and are set out in item 4 of the Schedule to the Mediation Agreement (ibid.)).

SPORTS DISPUTES MEDIATED

So far, the NSDC has been requested to intervene in a wide range of sports cases, including the following:

– Disputes between athletes and sports bodies over such matters as selection, discrimination, restraint of trade;
– Disputes between athletes or event promoters or organisations and sponsors over money due or alleged failure to perform under sponsorship agreements;
– Disputes over television broadcast rights;
– Disputes between sports federations at different levels (e.g. between a State and a National Organisation);
– Disputes between administrators and a sports organisation over employment issues;
– Disputes and appeals over penalties imposed by disciplinary tribunals including natural justice claims;
– Disputes between different sports over athletes involved in more than one sport over the use of venues;
– Damage claims by athletes for sports injuries.

In 2000, especially in the run up to the Sydney Olympics, according to Tim Frampton, the then Registrar of the NSDC:

'... there [has been] a flurry of requests for appointment of people to chair Tribunals to hear disputes concerning non-nomination for the Australian Olympic team ...'.

And according to Mark Fewel, a member of the Board of the NSDC, ADR, including mediation:

'... is ideally suited to situations where disputes arise quickly, and need to be resolved quickly ... [and] ... [t]he business of sport certainly fits into this category'.

MEDIATION IN 'RACIAL VILIFICATION'

Racial vilification has been a growing problem in Australian Football and Rugby leading to the introduction of so-called 'Vilification Codes' in an effort to combat this form of discrimination in sport. Mediation and conciliation processes have also been used successfully to deal with this problem.

In an interesting article, entitled, 'Combating vilification: The AFL and NRL Anti-vilification Rules'[34] Ian Warren discusses the role of ADR in general and mediation in particular in relation to dealing with breaches of the so-called 'Vilification Codes', introduced by the Australian Football League ('AFL') and Australian National Rugby League ('NRL'), to combat racial vilification.

This is defined in Rule 30 of the AFL Code as:

'conduct which threatens, disparages, vilifies or insults another ... on the basis of that person's race, religion, colour, descent or national or ethnic origin.'

And in similar, but more extensive terms, racial vilification is defined in Rule 2 of the NRL Code as:

'conduct which offends, insults, humiliates, intimidates, threatens, disparages or vilifies another person on the basis of that person's race, religion, colour, descent, nationality, ethnic origin, gender, sexuality, marital status, status as a parent, disability or HIV/AIDS status.'

As regards Rule 30, Warren notes in his article that it has become part of the AFL culture and, accordingly, racial vilification is no longer tolerated by the AFL He goes on to point out that, according to reports in 'The Australian' newspaper in April 1999, from the passage of this Rule in 1996 to the end of the 1997 season a total of 17 cases had been heard, all of which were successfully resolved by mediation.

He suggests that mediation has been successful because:

'Concepts of offence and harm often have subjective connotations, particularly within the context of sporting activity ... [and] ... [t]here is a vast range of behaviours, actions and words which might be deemed racially harmful in any given context. Conciliation [for which read "mediation"] processes are specifically aimed to consider these issues in an informal environment sensitive to the requirements of the parties.'

He also cites the case of the AFL player Sam Newman, who appeared on the nationally televised 'Footy Show' with his face painted black, after AFL star Nicky Winmar, who is black, failed to appear on the programme as scheduled. Newman and Winmar settled this racial slur by entering into a 'voluntary conciliation agreement' – again for 'conciliation' read 'mediation' independently of Rule 30 after complaints about the parody were made to both the network and the AFL

On the other hand, Warren points out that all cases falling under Rule 2 of the NRL Code are subject to 'preliminary conciliation conducted by an authorised

---

[34] The Australia New Zealand Sports Law Association Commentator, vol 9 no 4 March, 2000.

Complaints Officer' – again for 'conciliation', read 'mediation' and for 'Complaints Officer', read 'Mediator'.

Warren then goes on to make some interesting comments – worthy of consideration in a wider context – about the usefulness or otherwise of requiring confidentiality in dealing with complaints under both the AFL and NRL Codes as follows:

'It is difficult to compare the effectiveness of the AFL's and NRL's racial vilification codes. The critical issue lies in the frequency of complaints and the efficacy with which they are resolved. In this respect confidentiality requirements have a dual and often contradictory purpose. On the one hand they preserve the confidentiality of the victim's harm and the offender's shame at confronting that harm This is common justification for the requirement of confidentiality and informality under many models of alternative dispute resolution. On the other hand confidentiality is often compromised by extensive media and public scrutiny of suspected breaches of the Rules both before and after any mediation … As sports organisations become more accepting of legal representation in disciplinary proceedings, it is to be expected that greater synthesis of available information on the conduct and outcomes of these proceedings will be required to contest disputes in the future. This may erode the confidentiality rule with both positive and negative consequences.'

It is certainly true that, without sufficient information on mediations of sports disputes that have actually taken place and, in certain cases, without knowing either whether the mediation was successful or not, due to confidentiality constraints, it is very difficult, if not impossible, to make an evaluation of the efficacy of past mediations generally and whether to advise invoking the process in particular future cases. Precedent does have its uses. What works in one case may well work in another similar case (the Common Law *in consimili casu* principle).

Finally, he cites the interesting case of Peter Everitt and the novel and creative way in which he himself dealt with his admitted breach of Rule 30 for the second time. Again for 'conciliation' read 'mediation' and for 'deed of agreement' read 'settlement agreement'. He describes and explains the unusual resolution of this case as follows:

'After considerable debate over the availability of the conciliation process and the role of the Tribunal, Everitt offered his own punishment at a private meeting which was later ratified by the victim, the clubs concerned and the AFL in a formal "deed of agreement". Everitt agreed to step down from football for four matches and paid $20,000 of his football earnings to an indigenous development program in which he voluntarily participated. While this might be viewed as an unusual way to side-step the league's formal conciliation and tribunal procedures, it also suggests that clubs and individuals are willing and able to devise and implement their own forms of mediation and punishment alongside the League's formal rules.'

The case underscores the point that justice and honour can be done and seen to be done just as effectively through a mediation process as through a judicial process in a tribunal – in the right circumstances.

OTHER MATTERS HANDLED BY THE NSDC

The NSDC has also been involved in the following matters:

– Nominating an independent person to oversee the review of a sports organisation's decision in relation to a coaching appointment;
– Convening a panel for conducting hearings for breaches of doping policies;
– Conducting tribunal hearings in relation to selection appeals;
– Appointing experts to sit on disciplinary tribunals;
– Providing referrals to qualified sports lawyers; and
– Assisting in mediation processes for sports bodies and athletes.

As noted above (at page 19), 'expert determination' is a useful form of ADR akin to mediation and its success, particularly in the sports arena, depends upon the qualities, expertise and experience of the 'expert' appointed by the parties to settle their dispute. Apart from being competent to handle the particular sports dispute, the 'expert' also needs to command authority and respect in the sporting world. It is interesting to note, therefore, that one of the useful services offered by the NSDC is the selection of the appropriate 'expert' in a given case.

The FIFA Football Arbitration Tribunal

BACKGROUND

At its Congress in Buenos Aires on 5 July, FIFA[35], the World Governing Body of Football, announced the setting up of an 'independent' Arbitration Tribunal for Football (ATF) to deal with a variety of disputes as a final 'court of appeal'.

The ATF does not, however, have jurisdiction in respect of infringements of the 'Laws of the Game' or suspensions of up to four matches. And the amount in dispute must be 10,000 Sw.Frs. or more.

As a result of this decision, Article 63 of the FIFA Statutes[36] has been replaced by a new Article, the text of which is reproduced in Appendix XIII.

Although Football is part of the 'Olympic Programme', FIFA does not, like most

---

[35] Website: 'www.fifa.com'.

[36] See Section 2.11 of 'Basic Documents of International Sports Organisations' (1998) edited by Robert C. R. Siekmann & Janwillem Soek, Kluwer Law International The Hague The Netherlands at pp. 265-282.

International Olympic Sports Governing Bodies, refer disputes to the Court of Arbitration for Sport (CAS), set up by the IOC in 1983 – not even to the Appellate Division of the CAS, which hears appeals from International Sports Governing Bodies on disciplinary matters, particularly doping cases. However, during the Summer Games, football disputes, like all other sporting disputes arising during the Games, are required to be submitted to the so-called Ad Hoc Division of the CAS, which is in session throughout the Games to settle disputes within 24 hours of being referred. In fact, such references are a condition precedent for participation in the Games.[37]

To a large extent, the creation of the ATF was foreseen and necessitated by the new International Transfer Rules, agreed by FIFA, UEFA and The EU Commission in Brussels on 5 March 2001, following the Bosman case in 1995,[38] and approved by the FIFA Congress on 5 July 2001. However, initially the new Rules were challenged under EU Competition Rules and Belgian Labour Law by the International Football Players Union, FIFPro, in the Brussels High Court, in which an injunction was sought to prevent FIFA from implementing them. The dispute was amicably settled and the Court Proceedings withdrawn by FIFPro on 31 August 2001.

Under the new International Transfer Rules, set out in Appendix XIV, disputes, especially those concerning the amount of compensation to be paid to clubs for their 'investment' in players under 23, who move during the currency or at the end of their contracts, will be settled by this new Football Arbitration Tribunal.

FIFA CIRCULAR NO. 769

The new Rules came into effect on 1 September 2001 and on 24 August 2001, FIFA issued a Circular No. 769, entitled 'Status and Transfer of Players', summarising and explaining the main points of the Rules.[39] Section 6 of the Circular is headed 'Dispute resolution, disciplinary and arbitration system' and provides as follows:

'Without prejudice to the right of any player or club to seek redress before a civil court, a dispute resolution and arbitration system shall be established, which shall consist of the following elements:

– Conciliation facilities offered by FIFA, through which a low cost, speedy, confidential and informal resolution of any dispute will be explored with the parties by an independent mediator. If no such solution is found within one month, either party can bring a case before FIFA's Dispute Resolution Chamber.

---

[37] Bye-Law 5.1 of art. 49 of the Olympic Charter of 11 September, 2000.

[38] Case C-415/93 *Union Royale Belge des Societies de Football ASBL v. Bosman* [1995] ECR I-4921.

[39] The text of this Circular and the new Transfer Regulations themselves can be downloaded by logging on to the official FIFA website: 'www.fifa.com'.

- Dispute Resolution Chamber, with members chosen in equal numbers by players and clubs and with an independent chairman, instituted within FIFA's Player Status Committee, establishing breach of contract, applying sport sanctions and disciplinary measures as a deterrent to unethical behaviour (e.g., to sanction a club which has procured a breach of contract), determining financial compensation, etc. In addition, the Dispute Resolution Chamber can review disputes concerning training compensation fees and shall have discretion to adjust the training fee if it is clearly disproportionate in the individual circumstances. Rulings of the Chamber can be appealed by either party to the Football Arbitration tribunal.
- Football Arbitration Tribunal, with members chosen in equal numbers by players and clubs and with an independent chairman, according to the principles of the New York Convention of 1958.'

For the avoidance of doubt, the Dispute Resolution and Arbitration System will take account of all relevant arrangements, laws and/or collective bargaining agreements, which exist at national level, as well as the specificity of sport as recognised recently, for instance, in the relevant Declaration appended to the presidency Conclusions of the European Council at Nice in December 2000.

Particular reference should be made to section 7 of FIFA Circular No. 769, headed 'Dispute Settlement', which explains the relationship between FIFA's Dispute Resolution Chamber and the new Arbitration Tribunal for Football. As will be seen (para e.), FIFA offers 'low cost, speedy, confidential and mediation' for the settlement of disputes between a player and a club.

The text of section 7 is as follows:

'The key to the new dispute settlement provisions are the following elements:

a. Players and clubs have the choice to submit the triggering, contract-related elements of their disputes to national courts or to football arbitration.[40] Whatever the choice they make, the sportive sanctions envisaged in the present regulations can only be imposed by FIFA bodies, notably the Dispute Resolution Chamber. Decisions of this Chamber are subject to appeal to the Arbitration Tribunal for Football.

b. FIFA's Dispute Resolution Chamber will be composed of members chosen in equal numbers by players and clubs, as well as an independent chairman.[41] The same is true for the Arbitration Tribunal for Football whenever it hears appeals from decisions taken by FIFA's Dispute Resolution Chamber.[42]

c. If a party chooses to have its dispute resolved through football arbitration, the triggering, contract-related elements of the dispute will be handled by FIFA's Dispute Resolution Chamber at the request of this party, unless both parties have agreed in writing or it is provided in a collective bargaining agreement not to submit this part of the dis-

---

[40] See art. 42. 1 of the FIFA Transfer Regulations.
[41] See art. 42.1(b)(i), ibid. and art. 15 of the Application Regulations.
[42] See art. 42.1(c), ibid.

pute to FIFA's Chamber but rather to a national sportive arbitration tribunal. However, for this agreement or this provision to be recognized by FIFA, the national arbitration tribunal must also be composed of members chosen in equal numbers by players and clubs, as well as an independent chairman.[43]

d. Whenever a dispute between a player and a club is put to football arbitration, and an unjustified contractual breach is found, FIFA's Dispute Resolution Chamber is exclusively competent to establish the consequences of this finding (notably sportive sanctions, financial compensation), subject to appeal to the Arbitration tribunal for Football. The same is true for disputes relating to training compensation.[44]

e. Whenever a dispute between a player and a club arises, FIFA will offer low cost, speedy, confidential conciliation facilities available to the parties. The parties are free to accept mediation by an independent mediator. Any such conciliation will not delay or interfere with the formal dispute settlement procedures.[45]

f. Before reaching any decision in the matters discussed here, FIFA's Dispute Resolution Chamber will ask the national association which held the registration of the player before the dispute arose to give its opinion on the dispute'.[46]

THE INTERNATIONAL COURT FOR FOOTBALL ARBITRATION

The ATF will operate under the umbrella of a new Foundation created by FIFA, the International Court for Football Arbitration (ICFA), whose funding will be the responsibility of the FIFA Executive Committee, who will act as a 'funding agent'.

The ICFA follows the model of the International Council of Arbitration for Sport (ICAS), which was set up by the IOC in 1994, to fund and regulate the CAS, following the Elmar Gundel case in 1993,[47] in which the independence of the CAS was challenged in the Swiss Federal Tribunal. Although this legal challenge was rejected on the facts and circumstances of the particular case, the Tribunal did, however, express certain reservations in case the IOC was a party to proceedings before the CAS whilst the CAS was entirely funded by the IOC.

FINAL REMARKS

The exclusion in para. 6 of new Article 63 of the FIFA Statutes of the right to resort to the ordinary courts of law, being an attempt to oust the jurisdiction of the courts, is void under English Law – and also under many other Legal Systems around the world – as being contrary to 'public policy' ('*ordre public*').

---

[43] See art. 42.1(b)(i), ibid.
[44] See art. 42.1(b)(ii)-(v), ibid.
[45] See art. 42.1(a), ibid.
[46] See arts. 42-44, ibid.
[47] *Elmar Gundel v. FEI/CAS* [1993] I Civil Court (Swiss Fed Trib).

However, if reworded to the effect that recourse to the ordinary courts is only permitted after all procedures under the ATF have been exhausted, this is perfectly valid under the House of Lords ruling in the leading English case of *Scott v. Avery*.[48]

At the time of writing, the Rules to implement all these new arrangements have not yet been issued.

---

[48] [1856] 5 HL Cas 811.

CHAPTER VIII
AMERICAN ARBITRATION ASSOCIATION (AAA)

Background

In the United States, under the Ted Stevens Olympic and Amateur Sports Act of 1978 – usually referred to as the 'Amateur Sports Act' – National Governing Bodies (NGBs) of each sport are required to submit all disputes within the scope of this Act to binding arbitration by the American Arbitration Association (AAA).[49]

The Act also entitles Olympic, Pan American and Paralympic athletes and other parties dissatisfied with rulings of the United States Olympic Committee (USOC) to be reviewed by the AAA.

The decisions of NGBs, under the provisions of the USOC Constitution, are subject to arbitration by the AAA.

The AAA has an extensive experience of conducting Mediations and Arbitrations and the corresponding Rules are set out in full in Appendix XV.

Should CAS replace AAA?

Although the AAA has much experience of conducting Arbitrations of many kinds, in view of the developing role of the CAS in settling international sports disputes, there is a growing feeling, in some quarters, that the Amateur Sports Act should be amended to substitute the CAS for the AAA as the designated arbitral body to determine disputes between athletes and USOC and/or its NGBs.

For a view on this and the pros and cons of introducing such a requirement, the following contribution to this ongoing debate by American Lawyer, Paul H. Haagen, Professor of Law, Duke University School of Law, Durham, North Carolina, *'Have the Wheels Already been Invented? The Court of Arbitration for Sport as a Model of Dispute Resolution'*.[50]

The sports community faces the same problems that any other community faces when dealing with a dispute: how to resolve the matter in a way that is efficient and cost effective, and seen by interested parties to be fair. It faces those problems, however, in a context in which both the parties to the dispute and

---

[49] Website: 'www.adr.org'.
[50] 'www.e-global.es/arbitration/papersadr/paper_sports.pdf'.

interested third parties are likely to view any resolution through the jaundiced eye of partisanship. The cries of anguish that issue from the crowds at every sporting event, convinced that an injustice is perpetrated by each referee's call (and many non-calls), are only the most audible indication of the difficulty of adjudication in the context of intense competition.

In addition, there is often a need for a very rapid response. If the eligibility of an athlete is challenged on the eve of a competition, the question must either be decided very quickly or the competition will be seriously disrupted and distorted. Even when the context does not require an immediate decision, athlete careers are frequently so short that justice delayed is justice denied. In addition, the disputes are often about arcane matters, only poorly understood by persons outside the sports community, and take place against the background of legal norms that are relatively undeveloped. When we add to this that they can also involve very substantial amounts of money, and access to competitions that may define an athlete's sense of self, the potential intensity of the conflict becomes clearer.

The nature of many disputes in sports, moreover, precludes the easiest and happiest forms of dispute resolution. In general, they must be decided. They cannot merely be settled. There are few win/win situations, and a not inconsiderable number of lose/lose ones.

When these disputes take place not against the background of local or national competition, but international competition, each of the difficulties noted above is made more intense by the overlay of differing cultural and legal expectations, and increased levels of suspicion of the motives and good faith of others. Few competitors, and few of their supporters, are prepared to believe that anyone else's domestic adjudicatory process, whether in the courts or in some non-judicial forum, will produce fair or consistent results. They are certainly right to be skeptical. The handling of athletic disputes in domestic courts has not been among the greatest of judicial success stories. The individuals who run international sport have been vocal and open in their contempt for the interference of domestic tribunals, especially those of the United States, in the running of what they regard as their internal affairs.

Sixteen years ago, the IOC attempted to address these problems by creating the Court of Arbitration for Sport, or CAS. CAS was designed to be an international arbitral body capable of resolving disputes in the field of sports. It consists of two 'divisions': the Ordinary Arbitration Division, which handles matters of first instance, and the Appeals Arbitration Division, which deals with appeals from the decisions of federations, associations and other sports bodies. Sixty 'well-known jurists who also have a good knowledge of sports related issues' were appointed to serve as potential arbitrators. Both CAS and the arbitrators were, according to the pronouncements of the IOC, 'completely independent from the IOC, in the exercise of their duties'. If the IOC was impressed with the independence of CAS, others were not. Despite the pronouncement of independence, there were powerful indicia of dependence. The IOC had created CAS, it selected half of CAS's members, it administered and supervised CAS, it provided all of CAS's 'running costs', and CAS was physically located on the grounds of the IOC in Lausanne, Switzerland.

In 1993, the question of CAS's complete independence was challenged in court. The Swiss Federal Tribunal in the *Gundel* decision held that CAS did, in spite of the entanglements, offer 'the guarantees of independence upon which Swiss law makes conditional the valid exclusion of ordinary judicial recourse', but noted that the close ties between the IOC and CAS left open the question of whether it was sufficiently independent to serve as a valid arbitral body in a case involving the IOC. This opinion spurred a restructuring designed to make CAS more independent of the IOC. The critical reforms were the creation of ICAS, the International Council of Arbitration for Sport, to supervise and regulate CAS, the insulation of CAS from direct IOC supervision, and the change in the method of selection and an increase in the number of potential arbitrators. Under the reformed system, there are 150, 30 chosen from among those proposed by the IOC, 30 from among those proposed by the IF s, 30 from among those proposed by the NOCs, 30 chosen after appropriate consultations with a view to safeguarding the interests of athletes, and 30 chosen from among persons independent of the bodies responsible for proposing arbitrators.

In 1996, CAS added two additional courts, one at the National Dispute Resolution Center in Sydney, Australia and the other in Denver, Colorado, substantially increasing its potential attractiveness to non-European athletes.

The reformed CAS appears to address many of the most pressing problems surrounding the resolution of athletic disputes, and it has aroused considerable interest that it may provide a workable forum for adjudicating these disputes. It was recently proposed, for example, that the USOC externalize the adjudications process relating to doping by turning it over entirely to CAS.

In the remaining time, I want to raise the question of whether it will be possible to use CAS in this way and whether, given its current structure and modes of operation, such use would be desirable. As with most discussions of alternatives to current methods of dispute resolution, the answer depends in large measure on what one takes to be the baseline. It is easy to fall into the trap of comparing ideal litigation with actual arbitration, or the theoretical benefits of arbitration with the evident short comings of litigation. Here the analysis is complicated by the fact that to date there have been relatively few reported decisions from CAS, and even fewer involving difficult, contentious issues. That said, for those of you who like to look at the end of books first, my answer to the first question will be a qualified yes, and the answer to the second is that there will be some significant benefits and some significant problems.

1. The first issue to be faced is whether it is possible consistent with US law to require resort to CAS. At present, the answer is likely to be both no, but there is reason to believe that Congress may be willing to change the law. Although the language of the Amateur Sports Act is not entirely clear, the Act it is likely to be interpreted to require that arbitration of sports related disputes be AAA arbitration. If there is sufficient support for CAS in the American sporting community, it seems likely that the Act would be amended to permit the parties to agree to CAS arbitration.

2. The second issue is assuming that the Amateur Sports Act permits the use of CAS arbitration will CAS arbitration be available to deal with such disputes? Within the field of sport, CAS has very broad jurisdiction to hear cases in which the parties have agreed to submit their disputes to CAS.

   Until relatively recently, there was a substantial likelihood that the US courts would refuse to enforce pre-dispute arbitration agreements by denying a recalcitrant party access to the courts. The dramatic shift in attitude in the US courts toward arbitration and toward the enforceability of contracts to arbitrate makes it almost certain that they would be enforced today. Even adhesive contracts imposed on persons with no realistic alternatives but to sign them will be treated a enforceable agreements to arbitrate, at least in any situation in which the arbitration process meets at least minimal standards of due process.

   As a practical matter, getting the signed agreements from participating may be an administrative headache for the various federations. Attempting to solve the administrative problems may in turn raise legal issues. Will, for example, an agreement entered into on-line, but that is not followed up with a hard copy signature page, constitute a valid agreement enforceable agreement to arbitrate. There will also be serious questions about the enforceability of agreements entered into by or on-behalf of minors in those jurisdictions that do no by statute specifically provide that they are enforceable. Assuming that there are no problems relating to minors and theadministrative problems associated with actually getting valid signatures on the agreement to arbitrate, these agreements should be legally enforceable.

3. Assuming that CAS accepts the case will the Swiss courts treat CAS as a valid arbitral body? In light of the reforms, the answer is almost certainly yes. The *Gundel* case went a long way toward recognizing CAS as a valid arbitral body even under the old structure. It is difficult to believe that the reforms will not have removed their remaining doubts.

4. Assuming that the Swiss courts treat CAS as a valid arbitral body, will the US courts enforce the arbitral decisions without subjecting them to judicial review? Under the New York Convention, and the developing interpretation of arbitration law in the US, the answer is again almost certainly yes.

Thus we have in CAS a body able to render enforceable arbitral decisions.

Will this body deliver on the promise of speedy, cost effective justice, that is both fair to the parties and seen by the parties to be fair? No one knows. The record to date is too incomplete.

Is the structure of the organization such that it seems likely that it will? Here the answer seems to be mixed. There are some hopeful signs, and some reasons for concern.

The usual claims for arbitration are that it will be quick and relatively inexpensive. The CAS rules do, in fact, encourage quick resolution. They provide for relatively short time periods for the formation of the panels and for the rendering of opinions. There are a number of procedural devices that make it possible to deal with matters expeditiously. CAS has created special ad hoc bodies, such as the one at the Atlanta Olympics, where the need to timely adjudication was particularly acute.

Nothing guarantees that there will not be delays, but the structure favors quick resolution.

Similarly, the costs of proceeding through CAS seem reasonable for most situations. There will, however, be ones that raise serious concerns. CAS does not provide counsel for those unable to provide counsel for themselves, although at Atlanta it did encourage volunteers to provide free services. It also permits on a discretionary basis the apportioning of costs among the parties in accordance with their ability to pay. Whether this is enough to insure fairness is open to question, but then it should be borne in mind that many of these same criticisms could be leveled at the courts as well. What may be of more moment than the equitable concerns is the legal validity of any agreement to arbitrate that does not address them. Where employees are forced as a condition of employment to submit disputes with their employer to mandatory arbitration, the United States Court of Appeals has held that the employer must pay the costs of the arbitration in certain circumstances. It seems likely that the courts might hold federations that impose a requirement that competitors agree as a condition of participation to mandatory arbitration would be subject to a similar due process requirement, at least in any situation in which an athlete would be denied access to CAS because that athlete did not have the resources to bring the case.

Much of the attractiveness of CAS turns on the fact that the arbitrators are all persons ostensibly with expertise in sport. The value of expertise is immediately and intuitively obvious. Anyone who has ever litigated or arbitrated a case can tell horror stories of attempting to convey complex information to judges or arbitrators who are incompetent and uninformed. Expert panels can much more quickly focus on the issues genuinely in dispute, thus reducing costs and delay. They do not need to be brought up to speed. Many matters that would need to be explained to non-experts either will not need to be explained at all, or will be able to be explained much more efficiently.

Expertise is, however, a problematic concept. What constitutes expertise is left to the nominating bodies and ICAS. Nowhere is it defined. Nor is expertise, however defined, in one aspect of sport necessarily easily transferrable to another. A person expert in the organization of the International Olympic Committee may have no greater ability to deal with the science underlying a claimed challenge to a doping violation than any random member of the judiciary. Some may have less.

Experts are easily confused with persons who merely have a vested interest, and the unhappy history of expert courts in this country ought to serve as a caution.

President Taft created the Commerce Court for reasons that closely track those being given in favor of CAS – that it would permit the rapid and uniform resolution of often arcane regulatory disputes involving the Interstate Commerce Commission, a rapid and uniform resolution not available through the regular courts. Two and a half years later, the experiment was abandoned. The concentration of one type of dispute in a single body, it turned out, favored capture and corruption more than efficiency. One of the expert judges was discovered to have been accepting bribes from the railroads, and Congress or the Supreme Court ended up reversing virtually all of its decisions. The point here is not that CAS will so quickly fall prey to the same problems. The point is rather: 1) that expertise is not so easily established when we are dealing with an organization with as broad a mandate as CAS , that is for any relevant decisional group it may not be all that expert and 2) that expertise does not necessarily promote fairness.

These complaints notwithstanding, it seems likely that CAS arbitrators will have sufficient familiarity with sport related issues that they will be especially adept in dealing with cases that do not raise fundamental, structural questions. Was the handling of a particular urine sample compromised? – where the only question is one about establishing whether the taking of the sample conformed to standard procedures. Was the taking of a substance not specifically banned and about which there was lack of data about the performance enhancing effect grounds for stripping an athlete of an Olympic medal? Here the importance of familiarity with the usual ways of doing things, of the conventional understandings of athletes is enormously important.

Where the dispute does raise fundamental, structural questions, familiarity with and allegiance to the usual way of doing things is likely to be a hindrance. For example, if the question is whether existing tests for endogenous substances are adequate to constitute adequate proof of doping, then the question of meaning of expertise – and of genuine independence from the bodies with a vested interest in the regulation of sport becomes more pressing. To date, the reported decisions from CAS are reasonably comforting in their balance.

On the other hand, to date CAS has not ruled on hard questions that might affect the interests of federations, NGBs, NOCs or the IOC. One example of the experience to date may be illustrative of the current state of our information. In 1997, CAS reversed the decision of FINA to suspend for two years a water polo athlete who took a prescription drug to control asthma. Under FINA's rules, the athlete was entitled to take the drug, but was required to declare that he had done so. Operating under a misapprehension, caused in part by the failure of the IF to keep its various NGBs informed of changes in the rules, the athlete failed to report that he had used an inhaler to control asthma and was suspended from competition for two years from July 26 1995 to July 26 1997. The IF represented to CAS that it did not regard the athlete as a cheat. Rather, it believed that he had made a good faith mistake, but that it had no flexibility under its regulations to impose a lighter sanction or no sanction at all. CAS upheld the finding of a doping violation, but noted that it had greater authority with regard to the imposition of penalties and 'cancelled' the sanctions – or presumably only the three and a half months that were remaining of them. It is comforting that an athlete who took a substance that he was entitled to take, and whose only violation was the good faith failure to report the taking of it, and whose position was supported by both his national federation and the IF, could have the equity of his position vindicated. It was not a hard case. Whether the only partial independence of CAS will permit it the independence to take on the hard case and to protect athletes in accordance with the 'fundamental principles of law' that govern CAS proceedings remains an open question. Given the continuing control, albeit indirect, that the IOC exercises over CAS, there is strong reason to believe that such cases are not likely to get the serious review that they would get from a court or from a more independent, general body like AAA.

Searching review is, of course, only one value. Especially when we are talking about matters in international sports, the need for confidence in the consistency and uniformity of decisions may be equally pressing. What does CAS promise here? By centralizing decisions in a single body, and removing those decisions from both domestic and sport based tribunals, it may be possible to achieve greater uniformity. It should be noted, however, that not all federations are currently prepared to accept the jurisdiction of CAS either on matters of first instance or on appeal. Thus, even if CAS were to achieve consistency among those matters submitted to it, it could not deal with matters excluded by federations from its purview. What about consistency among those matters submitted to it.

There are a large number of potential arbitrators, drawn from around the world, and coming out of distinctly different legal traditions, who could be called on to decide any given case. It strains credulity to believe that they are likely to decide cases similarly. Moreover, like most arbitral bodies, CAS is not bound by precedent. Even if it were, it would be difficult for subsequent panels follow the lead of earlier panels, because of the incompleteness of the reported cases. This is admittedly a more pressing concern for persons trained in the Common Law, and especially those trained in the United States. Civil Lawyers have learned to live with sparse case reports. But if it is a more obvious concern for those of us trained in the Common Law, it is a more general problem as well. As Craig Masback has noted, there is a pressing need in international sports for what he has called a *lex sportiva*, a stable body of law that is transparent and consistent. Both the transparency and the consistency will certainly lead to greater confidence in and acceptance of decisions – especially those rendered by a body that is foreign to the participants, applying principles of law unfamiliar to them, and imposed on them by the very bodies that they are now in conflict with.

Has the wheel already been invented? Yes and no. The reformed CAS constitutes an important innovation in the search for a reliable, efficient forum for the resolution of sports related disputes. It has many of the positive features of sport specific arbitral bodies and has gone further than previous organizations to create the kind of externalization and independence that will be necessary to achieve credible results. It remains, however, closely tied to the IOC , the NOCs and the federations.

These ties will inevitably raise questions about the independence of CAS, particularly among those forced to resort to it.

The procedures established by CAS, like those of most arbitral bodies, have all of the advantages that come with greater informality and all of the disadvantages of them as well. There are questions about whether CAS has the authority to reach the full range of remedies available through the courts.

There is a wheel out there. How good it is remains to be seen.

Article 74 of the Olympic Charter

In any case, pursuant to article 74 of the Olympic Charter,[51] 'any dispute arising on the occasion of, or in connection with, the Olympic Games shall be submitted exclusively to the Court of Arbitration for Sport, in accordance with the Code of Sports-Related Arbitration'.

In practice, as a condition of entry to the Games, athletes are required to sign a waiver agreeing to the exclusive jurisdiction of the CAS for the settlement of such disputes pursuant to Bye-Law 5.1 of article 49 of the Olympic Charter.

Coaches, trainers and officials involved in the Games are also required to sign a similar declaration under Bye-Law 5.3 of the same article.

In fact, the wording of these two Bye-Laws is identical apart from the reference in the first line and the text is as follows:

---

[51] 11 September, 2000.

'Understanding that as a [competitor/coach/trainer/official] in the Olympic Games I am participating in an event which has ongoing international and historical significance, and in consideration of the acceptance of my participation therein, I agree to be filmed, televised, photographed, identified and otherwise recorded during the Olympic games under the conditions and for the purposes now or hereafter authorized by the International Olympic Committee ('IOC') in relation to the promotion of the Olympic Games and Olympic Movement.

I also agree to comply with the Olympic Charter currently in force and, in particular, with the provisions of the Olympic charter regarding the eligibility for the Olympic games (including Rule 45 and its Bye-law), the olympic movement Anti-Doping Code (Rule 48), the mass media (Rule 59 and its Bye-law), concerning the allowable trademark identification on clothing and equipment worn or used at the Olympic Games (Paragraph 1 of the Bye-law to Rule 61), and arbitration before the Court of Arbitration for Sport (Rule 74).

The relevant provisions and rules have been brought to my attention by my National Olympic Committee and/or my National Sports Federation.'

International Sports Arbitration Generally

On the subject of using Arbitration for settling sports disputes generally, a leading US Sports Lawyer and Academic, Prof James A.R. Nafziger of Willamette University College of Law, USA, and Vice President of the International Association of Sports Law, has written a most interesting article, entitled 'Arbitration of Rights and Obligations in the International Sports Arena'.[52]

It is reproduced in full as follows:

James A.R. Nafziger[*]
Arbitration of Rights and Obligations in the International Sports Arena

Arbitration of disputes related to international sports competition is a growth industry. Certainly one of the most important developments in sports law during the past few years has been the expanded role of the Court of Arbitration for

---

[*] Thomas B. Stoel Professor of Law, Willamette University College of Law; Vice President, International Association of Sports Law. This article is based on the author's remarks at a conference in Chicago on 2 and 3 November 2000, entitled, 'Arbitrating Sports Disputes: A World View' This conference was organized by the Valparaiso University School of Law. The author thanks Christopher Cipoletti and Steven J. Thompson for their assistance in the preparation of this article.

---

[52] Spring 2001, Valparaiso University Law Review, Vol. 35 No. 2, pp 357-377.

Sport ('CAS').[1] Business is also brisk for the American Arbitration Association and other national arbitral bodies around the world.[2] Many of the disputes have involved the eligibility of athletes on the eve of sanctioned international competition.[3]

I. GROWTH OF INTERNATIONAL SPORTS ARBITRATION

In 1988, not a single demand for arbitration was filed during the run-up to the Olympic Games in Seoul.[4] By contrast, in 2000, the docket prior to the Sydney Games numbered some eight cases in the United States alone[5] and six times that number in Australia.[6] Arbitration of international sports disputes in Europe is also common.[7] The growth industry of international sports arbitration is clearly multinational. Hailing, as I do, from the state that brought you Tonya Harding in 1994,[8] Mary Decker Slaney in 1996, 1997, 1998 and 1999,[9] and Matt Lindland in 2000[10] – three very different individuals, but all seasoned veterans of arbitration – I hope you appreciate that we Oregonians are doing our part to fuel this industry. And, as Matt Lindland's silver medal in Sydney attests, we are getting better at quality control within the industry.

What accounts for this 'A trendy Olympic event,'[11] this 'burgeoning Olympic sport of arbitration',[12] as it has been called? Several explanations are immedi-

---

[1] *See* Matthieu Reeb, *The Role of the Court of Arbitration for Sport, in* INTERNATIONAL LAW AND THE HAGUE's 750TH ANNIVERSARY 233 (Wybo P. Heere, ed., 1999); James A.R Nafziger, *The Court of Arbitration for Sport and the General Process of International Sports Law, in* INTERNATIONAL LAW AND THE HAGUE's 750TH ANNIVERSARY 239 (Wybo P. Heere, ed., 1999).

[2] Newspaper headlines tell the story. *See, e.g.,* Jess Bravin, *Ready, Set, Arbitrate!: Here is This Year's New Hot Olympic Event. Arbitration,* WALL ST. J., Aug. 18, 2000, at A1, A6; Vicki Michaelis, *Roster Disputes Go Down to the Wire,* USA TODAY, Aug. 24,2000, at 1C.

[3] *See, e.g.*, LAURI TARASTI, LEGAL SOLUTIONS IN INTERNATIONAL DOPING CASES: AWARDS BY THE IAAF ARBITRATION PANEL 1985-1999 (2000); RECUEIL DES SENTENCES DU TAS/DIGEST OF CAS AWARDS 1986-1998 (Matthieu Reeb ed., 1998).

[4] Bravin, *supra* note 2, at A1.

[5] Michaelis, *supra* note 2 at 1C.

[6] *Id.*

[7] *See, e.g.*, LUC SILANCE, LES SPORTS ET LE DROIT 406-08, 417-18 (1998) (referring particularly to Belgian and French practice).

[8] *See* James A.R. Nafziger, *International Sports Law as a Process for Resolving Disputes,* 45 INT'L & Comp. L.Q. 130,140-42 (1996).

[9] *See* TARASTI, *supra* note 3, at 155.

[10] *See infra* Parts II-III.

[11] Michaelis, *supra* note 2, at 1C.

[12] Jere Longman, *On the Olympics: Athletes Are Taking the Trials from the Arenas to the Courts,* N.Y. TIMES, Aug. 23, 2000, at C23.

ately apparent. Video taping and electronic records of trials and final events provide better evidence to resolve disputes and thereby encourage more challenges to decisions. More obviously, perhaps, issues involving doping and the use of other performance-enhancing agents have sparked a substantial amount of arbitration. Even though the identification, testing, and sanctioning of prohibited substances and techniques are more effective today than even five years ago, the circumstances of their procurement, distribution and use are subtle and often ambiguous, giving rise to more disputes. And speaking of agents, the growing role of professional agents and sports lawyers has given athletes a keener eye for infractions of their rights, procedures for implementing those rights, and alternative remedies for redressing their grievances. Today's athletes have a better idea of their rights and are prepared to act on them regardless of the traditional etiquette against doing so on the eve of competition. They also know that the stakes of eligibility are much higher than they used to be.

In responding to these developments, arbitration has become a preferred means for resolving sports-related disputes. In the United States, this trend is in part the result of the Ted Stevens Olympic and Amateur Sports Act[13] – otherwise known as the Amateur Sports Act which endorses arbitration to resolve disputes in the sports arena. The law requires National Governing Bodies ('NGBs') for each sport to agree to submit all disputes within the scope of the Act to binding arbitration by the American Arbitration Association ('AAA'). The law also entitles Olympic, Pan American and Paralympic athletes, or other parties aggrieved by decisions of the United States Olympic Committee ('USOC'), to a review of their grievances by the AAA.[14] Under the USOC Constitution, NGB decisions are subject to arbitration by the AAA.

Beyond the United States, at the global level, many international sports federations ('Ifs') have entered into agreements with the CAS for binding arbitration of disputes between them and their constituents. In turn, IFs normally require their member organizations to provide for arbitration of their disputes with athletes. Athletes selected for the Olympics and other international competition must now sign a waiver form by which they agree to exclusive CAS jurisdiction over au disputes involving doping and other issues of eligibility.[15] In *Ragheeb v. IOC*,[16]

---

[13] 36 U.S.C.A. §§ 220501-220509 (West Supp. 2000) ('Ted Stevens Olympic and Amateur Sports Act').

[14] 36 U.S.C.A. § 220529 (West Supp. 2000).

[15] OLYMPIC CHARTER 74 (2000).

[16] The decision of Ragheeb v. IOC is a decision of the Court of Arbitration for Sport. This decision is unpublished and on file with CAS in Lausanne, Switzerland. Ragheeb v. IOC, CAS (August 30, 2000) (on file with CAS).

the CAS confirmed that it could review an issue of eligibility only on the basis of such an arbitration agreement or a specific accreditation of an athlete for competition by the IOC. Because of the emerging role of the CAS in resolving these kinds of disputes at the international level, one commentator has suggested that the Amateur Sports Act should be amended to substitute the International Council of Arbitration for Sport, which is the parent organization of CAS, in place of the AAA as the designated arbitral body to hear all disputes between athletes and the USOC or its designated NGBs.[17]

For all these reasons, international sports arbitration is a growth industry. Litigation, on the other hand, is number two and, therefore, has to try harder. But courts have found it hard to try harder. Courts of law are, first of all, very reluctant to review eligibility and other decisions by sports bodies involving access to competition. When they do undertake such review, the process is often time-consuming and risky.[18] Although that may also be true for arbitration, on balance, arbitration is less costly, more expeditious, and more flexible in responding to new circumstances. The 1998 Amendments to the Amateur Sports Act that bar athletes from litigating eligibility decisions within twenty-one days before major competition also encourage arbitration unless the newly created USOC ombudsman is successful in facilitating a resolution of the dispute.[19]

---

[17] Edward E. Hollis III, Note, *The U.S.A. Olympic Committee and the Suspension of Athletes: Reforming Grievance Procedures Under the Amateur Sports Act of 1978,* 71 IND. L.J. 183, 200 (1995).

[18] *See generally,* James A.R. Nafziger, *International Sports Law: A Replay of Characteristics and Trends,* 86 Am. J. INT'L. 489,508-10 (1992).

[19] The amended law provides as follows:

    (a) General. [...] In any lawsuit relating to the resolution of a dispute involving the opportunity of an amateur athlete to participate in the Olympic Games, the Paralympic Games, or the Pan-American Games, a court shall not grant injunctive relief against the corporation within 21 days before the beginning of such games if the corporation, after consultation with the chair of the Athletes' Advisory Council, has provided a sworn statement in writing executed by an officer of the corporation to such court that its constitution and bylaws cannot provide for the resolution of such dispute prior to the beginning of such games.

    (b) Ombudsman.-

        (1) The ... ombudsman for athletes... shall -

            (A) provide independent advice to athletes at no cost about the applicable provisions of this chapter (citation omitted) and the constitution and bylaws of the corporation, national governing bodies, a paralympic sports organizations [Sic], international sports federations, the International Olympic Committee, the International Paralympic Committee, and the Pan-American Sports Organization, and with respect to the resolution of any dispute involving the opportunity of an amateur athlete to participate in the Olympic Games, the Paralympic Games, the Pan-American Games, world championship competition or other protected competition as defined in the constitution and bylaws of the corporation;

            (B) assist in mediating any such disputes.

    36 U.S.C.A. § 220509 (1994 & West Supp. 2000).

II. RECENT DEVELOPMENT: *LINDLAND V. U.S.A. WRESTLING*

Arbitration is not, however, without its problems. For one thing, any third-party settlement of grievances by athletes is apt to be controversial. After all, good sportsmanship is supposed to avoid squabbling. Disputes are supposed to be resolved on the playing field. But legal disputes are inevitable. When they do arise, any review process on the eve of major competition may affect team morale, compete for the attention of sports organizations at the expense of athletes, consume valuable training time for the competitors, and sap their energy.[20] Even so, the enthusiasm of Tammy Thomas, Lisa Raymond, Matt Lindland, Julie Smith and other claimants to pursue their rights to participate in international competition appeals to us more than the apathy of certain men's tennis and basketball players whom we might like to have seen in Sydney.

What, then, are the hurdles in the path of arbitration and how can they be cleared? In addressing this question, the dispute between Matt Lindland and the United States of America Wrestling Association ('U.S.A. Wrestling') is a good place to begin.

In one sense, the *Lindland* case is unusual because it does not involve the dominant theme in international sports arbitration of doping. The case does, however, raise a number of significant issues about the structure for resolving eligibility disputes and the role of arbitration in this structure. Lindland demonstrates what happens when function follows form in dispute resolution.

On 24 June 2000, in Bout 244 of the Greco-Roman Wrestling trials to determine the United States Olympic team, Keith Sieracki beat Matt Lindland 2-1 in a best-of-three series to gain a berth on the team in the seventy-six kilogram (167.5-pound) class.[21] In accordance with U.S.A. Wrestling rules, the three mat officials included a referee, a judge, and a mat chairman. Lindland immediately protested the officiating of his loss, claiming that Sieracki had applied an illegal hold by using his legs and had also attempted to flee a hold in violation of the rules of both the international wrestling federation ('FILA') and U.S.A.

---

[20] *See* Michaelis, *supra* note 2, at 2C.

[21] For a summary and chronology see Gary Mihoces, *Grappling with a Decision Lindland Goes to Sydney, While Sieracki Stays Home,* USA TODAY, Sept. 14, 2000, at 1C.

Wrestling.[22] Lindland's protest complied with the Protest Procedures of U.S.A. Wrestling and special procedures for the 2000 Olympic trials. The Protest Committee, however, refused to overturn the decision against Lindland on the basis that it involved judgment calls by mat officials that were beyond the Committee's competence to review. For good reason, mat decisions are simply not subject to change on review. Lindland appealed the denial of his protest to U.S.A. Wrestling's Standing Greco-Roman Sport Committee. He argued before this body, in a telephonic bearing on 13 July 2000, that the mat officials had not simply misinterpreted U.S.A. Wrestling rules, but had misapplied them. For proof of his claim, he demanded that the Committee view a videotape of the match despite an organizational rule against the use of videotaped evidence.

Six days later, on 19 July 2000, the Standing Committee denied Lindland's appeal, four to one, largely on the basis of the discretion vested in mat officials to make or not make penalty calls. As a result, U.S.A. Wrestling added Sieracki's name to the roster of nominations to be submitted to the USOC for the 2000 Olympic team. Lindland then brought a demand for arbitration in Chicago of his grievance against U.S.A. Wrestling,[23] as he was entitled to do under the Amateur Sports Act.[24] Such proceedings are usually referred to as Article IX arbitrations, after Article IX of the USOC Constitution.[25] In accordance with the Amateur Sports Act, the winner of the disputed event, Keith Sieracki, was not a party to the arbitration between Lindland and U.S.A. Wrestling.

---

[22] The Official Rules of FILA (the Fédération Internationale des Luttes Associées) (1999) are the international rules of wrestling. These rules have largely been adopted by U.S.A. Wrestling with some modifications. Article 61 of the FILA Rules provides as follows:

    A. In Greco-Roman Wrestling it is forbidden to grasp the opponent below the hips or to squeeze him with the legs. All pushing pressing or 'lifting' by means of contact with the legs on any part of the body of the opponent is also strictly forbidden.

    In Greco-Roman wrestling unlike Free Style wrestling it is necessary to accompany the opponent to the ground.

    B. In Free Style wrestling, a scissor lock with the feet crossed is forbidden on the head, the neck or the body.

FILA Rules, *available at* http://www.iat.uni-leipzig.de/iat/fila/RULES/drules.htrn (last visited March 27, 2001).

Article 57 of the FILA Rules provides as follows: 'Fleeing a hold occurs when the defending wrestler openly refuses contact in order to prevent his opponent from executing or initiating a hold'. *Id.* Article 59 of the FILA Rules ('Illegal Holds') establishes several duties of the referee in the event of a prohibited act by a competitor. *Id.* Lindland claimed the referee failed to fulfill these duties.

[23] Lindland v. United States Wrestling Ass'n, Inc., Am. Arb. Ass'n No. 30-190-00443-00 (Aug. 9,2000) (Burns, Arb.).

[24] U.S.C.A. § 220529 (West Supp. 2000).

[25] This provision implements the provision in the Amateur Sports Act for arbitration of grievances against the USOC. U.S. OLYMPIC COMMITTEE CONST., art. IX.

In the Chicago arbitration, Lindland argued that U.S.A. Wrestling had not provided procedures for the prompt and equitable resolution of his grievance, as the Amateur Sports Act requires.[26] This requirement formed the legal framework of the proceedings that followed. The gist of Lindland's arguments was that the Greco-Roman review committee had failed to follow U.S.A. Wrestling's own rules and had fashioned new ones to suit its interests, for example, by recusing four committee members who might have supported Lindland's claim. The arbitrator, Daniel Bums, agreed with Lindland and ordered a rematch between the two competitors. Sieracki participated in the rematch under protest. This time Lindland won 8-0. U.S.A. Wrestling, however, simply added Lindland to its Olympic eligibility list as an alternate, leaving Sieracki as its nominee to the USOC for the Olympic team. Lindland responded by seeking enforcement of the arbitral award in the federal District Court for the Northern District of Illinois. The court dismissed his action, without a written opinion, apparently for lack of federal jurisdiction.[27] Now, let us return to the arbitral award.

After the Chicago award but prior to the rematch, Sieracki filed his own arbitration demand in Denver before A. Bruce Campbell, seeking confirmation of his status as the sole nominee in his weight class for the Greco-Roman wrestling team.[28] Lindland counterclaimed to the opposite effect. So, we have the prospect of a rematch of dispute resolution as well as wrestling. As we shall see, however, the prospect of repetitive dispute resolution by virtue of a second round of arbitration in Denver was fuzzy because some of the issues in Denver were materially different from those in the Chicago arbitration. The Denver arbitrator first determined the arbitration was proper and allowed all evidence offered by the parties except the videotape of Bout 211. Sieracki won this second round of arbitration. After four conferences in which all parties in the overall dispute participated, Arbitrator Campbell determined that Sieracki was not bound by the Chicago Award because he had not been a party to it. He found no evidence that

---

[26] 36 U.S.C.A. § 220522(a)(13) (West Supp. 2000) ('An amateur sports organization is eligible ... to continue to to be recognized, as a national governing body only if it ... provides procedures for the prompt and equitable resolution or grievances of its members.'). 36 U.S.C. § 220503(8) assigns the following purpose to the USOC and therefore, by delegation, to the NGBS: 'to provide swift resolution of conflicts and disputes involving amateur athletes, national governing bodies, and amateur sports organizations, and protect the opportunity of any amateur athlete, coach, trainer, manager, administrator, or official to participate in amateur athletic competition.'

[27] See Lindland v. United States wrestling Ass'n, Inc., 230 F.3d 1036, 1038 (7th Cir. 2000).

[28] Sieracki v. United States Wrestling Ass'n, Inc., Am. Arb. Assn No. 30-190B00483-00 (Aug. 24, 2000) (Campbell, Arb.). Since this second arbitration did not fall within the prescribed process for reviewing a grievance under the Amateur Sports Act, it had the rather odd posture of a friendly action between the like-minded Sieracki and U.S.A. Wrestling as a means to confirm the latter's decision in Sieracki's favor, to challenge the fairness of the Chicago arbitration, and to question whether the notice and circumstances of the rematch were fair. See id.

the mat officials in Bout 244 had misapplied the rules or otherwise abused their authority. He also found that U.S.A. Wrestling's procedural arrangements, including the review committee's refusal to hear the team coach's testimony or to view video tape of the match, had not prejudiced either wrestler, did not constitute an irregularity or impropriety, and did not justify setting aside the grievance process. The Denver Award concluded by ordering U.S.A. Wrestling to withdraw Lindland's name from the eligibility list for the team and to confirm Keith Sieracki as the sole nominee on the team roster to be submitted to the USOC.

Just a few hours after the Denver Award, however, the Seventh Circuit Court of Appeals reversed the lower court in its refusal to enforce the Chicago Award in Lindland's favor and issued a mandate to U.S.A. Wrestling to enforce the award by nominating Lindland to the USOC.[29] When Lindland sought to enforce this decision, however, the district court refused again on the basis that it lacked jurisdiction.[30] Lindland then obtained a writ of mandamus from the Circuit Court that ordered the lower court to enforce the Chicago Award.[31] At this point U.S.A. Wrestling and the USOC were faced with what appeared to be contradictory orders.

Since arbitration is not normally subject to issue and claim preclusion,[32] each of the wrestlers therefore was free to seek judicial confirmation of the arbitral award in his favor under ' 9 of the Federal Arbitration Act.[33] Lindland, who was back in the federal courts for the second time, specifically requested a court order to compel the USOC to send his name to the IOC despite the USOC's argument that it could not do so because it had already sent Sieracki's name to the IOC. The Denver court, on the other hand, transferred the Sieracki action to the Chicago federal court, where the opposing federal actions were consolidated. (One might well ask what would have happened if the federal district court in Denver had not transferred the Sieracki action to the federal court in Chicago for consolidation of the two actions.)

After consolidation of the two actions, the Northern District of Illinois court, in the face of the mandamus order issued by the Seventh Circuit, directed the USOC to substitute Lindland for Sieracki as U.S.A. Wrestling's sole nominee to the USOC and denied Sieracki's petition to confirm the Denver Award in his

---

[29] *Lindland*, 230 F.3d at 1040
[30] Lindland v. United States Wrestling Ass'n., Inc., 227 F.3d 1000 (7th Cir. 2000).
[31] *Id.*
[32] Brotherhood of Maint. Of Way Employees v. Burlington N R.R., 24 F.3d 937, 939-41 (7th Cir. 1994).
[33] 9 U.S.C. § 9 (1994).

favor. In compliance with the district court order, the USOC requested the IOC to replace Sieracki with Lindland as a member of the Olympic team. It also appealed the court ruling that required it to take this action. U.S.A. Wrestling appealed each of the mandated district court decisions to the Seventh Circuit, which upheld both orders.[34] In the end, less than two weeks before the beginning of the Olympic Games, United States Supreme Court justice Stevens (also from Chicago, incidentally) denied a request by the USOC for a stay of the Seventh Circuit's mandamus order.[35]

From the record, it appears that the case was very ably, indeed admirably argued by counsel for the parties. In view of the time constraints, the advocacy was exemplary. And reasonable minds can certainly differ on the outcome of the case. I personally have no quarrel with it. But I do want to question several of its legal premises. Fundamentally, the Chicago Award was based on a determination that U.S.A. Wrestling's review of Lindland's protest was procedurally defective. The arbitrator found that the organization's rules were inadequate to deal with the issues that arose in the case concerning possible conflict of interest, recomposition of the review committee, and restrictions on testimony.[36] The materiality of these defects is questionable,[37] as was the advisability of ordering a rematch rather than a recomposition and reconvention of the Protest Committee.[38] Simple mathematics reveals that if Lindland's corner coach in

---

[34] Lindland v. United States Wrestling Ass'n, Inc., 227 F.3d 1000 (7th Cir. 2000).

[35] *See* Jess Bravin, *High Court Ensures Wrestler's Trip to Olympics,* WALL ST. J., Sept. 7, 2000, at B19 (noting that justice Stevens denied the request for review without comment).

[36] *See* Lindland v. United States Wrestling Ass'n, Inc., Am. Arb. Ass'n No. 30-190-00443-00 (Aug. 9, 2000) (Burns, Arb.).

[37] *See* Sieracki v. United States Wrestling Ass'n, Inc., Am Arb. Ass'n No. 30-190-00483-00 (Aug. 24, 2000) (Campbell, Arb.).

[38] In the Chicago arbitration, the justification in the 'Conclusion and Award' follows:

Changed situations of Committee participants, the question of the President of USA will attend and vote [sic], the exigencies of the present circumstances of final team selection, the fact that a crucial witness's testimony was chilled at the first hearing, the potential atmosphere of a reconvened full Committee, and the very lack of guidance in USA Wrestling by-laws and rules, when grouped together, are convincing that Lindland cannot be put back to the same position he was on July 12, and cannot receive the prompt and equitable resolution of his grievance that he has been promised. For example, one excluded member of the Committee was a fellow wrestler with a grievance *pending* at that time. That grievance has now been finally resolved. Another mistake made in fashioning the July 13 Committee, [sic] was the erroneous belief that some members of the Greco-Roman Sports Committee had also *voted* on that Protest Committee, and they were excluded for that reason. In fact, only one member had actually *voted* at the Protest Committee and that was the president of the USA Wrestling, who testified he was an *ad hoc* member of the Committee and may have attended one Committee meeting over the past several years. As significant is the lack of guidance and advance notice on these issues to Lindland, and Committee members, as he attempted to process his protest. Unfortunately, the same lack of guidance defeats any attempt to reconvene the Committee and provide a clean state to press his claim the short time before final team selection. *Lindland,* Am. Arb. Ass'n No. 30-190.00443-00.

Bout 244 had recused himself, as would surely be appropriate, and if all of the remaining three committee members who recused themselves had instead voted in Lindland's favor, the result at most would have been a tie, which would have been insufficient to reverse the original decision in favor of Sieracki.[39]

Even so, the bases for review within U.S.A. Wrestling, as the process developed, are murky. What is clear is that the by-laws and rules of U.S.A. Wrestling did not provide any real guidance on appropriate procedures for reviewing a protest of this sort.[40] As a result, simply reconvening the Protest Committee might not have overcome apprehensions about the fairness of the administrative process.

U.S.A. Wrestling's refusal to entertain videotaped evidence except for during-match viewing by mat officials and for viewing flagrant misconduct and allegations of brutality is also questionable. The rule against videotaped evidence is designed to shield judgment calls from endless challenge and dispute. The rule thus protects the integrity of officiating and avoids substituting arbitrators for referees. Nevertheless, excluding videotaped evidence clearly conflicts with the rules of FILA, the international wrestling federation.[41] Moreover, the governing law of the Amateur Sports Act seems to contemplate a freer evidentiary environment by stating that '[t]he parties may offer any evidence they desire and shall produce any additional evidence the arbitrators believe is necessary to an understanding and determination of the dispute. The arbitrators shall be the sole judges of the relevance and materiality of the evidence offered.'[42]

---

[39] *See Sieracki,* Am. Arb, Ass'n No. 30-190-00483-00, at &1 (f).

[40] The Chicago award found:

USA Wrestling has not provided any written rules, regulations, bylaws, or precedential authority justifying its actions and decisions regarding: 1) the determination of the number and identities of the Greco-Roman Sports Committee when hearing appeals such as Lindland's, 2) grounds for excluding sitting Committee members from participating and deliberating in appeals such as Lindland's; 3) limitations on the nature and extent of the testimony of witnesses; 4) who is permitted to appear and participate in the hearing.

Lindland, Am Arb. Ass'n No. 30-190-00483-00, at Findings of Fact &9.

[41] In the event of a protest, Article 63 of the Official Rules of FILA clearly encourages the use of videotape. *See* FILA Rules, *available at* http://www.iat.uni-leipzig.de/iat/fila/RULES/drules.htm (last visited March 27, 2001); *see supra* note 23. To the contrary, one of the few modifications of the FILA rules by U.S.A. Wrestling provides as follows: 'Under no circumstances shall the use of video tapes or films of a bout be considered or shown in the evaluation of any protest. Elements of the FILA Protest procedures may be applied as determined by the protest committee.' U.S.A. Modifications, Article 63, U.S.A. Wrestling Protest Procedures (1999), *available at* http://www.usawrestling.com.

The Denver Award wisely sidestepped the issue of whether U.S.A. Wrestling's rules are 'less or more wise' than those of FILA. *Sieracki,* Am. Arb. Ass'n No. 30-190-00483-00", at &II-6.

[42] 36 U.S.C.A. § 220529(5) (West Supp. 2000).

Reasonable minds may, of course, differ on the advisability of allowing video-taped evidence. What is hard to dispute, however, is the complexity of the legal process which extended over a period of two-and-one-half months and involved thirteen stages of dispute resolution.[43] Surely that was an unlucky thirteen, not just for Sieracki, but for the reputation of dispute resolution related to international sports competition. In the cogent words of Matt Lindland's wife, '[t]hey're probably going to have to change the rules after this one.'[44]

III. THE SEVENTH CIRCUIT OPINIONS

The formal process for resolving the *Lindland* dispute merits consideration. I would argue that, although the selection of Lindland to the Olympic team was a reasonable outcome of the dispute, the premises of the Seventh Circuit's orders to that effect are shaky. Indeed, *Lindland* is a good example of the difficulty that federal courts have had in defining their role in disputes involving the eligibility of athletes for international competition.[45]

At the heart of the Seventh Circuit's opinions, written by Judge Frank Easterbrook, is a conclusion that the Chicago Award was valid while the Denver Award was invalid.[46] The rationale was that because the Chicago Award had been upheld by a court of law, any later award, namely the one in Denver, could not purport to countermand it. Once the court had ordered U.S.A. Wrestling and the USOC to substitute Lindland for Sieracki on the Olympic team, that was it. Although the Seventh Circuit's confirmation of the Chicago Award is certainly reasonable, its negative conclusion about the Denver Award is much less compelling. While acknowledging the lack of issue and claim preclusion in arbitration, the court's opinion enlists two principal arguments against the Denver Award, concluding therefore that it was 'doubly flawed.'[47] First, Judge Easterbrook concluded that the Denver Award was, in his words, *ultra vires* because, unlike the Chicago Award, it was not conceived as an appeal of a USOC or NGB decision under the Amateur Sports Act. But he failed to appreciate that, unlike the Chicago arbitration, which was premised in the Amateur Sports Act, the Denver arbitration was brought under the USOC's Grievance Procedures for Code of Conduct and Team Selection 2000 Olympic Games.

---

[43] *See* Lindland v. United States Wresthng Assn., 230 F.3d 1036, 1037-38 (7th Cir. 2000) (noting the several stages of litigation); Michaelis, *supra* note 2, at 1C.

[44] Michaelis, *supra* note 2, at 1 C.

[45] *See* Nafziger, *supra* note 8, at 134-42 (discussing the *Reynolds and Harding cases*).

[46] Lindland v. United States Wrestling Ass'n, Inc., 227 F-3d 1000, 1005 (7th Cir. 2000).

[47] *Id.* at 1003.

Second, Judge Easterbrook construed Rule 48 of the Commercial Arbitration Rules of the American Arbitration Association to bar the Denver Award as a redetermination of the merits of a claim already decided.[48] But Rule 48 merely bars a redetermination of the merits in a *modification of a single award.* What makes the double arbitration in *Lindland* so interesting is that the two awards involved different parties and, to an extent, different issues. Not only did the Circuit Court minimize these differences, but it took Denver Arbitrator Campbell to task for deciding, in the courts words, to 'ignore' Rule 48 'utterly'[49] and thereby to flout the judicial confirmation of the Chicago Award. But Campbell had reason to ignore Rule 48 because it simply did not apply.

Judge Easterbrook's opinion emphasized that the winner of a contested event is normally not a party to an Article IX proceeding. That is certainly true and appropriate under the law. But there were four material differences between the Chicago and Denver arbitrations. First, the Denver claimant, Sieracki had been unable to appear formally in the Chicago arbitration. Although that did not in any way call into question the Chicago Award, by the same token it enabled him to demand relief in Denver from the mandatory rematch ordered by the Chicago Award. Judge Easterbrook seems to have been bothered by Sieracki's timing of this demand prior to the event itself. But what was Sieracki supposed to do to vindicate his position after the award in the Chicago arbitration to which he was not a party? Perhaps he should have waited a few days until he had lost the rematch before pursuing a judicial remedy. But, under the time constraints imposed by the Amateur Sports Act, it was probably wise for him to get off the mat and get moving again. In any event, he had standing under the 2000 Protest Rules to demand arbitration. Surely, the Denver arbitrator was acting properly in hearing the demand of an athlete whose original selection to the team was in jeopardy.

Although many Article IX disputes involving allegations against an athlete impact only indirectly on other identifiable competitors, an either-or eligibility issue of the sort at issue in *Lindland* is materially different. Article IX's exclusion of the disputed winner of an event in an arbitration of that dispute presents a serious issue. It is simply unfair to ignore the winner's interests on the basis that arbitration of a grievance under the Amateur Sports Act excludes the winner as a party. In the Denver arbitration, on the other hand, both of the contesting wrestlers, as well as U.S.A. Wrestling, made appearances.

---

[48] *Id.* at 1004.
[49] *Id.*

Second, the Denver arbitration, although it considered Lindland's protest *de novo,* also heard new issues related to the rematch that occurred while the Denver arbitration was pending. It simply is not correct to conclude, as the Seventh Circuit opinion does, that '[t]he whole point of the Campbell proceeding [Denver arbitration] was to redecide issues.'[50] That may have been part of the point but by no means the whole point. Judge Easterbrook's opinion itself acknowledges that Sieracki initiated his arbitration, 'protesting the result of the rematch.'[51] Moreover, unlike the issues raised by Lindland in the Chicago arbitration, Sieracki's demand in Denver sought a determination that he should be the sole nominee to the Greco-Roman Olympic team, to the exclusion of Lindland.

Third, it is reasonable to view the Denver arbitration as a fresh proceeding, unaffected in part by the Seventh Circuit order that confirmed the Chicago Award. After all, the rematch had converted Sieracki, the original winner, into a loser. Surely, Sieracki, the 'new' loser, so to speak, should have been entitled to the same right to demand the same kind of arbitration as Lindland, the 'old' loser, so to speak, had enjoyed. Thus, Sieracki could claim the arbitrability of his grievance under either the Code of Conduct and Team Selection or, arguably, under a theory that the results of the rematch could be contested as a fresh action and hence that the second arbitration in Denver was proper under the same provision of the Amateur Sports Act which Lindland had legitimately invoked.

Even if one does not accept the recharacterization of the Denver arbitration as a fresh action, perhaps because Sieracki had not exhausted the internal protest and grievance procedures required by law,[52] it nevertheless seems clear that the complex of dispute resolution was more of a muddle than the Seventh Circuit seems to have appreciated. For instance, the opinions failed to appreciate the very real dilemma faced by U.S.A. Wrestling and the USOC in the face of two inconsistent awards. Instead, one of judge Easterbrook's opinions intimates that NGB's like U.S.A. Wrestling are 'scofflaws',[53] chastises the USOC for insisting that 'it is entitled to do as it pleases – defying injunctions to its heart's content',[54] and surmises a conspiracy between U.S.A. Wrestling and the USOC in contempt of court.[55] These observations may or may not be correct, but that kind of

---

[50] *Id.*

[51] *Id.* at 1003.

[52] See 36 U.S.C.A. § 220529 (West Supp. 2000); Dolan v. U.S. Equestrian Team. Inc., 608 A.2d (N.J. Super. Ct. App. Div. 1992). Sieracki, on the other hand, was seeking to vindicate his initial victory under severe time constraints.

[53] Lindland v. United States Wrestling Ass'n, Inc., 227 F.3d 1000, 1008 (7th Cir. 2000).

[54] *Id.* at 1007.

[55] *Id.* at 1006.

fighting language by an appeals court, without adequate proof, is disconcerting.

That said, one of the Circuit Court opinions does hint at some productive new directions for resolving these kinds of disputes. In Judge Easterbrook's words, conflicting instructions may not be an 'irremediable evil. Injunctions create property rights, which may be altered by private agreements. Bargaining among Sieracki, Lindland and U.S.A. Wrestling could lead to a settlement that would relieve U.S.A Wrestling of any incompatible obligations.'[56] Judge Easterbrook caps this observation with a challenge: 'Definitive resolution of the right way to handle conflicting awards, after one has been confirmed, may await another day.'[57]

I am quite sure that that day has not yet arrived. I do want to ask, however, what can be done, specifically, to improve the process. Let me say again that I think both the Chicago and Denver arbitral awards in *Lindland* were creditable. Neither was spoiled by any of the defects of corruption, fraud or evident partiality for which the Arbitration Act allows an award to be set aside.[58] Even if one were to agree that a first award ordinarily should bar a second award, the two awards in this case differed substantially from each other.[59] Consequently, judge Easterbrook's misunderstanding of the express reach of the first award,[60] his caustic appraisal of the second award, and his injudicious name-calling were simply off the mat. The problem lay not in the arbitration itself but in the structure of dispute resolution that encourages proliferation and, worse yet, redundancy of proceedings.

IV. IMPROVING THE STRUCTURE OF DISPUTE RESOLUTION

Let me offer several suggestions to improve the structure. First, in reviewing arbitrations under federal law, the courts should proceed cautiously. Judicial relief from the decisions of sports bodies should be reserved for cases where due process violations are patent, and the violations dispositive, as they were not in

---

[56] *Id.* at 1003.

[57] *Id.*

[58] *See* 9 U.S.C. § 10(a) (supp. V 1999).

[59] *See supra* notes 50-51 and accompanying text

[60] Despite Judge Easterbrook's argument that the Denver Award purported to rescind the Chicago Awards order to place Lindland on the Olympic team not only does the Denver Award contain no such attempted rescission, but the Chicago Award, in the first instance, did not actually order Lindland's selection to the US.A. Olympic team. See Lindland v. United States Wrestling Asdn, Inc., Ani. Arb. Ass'n No. 30-190-00443-00 (Aug. 9, 2000) (Burns, Arb.).

Lindland. The financial stakes for athletes, absent issues of labor law,[61] do not alone provide a compelling basis for judicial intervention. To quote another Seventh Circuit judge, Richard Posner: '[T]here can be few less suitable bodies than the federal courts for determining the eligibility, or the procedure for determining the eligibility, of athletes ...'.[62] The *Harding* court in Oregon also had it right, I think, in cautioning that:

Intervention [by the courts] is appropriate only in the most extraordinary circumstances, where [a national governing body] has clearly breached its own rules, that breach will imminently result in *serious* and irreparable harm to the plaintiff, and the plaintiff has exhausted all internal remedies. Even then, injunctive relief is limited to correcting the breach of the rules. The court should not intervene in the merits of the underlying dispute.[63]

Second, repetitious proceedings and the complexity they entail, particularly in eligibility cases, could be avoided by amending the Amateur Sports Act and the USOC Constitution to enable an individual winner of a disputed competition to participate in a single arbitration alongside the individual claimant, NGB and, as appropriate, the USOC. It is simply unfair to presume that a contested winner's interests are fully represented by an NGB.[64] A unified arbitration would then bar subsequent arbitration. In team sports, the problem of standing to appear is considerably more complicated. Even so, as a starter, team members of a class potentially affected by an eligibility decision might simply elect one of their number to represent their common interests.

Third, the Amateur Sports Act should be interpreted or, if necessary, amended to avoid arbitration of a referee's decision so long as a claimant has had the benefit

---

[61] Compare the following timely observation:
U.S. courts and international federations must begin viewing amateur athletics in a more employment-related light, as substantial sums of money are at stake when suspensions of Olympic athletes occur. In the U.S.A., amateur athletes have traditionally not been viewed as 'employees' due to the strict NCAA regulations prohibiting college athletes from receiving financial rewards for their talents.
Mary K. Fitzgerald, *The Court of Arbitration for Sport: Dealing with Doping and Due Process During the Olympics,* 7 Sports Law. J. 213, 236 (2000).

[62] Michels v. United States Olympic Comm., 741 F.2d 155,159 (7th Cir. 1984).

[63] Harding v. United States Figure Skating Ass'n, 851 F. Supp. 1476,1479 (D. Or. 1994).

[64] U.S. Olympic Comm. Const., art IX, ' 2 (providing that a demand or arbitration must designate 'such USOC member', normally an NGB, as an adverse party). *See also* Lindland v. United States Wrestling Ass'n, Inc., 230 F.3d 1036, 1039 (7th Cir. 2000). As Judge Easterbrook's opinion points out, this is in keeping with the arrangement in labor arbitration that an employee who is discharged from employment may arbitrate a grievance with his employer but need not designate as an additional party a replacement who may be dischargeable by an award in favor of the grievant. *Id.*

of a full and fair review by the appropriate NCB, unless that body would itself permit such a review.[65] In *Lindland,* the Chicago Award steered clear of scrutinizing judgment calls. The Denver Award, on the other hand, seemed to comment fairly directly on the judgment of the mat officials. A procedural rule barring review of such judgment calls in all but the most egregious cases would help avoid understandable suspicions by the media and the public that arbitrators can make second caus. In the Lindland-Sieracki match, there were three mat officials, all of whom appear to have satisfied U.S.A. Wrestling's requirement that they understood the rules and avoided wrongful, dishonest, intentionally improper, or bad faith conduct.[66] Even if they failed to take account of illegal wrestling maneuvers in violation of the rules of the game, such bad judgment calls or inaction should not be subject to arbitration or litigation in the absence of evidence that they had simply failed to understand the rules or that they abused their authority.

Fourth, we should make it clear that the merits not only of judgment calls but of the rules of the game themselves are generally beyond the competence of arbitration or litigation. After all, technical rules are constantly under review and reform by the IOC, IFs and NGBs themselves. One commentator has therefore proposed that the Amateur Sports Act be amended to provide that the jurisdiction of courts under the Act should be limited to determinations of whether responsible sports organizations have complied with their own rules of eligibility, presumably within an acceptable margin of discretion. This proposal would bar courts from evaluating the merits of a dispute, confining their review to an evaluation of procedural due process.[67]

In drawing a line between nonreviewable game rules and reviewable rules, procedures and practices, two cases of the CAS are instructive. The first arose out of an incident during the 1996 Atlanta Games.[68] In reviewing a referee's disqualification of an athlete, known as 'Boxer M', for landing a below-the-belt punch on his opponent, the CAS applied international custom, particularly from the United States, France, and Switzerland. The CAS concluded from this general practice that a technical decision, standard or rule – in other words, a nonreviewable game rule – is shielded from arbitral or judicial scrutiny unless

---

[65] Longman, *supra* note 12, at D8 ('There is no quicker way to kill spectator interest than to have a game played and the outcome decided a month later by lawyers.').

[66] Sieracki v. United States Wresting Ass'n, Inc., Am. Arb. Ass'n No. 30-190-0m83-00, II-1, 2, (Aug. 24,2000) (Campbell Arb.).

[67] Hollis, *supra* note 17, at 200.

[68] Reeb, *supra* note 3, at 413 (M. v. Ass'n Internationale de Boxe Amateur) (CAS Ad Hoc Division, Atlanta 1996).

the rule or its application by sports officials is arbitrary, illegal, or the product of a wrong or malicious intent against an athlete.[69] In such cases, the rule or its application is reviewable. Sanctions appearing to be excessive or unfair on their face are also reviewable. The rationale for the *Boxer M* decision was two-fold: that IFs have the responsibility to enforce rules, and referees or ring judges are in a better position than arbitrators to decide technical matters.[70]

In the second CAS case, the AOC Advisory Opinion, the CAS considered the reviewability of a decision by the international swimming federation ('FINA'), less than a year before the 2000 Olympic Games, to approve the use of full-body ('long john') swimsuits.[71] These highly elastic suits, which were first marketed by Speedo, attempted to stimulate natural sharkskin. The suits were designed to increase a swimmer's speed and endurance, to reduce drag, and possibly to enhance the buoyancy of the swimmer. The FINA Bureau, after lengthy discussion, ruled that 'the use of these swimsuits does not constitute a violation of the FINA Rules'.[72] In response to this ruling, the Australian Olympic Committee ('AOC'), nervous about possible claims of unfairness at the Sydney Games, asked the CAS for an advisory opinion under its Rule 60. The AOC inquired whether the FINA ruling had complied with FINA's own rules and whether, in any event, use of the suits would raise contestable issues of fairness. In a thorough and thoughtful opinion, the CAS properly advised that FINA had reached its decision in compliance with its own rules and that its ruling which was tantamount to approval of bodysuits, did not raise any reviewable issues of unfair procedure, bad faith, conflict with general principles of law, or unreasonableness.[73]

Fifth, NGBs and other sports associations, under the supervision of IFs, should draft more explicit and uniform rules of eligibility and remedies for relief of legitimate grievances by athletes. Sheer chaos reigns today, and that is grossly unfair to athletes. For example, NGBs should clarify the precise weight that they will give to career records and recent international performance in determining eligibility when team tryouts alone are not determinative. Such clarification

---

[69] *Id.*

[70] *Id.*

[71] Advisory Opinion Delivered by the Ct. of Arbitration for Sport at the request of the Australian Olympic Committee, TAS 2000/C/267 ACO (Richard M. McLaren, Sole Arbitrator) (on file with author).

[72] *Id.* at 12.

[73] *Id.* at 19-21. *But see* Janwillem Soek, *You Don't Win Silver - You Miss the Gold,* INT'L SPORTS L.J., Sept. 2000, at 15 (criticizing the advisory opinion for assuming the existence of a dispute between the ACC and FINA and thereby failing to resolve the issue of fairness of the controversial bodysuits).

would have avoided the arbitration to determine the composition of the U.S. Women's softball team in Sydney and another arbitration involving the U.S. women's cycling team.[74] The demand by Tammy Thomas, winner of the 500-meter women's trial for the 2000 Olympics, against Christine Witty, whom the United States cycling federation selected on the basis of her superior two-year performance profile, was a variation on the *Lindland* case. Although an arbitrator ordered a ride-off to settle the controversy, much like the *Lindland* wrestling rematch, Witty, unlike Sieracki, simply refused to show up and promptly filed her own arbitration action.

Let me underscore the need, for reasons of fairness, to harmonize rules and remedies to make them as uniform and predictable as possible, across the range of sports. For example, serious questions of equity and due process arise whenever a track-and-field athlete is barred for life for ingesting a substance that is permitted (or was permitted) in baseball. Similarly, the Amateur Sports Act should make it clear that ad hoc measures, such as rematches, should be only a last resort when reconstitution of a defective eligibility review process would be grossly unfair or impossible.

V. OBLIGATIONS OF ATHLETES

Finally, my most far-reaching suggestion for reform is that arbitral awards should take account of obligations or duties as well as rights of athletes. We often forget that the framework for protection of human rights includes obligations or duties as well. It is a trade-off. Rights arise out of reciprocal relations within a community. They are confirmed by social contract. Article 29 of the Universal Declaration of Human Rights establishes that '[e]veryone has duties to the community in which alone the free and full development of his personality is possible.'[75] Similarly, the African Charter on Human and Peoples' Rights acknowledges obligations and duties of individuals toward society,[76] and the American Declaration of the Rights and Duties of Man establishes ten specific duties.[77]

---

[74] Bravin, *supra* note 2, at A1.

[75] Art. 29, UNIVERSAL DECLARATION OF HUMAN RIGHTS, G.A. Res. 217A, U.N. GAOR, 3rd Sess. Pt. 1, Resolutions, at 71, U.N. Doc. A/810 (1948); *see* Keba Mbaye, *Sport and Human Rights*, OLYMPIC REV., Dec. 1998-jan. 1999, at 8-12.

[76] AFRICAN CHARTER ON HUMAN AND PEOPLE'S RIGHTS, O.A.U. Doc. CAB/LEG/67/3 Rev. 5, arts. 27-29, (1981).

[77] AMERICAN DECLARATION OF THE RIGHTS AND DUTIES OF MAN, O.A.S. Res. XXX, O.A.S. Off. Rec. OEA/Ser. L/V/1.4, arts 29-38,(1965).

To be sure, this authority only confirms the reciprocal nature, in very general terms, of the social contract putting human rights into play. None of the human rights instruments comes close to identifying specific duties of athletes or to providing any specific legal basis for imposing duties on them. Still, the general authority provides a normative foundation for more specific requirements. The Olympic Charter, for example, establishes that '[t]he practice of sport is a human right.'[78] Several decisions of the CAS have elaborated on the obligation of athletes to serve the community interest in ensuring fairness and a level playing field for all. For example, in several doping cases, the CAS established a duty of athletes to disclose information coming to their attention about doping to the detriment of competition.[79]

Although the ideal of athletes as role models is often romanticized and exaggerated, athletes unquestionably influence young people.[80] Therefore, in reviewing claims, arbitrators should consider the special obligations or duties that athletes owe to society as well as their rights. In reviewing disputes involving the status of athletes, the issue ought to be what is in the best public interest, not just what is in the best interest of particular sports.[81] In that light, it is difficult to justify the outcome of the *Sprewell* arbitration. Latrell Sprewell's physical, indeed nearly homicidal, assault on Head Coach Peter Carlesimo and the Golden State Warriors' team trainer, followed by his angry return from the locker room to reiterate his threats and repeat his assaults, surely warranted the most severe penalty. Accordingly, the National Basketball Association ('NBA'), in consultation with the Warriors, imposed a one-year, 82-game suspension from NBA play without pay – the most severe sanction that the NBA had ever imposed on a player. The Warriors also terminated the remaining years in Sprewell's Uniform Player Contract with the Golden State Warriors.[82]

However, the arbitrator hearing Sprewell's demand for relief mitigated the suspension to the remaining 68 games of the season and reinstated Sprewell's

---

[78] OLYMPIC CHARTER, Fundamental Principle 8 (2000).

[79] Reeb, *supra* note 3, at 142,143,158.

[80] *See, e.g.,* René Lefort & Jean Harvey, *What's in a Game?,* THE UNESCO COURIER April 1999, at 18.

[81] *See* Paul C. Weiler & Gary R. Roberts, SPORTS AND THE LAW: TEXT, CASES, PROBLEMS 86 (#3) (2d ed. 1998).

[82] *See Latrell Sprewell Reinstatement Ruling, in* Walter T. Champion, jr., FUNDAMENTALS OF SPORTS LAW 442 (Cum. Supp. 1999).

contract with the Warriors.[83] The Grievance Arbitrator's generous treatment of Latrell Sprewell unfortunately minimized the social consequences of his decision. In all fairness, the Grievance Arbitrator was fundamentally concerned about the issue of due process insofar as there had been no precedent for the severe penalty of a one-year suspension and termination of Sprewell's guaranteed contract. Perhaps, though, precedent, like consistency, can be a hobgoblin. Perhaps serious physical assault should be treated the same in the sports arena and sports arbitration as on the streets.

By the same token, sports organizations have ethical obligations to society, too. This expectation underlies an arbitral decision that upheld the most severe penalty ever imposed by the NBA.[84] The Minnesota Timberwolves had received this sanction for secretly conspiring with an athlete to avoid the NBA's salary cap, a requirement that is further elaborated in the league's collective bargaining agreement with the players' association. Ethical issues of this sort are particularly serious when, as in this case, an athlete and a sports association conspire to violate fundamental organizational rules.

Although sports and athletes are special, their special status means a higher standard of conduct. In the words of one observer, 'players are highly visible in the community, and that carries a public obligation.'[85] Sport is also highly visible in the community. As we arbitrate rights and perhaps take account of obligations within the international sports arena, the public interest should be paramount. Surely that is an appropriate world view for arbitrating sports disputes in the early twenty-first century.

---

[83] Sprewell later brought action in the federal district court against the NBA and the Golden State Warriors claiming thirty million dollars in damages on the basis that the arbitral award against him was racially discriminatory. *See* Sprewell v. Golden State Warriors, C98-2053-VRW, 1999 WL 179682 (N.D. Ca. Mar. 26,1999). Sprewell's action and a revised version of it were both dismissed as meritless suits in 1998 and 1999, respectively. On review, the Ninth Circuit Court of Appeals upheld the lower court. Sprewell v. Golden St. Warriors, 231 F.3d 520 (9th Cir. 2000).

[84] *See* David DuPree and Vicki Michaelis, *Smith Cap Ruling Upheld,* USA TODAY, Nov. 10, 2000, at 1C (summarizing the arbitrator's approval of a penalty that denied the Timberwolves first-round draft picks during the next five NBA drafts and fined them $3.5 million).

[85] John Gibeaut, *When Pros Turn Cons,* ABA J., July 2000, at 108.

CHAPTER IX
THE INTERNATIONAL CHAMBER OF COMMERCE (ICC)

Introductory

As previously mentioned, sport is now a global business and, as such, many sports-related disputes are international in nature and scope. For almost eighty years, international business disputes of various kinds have been successfully referred to arbitration by the ICC,[53] based in Paris. The ICC International Court of Arbitration has gained a good reputation amongst business people. But, as disputes over the years have become more complex and, in turn, arbitration has become more technical, time-consuming and costly, other forms of dispute resolution have grown up and been developed by other organisations and also by the ICC.

In fact, since 1976, the ICC has operated an International Centre for Expertise, which appoints experts to issue non-binding reports on issues of a primarily technical nature, in order to help parties resolve related disputes amicably. Another form of 'expert determination'.

ICC Mediation Service

BACKGROUND

As part of this drive to offer new forms of dispute resolution, the ICC introduced on 1 January 1988, new rules on conciliation – the so-called ICC Rules of Optional Conciliation. These Rules were replaced with new so-called ICC ADR Rules on 1 July 2001. In effect, they are Mediation Rules and they are reproduced in Appendix XVI.

Before commenting on them, it is interesting to note, *en passant*, that, so far as the ICC is concerned, the idea of conciliation to settle commercial disputes is not that new. In fact, the very first dispute successfully resolved by the ICC, following the establishment of its Arbitration service in 1923, was settled by conciliation. The dispute, between French and Belgian parties concerning the quality of a consignment of walnut wood, was settled after an hour's discussion!

---

[53] Website: 'www.iccwbo.org'.

ICC MEDIATION RULES

The purpose of the ICC ADR Rules (ICC Mediation Rules) is set forth in the Preamble to them as follows:

> 'Amicable settlement is a desirable solution for business disputes and differences. It can occur before or during the litigation or arbitration of a dispute and can often be facilitated through the aid of a third party (the "Neutral") acting in accordance with simple rules. The parties can agree to submit to such rules in their underlying contract or at any other time.
>
> The International Chamber of Commerce ("ICC") sets out these amicable dispute resolution rules, entitled the ICC ADR Rules (the "Rules"), which permit the parties to agree upon whatever settlement technique they believe to be appropriate to help them settle their dispute. In the absence of an agreement of the parties on a settlement technique, mediation shall be the settlement technique used under the Rules'.

The ICC Mediation Rules are the product of extensive discussions between the ICC and dispute resolution experts and representatives of the business community from 75 countries around the world. Their aim is to offer an alternative method of resolving disputes amicably in the best way to suit the particular needs of the parties in dispute.

A distinctive feature of these Rules is the freedom offered to the parties to follow the dispute resolution mechanism most conducive to reaching a settlement in a given case. As will be seen, in the absence of a specific agreement to the contrary, the parties are taken to have opted for Mediation (article 5.2.).

Under article 5.3 of the Rules, the Mediator (the 'Neutral') is free to conduct the dispute settlement process 'as the Neutral sees fit', but must be 'guided by the principles of fairness and impartiality and by the wishes of the parties'. And each party is required to 'co-operate in good faith with the Neutral' (article 5.5.).

Article 3 of the Rules deals with the selection of the Mediator, who is required to provide the ICC with a CV and a 'statement of independence' (article 3.2.).

Likewise, the Mediation, including its outcome, is 'private and confidential' (article 7.1.) and conducted on a 'without prejudice' basis (article 7.2.). This latter article provides as follows:

> 'Unless required to do so by applicable law and in the absence of any agreement of the parties to the contrary, a party shall not in any manner produce as evidence in any judicial, arbitration or similar proceedings:
>
> a) any documents, statements or communications which are submitted by another party or by the Neutral in the ADR proceedings, unless they can be obtained independently by the party seeking to produce them in the judicial, arbitration or similar proceedings;

b) any views expressed or suggestions made by any party within the ADR proceedings with regard to the possible settlement of the dispute;

c) any admissions made by another party within the ADR proceedings;

d) any views or proposals put forward by the Neutral; or

e) the fact that any party had indicated within the ADR proceedings that it was ready to accept a proposal for a settlement'.

Furthermore, the Mediator must act impartially and, generally speaking, may not testify in '… any judicial, arbitration or similar proceedings concerning any aspect of the ADR proceedings' (article 7.4.).

The Mediation is started by a written Request under article 2.A.1., together with the payment of a 'non-refundable registration fee' pursuant to article 4.1. of US$1,500; and the parties are free to terminate the Mediation at any time after it has commenced, without being required to give any reason, and in the other circumstances specified in article 6.1.

Any settlement reached as a result of the Mediation is not binding on the parties unless and until it is incorporated into a 'settlement agreement' and signed by them (article 6. 1.a)).

As is usual nowadays, the Rules contain a 'Disclaimer' in article 7.5 in the following terms:

'Neither the Neutral, nor the ICC and its employees, nor the ICC National Committees shall be liable to any person for any act or omission in connection with the … proceedings'.

Of course, the extent to which, legally speaking, such a denial of liability will be valid and enforceable will depend upon the circumstances of each particular case and the applicable law.

As is also usual, the costs of the Mediation are shared equally by the parties, except as may be provided otherwise in any settlement agreement, and the parties are responsible for their own expenses (articles 4.5. & 4.6.). A Schedule of the Costs is contained in the Appendix to the Rules.

ADVANTAGES OF ICC MEDIATION RULES

In summary, as will be seen, the ICC Mediation Rules are:

− simple and concise (there are only 7 articles);
− flexible and user friendly (no procedural restraints are placed on either the Mediator or the parties);
− require full confidentiality from every person involved in the Mediation in whatever capacity;
− time effective (the Mediator can set time limits for the parties to present their

arguments); and
- cost effective (the costs are substantially lower than an ICC Arbitration and shall not, in any event, exceed US$10,000 (Appendix B.)).

As is normal, Mediation under the ICC ADR Rules should only be attempted and is only likely to be successful in appropriate cases where the parties in dispute are prepared to compromise, that is, are ready, able and willing to reach an amicable settlement of their dispute.

Anyone wishing to mediate under the ICC ADR Rules can include a corresponding clause in their contracts. The ICC offers a range of reference clauses to suit the parties' needs and the particular circumstances. These optional clauses are set out in Appendix XVI, including a very flexible and practical 'Optional ADR Clause' in the following terms:

'The parties may at any time, without prejudice to any other proceedings, seek to settle any dispute arising out of or in connection with the present contract in accordance with the ICC – ADR Rules'.

Why use ICC Mediation?

Mediation under such a prestigious, experienced, professional and independent body as the ICC – considered to be the world's leading business organisation – offers another reliable dispute resolution tool that is available to parties involved in all kinds of international commercial disputes, including sports-related ones, which, in relation to the latter, it is suggested, may be overlooked by them at their peril.

Furthermore, as doubts have been and continue, in some quarters, to be expressed about the independence of the CAS, despite the creation and interposition of the International Council for the Arbitration of Sport, pursuant to the 'Paris Agreement' of 22 June 1994, parties to international sports disputes may also wish to consider using the services of a completely independent, long established and respected body such as the ICC.

See the decisions of the Swiss Federal Tribunal in the cases of *Elmar Gundel v. FEI/CAS*[54] and *Raducan v. International Olympic Committee.*[55]

In view of their importance, English versions of these judgments are now reproduced for ease of reference:

---

[54] 15 March 1993 [1993] I Civil Court (Swiss Fed Trib).
[55] 4 December 2000 [2000] II Civil Court (Swiss Fed Trib).

Extract of the judgment of 15 March 1993, delivered by the 1st Civil Division of the Swiss Federal Tribunal in the case G. versus Fédération Equestre Internationale and Court of Arbitration for Sport (CAS) (public law appeal) (translation)

A. G. is a professional rider who is part of the German jumping team. He is a member of the Buchloe riding club and the holder of a licence for national and international competitions. On the occasion of the annual renewal of his licence, G. has each time undertaken to comply with the rules of the German Equestrian Federation, which refers to the rules enacted by the International Equestrian Federation for international competitions.

The International Equestrian Federation (FEI), which has its seat in Lausanne, is an association composed solely of National Federations (NF). It deals, in particular, with international competitions and establishes the rules governing the organization of international meetings. In the interest of the present case, it is appropriate to quote the following provisions from its statutes (18th edition, effective 21st March 1991):

'051 - PREAMBLE
1. The FEI is located in Switzerland, as an incorporated body under the Swiss Civil Code, Book 1, Title 11, Chapter III. In all matters of civil litigation, the FEI is subject to Swiss Law. All civil actions (litigations) shall be brought before the Swiss Courts of the city in which the FEI is located.
...
4. All Individuals and Bodies, National Federations and Organizing Committees, Officials, Horse Owners, Persons Responsible and Competitors involved in any activities within the jurisdiction of the Statutes, Regulations and Rules, undertake to recognize the authority and responsibilities of Officials, Ground Juries, Appeal Committees, the Judicial Committee and the CAS in the performance of the duties required of them under the Statutes, Regulations and Rules, and undertake not to resort to any other legal procedures in matters coming within the responsibilities of these bodies.
...
6. In order to ensure that the execution of these responsibilities is carried out according to the highest standards of justice and equity, the following bodies and procedures are established:
    6.1 A Judicial Committee to decide on all cases which are outside the competence of any other body established under the Statutes, Regulations and Rules.
    6.2 The Court of Arbitration for Sport (CAS) – created by the IOC – to hear all appeals against the decisions of any competent body established under the Statutes, Regulations and Rules.
    6.3 An Arbitration Procedure (Art. 057).

Article 052 - JUDICIAL COMMITTEE

...

4. The Judicial Committee shall decide all cases not in the competence of the Ground Jury and Appeal Committee of an International Equestrian Event submitted to it through the Secretary General. These cases may be:
    4.1 Cases of infringement of the Statutes, Regulations and Rules.
    4.2 Cases of violation of the common principles of behaviour, fairness and accepted standards of sportsmanship.
    4.3 Cases of disagreement on the interpretation of the Statutes, Regulations and Rules.

Article 053 - COURT OF ARBITRATION FOR SPORT (CAS)

1. The CAS shall hear all the admissible appeals reported by the Secretary General against decisions taken by Appeal Committees in the first instance and by the Judicial Committee (052.4). The parties concerned shall undertake to comply with the Statutes and Regulations of the CAS and to accent and enforce in good faith its decision.

...

6. There is no appeal against the decision of the Appeals Tribunal, except in the case of the expulsion of a National Federation which must be confirmed by the General Assembly.

Article 057 - ARBITRATION

1. Any dispute between National Federations or between National Federations and the Bureau or other body of the FEI which the Judicial Committee considers to be outside the scope of the Statutes, Regulations or Rules shall be settled definitively by a Court set up in accordance with the Statutes and Regulations of the "COURT OF ARBITRATION FOR SPORT".
2. The parties shall undertake to *conform* to the aforesaid Statutes and Regulations and to execute in good faith the award made.
3. The Court of Arbitration shall make a definitive award and the parties shall waive the right to any appeal, in accordance with Article 192 of the Swiss Federal Law on Private International Law (LDIP). The parties shall agree to have the seat of the Court of Arbitration at Lausanne (Switzerland) and to apply Swiss Law.'

In its General Regulations (GR) of 23rd July 1990, the FEI established the procedure to be followed in order to settle disputes, and fixed, in particular, the competence of its Judicial Committee (art. 168) and that of the CAS (art. 169), together with the conditions and terms and modalities of the appeal (art. 173). Annex F to the said GR contains the Statute and Regulations of the CAS, in which no distinction is made between the original and appellate jurisdiction.

B. G. took part with the horse 'Life is Life' in the international jumping event (CSIO) in Aachen between 16th and 19th June 1991. He won prize money representing a total of 40,000 marks. On the occasion of this event, the horse in question was designated for a medications control, which entailed the taking of a double sample of urine and blood. Analysis of the first sample of urine, performed by the Horseracing Forensic Laboratory Ltd in Newmarket (GB), revealed the presence of a prohibited substance, isoxsuprine. At the request of the German Equestrian Federation, an analysis of the second urine sample was performed in the presence of Professor Donike of Cologne; this gave the same result as the first.

In its decision of 5th December 1991, the FEI Judicial Committee, considering that isoxsuprine came under the category of substances prohibited by the FEI Veterinary Regulations, pronounced the disqualification of the rider G. and his horse 'Life is Life' from all the competitions of the Aachen CSIO and the withdrawal of the prize money won on this occasion. It further suspended the rider from international equestrian competitions for three months, imposed a fine of 1,500 francs on him and taxed the costs of the procedure to him.

Ruling on the appeal by G. on 10th September 1992, the CAS partially allowed this appeal in that it confirmed the disqualification of the rider and his horse, hut reduced the period of suspension to one month and the fine to 1,000 francs. As for the costs of the procedure, it taxed these 2/3 to the appellant and 1/3 to the FEI.

C. G. lodged a public law appeal in the meaning of arts. 191 para. 1 LDIP and 85 let. c OJ. He concluded in favour of the judgments pronounced on 5th December 1991 by the FEI and 10th September 1992 by the CAS being annulled. Accessorily, he requested the annulment only of the latter judgment and the fixing of a 30-day time limit to institute an ordinary action before the competent state court.

By presidential decision of 23rd September 1992, a request by the appellant for the granting of suspensive effect was rejected.

The exchange of documents was limited to the question of the admissibility of the appeal. In their respective answers, the FEI and the CAS both supported the argument of the admissibility of the appeal such as it relates to the judgment of the CAS of 10th September, excluding the FEI decision of 5th December 1991.

In Law

1. The public law appeal is inadmissible insofar as it relates to the decision taken on 5th December 1991 by the FEI Judicial Committee. Indeed, not only was it lodged late (art. 89 para 1 OJ), but it also relates to a decision which is not contestable by such means, given that the Committee, as a body of the FEI, merely expressed the will of this association, a party to the dispute, and

therefore did not pronounce, an international arbitral award which alone would have been subject to a public law appeal in the meaning of arts. 85 let. c OJ and 190 et seq. LDIP.

2. The appellant received, first of all, the operative provisions of the CAS award, dated 10th September 1992, the grounds of the award being sent to him later, viz. 15th October 1992. Written notification of the grounds of the award is provided under art. 61 of the CAS Statute. For this reason, both the first notice of appeal of 17th September 1992 and the two supplementary statements of case of 13th October and 6th November 1992 were lodged before expiry of the time for appeal (art. 89 para. 2 OJ; ATF 106 1a 239). Thus, the request made by the appellant in his document of 13th October 1992 for a second exchange of documents to be ordered becomes purposeless upon examination of the grounds cited in support of it.

3. The public law appeal is opened against the CAS award only on the double condition that such judgment actually be an international arbitral award in the meaning of arts. 176 et seq. LDIP, and that it concern points of law, and therefore that it does not have as its sole object games rules whose application is, in principle, outside all juridical control (ATF 118 11 15 et seq. preamble 2,108 11 15,103 1a 410 et seq.).

a) The seat of the CAS is in Lausanne and the appellant is domiciled in Germany. The condition of an international connection, laid down in art. 176 para. 1 LDIP, is thus fulfilled in this particular case.

b) The arbitral award, in the meaning of art. 189 LDIP, is a judgment pronounced, on the basis of an arbitration agreement, by a non-state court to which the parties entrust the task of settling a case of a patrimonial nature (art. 177 para. 1 LDIP) of an international nature (art. 176 para. 1 LDIP). According to the judicial practice of the Federal Tribunal, a true award, ranking with the judgment of a state court, presupposes that the arbitral tribunal pronouncing it offers sufficient guarantees of impartiality and independence as follow from art. 58 Cst. (ATF 117 1a 168 preamble 5a, 107 1a 158 preamble 2b). Failing this, the award would constitute merely a civil judgment enforceable in the whole of Switzerland (art. 61 Cst.; ATF 97 1 489 preamble 1). In this latter judgment, the Federal Tribunal, applying these principles, considered that an arbitral tribunal, which was the body of an association having the quality of party to the action did not offer sufficient guarantees of independence. The decisions taken by such bodies indeed constitute only a simple expression of will by the association concerned; such decisions are acts falling within the scope of administration and not judicial acts. Therefore it is not possible to consider them as arbitral awards, from the point of view of both the Concordat sur l'arbitrage (CIA) and chapter 12 of the LDIR. For this reason, such decisions cannot be contested either by means of a composition appeal (art. 36 CIA) or by the means of appeal provided under art. 190 LDIP (HEINI, Die gerichtliche Überprufung von Vereinsstrafen, in: Freiheit und Verantworturig im Recht, FS Arthur Meier-Hayoz, p. 223 et seq.; JOLIDON, Commentaire du Concordat suisse sur l'arbitrage, Introduction no. 68, and no. 235 ad art. 1; LALIVE/POUDRET/REYMOND, Le droit de l'arbitrage interne et international en Suisse, no. 1.2 ad art. 1 CIA and no. 2 ad art. 176 LDIP; CORBAT, Les peines statutaires, thesis Fribourg 1974, p. 130 et seq.). In fact, to pronounce an award in one's own case is quite simply not compatible with the guarantee of independence (ATF 52 1 75; HEINI, op. cit., p. 228; GULDENER, Schweizerisches Zivilprozessrecht, 3rd edition, p. 604), so that it matters little, in this respect, to know whether the personal independence of the members of the arbitral tribunal called upon to settle the dispute could be safeguarded by means of the rules on the challenge (of another opinion: JOLIDON, Arbitrage et sport, in: Recht und Wirtschaft heute, FS MAX KUMMER, p. 633 et seq., 643/644).

The above-mentioned principles apply also in the hypothesis where the person affected by the award of the body of the association is only indirectly a part of it, in other words when only associations or other artificial persons may become members, as sections, of the umbrella association. The indirect member may also contest the decisions of the association, pursuant to art. 75 CC, or have examined by the judge the punishments (penalties provided for by the regulations) which have been imposed upon him (RIEMER, Commentaire bernois ad art. 60 et seq. CC, Systematischer Teil no. 511,515 and 529, and no. 18 ad art. 75 CC). In the case of punishments, this juridical protection must be accorded even to the person who is not a member of the association, if such person is subject to the rules established by the association, for example when such a measure is a condition to be fulfilled in order to be able to take part in an event organized by the association. Here again, the contested decision must be open to free and independent juridical control, control which may be entrusted to an arbitral tribunal on condition that such tribunal constitutes a true judicial authority and not the simple body of the association interested in the outcome of the dispute (RIEMER, no. 18 and 85 ad art. 75 CC; HEINI, op. cit., p. 229; *passim,* Das Schweizerische Vereinsrecht, p. 55/56 and 60 et seq.; KUMMER, Spielregel und Rechtsregel, p. 48 et seq.; SCHERRER, Rechtsfragen des organisierten Sportlebens in der Schweiz, thesis Zurich 1982, p. 150 et seq.; BODMER, Vereinsstrafe und Verbandsgerichtsbarkeit, thesis St Gallen 1988, p. 204 et seq.; SCHWAB/WALTER, Schiedsgerichtsbarkeit, 4th edition, p. 274 et seq.). As indicated above, on the occasion of the annual renewal of his licence, the appellant undertook to respect the rules established by the German Equestrian Federation; in doing so, he indirectly submitted to the rules of conduct enacted by the International Equestrian Federation, in particular to the juridical procedure developed by such association to contest the penalties imposed by it. In conformity with these rules of procedure, after having brought an appeal against the decision of the Judicial Committee, he concluded a complementary arbitration agreement with the FEI in which he admitted the jurisdiction of the CAS to rule on his appeal. Consequently, in view of the above, the point of knowing whether the decision at present being contested is an arbitral award which can be brought before the Federal Tribunal depends on the juridical situation of the CAS with regard to the FEI.

The idea of creating an arbitral tribunal which would be seized of litigation directly or indirectly linked with sport was put forward in 1983 by Juan Antonio Samaranch, President of the International Olympic Committee (IOC). The CAS is an autonomous arbitral institution on an organizational level, but without artificial personality, whose seat is in Lausanne. Having a Statute, which entered into force on 30th June 1984, given to it by the IOC and completed by a set of Regulations adopted on the same date, it rules, by an arbitral award, on cases submitted to it by parties and bearing on rights which they freely dispose of (art. 3). *Ratione materiae,* it is competent to hear disputes of a private nature arising out of the practice or development of sport (art. 4). The CAS is composed of a maximum of 60 members, chosen, for a renewable period of four years, from among persons having had legal training and being recognized as competent in the field of sport (art. 6). The IOC, the International Federations (IFs) and the National Olympic Committees (NOCS) each appoint fifteen members from among their own members or from outside, while the final fifteen members, chosen by the IOC President, are necessarily from outside the IOC, IFs, NOCs and the Association grouping them (art. 7). Before taking office, all the CAS members sign a solemn individual declaration worded as follows (art. 10):

> 'I solemnly declare upon my honour and in all conscience that I shall fulfil properly and faithfully my duties as an arbitrator, that I shall observe secrecy concerning the deliberations and votes and that I shall act in all objectivity and in all independence.'

For each case, the CAS sits in a 'Panel' composed of one or three arbitrators mandatorily chosen from among its members (art. 11). Each of the two parties appoints one arbitrator and the two parties then come to an agreement as to the appointment of the third arbitrator. Failing such agreement, the third arbitrator is appointed by the President of the Federal Tribunal of the Swiss Confederation. If the parties choose to have a Panel with one arbitrator, they nominate him by mutual agreement (art. 12). The arbitrators may be challenged by the parties, on account, in particular, of the links between them and one or other of them or because they have already been involved with the dispute in another capacity (art. 16). The CAS has its own judicial organization which is characterized by the existence of pleadings and an oral presentation, an ordinary procedure and a summary procedure (art. 27 et seq.). The deliberations of the Panel take place in camera (art. 58 para. 1). The CAS award is reasoned and notified to the parties (art. 61 and 63). It may be the subject of an application for interpretation (art. 64) and, on condition that such has been provided for in the arbitration agreement, a request for review based on the appearance of new facts (art. 66 et seq.). The operating costs of the CAS are borne by the IOC (art. 71). In cases of a pecuniary nature, the parties contribute to the costs entailed by the resolution of the dispute in a proportion established by an agreement made between them and the President of the Panel (art. 72; for a general description of this arbitral institution, cf. MBAYE, Une nouvelle institution d'arbitrage: Le Tribunal Arbitral du Sport, in: Annuaire Français de Droit International, 1984, p. 409 et seq., also published in: COLLOMB, Sport, droit et relations internationales, p. 95 et seq.).

The provisions governing the conduct of proceedings before the CAS are clearly aimed at the so called initial or originating procedure, in the manner of what is provided under art. 057 of the FEI statutes. However, numerous international sports associations have also made use of the possibility offered to them to appoint the CAS as a body of appeal charged to examine the validity of the penalties pronounced by their organs. Such is the case of the FEI which opened the means of appeal to the CAS against the decisions pronounced by its Judicial Committee in particular (art. 053). This legal instrument is supposed to exclude recourse to any other legal procedure before a state judge (art. 051 para. 4; on this question cf. SCHWAAR, Nouvelles du Tribunal Arbitral du Sport, in: Bulletin ASA, 1989, p. 369 et seq.). In the opinion of its founders and its representatives, the CAS is a true arbitral tribunal independent of the parties, which freely exercises complete juridical control over the decisions of the associations which are brought before it, in particular over the penalties prescribed by the regulations which have been imposed on the appellant (MBAYE, op. cit., p. 424; passim, in: Tribunal Arbitral du Sport, p. 33; SCHWAAR, Le Tribunal Arbitral du Sport, in: Pratique juridique actuelle (PJA), 1992, p. 396 et seq.; passim in: Bulletin ASA, 1990, p. 144; passim, Tribunal Arbitral du Sport, in: La législation sportive en Europe: évolution et harmonisation, 1er Séminaire juridique, Moscou 1991 , p. 82/83; passim, in: Bulletin ASA, 1991, p. 201 et seq.; CARRARD, Au nom de la loi du sport, in: Revue Olympique, 1992, p. 614 et seq., this author nevertheless advocating more pronounced independence between the CAS and the IOC). Insofar as one can judge, this opinion is apparently unanimous in legal doctrine (SAMUEL/GERHART, Sporting Arbitration and the International Olympic Committee's Court of Arbitration for Sport, in: Journal of International Arbitration, 1989, p. 39 et seq.; NAFZIGER, International sports law: a replay of characteristics and trends, in: The American Journal of International Law,

1992, p. 489 et seq., 508; NETZLE, the Court of Arbitration for Sport, in: The Entertainment and Sports Lawyer, 1992, p. 1 et seq.; OSWALD, Le règlement des litiges et la répression des comportements illicites dans le domaine sportif, in: Mélanges en l'honneur de Jacques-Michel Grossen, p. 67 et seq., 80/81).

Such an opinion may be shared – not without hesitation, moreover, provided, at least, that it relates to proceedings conducted before the CAS in which the IOC does not appear as a party. This applies in this particular case. The CAS is not a body of the FEI; it does not receive instructions from this association and retains sufficient personal autonomy from the CAS insofar as it places at its disposal only three arbitrators of the maximum of sixty members of whom the CAS is composed (art. 053 eh. 3 of the FEI Statutes; from this point of view, the CAS can be distinguished from the sports tribunal of the Swiss Football Association (ASF), which the Vaud Cantonal Court refused to consider as a true arbitral tribunal, in: JT 1988 111 5 et seq.). Furthermore, art. 7 of the CAS Statute imposes the choice of at least fifteen members from outside the IOC, IFs and NOCs and the Association which regroups them, thereby offering the parties the possibility of designating as an arbitrator or umpire one of the fifteen persons belonging neither to the FEI nor to one of its sections. The guarantee of independence of the arbitrators in a concrete case is further assured by art. 16 of the CAS Statute relating to grounds for challenge. In these conditions, one may allow that the CAS offers the guarantees of independence upon which Swiss law makes conditional the valid exclusion of ordinary judicial recourse. His opinion is, moreover, corroborated by doctrinal opinion whereby the awards of the CAS may be the subject of international enforcement in conformity with the New York Convention on the subject (NAFZIGER, op. cit., p. 508). However, certain objections with regard to the independence of the CAS could not be set aside without another form of process, in particular those based on the organic and economic ties existing between the CAS and the IOC. In fact, the latter is competent to modify the CAS Statute; it also bears the operating costs of this court and plays a considerable role in the appointment of its members. The fact remains, however, that given, on the one hand, the possibility which exists of ensuring, by the remedy of challenge, the independence of the Panel called upon to hear a specific case and, on the other hand, the solemn declaration of independence signed by each CAS member before he takes office, such objections alone do not allow the CAS to be denied the quality of true arbitral tribunal (cf. JOLIDON, in: FS Kummer, p. 643 et seq.), even though it would be desirable for greater independence of the CAS from the IOC to be assured (CARRARD, Ibid.). Finally, the fact that the CAS is an institutionalized organization in no way prevents it from being considered as a true arbitral tribunal (ATF 107 la 152). Thus, from the procedural point of view, the decision contested is indeed an arbitral award of an international nature and may be the subject of a public law appeal in the meaning of art. 85 let. c OJ in conjunction with arts. 176 et seq. LDIR

c) The admissibility of the public law appeal presupposes, moreover, that the arbitral tribunal ruled on points of law and not solely on the application of games rules, which do not in principle lend themselves to juridical control (ATF 118 11 15 et seq. preamble 2,108 11 19 et seq. preamble 3, 103 la 412 preamble 3b). Such is indeed the case here. The withdrawal of prize money of the not inconsiderable sum of around 40,000 marks, in conjunction with the disqualification with retroactive effect from all competitions in which such prize money was won, together with the suspension from international equestrian competitions – a measure which indubitably affects the personal and economic sphere of a professional rider – go far beyond simple penalties intended to ensure the correct conduct of a game and constitute real penalties prescribed by the regulations which prejudice the juridical interests of the person whom they affect and which may, as a result, be subject to judicial control (ATF 108 11 21 preamble 3; KUMMER, op. cit., p. 48 et seq.; JOLIDON, FS Kummer, p. 651 et *seq; passim,* Le droit du sport en Suisse, in: RSJ 86/1990, p. 389 et seq.; *passim,* Ordre sportif et ordre juridique, in: RJB 127/1991 , p. 213 et seq., 231; OSWALD, op. cit., p. 71 et seq.).

d) Although the suspension imposed upon him has already ended, the appellant retains a current interest in it sufficient for the annulment of the contested award. Such is the unavoidable conclusion considering the personal and patrimonial effects which the penalty in question continues to produce. Moreover, the opposite conclusion would imply the impossibility of having suspensions of short duration examined by the appeals authority (ATF 118 la 53/54 preamble 3c).

e) Finally, seeing that the FEI has its headquarters in Switzerland, any exclusion prescribed by the regulations or fixed by contract of all recourse by the parties against the CAS award would be of no effect in the context of the present appeal procedure (art. 192 para. 1 LDIP).

This being so, it is appropriate to examine the subject matter.

4. (...)

5. Citing art. 190 para. 2 let. b LDIP, the appellant maintains that the CAS wrongly declared itself competent since the case at issue was not submissible to arbitration.

The plea of incompetence must be raised before the arbitral tribunal prior to any discussion of the merits (art. 186 paras. 1 and 2 LDIP). Failing this, it is no longer possible to claim lack of jurisdiction of the arbitral tribunal as a ground for appeal on the basis of art. 190 para. 2 let. b LDIP (LALIVE/POUDRET/REYMOND, op. cit., no. 10 ad art. 186 LDIP). The plea of inarbitrability of the dispute observes the same rule (LALIVE/POUDRET/

REYMOND, op. cit., no. 6 ad art. 177 LDIP). The appellant does not claim to have raised these exceptions before the CAS; it is rather the opposite which emerges from the contested award where the CAS notes that its own jurisdiction is recognized by all the parties. This first ground is therefore inadmissible.

The argument in question in any case appears unfounded:

a)The appellant maintains, first of all, that the litigious penalty prescribed by the rules comes within the meaning of criminal law and is hence under the jurisdiction of state justice. This opinion is erroneous. It is generally accepted that the penalty prescribed by regulations represents one of the forms of penalty fixed by contract, is therefore based on the autonomy of the parties and may thus be the subject of an arbitral award (RIEMER, no. 205 et seq., part of no. 226 ad art. 70 CC with numerous references; SCHWAB/WALTER, op. Cit., p. 281), on condition that, where international arbitration is concerned, it is of a patrimonial nature in the meaning of art. 177 para. 1 LDIP (on this point, cf. LALIVE/POUDRET/REYMOND, op. cit., no. 2 ad art. 177 LDIP). In other words, the penalty prescribed by regulations has nothing to do with the power to punish reserved by the criminal courts (HEINI, op. cit., p. 60; CORBAT, op. cit., p. 70), even if it is punishing behaviour which is also punished by the state (BGHZ 21 p. 374/5).

b) If one is to believe the appellant, Swiss work contract law would, moreover, exclude the possibility of having an arbitral tribunal settle the question of the validity of a litigious penalty prescribed by regulations. However, apart from the fact, according to prevailing opinion, art. 343 CO does not prohibit the submission of a dispute in matters of work to an arbitral tribunal (REHBINDER, no. 10/1 1 ad art. 343 CO; LALIVE/POUDRET/REYMOND, op. cit., no. 4 ad art 5 CIA), the appellant in no way demonstrates for what reason and to what extent the juridical relation in question would come within the meaning of the provisions of the Swiss law governing the work contract.

6. Citing art. 190 para. 2 let. a LDIP, the appellant further disputes that the arbitral tribunal which dealt with his case was properly appointed and composed. In support of this argument, he asserts that he was forced to choose an arbitrator from among the members of the CAS, and that, at least the two arbitrators designated by the parties and especially Mr Hans Ulrich Sutter, as President of the Swiss Equestrian Sports Federation, did not offer sufficient guarantees of independence to rule on his appeal.

It has already been indicated that the CAS in itself and the procedure for designating its members and arbitrators called upon to sit on a Panel fulfil the requirements which an arbitral tribunal must satisfy (cf. preamble 3 above). This state of affairs did not deprive the appellant of the right to lodge a motion challenging one or other, or even all the members of the Panel. However, for that he 'would have had to cite the ground for the challenge as soon as he knew of it, in accordance with the principle of good faith which also governs procedural law, under pain of being time-barred (ATF 113 la 67/68, 111 la 74/75 preamble 2b and 262 preamble 2b). Art. 180 para. 2 LDIP and art. 16 para. 3 of the CAS Statute furthermore give concrete form to the same idea. Consequently, the only grounds for challenge that may be cited, in the context of the argument provided under art. 190 para. 2 let. a LDIP – so long as they may be (cf. JOLIDON, no. 41/42 ad art. 36 CIA) –, are those which a party was not in a position to raise before the pronouncement of the arbitral award (LALIVE/POUDRET/REYMOND, op. cit., no. 5a ad art. 190 LDIP). This rule applies not only to the grounds for challenge which the interested party actually knew, but also to those which he could have known by showing the required attention. In this case, the appellant received, annexed to a letter from the CAS on 6th February 1992, the CAS booklet containing, among other texts, that of the Statute of the said court. From that moment, he could no longer be unaware that, of the sixty members of the CAS, only fifteen could not be part of a sports association affiliated to an IF or the IOC. Therefore, he should have informed himself, as soon as the Panel called upon to rule on his case was constituted, with regard to the identity of the arbitrators approached with a view to sitting and to any links they might have with an IF, so that he could immediately file a motion to challenge this. The abovementioned letter should have encouraged him all the more to take his investigations further, in that it expressly drew his attention to the fact that the arbitrators Klimke and Sutter, whose names were subsequently chosen, were specialists familiar with problems relating to equestrianism. Having omitted to seek some simple additional information on this subject at the time, the appellant is no longer entitled to cite today, with retroactive effect, the ground for challenge derived from the fact that two arbitrators belonged to associations or committees directly or indirectly linked with the FEI. As a result, the question of whether this latter circumstance would have sufficed to establish the appearance of bias of the interested parties may remain undecided.

7. According to the appellant, the CAS also violated his right to be heard (art. 190 para. 2 let. d LDIP) by imposing on the parties the obligation to bring their witnesses to the hearing, by not seeking the aid of the state judge to compel two defaulting witness to give evidence, by not of its own motion taking cognizance of the written report of one of the two witnesses and not adding to the file the photographs which had been produced.

a) The rules of procedure of the CAS authorize the parties to bring witnesses and have them heard at their own expense (art. 49 of the Statute, art. 49 et seq. of the Regulations). These come within the framework of the sphere of autonomy which art. 182 para. 1 LDIP reserves for the parties concerning the arbitral procedure, and manifestly do not prejudice the minimum guarantees which art. 182 para. 3 LDIP requires to be respected, whatever the procedure chosen.

b) If the aid of the state judiciary is necessary to the production of evidence, the arbitral tribunal, or the parties in agreement with it, may request the aid of the judge of the seat of the arbitral tribunal (art. 184 para. 2 LDIP). In order to be able to conclude that there was a violation of the parties' right to be heard, more precisely their right to collaborate in the production of evidence, it is not enough that the arbitral tribunal should not of its own motion seek the aid of the state judge without having been invited thereto by one of the parties; it is necessary rather that the tribunal should have refused without valid reason the request of one of the parties to obtain the aid of the state judiciary for the production of relevant evidence. It appears from the non-contested minutes of the hearing held on 10th June 1992 that the agent of the appellant added to the file a written declaration by Professor Donike, one of the witnesses whom he had asked to be heard, and indicated to the arbitrators that another witness, Dr Cronau, would not appear. On this occasion, the aid of the judge with a view to a hearing was not requested. On the contrary, it is mentioned in the said minutes that 'no measure of examination proceedings was requested'. The CAS therefore did not violate the appellant's right to be heard for the above-mentioned reasons.

c) The procedure applicable before the CAS is governed by the principle of hearings (art. 39 et seq. of the Statute, art. 41 et seq. of the Regulations). Also, by not of its own motion adducing evidence that the parties had not requested, in particular by not itself asking the witness Cronau to provide it with a written declaration, the CAS did not further fail to recognize the right to produce evidence cited by the appellant, since such a guarantee applies only to evidence asked for within the prescribed time and within the prescribed form (ATF 106 II 171 preamble 6b).

d) According to the non-contested minutes of the hearing of 9th September 1992, the CAS agreed, against the opinion of the opposing party, that the photographs produced by the agent of the appellant be added to the file and it listened to the comments made by this lawyer on them. The argument of violation is, on this point too, totally unfounded.

8. The appellant finally cites a violation of public policy (art. 190 para. 2 let. e LDIP).

a) As the Federal Tribunal has already had occasion to observe on many occasions, whatever the conception that one accepts, there are in all cases two elements which characterize the notion of public policy of art. 190 LDIP: on the one hand, the ground relating to it is more restrictive and narrower than the argument of arbitrariness based on art. 4 Cst. or on art. 36 let. f CIA; in addition, the said notion covers only the fundamental principles of the legal order taken into consideration. Thus, the manifestly erroneous application of a rule of law or the clearly false establishment of a point of fact are not yet sufficient to justify the annulment of an award under international arbitration (ATF 117 11 606 and references; non published judgment of 25th July 1990 in the case society v., preamble 2, reproduced in: SJ 1991 , p. 12 et seq.; kaufmann, in: Bulletin ASA 1992, p. 66 et seq.; poudret, in: Bulletin ASA 1992, p. 82183).

b) Under these conditions, it is fruitless for the appellant to seek to call into question the outcome of the preliminary procedure by challenging the modalities of the anti-doping control and the assessment of the result of such control. As for the opinion of the CAS, whereby it is sufficient that the analyses performed reveal the presence of a banned product for there to be presumption of doping and, consequently, a reversal of the burden of proof, this relates not to public policy but to the burden of proof and the assessment of evidence, problems which cannot be resolved, in private law matters, in the light of notions proper to criminal law, such as the presumption of innocence and the principle 'in dubio pro reo', and corresponding guarantees which feature in the European Convention on Human Rights. Nor is it contrary to public policy that the pertinent rules enacted by the FEI are characterized by great severity, in the opinion of the appellant, in that they prohibit products or amounts of a product which would not be likely to affect the performance of the horse. Indeed, whether they be appropriate or not, or even whether or not they stand up to the objection of arbitrariness, such rules do not in any case question the fundamental principles of the Swiss legal order in the area of relations of an international nature. In particular, there is no violation of public policy from the simple fact that the norms prescribed by the regulations relating to doping might be incompatible with certain statutory or legal provisions.

9. At the end of this examination, there is no alternative but to reject the appeal insofar as it is admissible.

Swiss Supreme Court , IInd Civil Court, 4 December 2000, 5P.427/2000
Raducan v. International Olympic Committee

Composition of the Court: Mr Bianchi, Chairman, Mr Raselli and
                                 Ms Nordmann, Justices.
Clerk: Mr Abrecht.

Ruling on the public law appeal lodged by

Andreea Raducan, domiciled in Rumania, represented with valid address for service by Messrs Jacques Michod and Olivier Rodondi, Attorneys-at-Law in Lausanne,
versus

the award rendered on 28 September 2000 by the ad hoc Division, constituted for the Sydney Olympic Games, of the Court of Arbitration for Sport, the seat of which is in Lausanne, in the cause opposing the appellant and the International Olympic Committee, in Lausanne, respondent;

(international arbitration in sports matters)
On the basis of the record, which evidences the following facts:

A. Andreea Raducan, a Romanian gymnast born on 30 September 1983, won the gold medal in the Gymnastics (Artistic) Women's Team Finals of the Sydney Olympics on 19 September 2000. She was not tested for doping at the end of that competition.
   On 20 September 2000, Andreea Raducan complained of a headache and of a runny nose to the doctor of the Rumanian gymnastics team, Dr Oana. The latter gave her a pill of 'Nurofen Cold and Flu', that she absorbed in the doctor's presence.
   On 21 September 2000, Andreea Raducan won the finals of the Gymnastics (Artistic) Women's Individual All-Around competition. Before the beginning of that competition, during her warm up, she again complained to Dr Oana that she was not feeling well. This doctor thereupon gave her a second pill of 'Nurofen Cold and Flu', that she absorbed.
B. After the competition of 21 September 2000, Andreea Raducan was taken to the anti-doping control station, in accordance with the anti-doping procedures adopted for the Sydney Olympics. She delivered, in three urine samples, between 11: 03 p.m. on 21 September and 12:20 a.m. on 22 September, a total urine quantity of 62 milliliters (ml).

Analyzing this urine, divided into samples 'A' and 'B', the Australian Sports Drug Testing Laboratory detected therein the presence of pseudoephedrine. The concentration of this substance was between 88 and 90.6 micrograms per miltilitre in sample 'A', which contained 80 ml of urine, and between 90.8 and 93.71 micrograms per millilitre in sample 'B', which contained 20 ml of urine.

C. The Olympic Movement Anti-Doping Code (hereinafter the Anti-Doping Code), amended on January 1, 2000, provides as follows:

'Chapter II: The Offence of Doping and its Punishment
Article 1
1. Doping contravenes the fundamental principles of Olympism and sports and medical ethics.
2. Doping is forbidden.
Article 2
Doping is:
1. the use of an expedient (substance or method) which is potentially harmful to athletes' health and/or capable of enhancing their performance, or
2. the presence in the athlete's body of a Prohibited Substance or evidence of the use thereof or evidence of the use of a Prohibited Method'.

Appendix A of the Anti-Doping Code, amended on 1 April 2000, contains the following provisions:

'I. Prohibited Classes of Substances
   A.   Stimulants
        Prohibited Substances in class (A) include the following examples:
        (...) ephedrines**, (..)
        **   For ephedrine and methylephedrine, the definition of a positive is a concentration in urine greater that 10 micrograms per millilitre. For phenlypropanolamine and pseudoephedrine, the definition of a positive is a concentration in urine of greater than 25 micrograms per millilitre'.

D. A report prepared on 27 September 2000 by Dr Richard Day and filed by Andreea Raducan at the hearing of the same day before the arbitral tribunal (see letter F below) establishes that a pill of 'Nurofen Cold and Flu' contains 30 mg of pseudoephedrine and that the concentration of this substance found in samples 'A' and 'B' is consistent with the absorption by Andreea Raducan of a pill of 'Nurofen Cold and Flu' on the evening of the competition of 21 September 2000.

E. By decision of 26 September 2000, the International Olympic Committee (hereinafter the IOC) disqualified Andreea Raducan from the Gymnastics (Artistic) Women's Individual All-Around competition for 'use of prohibited substances (Chapter II, Article 2.2 of the Olympic Movement Anti-Doping

Code)' and ordered the Romanian National Olympic Committee to withdraw and return the gold medal and the diploma awarded to Andreea Raducan for her first place in that competition.

F. On 26 September 2000, Andreea Raducan filed a request for arbitration with the Court of Arbitration for Sport (hereinafter the CAS), requesting that the IOC's decision be reversed and that she be reinstated as gold medalist.
By arbitral award, with reasons, of 28 September 2000, the CAS dismissed the request and confirmed the IOC's decision.

G. By way of a public law appeal before the Supreme Court, Andreea Raducan requests that this award be vacated, with costs.

Considering at Law:

1. The Supreme Court examines *ex officio* and with full scope of review the admissibility of appeals brought before it (ATF[56] 126 III 275, para. 1 and decisions referred to therein).

   a. The public law appeal against the CAS award is admissible only on the double condition that this ruling actually is an arbitral award rendered in international arbitration proceedings within the meaning of Articles 176 *et seq.* PIL Act[57] and that it pertains to legal issues, i.e. that it does not have as sole aim to decide on rules of the game, the application of which normally escapes all legal control (ATF 119 II 271 para. 3; 118 II 15, para. 2; 108 II 15; 103 Ia 410).

   b. The arbitral award, within the meaning of Article 189 PIL, is a judgment rendered on the basis of an arbitration agreement by a non-governmental tribunal which has been entrusted by the parties with the adjudication of a patrimonial matter (Article 177(1) PIL Act); a true award, equivalent to a judgment of a court, presupposes that the tribunal having rendered it offers all adequate guarantees of impartiality and independence, as these flow from Article 58 of the former Constitution and now from Article 30(1) of the Constitution (ATF 119 II 271 para. 3; 117 Ia 168 para. 5a; 107 Ia 158 para. 2b). The Supreme Court has held that the CAS can be considered as a true arbitral tribunal regarding proceedings to which the IOC is not a party, and where the CAS is mandated by an international sports association to act as the appellate body entrusted with examining the validity of sanctions pronounced by the bodies of these associations (ATF 119 II 271 para. 3b).

---

[56] 'ATF' is the French-language abbreviation for 'Supreme Court Decisions', i.e, the official report of Swiss Supreme Court decisions.
[57] 'PIL Act' is the English-language abbreviation for the Swiss Act on Private International Law of 1987.

c. The question whether the CAS can be considered as having rendered a true arbitral award within the meaning of Articles 176 *et seq* PIL Act when it has adjudicated a request for arbitration seeking the reversal of a decision of the IOC – the condition relating to the international connecting factor, set at Article 176(1) PIL Act, being met in this instance (see ATF 1 19 II 271 para. 3a) – does not need to be decided. Indeed, the public law appeal, supposing that it is admissible, would in any event be dismissed as will be seen below.

2. a. The Appellant argues firstly that Article 3.4 of the Anti-Doping Code, which prescribes a minimum urine quantity of 75 ml, has allegedly been breached in this instance. According to the appellant, the non-observation of this procedural rule allegedly violates the athlete's fundamental right to obtain a rigorous and infallible control of his or her physical condition and is allegedly contrary to public policy within the meaning of Article 190(2)(e) PIL Act. Indeed, in the context of anti-doping testing, the athlete is allegedly in a precarious situation, since the simple presence of a prohibited substance in his or her urine triggers a legal presumption of doping, which the athlete can rebut only by proving a malevolent act by a third party or an erroneous analysis result. The extreme rigor of this presumption of doping – which the Supreme Court has considered compatible with public policy (decision *in re* G. of 15 March 1993, para. 8b, not reported in ATF 119 II 271 but reproduced in ASA Bulletin 1993, p. 409) – should have as a corollary a very special rigor in the scrupulous application of the testing procedures issued by the sporting body.

b. The appellant also complains that her right to be heard in adversarial proceedings, within the meaning of Article 190(2)(d) PIL Act, has allegedly not been guaranteed. She alleges that, before the CAS, she argued that there was a 38 ml difference between the quantity of urine she delivered at the antidoping control station and that which arrived at the laboratory (80 ml in sample 'A' and 20 ml in sample 'B'). In its answer to this argument, the CAS stated that it was undisputed that the laboratory had received a sufficient volume of urine to undertake a valid analysis, and that the discrepancy between the quantity of urine delivered according to the report of the anti-doping control (62 ml) and that which results from the laboratory reports (100 ml) could not reasonably be considered to have had an impact on a correctly performed analysis (see award under appeal, para. 7.5 to 7.7, pp. 8-9). According to the appellant, the CAS allegedly did not answer her complaint, since the issue was not whether the laboratory had received a volume of urine that was sufficient to carry out the analysis of samples 'A' and 'B', but rather how and why a quantity of fluid that was greater than the 62 ml delivered by the appellant ended up in the laboratory.

c. Finally, the appellant argues that the award under appeal is contrary to public policy, within the meaning of Article 190(2)(e) PIL Act, to the extent that it violates the principles of good faith and equal treatment. Indeed, in an award rendered on 25 June 1992 in application of the General Regulations of the FEI *(Fédération Equestre Internationale)*, the CAS had established that certain jars containing urine samples had not been closed in accordance with the General Regulations of the FEI; considering that it had thus become possible to open the caps slightly and that one could thus not rule out the possibility of a manipulation and therefore a contamination of the jars' contents by a foreign substance, the CAS admitted that there remained a doubt that should benefit the appellant (see Matthieu Reeb (ed.), Collection of CAS Awards 1986-1998, Bern 1998, p. 99 *et seq.*). To treat differently this case, in which the only plausible explanation to the excess of fluid that had been observed, would allegedly constitute flagrantly unequal treatment, violating the principle of good faith to a degree that is incompatible with public policy within the meaning of Article 190(2)(e) PIL Act.

3. a. In the totality of the arguments summarized above, the appellant loses sight of an essential factor. Indeed, the appellant was punished for 'use of Prohibited Substances (Chapter II, Article 2.2 of the Olympic Movement Anti-Doping Code)'. Pursuant to this provision, doping is defined not only as 'the presence in the athlete's body of a Prohibited Substance', but also as 'evidence of the use thereof'.

In this instance, the IOC's decision was not confirmed by the CAS on the sole basis of the urine analysis, which revealed a concentration of pseudoephedrine three times greater than the threshold as of which a result is deemed positive. Indeed, the appellant admitted to having taken a pill of 'Nurofen Cold and Flu' – which contains 30 mg of pseudoephedrine – during her warm-up for the finals of the Gymnastics (Artistic) Women's Individual All-Around competition and this clearly falls within the definition of doping as per Article 2.2 of the Anti-Doping Code. In fact, it results from the award under appeal (para. 7.8-7.19, pp. 9-11) that the CAS considered that the presence of pseudoephedrine in the appellant's body was actually due to the absorption – admitted by the appellant – of that pill, which is confirmed by Dr Day's report of 27 September 2000.

b. Since it is established that the appellant took a pill of 'Nurofen Cold and Flu' containing 30 mg of pseudoephedrine just before the competition and that this explains the concentration of pseudoephedrine in her urine that is three times greater than the threshold defining doping, the CAS did not violate the appellant's right to be heard by merely stating, in reply to the argument based on the discrepancy between the quantity of urine delivered according to the doping control report and that resulting from the laboratory reports, that this discrepancy could not reasonably be deemed to have had an impact of the results of the analysis (see para. 2b above).

Again because it is established that the presence of pseudoephedrine in samples 'A' and 'B' in a concentration three times greater than the threshold set at Appendix A of the Anti-Doping Code is due to the absorption of a pill of 'Nurofen Cold and Flu' just before the competition, this case is totally different from that which was decided in the CAS award of 25 June 1992 to which the appellant refers, so that the complaint of unequal treatment in violation of public policy within the meaning of Article 190(2)(e) is ill-funded.

Finally, under these circumstances, one cannot argue, as the appellant does (see para. 2a above), that the failure to comply with Article 3.4 of the Anti-Doping Code, which prescribes the delivery of a minimum urine quantity of 75 ml, amounts to a violation of procedural public policy within the meaning of Article 190(2)(d) PIL Act.

4. The appeal is thus obviously without merit assuming that it can be considered admissible and must therefore be dismissed to the extent that it is admissible. In application of Article 156(1) FJO,[58] the appellant shall bear the court costs. However, no legal costs will be awarded to the respondent, who was not invited to make a submission and who thus has not incurred any costs in connection with the proceedings before the Supreme Court (Articles 159(1) and (2) FJO; Poudret/Sandoz-Monod, Commentaire de la loi fédérale d'organisation judiciaire, vol. V, 1992, n. 2 re art. 159 FJO).

For these reasons
the Supreme Court:
in view of art. 36a FJO:
1. Dismisses the appeal to the extent that it is admissible;
2. Orders that the appellant shall bear court costs in the amount of 5,000 Fr.;
3. Serves a copy of this decision on the parties and on the ad hoc Division, constituted for the Sydney Olympic Games, of the Court of Arbitration for Sport.

---

[58] 'FJO' is the English-language abbreviation for 'Federal Act on Judicial Organization', i.e., the act governing appeal proceedings before the Swiss Supreme Court.

CHAPTER X
MEDIATION IN SPORTS DISPUTES

Informal Survey on Sports Mediation by ISFs & NGBs

Dr. Robert Siekmann, the Managing Director of the International Sports Law Project at The TMC Asser Institute, The Hague, The Netherlands, conducted in the last quarter of 2001 an informal survey amongst several International Sports Federations and National Sports Governing Bodies on the use of Mediation in Sports Disputes.

525 of such Bodies, i.e., national sports organizations (Olympic sports) in the European Union, were sent a Questionnaire and 43 replied, that is 12%.

It appears from those Bodies, who did reply to the Questionnaire, that many of them do not have their own mediation rules, but rely on the arbitration and mediation rules of the CAS, to whom, in such cases, all disputes are exclusively referred.

For example, all disputes of the International Rowing Federation (FISA) are 'uniquely dealt with by the Court of Arbitration for Sport in Lausanne'.

Likewise the International Badminton Federation (IBF) does not have any specific rules on mediation but recognises the CAS under rule 2.4 of its Statutes, which provides as follows:

'Members of the Federation shall not be permitted to bring disputes with the Federation before a Court of Justice and membership of the Federation shall involve members in renouncing the right to take a dispute before the Courts. Any such dispute shall be referred to the Court of Arbitration for Sport, unless agreed otherwise by the parties in dispute'.

Likewise, the International Federation of Associated Wrestling Styles (FILA) provides:

'In the event of a sport dispute with a National Federation or an athlete, it is the CAS who is in charge of the mediation and of the arbitration if necessary'.

The International Motorcycling Federation (FIM) in article 9 of its Disciplinary and Arbitration Code (CDA) also provides for the mandatory reference of appeals to the CAS. The FIM also includes an unusual and interesting so-called 'Law of Mercy' provision ('*Droit de Clemence*') – a kind of mediation clause – in article 8 of its CDA.

This article provides as follows:

'The Management Council, after consultation with the CJI (International Judicial Panel) President or upon proposal of the latter, may mitigate or completely forgive the penalty of a person who has exhausted the appeal procedures'.

On the other hand, the International Ice Hockey Federation (IIHF) expressly recognises mediation as a first means of settling disputes within its own internal procedures, but also requires exclusive arbitration by the CAS in the event of any mediation proving to be unsuccessful. The IIHF Statutes provide as follows:

'45. Subject Matter of the Arbitration
Any dispute concerning the interpretation and/or application of the Statutes, Bylaws, Regulations and official rules or decisions of IIHF bodies or the decisions of any duly authorized representative of the IIHF and the appeal and/or the review processes within the IIHF having fully been exercised must be settled by arbitration – except of those specified in statutes 21 C. This also applies to disputes between and among the member national associations or between them and the IIHF bodies, if no amicable agreement has been reached.

46. Court of Arbitration for Sport
Any dispute to be settled by arbitration must be submitted exclusively by way of appeal to the Court of Arbitration for Sport (CAS) in Lausanne, Switzerland, which will resolve the dispute definitively in accordance with the Code of Sports-related Arbitration. The time limit for appeal is twenty-one days after receipt of the decision concerning the appeal'.

So, also does the French Sailing Federation (FFV) and this is perhaps not so surprising since mediation of sports disputes is quite well established in France. Indeed, the FFV expressly recommends the use of mediation in major events 'to reduce the number of protests' pointing out that 'through the mediation system, disputes may be solved very shortly, resulting in a lighter penalty'. An interesting sidelight on the value of mediation.

Again, in Title VI (comprising articles 95-114) of the Statutes of the Spanish Basketball Federation, there is provision for 'extrajudicial conciliation' of sporting disputes between the clubs themselves and between clubs and the Federation in certain prescribed circumstances and under certain formal conditions.

Also, the Italian Olympic Committee (Comitato Olimpico Nazionale Italiano – 'CONI') on 28 December 2000 approved the setting up of a special Chamber of Conciliation and Arbitration for Sport (Camera di Conciliazione e Arbitrato per lo Sport). Under article 3.5 of the Rules (Regolamento) of this Body, it is obligatory for the parties in dispute to first attempt conciliation before instituting an arbitration procedure. Conciliation is expressed to be conducted on a 'without prejudice' basis (art. 5.8, ibid.).

However, a number of Sports Bodies, for example, the British Triathlon Association, the Helenic Table Tennis Federation, the Portuguese Judo Federation (FPJ), the Irish Football Association and the European Swimming League (LEN), do not have any specific arbitration or mediation rules nor do they make any particular provision for the settlement of sports disputes in their Constitutions.

Others in the same situation, however, are aware of the need to make such provision. For example, the International Mountaineering and Climbing Federation (UIAA), which is based in Zollikon-Zurich in Switzerland, does not have any special rules on international sports disputes, giving as a probable reason for this that they 'have never been involved in a dispute of this kind so that the urgency for regulations is low'. However, Dr. Christoph Jezler, UIAA Attorney and Board Member, adds:

'We are aware that this might change, in particular in connection with lawsuits of athletes banned based on the doping regulations. We have not yet discussed this in the Board but my feeling is that we would refer to arbitration by the Court of Arbitration for Sport in Lausanne'.

And the Welsh Hockey Union commented:

'Whilst we have no definitive Arbitration and/or Mediation Rules at present (other than internal right of appeals etc.) as we are members of the Welsh Sports Association, that organisation is presently [September 2001] formulating a new Arbitration system that we would utilise. They will obviously be based on an independent based hearing and should be available to all National Governing Bodies in Wales within the next few months'.

The British Weightlifters' Association (BWLA) in its 2001 Disciplinary Code states in article 1: 'This Code has the overriding objective of enabling the Disciplinary Committee to deal with cases justly and efficiently'. It goes on in article 2 to elaborate on what, so far as is practical, dealing with a case justly involves as follows:

'2.1 Ensuring that the parties are on an equal footing;
2.2 Saving expense;
2.3 Dealing with a case that is proportionate
    2.3.1 To the importance of the case both to weightlifting and the world in general;
    2.3.2 To the complexity of the issues;
    2.3.3 To the financial resources of each party;
2.4 Ensuring it is dealt with expeditiously and fairly;
2.5 Allotting to it an appropriate share of resources while taking into account the need to allocate resources to other matters'.

Article 3 provides that:

'The Disciplinary Committee must seek to give effect to the overriding objectives when it exercises any powers given to it under this code or interprets any paragraph'.

And article 4 requires the parties who come before a Disciplinary Committee 'to help the Committee to further the overriding objectives'.

Appeals from the BWLA Disciplinary Committee go to an independent arbitrator (art. 67 of the Code). The arbitration is conducted according to English Law and expressly excludes the right of appeal, which is limited in any case, to the English High Court under sections 1 & 2 of the Arbitration Act, 1979. Before appointing an arbitrator, the parties in dispute must agree in writing to these requirements (art. 69, ibid.).

The International Cycling Union (UCI) has its own Disciplinary Commission for dealing with breaches of the UCI Regulations (art. 12.2.013 of the UCI Cycling Regulations). Appeals from decisions of the Disciplinary Commission are referred to the UCI Appeals Board (art. 12.2.022, ibid.).

As regards the Football Association of Ireland (FAI), under its Official Rule Book, effective from 6 June 1998, the FAI operates an Appeal Board to deal with contested decisions made by League and Divisional Associations of the FAI National League, as well as rulings of the FAI National League itself (art. 27 A & B). When all such appeal procedures of the FAI have been exhausted, article 28 provides for arbitration as follows:

'General

In pursuance of paragraphs 1 to 5 of Article 57 of the FIFA Statutes, members undertake not to refer disputes with other members, or the Association, to a court of law. Members agree to be bound by these rules and in the event of any differences or disputes under these rules the members agree to submit such disputes or differences to arbitration by a sole arbitrator to be appointed (in the absence of agreement between the members upon such appointment and on the application of either of them) by the President (or other Officer endowed with the functions of such President) for the time being of the Law Society of Ireland or (in the event of the President or other Officer as aforesaid being unable or unwilling to make such appointment) by the next Senior Officer of that Society who is so able and willing to make the appointment and such arbitration shall be governed by the Arbitration Acts 1954 and 1980.

The decision of the Arbitrator in respect of any dispute or difference under these Rules shall be final and conclusive and heretofore binding on the members'.

Finally, the Royal Belgian Federation for Equestrian Sports (KBRSF – FRBSE) refers appeals against decisions of the Board and the Technical and Disciplinary Committees to arbitration by the Belgian Arbitration Commission for Sport (BAS) of the Belgian Olympic and Interfederal Committee, which is based in Brussels.

As the mediation service provided by the CAS becomes better known and used and the advantages of mediation become more widely appreciated, many International and National Sports Bodies can be expected to include specific provisions for mediation of appropriate sports disputes by the CAS in their Statutes and Constitutions.

Such a so-called CAS arbitration 'clause by reference' in the Statutes of the International Equestrian Federation has been held in a ruling by the Swiss Federal Tribunal of 31 October 1996 in the case of *N. v Federation Equestre Internationale (FEI)*[59] to be perfectly valid and legal. In that case, the appellant signed a model agreement which contained an undertaking to abide by the rules of the FEI, but did not mention the arbitration clause for settling disputes which is contained in those Rules. However, the confirmation of eligibility that the appellant received contained the following express reference to CAS arbitration in the section headed 'General rules, regulations and conditions':

'An arbitration procedure is provided for under the FEI Statutes and General Regulations as referred to above. In accordance with this procedure, any appeal against a decision rendered by the FEI or its official bodies is to be settled exclusively by the Court of Arbitration for Sport (CAS) in Lausanne, Switzerland'.

The question before the Court was whether the reference to arbitration by the CAS was, in all the circumstances of the particular case, a legally valid one, from the formal point of view. The Court decided in the affirmative and dismissed the appellant's challenge.

There is no reason to suppose that a similar CAS mediation 'clause by reference' would also not be legal. Again, in view of its importance, the English text of this ruling of the Swiss Federal Tribunal of 31 October 1996 is now reproduced for ease of reference:

Extract of the judgment of 31st October 1996 delivered by the 1st Civil Division of the Swiss Federal Tribunal in the case N. versus Fédération Equestre Internationale (appeal) (translation)

A. N., a professional rider domiciled outside Switzerland, is a member of a local horse riding club attached to an equestrian association which comes under the control of a National Equestrian Federation, which is itself affiliated to the Fédération Equestre Internationale (FEI), whose headquarters are in Lausanne. On 18th September 1993, he took part in an international jumping event (CSIO) in San Marino.

On 30th May 1994, the Judicial Committee of the FEI, basing its action on the FEI statutes and general regulations, and considering that the analyses performed after the aforesaid competition revealed the presence of a prohibited substance in the urine and blood of the horse ridden by N., disqualified the rider

---

[59] I Civil Division Swiss Fed Trib 31 October 1996.

and his horse, demanded the return of any trophy and prize money won at the event in question, suspended the rider for six months, ordered him to pay the costs of the procedure and ordered the publication of such sanctions.

B. In his application of 24th June 1994, N. brought an action before the President of the Lausanne District Civil Court, within the meaning of art. 75 CC, seeking the setting aside of the sanctions. The FEI raised an objection of arbitration and submitted that the plaintiff's case be dismissed.

In his interlocutory order of 21st February 1995, the President of the Lausanne District Civil Court accepted the objection and instructed the plaintiff to take proceedings in the proper court. In an order dated 21st June 1995, the Appeals Division of the Vaud Cantonal Court rejected the appeal which N. had lodged against this judgment.

C. On appeal, the plaintiff invited the Federal Tribunal to annul the order of the cantonal court and reject the objection to jurisdiction. Subsidiarily, he called for the case to be referred to the cantonal authority for further inquiries into the facts and a new decision.

The defendant proposed that such appeal be rejected.

In Law

1. The present dispute relates to the punishments specified in the statutes which are imposed by an association whose headquarters are in Switzerland with a view to penalizing the behaviour of a non-Swiss participant in a competition held abroad; more precisely, it centres on establishing whether the jurisdiction of the state courts was validly excluded by an arbitration agreement, in which case the dispute should be settled pursuant to the procedure established by articles 176 et seq. LDIP (RS 291) which govern the area of international arbitration (art. 176 para. 1 LDIP). The international nature of the dispute, within the meaning of art. 1 para. 1 LDIP, is thus not in doubt. In consequence, the jurisdiction of the state court seized at the headquarters of the association in question must be examined in the light of the apposite provisions of the Swiss Code on private international law (art. 1 para. 1 letter a and para. 2 LDIP).

2. If the parties have concluded an arbitration agreement which applies to an arbitrable dispute, the Swiss court will decline to exercise jurisdiction, subject to any provisions to the contrary appearing in an international treaty (art. 1 para. 2 LDIP), unless it finds – this being the only reason taken into account in this particular case – that the arbitration agreement has lapsed, become ineffective or is not applicable (art. 7 letter b. LDIP). On this point, internal law coincides with art. II para. 3 of the New York Convention on the Recognition and Enforcement of Foreign Arbitral Awards (RS 0.277.12),

which is not, however, applicable in this particular case since the court of arbitration which would have to have cognizance of the dispute has its seat in Switzerland (ATF 122 III 139 section 2a; POUDRET, A propos de la validité d'une clause arbitrale – un arrêt pouvant prêter à confusion, in: JdT 1995 1 354 et seq., 355; POUDRET/COTTIER, Remarques sur l'application de l'article II de la Convention de New York, in: Bulletin de l'Association suisse de l'arbitrage [ASA] 1995, p. 383 et seq., 386 ch. 1).

According to the case law of the Federal Tribunal, if an objection of arbitration is referred to the state judge and the court of arbitration has its seat in Switzerland, he must decline to exercise jurisdiction if the summary examination of the arbitration agreement does not permit him to find that such agreement has lapsed, become ineffective or is not applicable (ATF 122 III 139 section 2b). In principle, there is no reason to go back over this case law, at least when – as in the case which is the subject of the above-mentioned order – it is the material validity of the arbitration agreement which is at issue, given that the authority to rule on this point lies primarily, or even exclusively, with the arbitration court (art. 186 para. 1 LDIP). The same cannot be said, however, when the point at issue is the formal validity of an arbitration agreement, that is to say establishing essentially whether the jurisdiction of the ordinary court has been replaced by that of a court of arbitration by an extension agreement which respects the legal requirements in terms of form. The effects of the arbitration agreement, in the same way as those of the choice of jurisdiction clause, are generally characterized by the exclusion of a given decision-making jurisdiction and the extension of another decision-making power. The efficacy of the exclusion presupposes that the competent court pursuant to objective law has been validly excluded. Now, even in cases which lend themselves to this, such exclusion may, among other reasons, face obstacles drawn from the formal provisions of procedural law (H.R. WALTER, Derogation c. Prorogation – Kollisionen aus interkantonal oder international vereinbarter Zuständigkeit im Zivilprozess, in: Rechtskollisionen, Festschrift für A. Heini, p. 509 et seq., 510 and references). Consequently, the court seized which is confronted with an incident raised in this connection, shall rule on the problem of form on the basis of its own jurisdiction, which the defendant intends to exclude, and not in terms of the extended competence of another jurisdiction. It should do this with full powers of examination, whether the extension agreement at issue seeks to establish the jurisdiction of another state court or that of a court of arbitration. Indeed, it alone has the power to pronounce a binding decision on the subject of the exclusion of its own jurisdiction, provided that a decision pronounced elsewhere which has the substantive force of *res judicata* has not already excluded such jurisdiction. The consequence of this is, *inter alia,* that a decision whereby a court (ordinary or arbitration) with extended jurisdiction declines jurisdiction is not alone sufficient to establish the jurisdiction of the court whose jurisdiction is supposed to have been excluded. Thus, once the state court before which the case has been brought is called upon to rule exclusively on the exclusion of its own jurisdiction and hence to pronounce a binding decision on this point, it must rule on the issue with full powers of examination, irrespective of whether it is the first or second court before which the objection to jurisdiction has been raised (in this sense, see also: POUDRET, op. cit., p. 356 et seq.; POUDRET/COTTIER, op. cit., p. 386 et seq.; for those holding the opposite opinion, see, lastly, C.U. MAYER, Die Überprüfung internationaler Schiedsvereinbarungen durch staatliche Gerichte. Überlegungen zu BGE 121 111 38 und BGE 122 III 139, in: Bull. ASA 1996, p. 331 et seq., 402/403 and 409 to 411, where the author argues in favour of a summary examination of the formal and material validity of arbitration agreements). Nor should one lose sight of the fact that formal provisions, where these perform a protective function, must ensure that waiving the legal protection provided by the state is not done lightly, but is the result of a well-established desire to do so (WENGER, Kommentar zum Schweizerischen Privatrecht, Internationales Privatrecht, Basle, n. 7 ad art. 178 LDIP and references). Consequently, the state court must make sure that only a validly agreed exemption excludes its effects.

3. According to the findings of the cantonal court, disputes such as the one which gave rise to the present action must be referred, pursuant to the provisions enacted by the FEI (statutes and regulations), to the Court of Arbitration for Sport (TAS; cf., in this connection, ATF 119 II 271) which the International Olympic Committee (IOC) made available to the federations affiliated to it, to the exclusion of state courts. In this case, the dispute concerns whether the plaintiff is subject to such jurisdiction by an arbitration agreement in the proper form.

The CAS, which is an institutionalized court of arbitration, has its seat in Lausanne (ATF 119 II 271 section 3a). This seat being in Switzerland, the formal validity of the arbitration agreement in dispute must be examined in the light of art. 178 LDIP, in accordance with what is today the majority opinion, and not on the basis of the stricter requirements (Cf. POUDRET Et POUDRET/COTTIER, ibid., who dispute the merits of the opinion expressed in ATF 121 III 38 section 2c p. 44) – laid down by art. II para. 2 of the New York Convention (see particularly LALIVE/POUDRET/REYMOND, Le droit de l'arbitrage interne et international en Suisse, n. 7 ad art. 178 LDIP; VOLKEN, in: IPRG-Kommentar, n. 9 et seq. ad art. 178 LDIP; WENGER, op. cit., n. 5 ad art. 178 LDIP; DUTOIT, Droit international privé suisse – Commentaire de la loi fédérale du 18 décembre 1987, n. 4 ad art. 178, and the references made by these authors, including the differing opinions of some of the legal authorities). In fact, even supposing the aforesaid convention had been applicable in this particular case, art. VII para. 1 thereof, which reserves the application of the more favourable national law would, in any case, have led to the application of art. 178 LDIP (VOLKEN, op. cit., n. 10 ad art. 178 LDIP; DUTOIT, ibid.; Lucius HUBER, Arbitration Clause 'By Reference', in: The Arbitration Agreement – Its Multifold Critical Aspects, ASA Special Series no 8, p. 78 et seq., 79).

a) Pursuant to art. 178 para. 1 LDIP, the arbitration agreement is valid, with regard to form, if it is concluded in writing, by telegram, telex, fax or any other means of communication which allows the proof of this to be established by a text.

b) The Appeals Division established finally (art. 63 para. 2 OJ) the following circumstances:
 – the plaintiff was already the subject of proceedings before the FEI Judicial Committee and himself lodged an appeal with the CAS against one of the decisions taken by such Committee;
 – when he was selected as a member of the national equestrian team, the plaintiff signed, on 25th January 1993, a model agreement under the terms of which he undertook, during such time as he belonged to the national squad, to abide by the provisions of the FEI regulations;
 on 27th August 1993, the National Federation concerned confirmed to the plaintiff that he was entered for the San Marino CSIO and sent him a copy of the programma relating to it, which contained, under the heading 'General rules, regulations and conditions', a figure 6 worded as follows:

> 'An arbitration procedure is provided for under the FEI Statutes and General Regulations as referred to above. In accordance with this procedure, any appeal against a decision rendered by the FEI or its official bodies is to be settled exclusively by the Court of Arbitration for Sport (CAS) in Lausanne, Switzerland.'

For the cantonal court, such circumstances and references are sufficient to establish the existence of an arbitration agreement valid with respect to form.

c) The model agreement signed by the plaintiff on 25th January 1993 refers to the FEI regulations, but without mentioning the arbitration clause which appears therein. The question of whether such a global reference satisfies the requirements as to form of art. 178 LDIP is disputed. In reality, it is not possible to answer this in any general way, only on the basis of the circumstances of the particular case (HUBER, op. cit., p. 81 and the authors referred to in footnote 11; WENGER, op. cit., n. 54 ad art. 178 LDIP; DUTOIT, op. cit., n. 6 ad art. 178 LDIP). In this respect, the starting point must be the principle whereby the requirement of a specified form, alongside the probative function assigned to it, essentially seeks to protect the parties and avoid their concluding arbitration agreements inadvertently (cf. VOLKEN, op. cit., n. 14 ad art. 178 LDIP). In the global reference accepted in writing, the problem consequently moves from the form to the consent and thus brings into play the principle of confidence, which is also applicable when settling disputes relating either to the consent required for an arbitration agreement to achieve its purpose, or the interpretation of such an act (ATF 121 III 38 section 3; POUDRET, op. cit., p. 358 et seq.; *the same,* in: Bull. ASA 1992, p. 31 ch. 6 and the decisions cited; POUDRET/COTTIER, op. cit., p. 391 et seq.; HUBER, op. cit., p. 83 et seq.). Thus, it is not admissible to hold that an arbitration agreement resulting from a global reference does not bind the person who, already knowing the existence of the arbitration clause when he signs the document referring to it and thereby satisfies the requirement of the written form, makes no objection to such a clause and further demonstrates, through his subsequent behaviour, that he regards himself as bound by it (see also a decision of the Commercial Court of the Canton of Zurich published in: ZR 1992-1993, no 23 section 2). A similar demonstration may result, especially with respect to the principle of confidence, from the acceptance without argument of an arbitration clause, the detailed text of which is subsequently brought to the attention of the party concerned. Such behaviour indeed allows the author of the communication logically to deduce that the arbitration agreement corresponds to the actual wish of the person to whom it was addressed at the time when he accepted, in the specified form, the global reference.

When considered in the light of the principle of confidence as thus understood, the arbitration agreement at issue is binding on the plaintiff. Equally, it is established that the plaintiff already knew the arbitration clause inserted in the FEI regulations when he signed the model agreement, and he actually made use of it to have recourse to the CAS on the occasion of a previous dispute. Moreover, the clause in question was communicated to him verbatim on the occasion of his selection for the competition in San Marino, without his finding fault with it. In view of these circumstances, and interpreting objectively (or prescriptively) – in other words according to the principle of confidence – the intent that he expressed in this respect, one is forced to conclude that the plaintiff agreed to submit to the arbitration agreement, validly giving his consent in formal terms by signing the model agreement, and confirming it by his unreserved acceptance of the arbitration clause contained *expressis verbis* in the documents sent to him when he entered for the competition in San Marino. Against, this conclusion, it is futile for the plaintiff to cite the so-called rule of the unusual (cf. ATF 119 II 443 section la p. 446). This notion indeed presupposes that one is dealing with something unexpected, an element which the person to whom the manifestation of intent is addressed had not reckoned with (JÄGGI/GAUCH, Commentaire zurichois, n. 472 ad art. 18 CO; KRAMER, Commentaire bernois, n. 204 et seq. ad art. 1 CO). This could not be so when, as in this particular case, the plaintiff already knew, and had approved, the content of the contract to which the subsequent agreement referred. Consequently, the Cantonal Court did not violate federal law in arguing as to the formal validity of the arbitration agreement at issue.

4. From the material point of view, the plaintiff holds that the arbitration agreement violates art. 27 CC and provisions of the antitrust law.

a) (...)

b) In as much as they are admissible, the material grounds put forward by the plaintiff will be the subject only of a summary examination for the reasons indicated above (section 2). The fact that they are new certainly does not prevent the Federal Tribunal from taking them into account, as it applies the law at its own discretion. However, only the facts established by the final cantonal authority may be taken into consideration in the framework of this analysis, since the plaintiff claims neither that they should be added to, owing to an allegedly incorrect application of the law by the previous judges, nor that he invoked, in this respect, before the cantonal authorities and in accordance with the formal requirements, relevant facts which were not recorded in the order being challenged (art. 64 OJ).

It does not emerge from the unappealable findings of the cantonal judges that the plaintiff would not have obtained his licence, and hence would not have been able to take part in equestrian events such as the one in San Marino, if he had not accepted the arbitration agreement. On the basis of these findings alone, there is therefore no question of accepting the existence of an inadmissible restriction on the freedom of the plaintiff. There is consequently no need to decide whether an arbitration agreement can in itself constitute such a restriction and thus fall within the ambit of art. 27 CC, nor whether the undertaking entered into, allegedly against his will, by the plaintiff should not be challenged exclusively by an action to set aside for vitiated consent. Be that as it may, it is appropriate to observe that, according to the case law of the Federal Tribunal, the CAS, even as initially organized, already enjoyed, generally speaking, sufficient independence for its awards to be treated as judgments by state courts (ATF 119 II 271), and that it has since been restructured, taking into account the reservations on this subject expressed in the above-mentioned order, so as now to be formally separated from the IOC and placed under the aegis of the International Council of Arbitration for Sport (ICAS), a body constituted as an autonomous foundation; it is moreover divided into two Divisions and has 150 arbitrators working for it, while it previously had only 60 (see, on this subject, STEPHAN NETZLE, Der Sportler – Subjekt oder Objekt, in: RDS 115 II 1 et seq., 72 s.). In these conditions, it is in all cases out of the question to treat as an excessive obligation, within the meaning of art. 27 CC, adoption by reference of the arbitration clause contained in the defendant's regulations.

Nor do the findings of the cantonal court reveal the existence of an antitrust-type interference with the economic freedom of the plaintiff. The claim that the arbitration clause violates art. 18 para. 1 aLCart, which was still in force at the time when the order being challenged was pronounced, is thus also seen to be without merit. In any case, the provision quoted could not be cited in the present case given both that art. 18 para. 3 aLCart excludes the application, on certain conditions, of objections brought before an international arbitration court, whether it has its seat in Switzerland or abroad and whatever the nationality of the arbitrators called upon to sit within it (for the interpretation of this Provision, Cf. SCHÜRMANN/SCHLUEP, Karteilgesetz – Preisüberwachungsgesetz, n. V ad art. 18 aLCart; HOMBERGER, Kommentar zum Schweizerischen Karteligesetz, n. 15 ad art. 18 aLCart), and that internal antitrust sanctions were not specified by the procedural provisions of art. 18 para. 1 aLCart (SCHÜRMANN/SCHLUEP, op. cit., n. VII ad art. 18 aLCart). Consequently, there could be no question of accepting, at least on the basis of a summary examination, that the arbitration agreement at issue violates antitrust law.

5. For all these reasons, the formal and material objections raised by the plaintiff with regard to the order being challenged are ill-founded, in as much as they can be taken into consideration. This finding implies the rejection of the present appeal, insofar as it is admissible, and affirmation of the decision appealed against.

In any case, there is nothing to stop 'ad-hoc' mediations being arranged if the parties in dispute so desire.

As far as the handling and settlement of disputes (referred to as 'Protests') by the International Paralympic Committee (IPC) is concerned, there are fairly detailed rules and procedures laid down in the IPC Handbook.

Section II of Part I of the Handbook contains General Regulations on Protests about classification disputes. Whilst Protests concerning eligibility issues are dealt with in Section II of Part I of the IPC Handbook.

Section IV of Part II of the Handbook deals in individual Chapters with Protests in the various Sports within the Paralympic Summer Games Programme. On the other hand, Protests in those Sports comprising the Paralympic Winter Games Programme are likewise dealt with in individual Chapters but in Section V of Part III of the Handbook.

All the above Rules and Regulations of the IPC are set out for ease of reference in Appendix XVII.

General Advantages of Sports Mediation

Perhaps the main advantage of using mediation to settle sports disputes is that the process preserves and even restores personal and business relationships.[60] It is well known that the sports world is a small one – everyone seems to know somebody – and relationships – and, indeed, reputations – are, therefore, more important and worth preserving. As Bernard Foucher, President of the French Board of Mediators, has put it:

'Mediation allows legal disputes to be resolved within "the family of sport".'[61]

As the process is not adversarial, there is no winner and, therefore, no loser. Or, at the very most, the parties share the 'pain'. Mediation reopens lines of communication, which have often broken down, requiring the parties to co-operate with one another in finding a solution to their problems. Mediation provides the opportunity for co-operative problem solving.

Through careful probing by the mediator, the actual underlying reasons for the particular dispute can be identified and addressed. This goes a long way towards finding an appropriate solution to the parties' problems.

Dispute settlement through the courts or arbitration is backward looking, the decision or award being reached on the basis of past facts and historical background. Mediation, on the other hand, is forward looking, having regard to the future and future possibilities. Mediation is not seeking to apportion blame or fault, but to reach a solution.

Mediation is more flexible than traditional forms of litigation and even arbitration, which has become rather technical and specialised. There are no set rules of procedure to get in the way. The approach is informal and flexible.

Mediation is swift, and this is a particular advantage to sports persons, who often

---

[60] See I. Blackshaw, 'Resolving sports disputes the modern way – by mediation' (2000) 18(1) Sport and the Law Journal; I. Blackshaw, 'Sporting settlements' (2001) 145 (27) SJ; C. Newmark, 'Is mediation effective for resolving sports disputes?' (2000) 5/6 International Sports Law Journal 37; W. Slate, 'The Growth of mediation and mediation in Sports Disputes in the US' (2000) Paper presented at the CAS Symposium on Mediation in Lausanne, Switzerland, 4 November 2000.

[61] B. Foucher, 'La Conciliation Comme Mode de Reglement des Conflits Sportifs en Droit Francais' (2000) Paper presented at the CAS Symposium on Mediation in Lausanne, Switzerland, 4 November 2000.

have pressing event and other commitments and commercial deadlines.

This was one of the factors why a dispute in 1999 between Frank Warren, the well-known boxing promoter, and Richie Woodhall, the former WBO super middleweight world champion, was successfully resolved by mediation. The case also illustrates other reasons for opting to settle disputes by mediation.

Case Study: The Woodhall/Warren Case

In this case, in April 1999, Richie Woodhall sought to terminate his management and promotion agreements with Frank Warren, claiming that Warren was in breach of them and also that the agreements were unenforceable. Woodhall refused to fight for Warren, and also started approaches to other boxing promoters.

On the other hand, Warren refused to let Woodhall go, claiming that contracts were valid; that there was still some considerable time to run on them; and that he was not in breach of them. The parties were adamant in their respective positions.

Woodhall, therefore, started proceedings in the High Court in June 1999. He requested an early hearing of the case to enable him to fight the defence of his world title by September, as required by the rules of the World Boxing organisation. As the agreements required that any disputes were to be referred to the British Boxing Board of Control, Warren, for his part, sought an order from the Court to that effect.

This dispute had all the makings of a full-blown legal fight in the Courts with lots of blood on the walls – and in the full glare of the media. As such, it would not only be time consuming and expensive to both parties, but also potentially damaging for their reputations. In addition, Woodhall was anxious to get back in the ring and, if he were to continue to be of any value to Warren, he needed to fight his mandatory defence to his world title within a short period of time. So, in all these circumstances, the question arose as to whether the Court was the best forum in which to resolve this bitter dispute. It was decided to refer the dispute to mediation. And the Court was prepared to adjourn the proceedings, for a short time, to enable the parties to see if they could, in fact, settle their differences by this method.

A hastily arranged mediation was set up and conducted by CEDR. Within 72 hours later, the dispute was resolved, and Woodhall signed a new deal with Warren and continues to box for him. Unfortunately, as mediation is confidential and there is no official record or transcript of the process, it is not possible to have a 'blow by blow' account of what was said, what arguments were adduced and exactly why a settlement was reached (e.g. what leverage the mediator was able to apply to reach a compromise) and what precisely were its actual terms. One thing can, however, be deduced from the brief facts and circumstances of this dispute, there were some sporting and commercial deadlines to concentrate the minds of the parties and act as a spur to reaching a compromise. There was also a pressing need for the parties not to 'wash their dirty linen in public'!

Other Sports Mediation Cases

For many years now, many labour disputes have been settled by mediation through private and official bodies, such as ACAS (Arbitration and Conciliation Advisory Service). With more and more sports persons, especially footballers, being paid more and more for their services, more and more disputes are arising under their employment and service contracts. This is, therefore, a field in which many such disputes are capable of being successfully settled by mediation. This has certainly been the experience in the States where labour disputes in the sporting context are quite commonplace.

The Amateur Swimming Association (ASA) encourages 'informal mediation' in settling cases of alleged breaches of their Code of Ethics in 'suitable cases'. Also the ASA operates a 'Quick Justice' system (a kind of mediation) for charges of 'brutality' in water polo. Cases must be brought within 30 days.

A schedule of some other sports disputes mediated by CEDR in the last few years, giving brief details of the nature of the dispute, the parties and the amounts involved, as well as the outcomes, follows:

- Frank Warren boxing contract - £3000,000 – settled in 1 day.
- Golf club fees - £20,000 – settled in 1 day.
- Aircraft leasing in a parachute club - £340,000 – settled in 2 days.
- Rugby club contract and the Rugby Football League - £340,000 – settled in 1 day.
- Contract concerning a yachting club - £1.5m – settled in 1 day.
- Defamation case between an English Premier League football club and national broadsheet newspaper – settled in 1 day.
- Land dispute with Formula One company - £350,000 – settled in 1 day.
- Football club contract - £400,000 – settled in 1 day.
- Gliding club contract - £50,000 – settled in 1 day.
- Ground dispute between two rugby clubs - £500,000 – settled in 1 day.
- Shooting club and game (pheasant supplier) - £120,000 – settled in 1 day.

Of course, not all disputes submitted to mediation have successful outcomes, but the majority of them do.

Likewise, brief details of some sports disputes and their outcomes mediated by the ADR Group during the last couple of years:

- Personal injury claim against a sports body by a sportswoman injured in a track and field event, valued at around £150,000, was referred to mediation, but did not proceed due to the parties reaching a settlement after mediation had been proposed.
- Personal injury claim in excess of £200,000 brought by a female spectator at a sports event, who suffered severe back injury as a result of a seat collapsing, against a Trust responsible for the stadium was successfully settled within three weeks of being referred to mediation.

- Dispute, valued at around £80,000, between a sports clothing manufacturer and a high street sports retailer under a sale and distribution agreement was referred to mediation, but did not settle on the day, but within a month afterwards. The parties chose mediation because they wanted to preserve their existing business relationship. The mediation helped the parties to narrow the issues in dispute.
- Claim for £75,000 brought by a Premiership rugby football player against his club for breach of an employment contract was successfully mediated within one day.
- Claim of £450,000 for breach of an architectural/engineering/construction contract relating to the building of a football stadium was also successfully settled by mediation within one day.

So, mediation was a great success in the Woodhall/Warren case and the majority of the other CEDR and ADR Group mediated sports disputes mentioned above. Even in those cases where mediation did not immediately result in the settlement of the dispute concerned, the process of mediation helped to bring the parties closer together on the issues and paved the way to an ultimate amicable settlement. But, it must be said, mediation does have some intrinsic limitations.

What are they?

Sports Mediation Limitations

Mediation, as a method of settling sports disputes, is not a panacea. Although it works in most cases, it does not work in all cases.

Mediation is not suitable in those cases in which a legal precedent or an injunction is required – it is not, as previously noted, a legally based process.

Neither is mediation appropriate where a sports body needs to make a public example of another party to the dispute in order to act as a deterrent to others. This point is illustrated by the banning on 10 October 2000 by the English Football Association (FA) of the Arsenal manager, Arsene Wenger, from the touchline for four weeks for 'threatening behaviour and physical intimidation' of an official. He was also fined four weeks' wages amounting to £100,000! This sort of case raises a point of principle on which the FA is unlikely to compromise in a mediation, especially as the FA wishes to enforce its new hard-hitting disciplinary code of conduct designed to preserve the integrity of the game of football.

Being a voluntary and non-binding process until a settlement is agreed, written down and signed by the parties, it is not suitable either in those cases where the parties are not interested in trying to find a settlement by mediation or extra-judicial means. For example, the Rugby Football Union (RFU) is attempting to resolve a major dispute between the two top divisions in English Rugby Union involving 26 professional clubs and has suggested mediation. The chairman of the RFU considers that appointing an independent third party with specialist skills in resolving difficult disputes is the right way forward, whilst the head of English First Division Rugby is reported in The Guardian on 20 October, 2000 as saying:

'It wouldn't make any difference if they brought the Queen in to arbitrate'.

The RFU may consider that mediation is a good idea, but if the teams in dispute do not, mediation will not work in such a case.

Again, if the full glare of publicity is important, mediation is not the kind of dispute resolution method to adopt. It is an entirely confidential process.

Neither is mediation suitable for resolving doping and other disciplinary cases. Indeed, as has previously been noted, the mediation procedure of the CAS is expressly excluded for dealing with such cases, and this is also the considered opinion of David Richbell, Training Director of CEDR. Mediation may, however, be useful for dealing with the commercial fall out from such cases – for example, claims for financial compensation for losses suffered as a result of a wrongful 'conviction'.

The well-known Dianne Modahl doping case would be a good example for mediation in relation to the financial claims and losses the athlete sought to recover through the Courts, as a result of having been exonerated from taking a banned performance enhancing substance, from her World Governing Body, the International Amateur Athletic Federation, that wrongly imposed the suspension from competition in the first place. Her claim for compensation of £1 million against the British Athletic Federation for an unlawful doping ban imposed on her eventually ended in failure in the English Court of Appeal on 12 October 2001.[62]

As Kenneth Kressel has pointed out in 'The Handbook of Conflict Resolution: Theory and Practice'[63]:

'While mediation is generally useful in many types of conflicts, it is certainly no magic bullet. Even if mediation does not succeed in producing an agreement, parties still benefit when the process helps clarify issues, or "humanize" the disputants, or help reach a partial agreement. The following factors are key obstacles to a successful mediation:

– High levels of Conflict. The measures of conflict intensity that correlate negatively with settlement include the severity of prior conflict between the parties; a perception that the other is untrustworthy, unreasonable, angry, or impossible to communicate with; and the existence of strong ideological or cultural differences.
– Low Motivation to Reach Agreement.
– Low Commitment to Mediation.
– Shortage of Resources. Resource scarcity presumably limits the range of mutually

---

[62] *Modahl v. British Athletic Federation* [2001] All ER (D) 181 (Oct). See also I. Blackshaw, 'Modahl Loses Appeal For Compensation' in the November/December, 2001 issue of the Sports Law Bulletin, vol. 4 no. 6 at pp. 1, 3 & 4.

[63] Edited by Morton Deutsch and Peter T. Coleman, 2000, San Francisco: Jossey-Bass (www.josseybass.com).

acceptable solutions and may reduce the motivation of both the parties and the
mediator.
– Disputes Involving Fundamental Principles.
– Parties of Unequal Power'.

Criteria for Mediating

In deciding, however, whether mediation is suitable or not, it is often said by
protagonists of mediation, including David Richbell, Former Training Director of
CEDR, that the question to be asked is not 'is mediation appropriate?' but rather
'why is mediation not appropriate?' Each case should be considered on its own
particular merits.

However, in an insightful and practical article, entitled 'Ready ... Set ...
Mediate'.[64] Peter J. Comodeca, a Partner at Calfee, Halter & Griswold, Cleveland,
Ohio, USA and a member of the American Arbitration Association Panel of
Neutrals, identifies a number of key factors that disputants and their counsel must
consider before pursuing mediation. The text of his article is as follows:

Peter J. Comodeca[65]
Ready ... Set ... Mediate

While it's no secret that more and more people are discovering the benefits of
mediation, it is not always clear why some parties are more successful at it than
others. This article by Peter Comodeca identifies a number of key factors that
disputants and their counsel must consider before pursuing mediation.

Regardless of one's position on mediation, it has become an integral part of the
legal process in the United States. Given the crowded dockets most courts must
contend with, the use of alternative dispute resolution methods, such as
mediation, is only likely to increase in the future.
It is imperative that lawyers and clients be familiar with the fundamental aspects
of mediation. They must be able to recognize when it may be in their best interest
to mediate, or how to proceed when required to mediate by court order. Proper
knowledge of mediation techniques can help an attorney avoid unnecessary
surprises in the process.

---

[64] Dispute Resolution Journal, Nov. 2001/Jan. 2002, at pp. 32 – 38.

[65] The author is a partner at Calfee, Halter & Griswold in Cleveland, Ohio. He serves on the AAA's
roster of neutrals; his arbitration and mediation experience is primarily in the construction, commercial
and international arenas. He is a member of several professional associations including the American
Bar Association (Public Contract Law Section) and the International Bar Association.

This article will help attorneys identify issues to consider before agreeing to mediation.

Parties involved in a dispute participate in mediation either voluntarily or involuntarily. Often, parties recognize the benefits of mediation and choose to mediate voluntarily. The most common method used to commence mediation is by entering into a contract or agreement identifying mediation as a dispute resolution mechanism.

In the absence of a contract requirement, the parties may agree, after a dispute arises, to pursue mediation to resolve the dispute. However, mediation is not always chosen by the parties. It can be imposed involuntarily. Generally, this occurs pursuant to a court order or directive.

Involuntary mediation also occurs when the parties are subject to a governing policy or regulation requiring mediation of which they were unaware. For example, some standing court procedural rules require mediation as a preliminary step to either arbitration or litigation.

Appropriate Mediation Clause

Parties to a contract often choose to include a mediation clause applicable to any dispute that arises under the contract. Contractual mediation clauses are generally connected with other dispute resolution procedures. Often, mediation is required as a precursor to arbitration or litigation. Also, mediation is commonly used in conjunction with nonbinding negotiations between the parties. Thus, many different issues must be considered in drafting the appropriate mediation clause for each individual contract.

First, a determination must be made whether the mediation should be binding or nonbinding. If the clause mandates binding mediation, a provision should be included in the contract permitting an entry of judgment by either party to enforce the mediation result. If the clause mandates nonbinding mediation, the clause should be clear as to whether or not mediation is required prior to the pursuit of arbitration or litigation.

Next, the parties must consider the scope of claims to be governed by the mediation. Mediation may not be appropriate for all claims that may arise related to the agreement. Thus, for various issues under the contract, the parties may wish to narrow the application of the mediation clause.

The clause may also limit mediation to certain categories of claims such as international, intellectual property, labor, or valuation issues. Additionally, mediation does not have to address the entire dispute. For example, mediation can be used as a method to resolve disputes and minimize costs of parallel proceedings by achieving agreements on discovery, stipulations, or protective orders.

The parties must also decide what types of damage claims may be considered by the mediator. Regardless, when attempting to limit the scope of the mediation clause the parties must clearly delineate the claims to which the mediation clause is applicable in order to avoid unnecessary confusion should a dispute arise.

Another issue to be considered by the parties is whether or not to extend the mediation clause to include disputes involving third parties. If the parties to a contract desire to include third parties in any mediation, it may be necessary to modify third-party contracts to require the third parties to participate in any mediation pursued by the parties to the core agreement.

An example of such a scenario would be a construction dispute between the project owner and the general contractor. A mediation clause could be drafted to require subcontractors to participate to the extent relevant to the dispute. The general contractor would then include this requirement in the subcontracts.

The parties must choose the manner in which the mediator will be selected. Mediation is often described as a process where the mediator functions as a neutral facilitator. To ensure fairness and neutrality, the mediation clause should include provisions describing how the mediator will be chosen.

The clause should provide, or refer to existing rules that provide, that the mediator shall be neutral and shall fully disclose any and all relationships he or she may have to the parties and/or to counsel involved in the mediation.

In some instances, it may be prudent to specifically identify in advance an agreed upon mediator by name. This could be done in the contract or by separate agreement referring to the contract.

Discovery in the United States under any alternative method of dispute resolution is generally less extensive than with litigation. However, some form of discovery, though limited, may be necessary to make a mediation effective. Thus, the mediation clause may also address what, if any, discovery will be required prior to conducting the actual mediation.

Generally, mediation clauses are silent on the scope of discovery. However, there are many situations where a requirement for the exchange of all related and relevant documents may be beneficial. This can be especially important in mediations involving international parties. For example, one party's legal system may provide for a full exchange of documents while the other party's legal system may not have a similar provision. In such situations, directly addressing discovery in the contract may help prevent ambiguity should a dispute arise, fostering a better climate for mediation.

There are many general issues to be considered in drafting a mediation clause. The parties may want to select which jurisdiction's law will govern the mediation. Additionally, the parties should select a mutually acceptable location for the mediation to take place. In an attempt to prevent unnecessary delay, the parties should also set forth a specific time frame for the mediation to commence and conclude relative to the acknowledgment of the dispute.

Mediation is generally a confidential process. However, to further protect against disclosure of statements or positions discussed during the mediation, the parties may wish to contractually define information exchanged and discussed during mediation as confidential. Such information would include presentations, statements, and positions advocated. Therefore, such information could not be used in any subsequent proceedings other than an action for breach of the mediation agreement.

For example, the parties could include a clause stating, 'The mediation process is confidential. Neither a party nor the mediator may disclose the existence, contents, or results of any mediation unless the parties agree in writing to such disclosure or unless such disclosure is required by law.'

When drafting a mediation clause, consideration should be given to the rules that will govern the mediation process. Many alternative dispute resolution organizations have developed their own rules governing mediation, such as the American Arbitration Association (AAA), the Center for Public Resources (CPR), and the International Chamber of Commerce (ICC). Choosing one of these organizations to conduct the mediation will save the parties from having to draft their own rules, while at the same time helping to ensure fairness and neutrality. Selecting the organization that will better suit the needs of the parties will depend upon the specific interests of the parties to the agreement.

Finding a Mediator

Generally, the agreement will establish a mechanism for selection of the mediator. If the parties have selected an alternative dispute resolution organization to conduct the mediation, such as the AAA, the CPR, or the ICC, then the clause may permit the selected organization to provide the parties with a roster of potential mediators. As mentioned above, the parties can also identify a particular mediator by name in the mediation clause.

If the mediation agreement remains silent as to the method of selecting a mediator, there are several ways that the mediator may be selected after a dispute arises. The parties may negotiate to select a mediator on their own. The parties may also agree to submit a request to an alternative dispute resolution organization for a proposed roster of mediators from which a selection will be made. From this list, the parties can negotiate a selection, or the selected organization may be asked to appoint a mediator.

The parties may also ask the ADR organization to provide a shortened roster of proposed mediators. Once this list is provided, the parties can rank the potential mediators in order from most desirable to least desirable. The intersection of the parties' respective rankings becomes the selected mediator. Or, the parties may choose, to strike names from the list in turn until only one mediator remains.

Often, if mediation is unsuccessful, the parties will proceed to arbitration. Thus, the parties must evaluate, should mediation fail, whether or not the chosen mediator can also later serve as the arbitrator. As a general rule, this is not advisable because of the structure and process of mediation, which necessitates frank and candid discussions between the parties. If the parties know that the same mediator will be used for any subsequent arbitration, it may have a chilling effect on the discussions between the parties during the mediation process.

The process of selecting a mediator is much more efficient if biographies are available to the parties for the potential mediators. Ideally, conflict disclosures by the potential mediators should be made prior to selection. Regardless, upon appointment of the mediator the parties should require him or her to fully disclose any potential conflicts which might affect his or her services as the mediator.

Factors to Consider in Mediator Selection

There are many factors to consider when selecting a mediator. Generally, a mediator must be skilled in dealing with people as well as the processes of mediation. It is also beneficial if a mediator has subject matter expertise regarding the issues involved in the dispute.

The ability to relate well with others is paramount to being a good mediator. Such abilities should be evaluated in light of the personalities of the parties, the requirement for overall fairness and integrity of the mediator, and the coercive factors that may be necessary to effectuate a successful mediation.

Needless to say, the mediator should be familiar with the process of mediation. The mediator must be able to facilitate sessions with the parties jointly, as well as private caucus sessions. A good mediator will be able to encourage innovative thought and compromise. Process skills must also include an overriding sense of fairness to each side with regard to their abilities to present argument and speak on the relevant issues.

While many people involved with mediation feel that subject matter expertise is an essential criteria for mediator selection, others argue that it is not. The need for subject matter expertise generally depends upon the theories argued in each individual case.

If the nature of the dispute hinges on the comprehension of a specific industry, subject matter expertise in that industry may be relevant to facilitating a successful mediation. If the dispute focuses on legal arguments, a mediator with expertise in the governing law would be more desirable. Since the parties will often argue different theories in a single case, they will frequently have a different conception of what qualities comprise the 'ideal' mediator.

Additionally, the nature of a dispute can be very different depending on whether the dispute is of a business nature or has emotional aspects. Thus, the parties would want to be careful to choose a mediator who is skilled at dealing with the specific type of dispute at issue.

Mediation has both an evaluative and facilitative function. The mediator must attempt to evaluate the dispute, and determine what a proper range of resolution might be. The mediator must also act as a facilitator, to guide the parties toward resolution.

These two criteria may be in conflict during the mediation. For example, there are times when a rational evaluation of the dispute results in favoring one party over the other. This may conflict with the facilitative role of the mediator. If this occurs, it should be handled tactfully by the mediator, avoiding the appearance of favoritism.

The style of mediation that the parties desire may also affect mediator selection. If the parties wish to have the mediator shuttle between them, they will want to choose a mediator that will be able to do this effectively. If the dispute requires a more forceful presence, that will also factor into the mediation selection process. Thus, the parties must consider whether they want a mediator that will aggressively push them towards compromise or one that will take a more relaxed approach.

Pre-Mediation Consideration

A mediator comes to the dispute with, at best, two-dimensional knowledge. While the mediator may have some level of subject matter expertise relating to the dispute, the mediator is unaware of the history and evolution of the dispute and the emotional implications that it may have on the parties.

Party advocates assume a different role in mediation than the roles adopted in other forums. The style of advocacy expected in arbitration or litigation is out of place in mediation.

In mediation, party advocates must take care to maintain credibility with the mediator at all times during the process. Advocates should view their roles as being partners to the process. They can enhance the process of mediation by presenting their client's case in a straightforward manner.

More importantly, party advocates can assist by presenting information to the mediator that may be helpful in persuading the opponent to believe that settlement will be more beneficial than proceeding to arbitration or litigation.

Party advocates should attempt to present the mediator with pre-mediation written submissions. The submissions should clearly include a statement of the facts of the case, as well as an argument that is based on those facts and supported by the governing law. At the very least, key documents as well as the text of relevant cases or statutes should be provided to the mediator prior to the mediation session.

Pre-mediation submissions are an important tool both for assisting the mediator in grasping the subtleties of the dispute at hand and for educating the opposing party. A compromise cannot be expected unless each party has a full understanding of the opposing arguments. The opportunity to evaluate and test the merit of the opposition's arguments is an essential facet of the mediation process.

Successful mediation requires the presence of a client representative with full settlement authority. This provides the best opportunity to take advantage of the dynamics, of mediation. It can be quite costly if an agreement is reached through mediation but is later vetoed by someone at a higher level who did not participate in the mediation.

Additionally, to ensure a knowledgeable response to the ebb and flow of mediation, the client should consider and prepare possible concessions in position as well as potential fallback positions prior to the mediation. Advance preparation for position movement allows for less stress and better understanding of the opposition's concerns during the mediation.

Basic Misconceptions

Mediation is not simply an opening statement followed by negotiation. Mediation is fundamentally different from arbitration/litigation. In mediation, the parties reach an agreement facilitated by the mediator. Conversely, in arbitration/litigation, the arbitrator, judge, or jury reaches the decision and imposes it upon the parries. Thus, the opening statement in mediation is not principally directed toward the mediator, hut rather to the opposing party.

Mediation is not the same as negotiation. Generally, mediation is commenced after an unsuccessful negotiation. Additionally, the distinction between mediation and negotiation is highlighted by the role of the mediator. The mediator's ultimate goal is to facilitate an agreement between the parties.

Preliminary steps towards reaching such an agreement involve minimizing the advocacy and posturing between the parties and focusing on the facts and law which are related to the dispute. In negotiation, party advocacy and posturing remain largely untempered, and may operate to aggravate the dispute.

Mediation is focused on achieving a settlement. In any dispute, an assessment of the risks and costs involved determine whether or not a party will settle. In mediation, an important goal is to encourage that such an assessment be done objectively. While counsel may initially advocate their client's position during a mediation, one goal of the mediator is to convert such advocacy to more objective counseling and advice to the client. Many party advocates hesitate to make this transition during mediation for fear of appearing to lack the appearance of zealously representing their client.

Mediation is not always the answer. In some cases, a party may steadfastly refuse to consider any position reflected in opposing arguments. Mediation is probably not appropriate in such scenarios. Also, because the results of mediation do not add to the common law, mediation is not appropriate if a party seeks to create legal precedent that will govern prospective or parallel disputes.

Conclusion

Mediation can be an effective tool for ensuring efficient, fair dispute resolution. Correctly drafted, a contractual mediation clause can help to protect the rights of the parties involved in the dispute by fully defining the scope of the process.

In order for mediation to be successful, however, the parties must be aware of the various concerns that need to be addressed prior to beginning the process. With careful consideration, the final result – a mutual agreement – will be acceptable, and even welcome, to all parties involved.

CHAPTER XI
SPORTS MEDIATION IN THE PEOPLE'S REPUBLIC OF CHINA

Background to the New Chinese Sports Law

Beijing put in a strong bid in Monaco in 1993 to host the Millennium Olympic Games of 2000, but was narrowly beaten by Sydney by two votes (45-43). The deciding factor seems to have been human rights and, in particular, the massacre in Tiananmen Square of June 1989. However, in Moscow on 16 July 2001, the IOC accepted Beijing's bid – widely regarded objectively as being the best of the bids – to host the Summer Games of 2008, but not without controversy and active opposition from human rights' campaigners.

China's profound disappointment in being rejected by the IOC in 1993 accelerated the completion of a new comprehensive Chinese Sports Law, which was published on 29 August 1995 and took effect on 1 October 1995.

An English translation of this important Law will be found in Appendix XVIII.

In an article entitled, 'China's Sports Law',[66] Professor James Nafziger of Willamette University, USA and Li Wei, a former Assistant Professor of Law at Shanghai University, China, critically review – in some depth – this new Law, which they say 'reflects the complexity of a legal system in transition, giving new meaning to the concept of Market-Leninism'.

They add:

> 'On the one hand, the legislation confirms state control over sports by relying heavily on standard political ideology, centralized policy-making, and traditional administrative practice to help the national government achieve several major objectives. These objectives include gaining greater international prestige from the success of Chinese athletes; creating a structure of dynamic sports organizations; providing reliable sources of funding for sports; and deterring the use of banned drugs in sports activities, bribery of athletes and sports officials, and gambling on sports events. On the other hand, the Sports Law shifts much of the day-to-day control over sports to non-governmental initiatives. In particular, it has formalized the establishment of market-oriented, western-style sports associations to carry out national sports policy, develop new sources of funding, and impose sanctions against athletes for non-criminal violation of anti-doping and other organizational rules'.

---

[66] The American Journal of Comparative Law Summer 1998, vol. XLVI no. 3 at pp. 453-483.

En passant, it may be noted that the new Chinese Sports Law legalises the commercialisation of and investment in sports, including sports sponsorship (see articles 3 & 42), which has become a popular marketing tool not only for major Chinese companies but also foreign ones doing business in or with China. Also, a National Sports Lottery to raise funds for sports has also been established pursuant to the provisions of the new Sports Law.

New Chinese Sports Mediation and Arbitration Body

The new Sports Law also provides for the establishment of a special body to mediate and arbitrate disputes arising in competitive sports. This, as the authors point out, is very much in line with the Chinese normal preference for mediation and arbitration over adjudication. This new body shares authority over dispute resolution with the non-governmental sports associations. And this very much reflects the growing trend internationally of settling sports disputes by a combination of administrative review by sports bodies and specialised arbitration and mediation.

Article 33 of the Chinese Sports Law provides that:

'Any disputes arising in competitive sports shall be subject to mediation and arbitration by a sports arbitration body.

Rules governing the establishment of a sports arbitration body and the scope of its mandate shall be adopted by the State Council'.

This extra-judicial form of dispute resolution reflects traditional Chinese mechanisms of dispute resolution but, as James Nafziger and Li Wei also point out, it is also progressive 'in its reliance on a specialized process in which nongovernmental sports ... will play a decisive role ... [and] ... in line with official endorsement of nongovernmental (private) tribunals to arbitrate disputes'.

However, they also draw attention to a possible conflict of interest problem, namely: 'if dispute resolution is largely left up to the sports associations or bodies closely related to them, the body that applies sanctions might be the same as, or closely associated with, a party to a dispute'. In other words, one of the fundamental principles of 'natural justice', namely 'no person may be a judge in their own cause' ('ncmo judex in causa sua potest') – the so-called 'rule against bias' – may be breached.

Evaluation of Article 33 of the New Chinese Sports Law

Evaluating article 33 of the new Chinese Sports Law, James Nafziger and Li Wei have this to say:

'it is noteworthy ... that the Sports Law rejects any recognition of the adjudicable rights of athletes, although it does entitle them to financial, educational and other privileges. In lieu of litigation, article 33 ... prescribes mediation and arbitration. ... In this respect, China, doing what comes naturally, is in the vanguard of a global trend toward shunning the courtroom to resolve disputes involving athletes and sports activity. Taking an approach that is traditional for it but progressive for the global system, China may better avoid the risks and complexity of dispute avoidance and resolution that so beset the sports arena in other countries'.

And go on to conclude as follows:

'On the other hand, China's refusal to adjudicate any rights of individual athletes denies them an appropriate remedy for the most serious breaches of fairness and justice that more informal methods of dispute resolution do not always rectify. The Sports Law has accorded individual athletes many privileges and a measure of autonomy from the bureaucracy as members of the newly empowered sports associations, but their standing to vindicate fundamental rights remains doubtful. The legislation is thus a product of China's policy of Market-Leninism'.

It will be interesting to see how this new Chinese Sports Law develops and is applied in practice, particularly its dispute resolution provisions, in the run up to the 2008 Summer Olympic Games in Beijing. The eyes of the world in general and sport in particular will be keeping a close watch on the Chinese!

CHAPTER XII
SPORTS OMBUDSMAN

For the sake of completeness, a word or two about a novel idea for settling sports disputes extra-judicially à la mediation: a Sports Ombudsman.

Background

This has been put forward by Philip Morris of the University of Stirling, who is an Associate Member of the British and Irish Ombudsman Association. He suggests that sports lawyers should think seriously about using the Ombudsman technique as a form of dispute resolution mechanism.

He points out:

'No longer confined to the province of government, Ombudsmen are now well entrenched in the professions and in the financial services sector in the UK and abroad. Indeed, this year has witnessed the creation of a "super" Financial Services Ombudsman scheme for the UK'.

And he goes on to say:

'In principle, there is no reason why, albeit on a self-regulatory and much smaller scale, this model could not be replicated by major UK sports governing bodies'.

Advantages

Whilst recognising that the arbitration and mediation services offered by the SDRP and CAS may make a Sports Ombudsman redundant, he mentions a number of advantages that an Ombudsman could offer in the sporting context. Amongst them are the following:

– An Ombudsman can draw on his/her own notions of fairness and good administration thus enhancing the protection of athletes.

– An Ombudsman in performing his/her conciliation functions can not only provide redress, but also use a complaint for improving practices within the sports 'industry' [the so-called 'quality control' dimension].

– An Ombudsman acts totally independently of any sports bodies or interests.

The author of this book, having had a good and wide professional experience of the work of Ombudsmen in the Scandinavian countries in settling consumer disputes in relation to advertising and marketing complaints, considers that the idea of a Sports Ombudsman is generally worth pursuing.

This is especially so if, as Philip Morris also suggests, Ombudsman schemes are established in other sporting nations as part of what he calls 'an international extra-judicial resolution structure'. He goes on to propose that such schemes incorporate a final right of appeal to the CAS where the dispute 'involves important or novel issues of sports law or policy'. Such arrangements, he concludes, could 'extend and strengthen [the] role [of CAS] as a pivotal institution in the development of a coherent and sophisticated corpus of sports law jurisprudence'.

Certainly, as sport has become transnational, there is a need for a coherent international sports disputes structure, which relies on effective alternative forms of dispute resolution whenever and wherever appropriate.

The Role of the Sports Ombudsman

Because of its novelty and interest, we reproduce the complete text, from which the above extracts are taken, of a recent article written by Morris and entitled, '*The Role of the Ombudsman in Sporting Disputes: Some Personal Thoughts*'[67] in which he expounds his ideas for a Sports Ombudsman:

> The apparently relentless juridification of much professional sport both in the United Kingdom and abroad, which is an inevitable consequence of the massive commercial interests in the structures, processes and outcomes of modern sport, has prompted debate about the appropriate mechanisms for dispute resolution. The initial enthusiasm which accompanied increasing judicial intervention in sports administration has begun to wane, largely because of an increasing realisation that high profile, bitterly fought court battles between athletes and governing bodies do not necessarily serve the long term interests of sports governing bodies, athletes or indeed the sport itself. While academic and practising lawyers may view long running legal conflicts involving the likes of Jean-Marc Bosman, Butch Reynolds, Tonya Harding and Diane Modahl as providing fertile ground for research projects and fee income, these disputes leave significant problems in their wake.
>
> While I can accept that some sporting disputes may make a significant and lasting contribution to the development of national and international sports law jurisprudence as well as leading to structural changes in a particular sport for the

[67] P. Morris, 'The Role of the Ombudsman in Sporting Disputes: Some personal Thoughts', (2000) Sports Law Bulletin, Vol. 3 No. 4, July/August 2000.

enduring benefit of athletes (Bosman is perhaps the outstanding example of this) I would, on an objective cost-benefit analysis, express serious concerns about the utility of court involvement in most sporting disputes. The costs, antagonism, bad publicity and (all too frequently) ineffectual remedies awarded all make a compelling case for confining court intervention to disputes raising novel or crucial issues of sporting or legal policy where a clear, binding precedent is of overriding importance. To argue in favour of a shift toward a greater measure of self-regulation is of course not new. What is now urgently needed though is a balanced assessment of the various modes of alternative dispute resolution potentially on offer, the interaction between them and whether it might be possible to design an integrated national and international sports dispute resolution structure.

Completion of this project requires sports lawyers to think seriously about the utility of the Ombudsman technique as a mechanism of redress. No longer confined to the province of government, Ombudsmen are now well entrenched both in the professions and in the financial services sector both in the United Kingdom and abroad. Indeed this year has witnessed the creation of a 'super' Financial Services Ombudsman scheme for the United Kingdom. The scheme is the largest Ombudsman institution in the world with 330 employees and an annual operating budget expected to exceed £20million. In principle there is no reason why, albeit on a self-regulatory and much smaller basis, this model could not be replicated by major United Kingdom sports governing bodies. The obvious objection is that there is no room or need for the Ombudsman technique given the existence of distinct arbitration schemes operated by some governing bodies, the recent launch of the United Kingdom Sports Dispute Resolution Panel and, on the international plane, the increasingly important contribution of the Court of Arbitration for Sport.

Without wishing to understate the work of these bodies there are key advantages, I believe, offered by the Ombudsman model in the sporting context:

An Ombudsman, unlike arbitration techniques, is not confined to strict legal standards but can draw upon his/her own subjective notions of fairness and good administration which together furnish athletes with enhanced protection.

In performance of his/her adjudication and conciliation functions an Ombudsman does not characteristically focus on redress of individual grievance but may also use a complaint as a vehicle for improving administrative practices within the industry (the so-called 'quality control' dimension of an Ombudsman's work).

Arbitration mechanisms continue to suffer from the lingering suspicion by athletes (even one as prestigious and well established as the Court of Arbitration for Sport) that they are not truly independent of governing bodies whereas Ombudsmen schemes can be designed, as the United Kingdom financial services industry experience shows, in such a way as to allay any such fears.

Unlike arbitration, with its reliance on formal, court like hearings, Ombudsmen tend to prefer the use of inquisitorial, paper-based investigations which are user-friendly and more conducive to continuing harmonious relations between the athlete and the governing body.

Where a dispute raises legal or policy issues more appropriately determined by a court it is possible, by use a 'test cases' clause in the Ombudsman's terms of reference, to provide for the timely transfer of the dispute to a court provided the complainant consents and with the sports governing body meeting the erstwhile complainant's legal costs.

If one accepts the case for United Kingdom Sports Ombudsman the next issue is to delineate its main features. It could, I think, be created on a self-regulatory basis using the same 'blue print' as existing private sector schemes, that is to say membership of a private company, an independent Ombudsman Council to perform a 'buffer' function between the sponsoring governing bodies and the Ombudsman and a separate Board, composed of a majority of sports' governing bodies representatives, raising the finance for the scheme which would take the form of a fixed levy and a case fee for every formal complaint lodged with the Ombudsman.

Given the self regulatory character of the scheme, achieving comprehensive membership by United Kingdom governing bodies would rest, ultimately, on persuading them of the benefits of membership in terms of cheapness, speed, informality and privacy compared with litigation and traditional arbitration. To avoid charges of ousting the athlete's 'constitutional' right of access to court for a determination as to his/her legal rights, use of the Ombudsman should be voluntary with a right to reject the Ombudsman's eventual recommendation and pursue the matter in court. I very much doubt whether many would opt to do so given that the Ombudsman unlike a court enjoys the capacity to transcend the parameters of legality by applying any relevant code of practice and his own subjective standards of fairness and good administrative practices.

Finally, if Ombudsman schemes along similar lines were established in other sporting nations an embryonic international extra-judicial dispute resolution structure could emerge by incorporating a final right of appeal for either party to the Court of Arbitration for Sport on the ground that the dispute involves important or novel issues of sports law or policy. The proliferation of national Sporting Ombudsmen and their integration with the Court in this manner could extend and strengthen its role as a pivotal institution in the development of a coherent and sophisticated corpus of sports law jurisprudence.

The Athletes Ombudsman

It should be added that the idea of a Sports Ombudsman as proposed by Morris is not entirely new. Under amendments passed in 1998 to the US Amateur Sports Act, an Ombudsman for Athletes has been established under the auspices of the United States Olympic Committee.

The Athletes Ombudsman has the two following functions:

'(A) to provide independent advice to athletes at no cost about the applicable provisions of [the Amateur Sports Act] ... and the constitution and bylaws of the corporation, national governing bodies, a paralympic sports organisations [sic], international sports federations, the International Olympic Committee, the International Paralympic Committee, and the Pan-American Sports Organization, and with respect to the resolution of any dispute involving the opportunity of an amateur athlete to participate in the Olympic Games, the Paralympic Games, the Pan-American Games, world championship competition as defined in the constitution and bylaws of the corporation; and (B) to assist in mediating any such disputes.'

CHAPTER XIII
EVALUATION OF SPORTS MEDIATION

Although it has certain limitations, mediation is generally proving itself to be a modern effective alternative method of resolving disputes in general. As the Woodhall/Warren and other sports cases show (e.g., the dispute between Ellery Hanley, the Rugby League coach, and his club's directors over some unflattering remarks he made publicly about them in 2000), mediation can be a most suitable way of settling sports disputes quickly, effectively and relatively cheaply.

The success of mediation in the Woodhall/Warren case[68] is a clear sign that resort to the Courts is no longer the only and perhaps not the best way of resolving disputes. And it also shows that opting for mediation should no longer be regarded as a sign of weakness on the part of any of the parties. As Frank Warren remarked:

'It was important to all concerned to have brought this matter to a speedy conclusion. We have shaken hands and look forward to resuming our successful partnership'.

For Richie Woodhall, speed was also 'of the essence':

'I am pleased this episode has now come to an end. I can tell my fans that I will be back in the ring within the next few weeks'.

Mediation generally offers so many advantages over traditional dispute resolution methods. In the sports field, in particular, the attraction of mediation has been well summarised by Frank Warren's Lawyer, Dominic Bray, in the following terms:

'Mediation can have real benefits, not only in terms of savings of management time and money, but also, and perhaps more significantly, in the preservation of ongoing relationships between the parties. These relationships are fundamental to any business, but particularly so in the sporting context.'

Not only must the case be suitable for mediation, but the success of the mediation will also, to a large extent, depend upon the qualities and skills of the mediator. On this point, Richie Woodhall's Lawyer, Richard Cramer, remarked:

'The mediator proved to be a very positive feature and focused the parties' minds on settlement.'

---

[68] See CEDR Press Release of 21 July 1999.

He or she needs to have knowledge and understanding of sport as well as being a good mediator.

As Robert Barker, a former Senior International In-house Counsel of The Coca-Cola Company, one of the world's major sponsors of major international sports events, including the Summer and Winter Olympic Games, but now a partner in the Atlanta Office of the US Law Firm of Smith Helms Mulliss & Moore, has remarked in relation to the handling of sports disputes:[69]

> 'If mediation ... [is] required ... traditional mediators ... may not serve you well ... [t]hey are not skilled in the industry of sports ...'

These remarks are made in an interesting article written for the Center for Public Resources ('CPR') entitled, 'Resolving Sports Conflicts Centers On Rights' Analysis', in which Barker is in no doubt that:

> '... sport is a unique industry ... [and] ... produces a product – a sporting event – that excites emotion in the industry's consumers. Emotion is a contributing factor to its uniqueness.'

In view of sport's uniqueness, he points out that, if, for instance, an intellectual property issue arises in connection with a sports dispute:

> '... traditional mediators ... are not skilled in the finer issues of intellectual property ... [which] ... is its own law merchant, and it probably does little good to have a [mediator] who will not recognise an IP right just because it might not be recognised at law ... Like our judicial system today, traditional neutrals [i.e., mediators] tend to want to render equitable rulings, rather than enforcing the rights in a contract – particularly if those rights are hard fought and harsh.'

And on the subject of using ADR generally in sports matters, he adds rather perceptively:

> 'There is a need for a global solution to sport problems, not just solutions based on a case-by-case negotiation. If you are acting in a particular sector or sub-industry, encourage those in the industry to create a standard for mediation ... Some sports lawyers are lucky enough today to be defining the rules for new leagues and sports for tomorrow. They should consider writing ADR into the governing documents of their leagues – and make it condition for all contracts with outsider parties'.

It is in the light of remarks such as these that suitably qualified mediators need to be chosen if the mediation is to be a successful one.

---

[69] 'Alternatives' Center for Public Resources/CPR Legal, May 2000.

Reference was made earlier to the gender of the mediator and, according to the nature and circumstances of the particular dispute, this may also be a relevant consideration in choosing a suitable mediator to act in an individual case. Of course, much continues to depend on the skills and experience of the mediator generally and, in particular, his or her knowledge and understanding of the sports industry. In this connection, there are a number of women involved in the administration of sport and the practice of sports law internationally. In the author's experience, women generally do tend to have more patience and a better understanding of and insight into human nature than men! On the other hand, women also have a tendency to be swayed by emotion – to decide more according to their hearts than their heads! It is interesting to note that the SDRP Panel of Mediators, out of a total of 36 people, contains only two women – one in the section of Mediators and the other in the section on Associate Mediators (whatever they might be!). Beyond these brief remarks on the subject of women mediators, it is not prudent to venture any further into such a controversial minefield!

According to Maitre Paul Dahan, a leading French Sports Lawyer, based in Cannes, mediation is usually attempted in disputes between leading footballers (e.g., d'Anelka, Ginola and Vieira) and French and European Football Clubs, through the competent National Federations and/or FIFA, before invoking EU Law. In France, there is a special Law of 13 July 1992 relating to the Settlement of Sports Disputes by Arbitration and Mediation. This Law has been strengthened by another Law of 6 July 2000.

In Germany, according to Dr. Markus Buchberger, a Sports Lawyer from Dortmund, who specialises in sports litigation, most of the German Sports Bodies, including the German Football Association, now include mediation in their Statutes as a dispute resolution procedure, although, to date, mediation has not been widely used in sports cases. However, he expects the practice to grow in the future.

Surprisingly, in the States – the home of ADR – mediation in sports disputes is also still – relatively speaking – virgin territory, although because of its confidential nature, it is difficult to get a true picture of the actual extent of sports mediation. As Professor James A.R. Nafziger, Thomas B. Stoel Professor of Law at Willamette University College of Law, USA recently told the author:

'… mediation merits much greater attention than it has had as an alternative to both forms of adjudication – arbitration and litigation. In fact, of course, much informal mediation does go on, but is seldom reported'.

However, in the States, a Uniform Mediation Act has been recently approved in August 2001 to replace the patchwork of State Laws on Mediation with a uniform code. In particular, the Act includes a new provision to prevent disclosure of communications during any subsequent legal procedures, which reads as follows:

'Unless subject to the [open meetings act/open records act], mediation communications are confidential to the extent agreed by the parties or provided by other laws or rules of this State'.

William K. Slate II, President and Chief Executive Officer of the American Arbitration Association has welcomed this new provision in the following terms:

'By protecting the confidentiality of mediator, party, and non-party communications, the Act meets the expectations of all participants to the mediation process'.

The New US Uniform Mediation Act will lead to more mediations.

Contrasting the apparent slow take up to date of mediation in sports-related disputes in the States, Professor Nafziger, in a joint article with Li Wie, on 'China's Sports Law'[70] points out that China, where a National Sports Policy is developing, is 'in the vanguard of the global trend' as far as the use of ADR, as a primary form of dispute resolution, is concerned (see previous Chapter).

---

[70] The American Journal of Comparative Law, vol. XLVI no. 3, Summer, 1998.

CHAPTER XIV
FINAL REMARKS

Mediation, as an alternative method of dispute resolution, has something valuable to offer to the world of sport in appropriate cases, including speed, confidentiality and cheapness. Many sports bodies and other organisations have recognised this and are offering – and also promoting – mediation services at the national and the international levels.

Much depends, as we have seen, on the personal skills and experience of the mediators, but the success of mediation equally depends on the willingness of the parties to settle their disputes amicably, if at all possible.

One of the main advantages of mediation is that it is a 'without prejudice' process and so little, if anything, is lost if it fails. It is very much a case of: 'nothing ventured nothing gained!' For as David Richbell, former Director of Training at CEDR, has recently put it:

> 'Even if a settlement agreement is not reached, nothing is lost, as the parties are better informed, issues are narrowed down and the dispute is moved significantly towards resolution as a result'.

Mediation is not a universal solution for dispute settlement. It is very much, to use the sporting metaphor, a case of 'horses for courses'.

Neither is it cost-free. But savings in time are also saving in monetary terms and management resources.

However, although mediation of sports disputes – both nationally and internationally – is still, in many respects, in its infancy, the cases, in which it has been used successfully to date, clearly demonstrate its potential and usefulness as an alternative dispute resolution method.

In the author's view, therefore, it is only a matter of time – and a short time at that – as well as education before sports mediation – in its widest sense – comes into its own and is more widely and regularly practised and used and also recognised as an effective alternative dispute resolution mechanism in sport around the world.

APPENDICES – DOCUMENTATION

APPENDIX I
ADR GROUP CODE OF PRACTICE FOR SOLICITORS

All ADR Group accredited mediators are lawyers and subscribe to The Law Society's code of practice ('Code of Practice') for civil/commercial mediation (Annex 22A). The Law Society recommends that all solicitors who offer ADR services (including mediation) comply with a code of practice.

1. **Objectives of Civil/Commercial Mediation**
    Civil commercial mediation is a process in which:
    1.1   two or more parties in dispute
    1.2   whether or not they are legally represented
    1.3   and at any time, whether or not there are or have been legal proceedings
    1.4   agree to the appointment of a neutral third party (the mediator)
    1.5   who is impartial
    1.6   who has no authority to make any decisions with regard to their issues
    1.7   which may relate to all or any part of a dispute of a civil or commercial nature
    1.8   but who helps them reach their own decisions
    1.9   by negotiation
    1.10 without adjudication.

2. **Qualifications and Appointment of mediator**
    2.1   Every mediator must comply with the criteria and requirements for mediators stipulated from time to time by the Law Society, including those relating to training, consultancy, accreditation and regulation.
    2.2   Save where appointed by or through the court, a mediator may only accept appointment if both or all the parties to the mediation so request, or agree.
    2.3   Whether a mediator is appointed by the parties or through the court or through any other agency, he or she may only continue to act as such so long as both or all parties to the mediation wish him or her to do so. If any party does not wish to continue with the mediation, the mediator must discontinue the process as regards that party and may discontinue the process as regards all parties. Also, if the mediator considers that it would be inappropriate to continue the mediation, the mediator shall bring it to an end, and may, subject to the terms of the mediation agreement, decline to give reasons.

3. **Conflicts of interest, confidential information and the impartiality of the mediator**
    3.1   The impartiality of mediator is a fundamental principle of mediation.
    3.2   Impartiality means that:
        3.2.1   the mediator does not have any significant personal interest in the outcome of the mediation;

3.2.2 the mediator will conduct the process fairly and even-handedly, and will not favour any party over another

3.3 Save as set out in 3.2 above, a mediator with an insignificant interest in the personal outcome of the mediation may act if, full disclosure is made to all of the parties as soon as it is known, and they consent.

3.4 The mediator must not act, or, having started to do so, continue to act:

3.4.1 in relation to issues on which he or she or a member of his firm has any act for any party;

3.4.2 if any of the circumstances exist which may constitute an actual or potential conflict of interest

3.4.3 if the mediator or a member of his or her firm has acted for any of the parties in issues not relating to the mediation, unless that has been disclosed to the parties as soon as it is known and they consent.

3.5 Where a mediator has acted as such in relation to a dispute, neither he or she nor any member of his or her firm may subsequently for any party in relation to the subject matter of the mediation.

4. Mediation Procedures

4.1 The mediator must ensure that the parties agree the terms and conditions regulating the mediation before dealing with the substantive issues. This should be in written agreement which should reflect the main principles of this code. Such agreement should also contain the remuneration of the mediator.

4.2 The procedure for the conduct of the mediation is a matter for the decision of the mediator. Insofar as the mediator establishes an agenda of matters to be covered in the mediation, the mediator shall be guided by the needs, wishes and priorities of the parties in doing so.

4.3 In establishing any procedures for the conduct of the mediation, the mediator must be guided by a commitment to procedural fairness and a high quality of process.

5. The decision making process

5.1 The primary aim of the mediation is to help the parties to arrive at their own decisions regarding the disputed issues.

5.2 The parties should be helped to reach such resolution of such issues which they feel are appropriate to their particular circumstances. Such resolution may not necessarily be the same as that which may be arrived at in the event of adjudication by the court. That allows the parties to explore and agree upon a wider range of options for settlement that might otherwise be the case.

5.3 The mediator may meet the parties individually and/or together. Solicitors, barristers or other professional advisers acting for the individual parties may, but need not necessarily, participate in the mediation process if the parties so wish. Such solicitors and/or advisers may take part in discussions and meetings, with or without the parties, and in other communication and representation, in such manner as the mediator may consider useful and appropriate.

5.4 Parties are free to consult with the individual professional advisers as the mediation progresses. The mediator may make suggestions to the parties as to the appropriateness of seeking further assistance from professional advisers such as lawyers, accountants, expert valuers or others.

5.5 The mediator must not seek to impose his or her preferred outcome on the parties.

5.6 The mediator shall be free to make management decisions with regard to the conduct of the mediation process.

5.7 The mediator may suggest possible solutions and help the parties to explore these, where he or she thinks this would be helpful to them.

5.8 The mediator must recognise that the parties can reach decisions on any issues at any stage of the mediation.

5.9 Agreements reached in mediation fall into three categories:
5.9.1 non-binding agreement
5.9.2 binding agreements (which would be enforceable by a court)
5.9.3 binding agreements enshrined in a court or arbitration order
The mediator should ascertain how the parties wish their agreement to be treated. Where the parties do not wish to have a legally binding solution (for example where they have resolved personal rather than legal issues), their wishes should be respected.

5.10 At the end of the mediation or at any interim stage, the mediator and/or the parties or their representatives may prepare a written memorandum or summary or any agreements reached by the parties, which may, where considered by the mediator to be appropriate, compromise draft heads of such agreements for formalisation by the legal advisers acting for the parties.

5.11 If the parties wish to consult their respective individual legal advisers before entering into any binding agreement, then any terms which they may provisionally propose as the basis for resolution will not be binding on them until they have each had the opportunity of taking advise form such legal advisers and have thereafter agreed, in writing, to be bound.

5.12 Mediation does not provide for the disclosure and inspection of documents in the same way or to the same extent as required by court rules. The parties may voluntarily agree to provide such documentation, or any lesser form of disclosure considered by them to be sufficient. This should be considered in advance of the mediation. The mediator may indicate any particular documents that he or she considers should be bought to the mediation.

5.13 The mediator may assist the parties, so far as appropriate and practicable, to identify what information and documents will help the resolution of any issue(s), and how best such information and documents should be obtained. However, the mediator has no obligation to make independent enquiries or undertake verification in relation to any information or documents sought or provided in the mediation.

5.14 If, in cases where one or more parties is unrepresented at the mediation and the parties are proposing a resolution which appears to the mediator to be unconscionable, having regard to the circumstances, then the mediator must inform the parties accordingly and may terminate the mediation and/or refer the parties to their legal advisers.

6. Dealing with power imbalances

6.1 The mediator should be alive to power imbalances existing between the parties. If the such imbalances seem likely to cause the mediation process to become unfair or ineffective, the mediator must take reasonable steps to try to prevent this.

6.2 The mediator must seek, in particular, to prevent abusive or intimidating behaviour by any of the parties.

6.3 If the mediator believes that, because of power imbalances, the mediation would not be able to be fairly and effectively conducted, he or she may discuss this with the parties, recognising that the mediation may have been bought to any end and/or the parties referred to their lawyers.

7. Confidentiality and privilege

7.1 Before the mediation commences, the parties should agree in writing as to the provisions concerning confidentiality and privilege that will apply to the mediation process itself and any resultant mediation agreement, save as otherwise agreed in the mediation settlement agreement.

7.2 The mediator must maintain confidentiality in relation to all matters dealt with in the mediation. The mediator may disclose:

7.2.1 matter which the parties and the mediator agree may be disclosed;

7.2.2 matters which are already public;

7.2.3 matter which the mediator considers appropriate where he or she believes that if the life or safety of any person is or may be at serious risk;

7.2.4 matters where the law imposes an overriding obligation of disclosure on the mediator.

7.2.5 Subject to paragraph 7.2 above, where the mediator meets the parties separately and obtains information from any party which is confidential to that party, the mediator must maintain the confidentiality of that information from all other parties, except to the extent that the mediator has be authorised to disclose any such information.

7.3 Mediators should note that the mediation privilege will not ordinarily apply in relation to communications indicating that a person is suffering or likely to suffer serious bodily harm, or where other public policy considerations prevail, or where for any other reason, the rules of evidence render privilege inapplicable.

7.4 The mediator should remind the parties that (unless the mediation agreement provides otherwise) the confidentiality and privilege attaching to the mediation process may not extend to the provisions of any settlement agreement which results. The mediator should suggest to the parties that they consider the extent to which they wish the terms of the resulting settlement to be discloseable – and to provide accordingly in the agreement itself.

8. Professional indemnity cover

8.1 All solicitor mediators must carry professional indemnity cover in respect of their acting as mediators.

8.1.1 Solicitors who practise as mediators will be covered by the Solicitor's Indemnity Fund in respect of their acting as a mediator, provided they are doing so in their capacity as a member of their firm

8.1.2 If a solicitor is acting as a mediator as a separate activity outside his or her legal practise, separate indemnity insurance must be obtained.

9.   Promotion of mediation

9.1   Solicitor mediators may promote their practice as such, but must always do so in a professional, truthful and dignified way. They may reflect their qualification as a mediator and their membership of any other relevant mediation organisation.

9.2   Solicitor mediators must comply with the Solicitors' Publicity Code 1990.

APPENDIX II
ADR GROUP MEDIATION PROCEDURE

ADR Group mediations shall be governed by the following procedure ('the Mediation Procedure'), as amended by ADR Group from time to time) and the parties shall be taken to have agreed that the mediation shall be conducted in accordance with the Mediation Procedure.

1. **Mediation Procedure**
   1.1 The parties to a dispute or negotiation in question will attempt to settle it by mediation. Representatives of the parties including their advisers (legal representatives) and the mediator will attend the mediation sessions. Any and all communications relating to, and at, the mediation are private & confidential and will be without prejudice.
   1.2 The representatives of the parties must have the necessary authority to settle the dispute. If a party is a natural person, that person must attend the mediation session. If a party is not a natural person it must be represented at the mediation session by an officer or employee with full authority to make binding agreements settling the dispute. If that person comes with 'limited' authority, that is, authority up to a certain amount, he or she must disclose this information to the mediator prior to the mediation.
   1.3 The procedure at the mediation will be determined by the mediator.
   1.4 The parties will agree to the appointment of an ADR Group accredited mediator. ADR Group will provide to the parties, in advance of the mediation, details of recommended mediators drawn from ADR Net Limited's panel of mediators. If the parties are unable to agree to the appointment of a mediator, ADR Group will appoint a mediator if requested to do so.

2. **Mediation Agreement**
   2.1 The parties and ADR Group will enter into and sign an agreement ('Agreement to Mediate') in advance of the mediation and which agreement shall govern the relationship between the parties before, during and after the mediation.
   2.2 Each party, in signing the Agreement to Mediate, will be deemed to be agreeing on behalf of both itself and all such other persons to be bound by the confidentiality provisions of the Mediation Procedure.

3. **The Mediator**
   3.1 The mediator will:
      (a) attend any meetings with any or all of the parties preceding the mediation, if requested to do so, or if the mediator decides it is appropriate;
      (b) prior to the commencement of the mediation read and familiarise him/herself with each party's Position Statement and any documents provided in accordance with paragraph 6.1 below;

(c)   determine the procedure (see paragraph 1.3 above);

(d)   assist the parties in drawing up any written settlement agreement;

(e)   abide by the terms of the Mediation Procedure, the Agreement to Mediate and the Solicitors Code of Practice (as amended from time to time) ('Code of Practice')

3.2   The mediator will not:

(a)   impose a settlement on the parties;

(b)   offer legal advice or act as legal adviser to any party;

(c)   analyse an party's legal position or rights.

3.3   The parties and mediator acknowledge that the mediator is an independent contractor and is not appointed as an agent or employee of any of the parties or ADR Group. Neither the mediator nor a member of his or her firm will act, or have acted, as a professional adviser, or in any other capacity, for any of the parties individually in connection with the dispute either during the currency of the mediation or at any time thereafter.

4.   Mediation arrangements

4.1   ADR Group, will in consultation with the parties and the mediator, make the necessary arrangements for the mediation including, as appropriate:

(a)   recommend mediators with regard to, inter alia, nature of the dispute, degree of complexity, location of parties etc and drawing up the Agreement to Mediate;

(b)   liaise between the parties to agree suitable date and venue;

(c)   assist the parties in preparing their Position Statement (see paragraph 6) and supporting documentation;

(d)   discuss or meet with any or all of the parties or their representatives (and the mediator if appropriate), either together or separately, on any matter pursuant to the proposed mediation;

(e)   general administration in relation to the mediation.

5.   Representation

5.1   Parties do not require legal representation to attend the mediation.

5.2   Where a party is un-represented, ADR Group encourages such party to obtain independent legal advice pursuant to the mediation.

5.3   Each party is required to notify ADR Group and other parties involved in the mediation of the names of those people intended to be present on its behalf at the mediation.

6.   Position Statements & Documentation

6.1   Each party will be required to prepare and deliver to the mediator, within seven (7) days of the mediation, a concise summary ('Position Statement') of the case in dispute and copies of any and all documents referred to in the Position Statement and which it will be seeking to refer to during the mediation.

6.2   ADR Group do not impose any obligation on the parties to exchange Position Statements, but parties are free to agree to the simultaneous exchange of the Position Statements, if so agreed or if considered appropriate.

6.3   The Position Statement is private and confidential and will not be disclosed (by the mediator) to any other third party unless expressly authorised to do so. ADR Group will provide to the parties, upon request, a guide to position statement preparation.

6.4   Parties are encouraged to prepare and agree a joint bundle of documents where appropriate.

7.   The Mediation

7.1   No formal record or transcript of the mediation will be made.

7.2   The mediation session is for the purpose of attempting to achieve a negotiated settlement and all information provided during the mediation session is without prejudice and will be inadmissible in any litigation or arbitration of the dispute. Evidence, which is otherwise admissible, shall not be rendered inadmissible as a result of its use in the mediation session.

7.3   If the parties are unable to reach a settlement during the mediation, the mediator may, if requested to do so, facilitate further negotiation after the mediation session itself has ended.

8.   Settlement Agreement

Any settlement reached in the mediation will not be legally binding until it has been recorded in writing and signed by, or on behalf of, the parties.

9.   Termination

9.1   Any of the parties may withdraw from the mediation at any time and shall immediately inform the mediator and the other representatives either orally or in writing. The mediation will terminate when:

(a)   a party voluntarily withdraws from the mediation; or

(b)   a written settlement agreement is concluded; or

(c)   the mediator elects, in his/her sole discretion, that continuing the mediation is unlikely to result in a settlement; or

(d)   the mediator decides that he/she should retire for any of the reasons set out in the Code of Practice.

10.   Effect on legal proceedings

Where the dispute has been referred to mediation by the Court or where the Court has ordered that the parties consider mediation (under the current civil procedure legislation (as amended from time to time)), and the mediation does not achieve settlement, the current litigation or arbitration in relation to the dispute may be commenced or continued, notwithstanding the mediation, unless the parties agree otherwise.

11.   Confidentiality

11.1   Every person involved in the mediation will keep confidential and not use for any collateral or ulterior purpose:

(a)   the fact that the mediation is to take place or has taken place; and

      (b)   all information, (whether given orally or in writing or otherwise), produced for, or arising pursuant to, the mediation including the settlement agreement (if any) arising out of it

except in so far as is necessary to implement and enforce any such settlement agreement.

11.2 All documents (which include anything upon which evidence is recorded including tapes or computer discs) or other information produced for, or arising in relation to, the mediation will be privileged and not admissible as evidence or discoverable in any litigation or arbitration connected with the dispute (see paragraph 11.1 (b) above). This does not apply to any information, which would in any event have been admissible or discloseable in any such proceedings.

11.3 The parties will not subpoena or otherwise require the mediator, ADR Group (or any employee, consultant, director or representative of ADR Group) or any other person attending the mediation under the auspices of ADR Group to testify or produce records, notes or any other information or material whatsoever in any future or continuing proceedings.

12. Mediation Costs

12.1 It is usual that the costs of the mediation are borne equally between the parties.

12.2 Payment of these costs will be made to ADR Group in accordance with its fee schedule and terms and conditions of business (as amended from time to time).

12.3 Each party attending the mediation is to bear its own costs and expenses of its participation in the mediation (including legal representative costs) and unless agreed otherwise, such costs will be costs in the cause.

13. Waiver of Liability

Neither the mediator nor ADR Group shall be liable to the parties for any act or omission in connection with the services provided by them in, or in relation to, the mediation, unless the act or omission is fraudulent or involves wilful misconduct.

14. Human Rights

The referral of a dispute to mediation does not affect any rights that may exist under Article 6 of the European Convention of Human Rights. Should the dispute not settle through the process of mediation, the parties' right to a fair trial shall remain unaffected.

APPENDIX III
CPR INSTITUTE FOR DISPUTE RESOLUTION:
MODEL MEDIATION AGREEMENT: EUROPE

Agreement made _____, 19__
Between _____ A Company _____
represented by _____
and _____ B Company_____
[and _____ C Company represented by _____]
represented by _____
and _____
(the Mediator) _____
(the Trainee)

A dispute has arisen between the parties (the 'Dispute') [sentence(s) describing Dispute]. The parties have agreed to participate in a mediation proceeding (the 'Proceeding') under the [CPR Model Procedure for Mediation of Business Disputes in Europe], [as modified by mutual agreement] (the 'Procedure') . The parties have chosen the Mediator for the Proceeding. The parties and the Mediator agree as follows:

A. Duties and Obligations

1. The Mediator and [the Trainee] and each of the parties agree to be bound by and to comply faithfully with the Procedure, including without limitation the provisions regarding confidentiality.

2. The Mediator and [the Trainee] have no previous commitments that may significantly delay the expeditious conduct of the proceeding and will not make any such commitments.

3. The Mediator and [the Trainee], the CPR Institute for Dispute Resolution ('CPR') and their employees, agents and partners shall not be liable for any act or omission in connection with the Proceeding, other than as a result of its/his/her own willful misconduct or gross negligence. Neither party shall seek to require the mediator to give evidence in any subsequent litigation about the dispute except in the case of an allegation of misconduct during the mediation proceedings.

B. Disclosure of Prior Relationships

1. The Mediator [and the Trainee] have made a reasonable effort to learn and has/have disclosed to the parties in writing (a) all business or professional relationships the Mediator's and/or the Trainee's firm has/have had with the parties or their lawyers within the past five years, including all instances in which the Mediator [or the Trainee] or the Mediator's [or the Trainee's firm] served as a lawyer for any party or adverse to any party; (b) any financial interest the Mediator [and the Trainee] has in any party; (c) any significant social, business or professional relationship the Mediator [or the Trainee] has/have had with an officer or employee of a party or with an individual representing a party in the Proceeding; and (d) any other circumstances that may create doubt regarding the Mediator's [and the Trainee's] impartiality in the Proceeding.

2. Each party and its lawyer has made a reasonable effort to learn and has disclosed to every

other party and the Mediator [and the Trainee] in writing any relationships of a nature described in paragraph B.1. not previously identified and disclosed by the Mediator [and the Trainee].

3. The parties and the Mediator [and the Trainee] are satisfied that any relationships disclosed pursuant to paragraphs B.1. and B.2. will not affect the Mediator's [or the Trainee] independence or impartiality. Notwithstanding such relationships or others which the Mediator [and the Trainee] and the parties did not discover despite good faith efforts, the parties wish the Mediator [and the Trainee] to serve in the Proceeding, waiving any claim based on said relationships, and the Mediator [and the Trainee] agrees to so serve.

4. The disclosure obligations in paragraphs B.1. and B.2. are continuing until the Proceeding is concluded. The ability of the Mediator [and the Trainee] to continue serving in this capacity shall be explored with each such disclosure.

C. Future Relationships

1. The Mediator, [the Trainee,] the Mediator's firm [and the Trainee's firm] shall not undertake any work for or against a party regarding the Dispute, and pending the mediation proceedings, any other matter.

2. Neither the Mediator [or the Trainee] nor any person assisting the Mediator [or the Trainee] with this Proceeding shall personally work on any matter for or against a party, regardless of specific subject matter, prior to [six] months following cessation of the Mediator's [and the Trainee's] services in the Proceeding without the consent of both (all) parties.

D. Remuneration

1. The Mediator shall be remunerated for time expended in connection with the Proceeding at the rate of _____, plus reasonable travel and other out-of pocket expenses. The Mediator's fee shall be shared equally by the parties. No part of such fee shall accrue to CPR. No fee is payable to the Trainee.

2.   ...

E. Governing Law and Jurisdiction

This agreement is governed by appropriate law and shall be subject to the [non exclusive] jurisdiction of the appropriate country's courts.

Party
by _____
Party's Lawyer

Party
by _____
Party's Lawyer

---

by Mediator

Trainee

APPENDIX IV
CPR INSTITUTE FOR DISPUTE RESOLUTION: MODEL MEDIATION PROCEDURE FOR BUSINESS DISPUTES IN EUROPE

1. Proposing Mediation

Mediation can be used in disputes including those where numerous parties are involved. Any party to a business dispute may propose the use of mediation to the other party or parties. If the parties have made a contractual commitment to mediate disputes between them, or if they have subscribed to another commitment to engage in alternative dispute resolutions (ADR), that commitment or policy may be invoked. Sometimes a neutral organisation may help persuade a party to engage in mediation. CPR may be requested to play that role.

2. Selecting the Mediator

Unless the parties promptly, as part of their agreement to mediate, agree on a mediator, they will notify CPR of their need for assistance in selecting a mediator, informing CPR of any preferences as to matters such as candidates' mediation style, technical and/or legal expertise, competence in certain languages or geographic location. In international disputes, CPR will endeavour to appoint a mediator from a country other than that of either of the parties, unless the parties agree otherwise.

CPR will convene the parties, in person or by telephone, to attempt to select a mediator by agreement. If the parties do not promptly reach agreement, CPR will submit to the parties the names of not less than three candidates, with their resumes and hourly rates. If the parties are unable to agree on a candidate from the list within seven days following receipt of the list, each party will, within 10 days following receipt of the list, send to CPR the list of candidates ranked in descending order of preference. The candidate with the lowest combined score will be appointed as the mediator by CPR. CPR will break any tie.

Before proposing any mediator candidate, CPR will request the candidate to disclose any circumstances known to him or her that would cause reasonable doubt regarding the candidate's impartiality. If a clear conflict is disclosed, the individual will not be proposed and CPR will promptly propose another candidate. Other circumstances a candidate discloses to CPR will be disclosed to the parties. A party may challenge a mediator candidate if it knows of any circumstances giving rise to reasonable doubt regarding the candidate's impartiality.

The mediator's fees will be determined before appointment. Those fees, and any other costs of the process, will be shared equally by the parties unless they otherwise agree. If a party withdraws from a multiparty mediation but the procedure continues, the withdrawing party will not be responsible for any costs incurred after it has notified the mediator and the other parties of its withdrawal. Shared costs will not include costs that each party incurs in preparing its own case, attending meetings and instructing representatives. The parties will bear these costs themselves.

Before appointment, the mediator will assure the parties of his or her availability to conduct the proceeding expeditiously. It is strongly advised that the parties and the mediator enter into a mediation agreement. A model agreement is attached.

3. Ground Rules of Proceeding

The following ground rules will apply, subject to any changes on which the parties and the mediator agree.

3.1 The process is voluntary and depends on the co-operation of the parties. The mediator does not issue a binding decision.

3.2 Each party may withdraw at any time by written notice to the mediator and the other party or parties.

3.3 The mediator is neutral, independent and impartial.

3.4 The mediator controls the procedural aspects of the mediation. The parties cooperate fully with the mediator.

    (a)   The mediator is free to meet and communicate separately with each party.

    (b)   The mediator decides when to hold joint meetings with the parties and when to hold separate meetings. The mediator fixes the time and place of each session and its agenda in consultation with the parties. There is no formal written, audio or video record of any meeting. Formal rules of evidence or procedure do not apply.

    (c)   Unless otherwise agreed by the parties, the mediator decides, if necessary, the language in which the mediation is to be conducted and whether any documents should be translated.

3.5 Each party is represented at each mediation conference by a business executive authorized to negotiate a resolution of the dispute and to execute a settlement agreement. Each party may be represented by more than one person, e.g. a business executive and a lawyer. The mediator may limit the number of persons representing each party.

3.6 The process is to be conducted expeditiously. Each representative undertakes to make every effort to be available for meetings.

3.7 The mediator does not transmit information received in confidence from any party to any other party or any third party, unless authorised to do so by the party transmitting the information, or unless ordered to do so by a court of competent jurisdiction.

3.8 The mediator and any persons assisting the mediator is disqualified as a witness, consultant or expert in any pending or future investigation, action or proceeding relating to the subject matter of the mediation (including any investigation, action or proceeding which involves persons not party to this mediation) .

3.9 If the dispute goes into arbitration, the mediator will not serve as an arbitrator.

3.10 The mediator may obtain assistance and independent expert advice, with the prior agreement of and at the expense of the parties. Any candidate proposed as an independent expert will also be required to disclose any circumstances known to him or her that would cause reasonable doubt regarding the candidate's impartiality.

3.11 Neither CPR nor the mediator is liable for any act or omission in connection with the mediation, except for its/his/her own wilful misconduct or gross negligence.

3.12 The mediator may withdraw at any time by written notice to the parties. Either party may seek assistance from CPR in such a situation.

3.13 At the inception of the mediation process, each party and representative agrees in writing to all provisions of this Model Procedure, as modified by agreement of the parties. A model mediation agreement is attached.

3.14 With the approval of the parties, the mediator may sit with a trainee mediator, who may observe the process, but takes no active part in it and charges no fee. The trainee will be bound by the same obligations of confidentiality as the mediator.

4. Exchange of Information

Each party shall produce the documents it relies on in the mediation and may, but shall not be obliged to, produce any further documents requested by the mediator or the other party.

At the conclusion of the mediation process, upon the request of a party which provided documents or other material to one or more other parties, the recipients undertake to return them to the originating party without retaining copies thereof. All documents and other information provided to a party, in the course of a mediation, shall be used by that party exclusively for the purposes of the mediation.

5. Presentation to the Mediator

Before dealing with the substance of the dispute, the parties and the mediator discuss preliminary matters, such as possible modification of the ground rules, place and time of meetings, and each party's need for documents or other information in the possession of the other.

At least five business days before the first substantive mediation conference, unless otherwise agreed, each party submits to the mediator a written statement summarising the background and present status of the dispute and such other material and information as it deems helpful to familiarise the mediator with the dispute. The parties may agree to submit jointly certain other materials. The mediator may request any party to provide clarification and additional information. The mediator may limit the length of written statements and supporting material. The mediator may direct the parties to exchange concise written statements and other materials they submit to the mediator to further each party's understanding of the other party's viewpoints.

Except as the parties otherwise agree, the mediator keeps confidential any written materials or information that are submitted to him or her. The parties and their representatives are not entitled to receive or review any materials or information submitted to the mediator by another party or representative without the concurrence of the latter. At the conclusion of the mediation process, upon request of a party, the mediator without retaining copies returns to that party all written materials and information which that party had provided to the mediator.

6. Negotiation of Terms

The mediator may promote settlement in any manner the mediator believes is appropriate. The mediator helps the parties focus on their underlying interests and concerns, explore resolution alternatives and develop settlement options. The mediator decides when to hold joint meetings, and when to confer separately with each party.

The mediator expects the parties to make settlement proposals.

Finally, if the parties fail to develop mutually acceptable settlement terms, before terminating the procedure, and only with the consent of the parties, (a) the mediator may submit to the parties a final settlement proposal which the mediator considers fair and equitable to all parties; and (b) if the mediator believes he/she is qualified to do so, the mediator may give the parties an evaluation (which if the parties choose will be in writing) of the likely outcome of the case if it were tried to final judgment. Thereupon, the mediator may suggest further discussions to explore whether the mediator's evaluation or proposal may lead to a resolution.

Efforts to reach a settlement continue until (a) a written settlement is reached, or (b) the mediator concludes and informs the parties that further efforts would not be useful, or (c) one of the parties or the mediator withdraws from the process. However, if there are more than two parties, the remaining parties may elect to continue following the withdrawal of a party.

7. Settlement

If a settlement is reached, the representatives of the parties draft a written settlement document incorporating all settlement terms, which may include mutual general releases from or discharges of all liability relating to the subject matter of the dispute. This draft will be circulated among the parties and the mediator, amended as necessary, and formally executed. Initially, a preliminary memorandum of understanding may be prepared at the mediation and executed by the parties; the memorandum should make it expressly clear whether it is intended to be binding or not.

If litigation is pending, the settlement may provide that the parties will request the court to make an appropriate order disposing of the case promptly upon execution of the settlement agreement. The settlement agreement may also be entered as a consent judgment.

8. Failure to Agree

If a resolution is not reached, the mediator discusses with the parties the possibility of their agreeing on arbitration or another form of ADR. If the parties agree in principle, the mediator may offer to assist them in structuring a procedure designed to result in a prompt, economical process.

9. Confidentiality

For, Austrian, Belgian, Dutch, English, French, German, Italian, Scottish, Spanish, Swedish and Swiss mediations: The parties agree that the mediation process, and all negotiations, statements and documents expressly prepared for the purposes of the mediation shall be 'without prejudice'. The entire mediation process is confidential. Unless agreed among all the parties or required by law or ordered by the Court, the parties and the mediator may not disclose to any person any information regarding the process (including pre-process exchanges and agreements), contents (including written and oral information), settlement terms or outcome of the proceeding. If litigation is pending, the participants may, however, inform the court of the schedule and overall status of the mediation for purposes of litigation management.

APPENDIX V
THE CAS CODE OF SPORTS-RELATED ARBITRATION

PROCEDURAL RULES

A – GENERAL PROVISIONS

R27 – Application of the rules
1. These Procedural Rules apply whenever the parties have agreed to refer a sports-related dispute to the CAS. Such disputes may arise out of a contract containing an arbitration clause or be the subject of a later arbitration agreement (ordinary arbitration proceedings) or involve an appeal against a decision given by the disciplinary tribunals or similar bodies of a federation, association or sports body where the statutes or regulations of such bodies, or a specific agreement provides for an appeal to the CAS (appeal arbitration proceedings).
2. Such disputes may involve matters of principle relating to sport or matters of pecuniary or other interests brought into play in the practice or the development of sport and, generally speaking, any activity related or connected to sport.
3. These Procedural Rules also apply where the CAS is called upon to give an advisory opinion (consultation proceedings).

R28 – Seat
The seat of the CAS and of each Arbitration Panel ('Panel') is in Lausanne, Switzerland. However, should circumstances so warrant, and after consultation with all parties, the President of the Panel or, failing him, the President of the relevant Division may decide to hold a hearing in another place.

R29 – Language
1. The CAS working languages are French and English. In the absence of agreement between the parties, and taking into account all pertinent circumstances, the President of the Panel shall select one of these two languages as the language of the arbitration at the start of the proceedings before the Panel.
2. The parties may choose another language provided that the Arbitration Panel agrees. The parties shall advise the CAS of such a choice. In the event of such a choice, the Panel may order that the parties bear all or part of the translation and interpreting costs.

R30 – Representation and assistance
The parties may be represented or assisted by persons of their choice. The names, addresses, telephone and facsimile numbers of the persons representing the parties shall be communicated to the Court Office, the other party and the Panel after its formation.

R31 – Notifications and communications
1. All notifications and communications that the CAS or the Panel intend for the parties shall be made through the Court Office. The notifications and communications shall be written in French or in English and sent to the address shown in the arbitration request,

statement of appeal or application for an opinion, or to any other address specified at a later date.

2. All arbitration awards, orders, and other decisions made by the CAS and the Panel shall be notified by any means permitting proof of receipt.

3. All communications from the parties intended for the CAS or the Panel, including the arbitration request, statement of appeal, application for an opinion and request for participation of a third party, as well as the reply shall be sent to the CAS in as many copies as there are parties, counsel and arbitrators, together with one additional copy for the CAS itself

R32 – Time-limit
Upon application on justified grounds, either the President of the Panel or, failing him, the President of the relevant Division, may extend the time-limits provided in these Procedural Rules, if the circumstances so warrant.

R33 – independence and qualifications of arbitrators
1. Every arbitrator shall be and remain independent of the parties and shall immediately disclose any circumstances likely to affect independence with respect to any of the parties.

2. Every arbitrator shall appear on the list drawn up by the ICAS in accordance with the Statutes which are part of this Code and shall have the availability required to expeditiously complete the arbitration.

R34 – Challenge
1. An arbitrator may be challenged if the circumstances give rise to legitimate doubts over his independence. The challenge shall be brought immediately after the ground for the challenge has become known.

2. Challenges are in the exclusive power of the ICAS which may exercise such power through its Board in accordance with the Statutes which are part of this Code. The challenge shall be brought by way of a petition setting forth the facts giving rise to the challenge. The ICAS or its Board shall rule on the challenge after the other parties, the challenged arbitrator and the other arbitrators have been invited to submit written comments. It shall give brief reasons for its decision.

R35 – Removal
An arbitrator may be removed by the ICAS if he refuses to or is prevented from carrying out his duties. The ICAS may delegate this function to its Board. The Board shall invite the parties, the arbitrator in question and the other arbitrators to submit written comments and shall render a brief reasoned decision.

R36 – Replacement
In the event of resignation, death, challenge or removal of an arbitrator, such arbitrator shall be replaced in accordance with the provisions applicable to his appointment. Unless otherwise agreed by the parties or otherwise decided by the Panel, the proceedings shall continue without repetition of the procedure which took place prior to the replacement.

R37 – Provisional and conservatory measures

1. No party may apply for provisional or conservatory measures under these Procedural Rules before the request for arbitration or the statement of appeal, which implies the exhaustion of internal remedies, has been filed with the CAS.

2. The President of the relevant Division, prior to the transfer of the file to the Panel, or thereafter the Panel may, upon application by one of the parties, make an order for provisional or conservatory measures. In agreeing to submit to these Procedural Rules any dispute subject to appeal arbitration proceedings, the parties expressly waive their rights to request such measures from state authorities. This waiver does not apply to provisional or conservatory measures in connection with disputes subject to ordinary arbitration proceedings.

3. If an application for provisional measures is filed, the President of the relevant Division or the Panel invites the opponent to express his position within fifteen days or within a shorter time-limit if circumstances so require. The President of the relevant Division or the Panel shall issue an order within a short time. In case of utmost urgency, the President of the relevant Division prior to the transfer of the file to the Panel, or thereafter the President of the Panel may issue an order upon mere presentation of the application, provided that the opponent shall be heard subsequently.

4. Temporary and conservatory measures may be made conditional upon the provision of security.

B – SPECIAL PROVISIONS APPLICABLE TO THE ORDINARY ARBITRATION PROCEEDINGS

R38 – Request for Arbitration

1. The party intending to submit a reference to arbitration under these Procedural Rules shall file a request with the CAS containing:
   - a brief statement of the facts and legal argument, including a statement of the issue to be submitted to the CAS for determination;
   - the claimant's request for relief;
   - a copy of the contract containing the arbitration agreement or of any document providing for arbitration in accordance with these Procedural Rules;
   - any relevant information about the number and choice of the arbitrator(s), in particular if the arbitration agreement provides for three arbitrators, the name and address of the arbitrator chosen by the claimant from the CAS list of names.

2. Upon filing its request, the claimant shall pay the fee provided in Article R64.1.

R39 – Initiation of the arbitration by the CAS and answer

Unless it is apparent from the outset that there is manifestly no agreement to arbitrate referring to the CAS, the Court Office shall take all appropriate actions to set the arbitration in motion. To this effect, it in particular communicates the request to the respondent, calls upon the parties to express themselves on the law applicable to the merits of the dispute and sets time-limits for the respondent to submit any relevant information about the number and choice of the arbitrator(s), in particular to appoint an arbitrator from the CAS list, as well as to file an answer to the request for arbitration. The answer shall contain:
   - a brief statement of the defence;

- any defence of lack of jurisdiction;
- any counterclaim.

R40 – Formation of the Panel
R40.1 – Number of arbitrators
The Panel is composed of one or three arbitrators. If the arbitration agreement does not specify the number of arbitrators, the President of the Division shall determine the number taking into account the amount in litigation and the complexity of the dispute.

R40.2 – Appointment of the arbitrators
1. The parties may agree on the method of appointment of the arbitrators. In the absence of an agreement, the arbitrators shall be appointed in accordance with the following paragraphs.
2. If, by virtue of the arbitration agreement or a decision of the President of the Division, a sole arbitrator is to be appointed, the parties may select him by mutual agreement within a time-limit of twenty days set by the Court Office upon receipt of the request. In the absence of an agreement within such time-limit, the President of the Division shall proceed with the appointment.
3. If, by virtue of the arbitration agreement or of a decision of the President of the Division, three arbitrators are to be appointed, the claimant shall appoint its arbitrator in the request or within the time-limit set in the decision on the number of arbitrators and the respondent shall appoint its arbitrator within the time-limit set by the Court Office upon receipt of the request. In the absence of such appointment, the President of the Division shall proceed with the appointment in lieu of the parties. The two arbitrators so appointed shall select the President of the Panel by mutual agreement within a time-limit set by the Court Office. In the absence of an agreement within such time-limit, the President of the Division shall appoint the President of the Panel in lieu of the two arbitrators.

R40.3 – Confirmation of the arbitrators and transfer of the file
1. Any arbitrator selected by the parties or by other arbitrators shall only be deemed appointed after confirmation by the President of the Division. Before proceeding with such confirmation, the latter shall ascertain that the arbitrator fulfils the requirements of Article R33.
2. Once the Panel is formed, the Court Office takes notice of the formation and transfers the file to the arbitrators.

R41 – Multiparty arbitration
R41.1 – Plurality of claimants / respondents
1. If the request for arbitration names several claimants and/or respondents, the CAS shall proceed with the formation of the Panel in accordance with the number of arbitrators and the method of appointment agreed by all parties. In the absence of such an agreement, the President of the Division shall decide on the number of arbitrators in accordance with Article R40.1.
2. If a sole arbitrator is to be appointed, Article R40.2 shall apply. If three arbitrators are to be appointed and there are several claimants, the claimants shall jointly appoint an arbi-

trator. If three arbitrators are to be appointed and there are several respondents, the respondents shall jointly appoint an arbitrator. In the absence of such a joint appointment, the President of the Division shall proceed with the appointment in lieu of the claimants/respondents. If (i) three arbitrators are to be appointed, (ii) there are several claimants and several respondents, and (iii) either the claimants or the respondents fail to jointly appoint an arbitrator, then both co-arbitrators shall be appointed by the President of the Division in accordance with Article R40.2. In all cases, the co-arbitrators shall select the President of the Panel in accordance with Article R40.2.

R41.2 – Joinder
If a respondent intends to cause a third party to participate in the arbitration, it shall so state in its answer, together with the reasons therefore, and file an additional copy of its answer. The Court Office shall communicate this copy to the person the participation of which is requested and set such person a time-limit to state its position on its participation and to submit a response pursuant to Article R39. It shall also set a time-limit for the claimant to express its position on the participation of the third party.

R41.3 – Intervention
If a third party intends to participate as a party in the arbitration, it shall file with the CAS an application to this effect, together with the reasons therefore within the time-limit set for the respondent's answer to the request for arbitration. To the extent applicable, such application shall have the same contents as a request for arbitration. The Court Office shall communicate a copy of this application to the parties and set a time-limit for them to express their position on the participation of the third party and to file, to the extent applicable, an answer pursuant to Article R39.

R41.4 – Joint provisions on joinder and intervention
1. A third party may only participate in the arbitration if it is bound by the arbitration agreement or if itself and the other parties agree in writing.
2. Upon expiration of the time-limit set in Articles R41.2 and R41.3, the President of the Division shall decide on the participation of the third party, taking into account, in particular, the prima facie existence of an arbitration agreement as referred to in Article R39 above. Such decision shall be without prejudice to the decision of the Panel on the same matter.
3. If the President of the Division accepts the participation of the third party, the CAS shall proceed with the formation of the Panel in accordance with the number of arbitrators and the method of appointment agreed by all parties. In the absence of such an agreement, the President of the Division shall decide on the number of arbitrators in accordance with Article R40.1. If a sole arbitrator is to be appointed, Article R40.2 shall apply. If three arbitrators are to be appointed, the co-arbitrators shall be appointed by the President of the Division and shall choose the President of the Panel in accordance with Article R40.2.
4. Regardless of the decision of the Panel on the participation of the third party, the formation of the Panel cannot be challenged. In the event that the Panel accepts the participation, it shall, if required, issue related procedural directions.

R42 – Conciliation

The President of the Division, before the transfer of the file to the Panel, and thereafter the Panel may at any time seek to resolve the dispute by conciliation. Any settlement may be embodied in an arbitral award rendered by consent of the parties.

R43 – Confidentiality

Proceedings under these Procedural Rules are confidential. The parties, the arbitrators and the CAS undertake not to disclose to any third party any facts or other information relating to the dispute or the proceedings. Awards shall not be made public unless the award itself so provides or all parties agree.

R44 – Procedure before the Panel
R44.1 – Written submissions

1. The procedure before the Panel comprises written submissions, if the Panel deems it appropriate, and an oral hearing. Upon the receipt of the file, the President of the Panel, if appropriate, shall issue directions in connection with the written submissions. As a general rule, there shall be one statement of claim, one response and, if the circumstances so require, one reply and one second response. The parties may, in the statement of claim and in the response, raise claims not contained in the request for arbitration and in the answer to the request. Thereafter, no party may raise any new claim without the consent of the other party.
2. Together with their written submissions, the parties shall produce all written evidence upon which they intend to rely. After the exchange of the written submissions, the parties shall not be authorized to produce further written evidence, except by mutual agreement or if the Panel so permits on the basis of exceptional circumstances.
3. In their written submissions, the parties shall specify any witnesses and experts which they intend to call and state any other evidentiary measure which they request.

R44.2 – Hearing

1. Once the exchange of pleadings is closed, the President of the Panel shall issue directions with respect to the hearing and in particular set the hearing date. As a general rule, there shall be one hearing during which the Panel hears the parties, the witnesses and the expert as well as the parties' final oral arguments, for which the respondent has the floor last.
2. The President of the Panel shall conduct the hearing and ascertain that the statements made are concise and limited to the subject of the written presentations, to the extent that these presentations are relevant. Except if the parties agree otherwise, the hearings are not public. There shall be minutes of the hearing. Any person heard by the Panel may be assisted by an interpreter at the cost of the party which called such upon.
3. The parties may call to be heard by the Panel such witnesses and experts which they have specified in their written submissions.
4. Before hearing any witness, expert or interpreter, the Panel shall solemnly invite such persons to tell the truth, subject to the sanctions of perjury.
5. Once the hearing is closed, the parties shall not be authorized to produce further written pleadings, except if the Panel so orders.

R44.3 – Evidentiary proceedings ordered by the Panel

1. A party may request the Panel to issue an order that the other party produces documents in its custody or under its control. The party seeking such production shall demonstrate that the documents are likely to exist and to be relevant.
2. If it deems it appropriate to supplement the presentations of the parties, the Panel may at any time order the production of additional documents or the examination of witnesses, appoint and hear experts, and proceed with any other procedural act.
3. The Panel shall consult the parties with respect to the appointment and terms of reference of such expert. The expert appointed by the Panel shall be and remain independent of the parties and shall immediately disclose any circumstances likely to affect independence with respect to any of the parties.

R44.4 – Expedited procedure

With the consent of the parties, the Panel may proceed in an expedited manner for which it shall issue appropriate directions.

R45 – Law applicable to the merits

The Panel shall decide the dispute according to the rules of law chosen by the parties or, in the absence of such a choice, according to Swiss law. The parties may authorize the Panel to decide ex aequo et bono.

R46 – Award

1. The award shall be made by a majority decision, or, in the absence of a majority, by the President alone. The award shall be written, dated and signed. Unless the parties agree otherwise, it shall briefly state reasons. The signature of the President of the Panel shall suffice.
2. The award shall be final and binding upon the parties. It may not be challenged by way of an action for setting aside to the extent that the parties have no domicile, habitual residence, or business establishment in Switzerland and that they have expressly excluded all setting aside proceedings in the arbitration agreement or in an agreement entered into subsequently, in particular at the outset of the arbitration.

C – SPECIAL PROVISIONS APPLICABLE TO THE APPEAL ARBITRATION PROCEEDINGS

R47 – Appeal

A party may appeal from the decision of a disciplinary tribunal or similar body of a federation, association or sports body, insofar as the statutes or regulations of the said body so provide or as the parties have conclude a specific arbitration agreement and insofar as the appellant has exhausted the legal remedies available to him prior to the appeal, in accordance with the statutes or regulations of the said sports body.

R48 – Statement of appeal

1. The appellant shall submit to the CAS a statement of appeal containing:
    –   a copy of the decision appealed from;
    –   the appellant's request for relief;

> – the appointment of the arbitrator chosen by the appellant from the CAS list, unless the parties have agreed to the Panel composed of a sole arbitrator;
> – if applicable, an application to stay the execution of the decision appealed from, together with reasons;
> – a copy of the provisions of the statutes or regulations or the specific agreement providing for appeal to the CAS.

2. Upon filing the statement, the appellant shall pay the fee provided for under Article R65.2.

R49 – Time-limit for appeal

In the absence of a time-limit set in the statutes or regulations of the federation, association, sports body concerned, or of a previous agreement, the time-limit for appeal shall be twenty-one days from the communication of the decision which is appealed from.

R50 – Number of arbitrators

The appeal shall be submitted to a Panel of three arbitrators, except if the appellant establishes at the time of the statement of appeal that the parties have agreed to a Panel composed of a sole arbitrator or if the President of the Division considers that the matter is an emergency and the appeal should be submitted to a sole arbitrator.

R51 – Appeal brief

Within ten days following the expiration of the time-limit for the appeal, the appellant shall file with the CAS a brief stating the facts and legal arguments giving rise to the appeal, together with all exhibits and specification of other evidence upon which he intends to rely, failing which the appeal shall be deemed withdrawn.

R52 – Initiation of the arbitration by the CAS

Unless it is apparent from the outset that there is manifestly no agreement to arbitrate referring to the CAS, the CAS Shall take all appropriate actions to set the arbitration in motion. To this effect, the Court Office shall, in particular, communicate the statement of appeal to the respondent, and the President of the Division shall proceed with the formation of the Panel in accordance with Articles R53 and R54. If applicable, he shall also decide promptly on an application for a stay.

R53 – Appointment of arbitrator by respondent

Unless the parties have agreed to a Panel composed of a sole arbitrator or the President of the Division considers that the appeal is an emergency and must be submitted to a sole arbitrator, the respondent shall appoint an arbitrator within ten days after the receipt of the statement of appeal. In the absence of an appointment within such time-limit, the President of the Division shall proceed with the appointment in lieu of the respondent.

R54 – Appointment of the sole arbitrator or of the President and confirmation of the arbitrators by the CAS

1. If, by virtue of the parties' agreement or of a decision of the President of a Division, a sole arbitrator is to be appointed, the President of the Division shall appoint the sole arbitrator upon receipt of the motion for appeal.

2. If three arbitrators are to be appointed, the President of the Division shall appoint the President of the Panel upon appointment of the arbitrator by the respondent. The arbitrators selected by the parties shall only be deemed appointed after confirmation by the President of the Division. Before proceedings with such confirmation, the President of the Division shall ascertain that the arbitrators fulfil the requirements of Article R33.

3. Once the Panel is formed, the Court Office takes notice of the formation of the Panel and transfers the file to the arbitrators.

R55 – Answer of respondent

Within twenty days from the receipt of the grounds for the appeal, the respondent shall submit to the CAS an answer containing:
–   a statement of defence;
–   any defence of lack of jurisdiction;
–   any exhibits or specification of other evidence upon which the respondent intends to rely.

R56 – Statement of appeal and answer complete

Unless the parties agree otherwise or the President of the Panel orders otherwise on the basis of exceptional circumstances, the parties shall not be authorized to supplement their argumentation, nor to produce new exhibits, nor to specify further evidence on which they intend to rely after the submission of the grounds for the appeal and of the answer.

R57 – Scope of Panel's review, hearing

The Panel shall have full power to review the facts and the law. Upon transfer of the file, the President of the Panel shall issue directions in connection with the hearing for the examination of the parties, the witnesses and the experts, as well as for the oral arguments. He may also request communication of the file of the disciplinary tribunal or similar body, the decision of which is subject to appeal. Articles R44.2 and R44.3 shall apply.

R58 – Law applicable

The Panel shall decide the dispute according to the applicable regulations and the rules of law chosen by the parties or, in the absence of such a choice, according to the law of the country in which the federation, association or sports body is domiciled.

R59 – Award

1. The award shall be rendered by a majority decision, or in the absence of a majority, by the President alone. It shall be written, dated and signed. The award shall state brief reasons. The signature of the President shall suffice.

2. The Panel may decide to communicate the holding of the award to the parties, prior to the reasons.

3. The award shall be final from such written communication. The award shall be final and binding upon the parties. It may not be challenged by way of an action for setting aside to the extent that the parties have no domicile, habitual residence, or business establishment in Switzerland and that they have expressly excluded all setting aside proceedings in the arbitration agreement or in an agreement entered into subsequently in particular at the outset of the arbitration.

4. The holding of the award shall be communicated to the parties within four months after the filing of the statement of appeal. Such time-limit may be extended by the President of the Appeals Arbitration Division upon a motivated request from the President of the Panel.

5. The award or a summary setting forth the results of the proceedings shall be made public by the CAS, unless both parties agree that they should remain confidential.

D – SPECIAL PROVISIONS APPLICABLE TO THE CONSULTATION PROCEEDINGS

R60 – Request for opinion
The IOC, the IFs, the NOCs, the associations recognized by the IOC, the OCOGS, may request an advisory opinion from the CAS about any legal issue with respect to the practice or development of sports or any activity related to sports. The request for an opinion shall be addressed to the CAS and accompanied by any document likely to assist the Panel entrusted with giving the opinion.

R61 – Initiation by the CAS
When a request is filed, the CAS President shall review whether it may be the subject of an opinion. In the affirmative, he shall proceed with the formation of a Panel of one or three arbitrators from the CAS list and designate the President. He shall formulate, in his own discretion, the questions submitted to the Panel and forward these questions to the Panel.

R62 – Opinion
Before rendering its opinion, the Panel may request additional information. The opinion may be published with the consent of the party which requested it. It does not constitute a binding arbitral award.

E – INTERPRETATION

R63
1. A party may apply to the CAS for the interpretation of an award issued in an ordinary or appeals arbitration, whenever the holding of the award is unclear, incomplete, ambiguous or whenever its components are contradictory among themselves or contrary to the reasons, or whenever it contains clerical mistakes or a miscalculation of figures.

2. When an application for interpretation is filed, the President of the relevant Division shall review whether there is ground for interpretation. If there is ground, he shall submit the request to the Panel which has rendered the award for interpretation. The arbitrators of the Panel who are unable to act shall be replaced in accordance with Article R36. The Panel shall rule on the request within one month following the submission of the request to the Panel.

F – COSTS OF THE PROCEEDINGS

R64 – Ordinary arbitration
R64.1

Upon filing of the request, the claimant shall pay a minimum fee of Swiss-francs 500.—, without which the CAS shall not proceed. The CAS shall in any event keep this fee. The Panel shall take it into account when assessing the final amount of the fees.

R64.2
1. Upon formation of the Panel, the Court Office shall fix, subject to later changes, the amount and the method of payment of the advance of costs. The filing of a counter-claim or a new claim shall result in the determination of separate advances.
2. To determine the amount of the advance, the Court Office shall fix an estimate of the costs of arbitration, which shall be borne by the parties in accordance with Article R64.4. The advance shall be paid in equal shares by the claimant and the respondent. If a party fails to pay its share, the other may substitute for it; in the absence of substitution, the claim to which the unpaid share relates shall be deemed withdrawn.

R64.3
1. Each party shall advance the cost of its own witnesses, experts and interpreters.
2. If the Panel appoints an expert, retains an interpreter or orders the examination of a witness, it shall issue directions with respect to an advance of costs, if appropriate.

R64.4

At the end of the proceedings, the Court Office shall determine the final amount of the cost of arbitration, which shall include the fee of the CAS, the costs and fees of the arbitrators computed in accordance with the CAS fee scale, the contribution towards the costs and expenses of the CAS, and the costs of witnesses, experts and interpreters.

R64.5

The foregoing costs shall be stated in the arbitral award, which shall also determine which party shall bear such costs or in which portion the parties shall share them. As a general rule, the award shall grant the prevailing party a contribution towards its legal fees and other expenses incurred in connection with the proceedings and, in particular, the costs of witnesses and interpreters. When granting such contribution, the Panel shall take into account the outcome of the proceedings, as well as the conduct and the financial resources of the parties.

R65 – Appeals arbitration
R65.1
1. Subject to Articles R65.2 and R65.4, the proceedings shall be free.
2. The fees and costs of the arbitrators, calculated in accordance with the CAS fee scale, together with the costs of the CAS are borne by the CAS.

R65.2
Upon submission of the statement of appeal, the appellant shall pay a minimum fee of Swiss francs 500.- without which the CAS shall not proceed and the appeal shall be deemed withdrawn. The CAS shall in any event keep this fee.

R65.3
The costs of the parties, witnesses, experts and interpreters shall be advanced by the parties. In the award, the Panel shall decide which party shall bear them or in what proportion the parties shall share them, taking into account the outcome of the proceeding, as well as the conduct and financial resources of the parties.

R65.4
If all circumstances so warrant, the President of the Appeals Arbitration Division may decide to apply Articles R64.4 and R64.5 to an appeals arbitration.

R66 – Consultation proceedings
The Court Office shall determine, after consultation with the person requesting the opinion, to what extent and upon what terms such person shall contribute towards the costs of the consultation procedure.

G – MISCELLANEOUS PROVISIONS

R67
The arbitration agreements entered into prior to November 22, 1994 shall be deemed to refer to the present Rules, unless both parties request the application of the Rules in force prior to November 22, 1994.

R68
The French text and the English text are authentic. In the event of any discrepancy, the French text shall prevail.

R69
The Procedural Rules may be amended by the decision of the Council, in conformity with Article S8.

APPENDIX VI
THE CAS MEDIATION RULES

Pursuant to Articles S2 and S6 paragraph 10 of the Code of Sports-related Arbitration, the International Council of Arbitration for Sport adopts the present Mediation Rules.

A. Definitions

Article 1
CAS mediation is a non binding and informal procedure, based on a mediation agreement in which each party undertakes to attempt in good faith to negotiate with the other party, and with the assistance of a CAS mediator, with a view to settling a sports-related dispute.

CAS mediation is provided solely for the resolution of disputes related to the CAS ordinary procedure. A decision passed by the organ of a sports organization cannot be the subject of mediation proceedings before the CAS. All disputes related to disciplinary matters, as well as doping issues, are expressly excluded from CAS mediation.

Article 2
A mediation agreement is one whereby the parties agree to submit to mediation a sports-related dispute which has arisen or which may arise between them.

A mediation agreement may take the form of a mediation clause inserted in a contract or that of a separate agreement.

B. Scope of application of rules

Article 3
Where a mediation agreement provides for mediation under the CAS Mediation Rules, these Rules shall be deemed to form an integral part of such mediation agreement. Unless the parties have agreed otherwise, the version of these Rules in force on the date when the mediation request is filed shall apply.

The parties may however agree to apply other rules of procedure.

C. Commencement of the mediation

Article 4
A party wishing to institute mediation proceedings shall address a request to that effect in writing to the CAS Court Office, and at the same time send a copy of this to the other party.

The request shall contain: the identity of the parties and their representatives (name, address, telephone and fax numbers), a copy of the mediation agreement and a brief description of the dispute.

Upon filing its request, the party shall pay the administrative fee stipulated in Article 14 of the present Rules.

The day on which the mediation request is received by the CAS Court Office shall be considered as the date on which the mediation proceedings commence.

The CAS Court Office shall immediately inform the parties of the date on which the mediation commences, and shall fix the time limit by which the other party shall pay its share of the administrative costs pursuant to Article 14 of the present Rules.

D. Appointment of the mediator

Article 5
The ICAS draws up the list of mediators chosen from the list of CAS arbitrators or from outside.
The personalities whom the ICAS chooses appear on the list of mediators for a four-year period, and are thereafter eligible for reselection.

Article 6
Unless the parties have agreed between themselves on who the mediator will be, he shall be chosen by the CAS President from among the list of CAS mediators and appointed after consultation with the parties.
In accepting such appointment, the mediator undertakes to devote sufficient time to the mediation proceedings as will allow these to be conducted expeditiously.
The mediator shall be and must remain independent of the parties, and is bound to disclose any circumstances likely to compromise his independence with respect to any of the parties.
Having duly been informed thereof, the parties may however authorize the mediator to continue his mandate, by means of a signed separate or joint declaration.
In the event of an objection by any of the parties, or at his own discretion if he deems himself unable to bring the mediation to a successful conclusion, the mediator shall cease his mandate and inform the CAS President accordingly, whereupon the latter will make arrangements to replace him, after consulting the parties.

E. Representation of parties

Article 7
The parties may be represented or assisted in their meetings with the mediator.
If a party is being represented, the other party and the CAS must be informed beforehand as to the identity of such representative.
The representative must have full authority to settle the dispute alone, without consulting the party he is representing.

F. Conduct of mediation

Article 8
The mediation shall be conducted in the manner agreed by the parties. Failing such agreement between the parties, the mediator shall determine the manner in which the mediation will be conducted.
As soon as possible, the mediator shall establish the terms and timetable for submission by each party to the mediator and to the other party of a statement summarizing the dispute, including the following details:

1. a brief description of the facts and points of law, including a list of the issues submitted to the mediator with a view to resolution;
2. a copy of the mediation agreement.

Each party shall cooperate in good faith with the mediator and shall guarantee him the freedom to perform his mandate to advance the mediation as expeditiously as possible. The mediator may make any suggestions he deems appropriate in this regard. He may meet with separately with one of the parties, if he deems it necessary to do so.

G. Role of the mediator

Article 9

The mediator shall promote the settlement of the issues in dispute in any manner that he believes to be appropriate. To achieve this, he will:

a. identify the issues in dispute;
b. facilitate discussion of the issues by the parties;
c. propose solutions.

However, the mediator may not impose a solution of the dispute on either party.

H. Confidentiality

Article 10

The mediator, the parties, their representatives and advisers, experts and any other persons present during the meetings between the parties may not disclose to any third party any information given to them during the mediation, unless required by law to do so.

Under their own responsibility, the parties undertake not to compel the mediator to divulge records, reports or other documents, or to testify in regard to the mediation in any arbitral or judicial proceedings.

Any information given by one party may be disclosed by the mediator to the other party only with the consent of the former.

No record of any kind shall be made of the meetings. All the written documents shall be returned to the party providing these upon termination of the mediation, and no copy thereof shall be retained.

The parties shall not rely on, or introduce as evidence in any arbitral or judicial proceedings:

views expressed or suggestions made by a party with respect to a possible settlement of the dispute;

admissions made by a party in the course of the mediation proceedings;

documents, notes or other information obtained during the mediation proceedings;

proposals made or views expressed by the mediator; or

the fact that a party had or had not indicated willingness to accept a proposal.

I. Termination

Article 11

Either party or the mediator may terminate the mediation at any time.

The mediation shall be terminated:

by the signing of a settlement by the parties;

by a written declaration of the mediator to the effect that further efforts at mediation are no longer worthwhile; or
by a written declaration of a party or the parties to the effect that the mediation proceedings are terminated.

J. Settlement

Article 12
The settlement is drawn up by the mediator and signed by the mediator and the parties.
Each party shall receive a copy thereof. In the event of any breach, a party may rely on such copy before an arbitral or judicial authority.
A copy of the settlement is submitted for inclusion in the records of the CAS Court Office.

K. Failure to settle

Article 13
The parties may have recourse to arbitration when a dispute has not been resolved by mediation, provided that an arbitration agreement or clause exists between the parties.
The arbitration clause may be included in the mediation agreement. In such a case, the expedited procedure provided for under Article 44, paragraph 4 of the Code of Sports-related Arbitration may be applied.
In the event of failure to resolve a dispute by mediation, the mediator shall not accept an appointment as an arbitrator in any arbitral proceedings concerning the parties involved in the same dispute.

L. Costs

Article 14
Each party shall pay the CAS Court Office the administrative fees fixed by the Court within the time limit provided in Article 4 of the present Rules. In the absence of such payment, the mediation proceedings will not be not set in motion.
The parties will pay their own mediation costs.
Unless otherwise agreed between the parties, the final costs of the mediation, which include the CAS fee, the fees of the mediator calculated on the basis of the CAS fee scale, a contribution towards the costs of the CAS, and the costs of witnesses, experts and interpreters, will be borne by the parties in equal measure.
The CAS Court Office may require the parties to deposit an equal amount as an advance towards the costs of the mediation.
Recommended clause for CAS mediation to be inserted in a contract

'Any dispute, any controversy or claim arising under, out of or relating to this contract and any subsequent amendments of or in relation to this contract, including, but not limited to, its formation, validity, binding effect, interpretation, performance, breach or termination, as well as noncontractual claims, shall be submitted to mediation in accordance with the CAS Mediation Rules. The language to be used in the mediation shall be ...'

Additional clause in the absence of settlement of the dispute

'If, and to the extent that, any such dispute has not been settled within 90 days of the commencement of the mediation, or if, before the expiration of the said period, either party fails to participate or continue to participate in the mediation, the dispute shall, upon the filing of a Request for Arbitration by either party, be referred to and finally settled by CAS arbitration pursuant to the Code of Sports-related Arbitration. When the circumstances so require, the mediator may, at his own discretion or at the request of a party, seek an extension of the time limit from the CAS President.'

APPENDIX VII
THE SDRP MEDIATION PROCEDURE

The following procedure ('the Mediation Procedure') (as amended by the SDRP from time to time) shall govern the mediation of any dispute and the parties shall he taken to have agreed that the mediation shall be conducted in accordance with the Mediation Procedure.

1. Mediation Procedure

1.1 The parties to a dispute or negotiation in question will attempt to settle it by mediation. Representatives of the parties including their advisers and the mediator will attend mediation meetings. All communications relating to, and at. the mediation will be without prejudice.

1.2 The representatives of the parties must have the necessary authority to settle the dispute. The procedure at the mediation will be determined by the mediator after consultation with those representatives.

1.3 The parties will appoint a mediator or mediators from the SDRP's list of mediators. If they cannot agree as to who should be appointed, the mediator shall be appointed by the Chairman of the SDRP.

2. Mediation Agreement

2.1 The parties, the mediator and the SDRP will enter into an agreement ('mediation Agreement') based on the SDRP Model Mediation Agreement ('the Model Agreement') in relation to the conduct of the mediation.

3. The Mediator

3.1 The mediator will:

    (a) attend any meetings with any or all of the parties preceding the mediation, if requested or if the mediator decides this is appropriate;

    (b) read before the mediation each Summary and all the Documents sent to him/her in accordance with paragraph 6.1 below;

    (c) determine the procedure (see paragraph 1.2 above);

    (d) assist the parties in drawing up any written settlement agreement;

    (e) abide by the terms of the Mediation Procedure, the Mediation Agreement and any code of conduct adopted from time to time ('the Code of Conduct').

3.2 The mediator and any member of a firm or company associated with the mediator will not act for any of the parties individually in connection with the dispute in any capacity either during the currency of the Mediation Agreement or at any time thereafter. The parties accept that in relation to the dispute neither the mediator nor the SDRP is an agent of, or acting in any capacity for, any of the parties. The parties and the mediator accept that the mediator is acting as an independent contractor and not as agent or employee of the SDPP.

4. The SDRP

4.1 The SDRP, in conjunction with the mediator, will make the necessary arrangements for the mediation including, as necessary:

    (a)   assisting the parties in appointing the mediator and in drawing up the Mediation Agreement;

    (b)   organising a suitable venue and dates;

    (c)   organising exchange of the Summaries and Documents;

    (d)   meeting with any or all of the representatives of both parties (and the mediator if he/she has been appointed) either together or separately, to discuss any matters or concerns relating to the mediation;

    (e)   general administration in relation to the mediation.

4.2   If a dispute is referred to the SDRP as a result of a mediation (or other Alternative Dispute Resolution ('ADR') clause in a contract, and if there is any issue with regard to the conduct of the mediation (including as to the appointment of the mediator) upon which the parties cannot agree within a reasonable time from the date of the notice initiating the mediation ('the ADR notice') the SDRP will, at the request of any party, decide the issue for the parties, having consulted with them.

5.   Other Participants

Each party wilt notify the other party or parties, through the SDRP, of the names of those people that it intends will be present on its behalf at the mediation. Each party, in signing the Mediation Agreement, will be deemed to be agreeing on behalf of both itself and all such persons to be bound by the confidentiality provisions of the Mediation Procedure.

6.   Exchange of Information

6.1   Each party will, simultaneously through the SDRP, exchange with the other and send to the mediator at least two weeks before the mediation or such other date as be agreed between the parties:

    (a)   a concise summary ('the Summary') stating its case in the dispute;

    (b)   copies of all documents to which it refers in the Summary and to which it may want to refer in the mediation ('the Documents').

In addition, each party may send to the mediator (through the SDRP and/or bring to the mediation further documentation which it wishes to disclose in confidence to the mediator but not to any other party, clearly stating in writing that such documentation is confidential to the mediator and the SDRP.

6.2   The parties will, through the SDRP, agree the maximum number of pages of each Summary and of the Documents and try to agree a joint set of documents from their respective Documents.

7.   The Mediation

7.1   No formal record or transcript of the mediation will be made.

7.2   If the parties are unable to reach a settlement in the negotiations at the mediation and only if all the parties request and the mediator agrees, the mediator will produce for the parties a non-binding written recommendation on terms of settlement. This wilt not attempt to anticipate what a court might order but will set out what the mediator suggests are appropriate settlement terms in all of the circumstances.

8. Settlement Agreement

Any settlement reached in the mediation will not be legally binding until it has been reduced to writing and signed by, or on behalf of, the parties.

9. Termination

Any of the parties may withdraw from the mediation at any time and shall immediately inform the mediator and the other representatives in writing. The mediation will terminate when:

(a)   a party withdraws from the mediation; or

(b)   a written settlement agreement is concluded; or

(c)   the mediator decides that continuing the mediation is unlikely to result in a settlement; or

(d)   the mediator decides he should retire for any of the reasons set out in the Code of Conduct.

10. Stay of Proceedings

Any litigation or arbitration in relation to the dispute may be commenced or continued notwithstanding the mediation unless the parties agree otherwise.

11. Confidentiality

11.1 Every person involved in the mediation will keep confidential and not use for any collateral or ulterior purpose:

(a)   the fact that the mediation is to take place or has taken place; and

(b)   all information, (whether given orally, in writing or otherwise), produced for, or arising in relation to, the mediation including the settlement agreement (if any) arising out of it,

except insofar as is necessary to implement and enforce any such settlement agreement.

11.2 All documents (which include anything upon which evidence is recorded including tapes and computer discs) or other information produced for, or arising in relation to, the mediation will be privileged and not be admissible as evidence or discoverable in any litigation or arbitration connected with the dispute except any documents or other information which would in any event have been admissible or discoverable in any such litigation or arbitration.

11.3 None of the parties to the Mediation Agreement will call the mediator or the SDPP (or any employee, consultant, officer or representative of the SDRP) as a witness, consultant, arbitrator or expert in any litigation or arbitration in relation to the dispute and the mediator and the SDRP will not voluntarily act in any such capacity without the written agreement of all the parties.

12. Fees, Expenses and Costs

12.1 Unless otherwise agreed, the SDRP's fees (which include the mediator's fees) and the other expenses of the mediation will be borne equally by the parties. Payment of these fees and expenses will be made to the SDRP in accordance with its fee schedule and terms and conditions of business.

12.2 Unless otherwise agreed, each party will bear its own costs and expenses of its partici-
     pation in the mediation.

13. Waiver of Liability

Neither the mediator nor the SDRP shall be liable to the parties for any act or omission in
connection with the services provided by them in, or in relation to, the mediation, unless the
act or omission is fraudulent or involves wilful misconduct.

APPENDIX VIII
THE SDRP MODEL MEDIATION AGREEMENT

Date:

Parties

1:    [details to be provided]

('Party A')

2:    [details to be provided]

('Party B')

(jointly 'the Parties')

3:    [Mediator to be agreed] c/o SDRP, Francis House, Francis Street, London SW1P 1DE
      ('the Mediator')

4:    **Sports Dispute Resolution Panel Limited**, Francis House, Francis Street, London
      SW1P 1DE
      ('SDRP')

Dispute ('the Dispute')

[Description of dispute]

Participation in the Mediation

1.   The Parties will attempt to settle the Dispute by mediation ('the Mediation'). The
      SDRP Model Mediation Procedure ('the Mediation Procedure') as varied by this
      agreement will determine the conduct of the Mediation and is incorporated into, and
      forms part of, this agreement.

The Mediator

2.   The Mediator will be:

The Representatives

3.   The representatives for each of the Parties at the Mediation will be:

Party A:

Party B:

(jointly 'the Representatives')

A Party will immediately notify the other Party, SDRP and the Mediator of any change to the above.

4. Each Representative in signing this agreement is deemed to be agreeing to the provisions of this agreement on behalf of the Party he/she represents and all other persons present on that Party's behalf at the Mediation.

Other Participants

5. The following, in addition to the Representatives, will be present on behalf of each of the Parties at the Mediation:

Party A:

Party B:

A Party will immediately notify the other Party, SDRP and the Mediator of any change to the above.

Place and Time

6. The Mediation will take place at

At:
On:
Starting at:

Confidentiality

7. Each Representative in signing this agreement is deemed to be agreeing to the confidentiality provisions of the Mediation Procedure (paragraph 11) on behalf of the Party he/she represents and all other persons present on behalf of that Party at the Mediation.

Amendments to Mediation Procedure

8. Paragraph 12.1 – Fees and expenses
    As set out in paragraph 12.1 of the Mediation Procedure, the fees and other expenses will be borne equally by the Parties.

Law and Jurisdiction

9. This agreement shall be governed by, construed and take effect in accordance with
    English law. The courts of England and Wales shall have exclusive jurisdiction to settle
    any claim, dispute or matter of difference which may arise out of or in connection with
    the mediation.

Signed

(On behalf of Party A)

(On behalf of Party B)

(The Mediator)

(On behalf of SDRP)

APPENDIX IX
THE CEDR CODE OF CONDUCT FOR MEDIATORS AND OTHER THIRD PARTY NEUTRALS

Introduction

1. This Code applies to any person who acts as a neutral third party ('the Mediator') in an ADR procedure (such as mediation or executive tribunal – 'Mediation') under the auspices of the Centre for Effective Dispute Resolution ('CEDR Solve').

Impartiality and conflict of interest

2. The Mediator will at all times act, and endeavour to be seen to act, fairly and with complete impartiality towards the Parties in the Mediation without any bias in favour of any Party or any discrimination against any Party.

3. Any matter of which the Mediator is aware, which could be regarded as involving a conflict of interest (whether apparent, potential or actual) in the Mediation, will be disclosed to the Parties. This disclosure will be made in writing to all the Parties as soon as the Mediator becomes aware of it, whether the matter occurs prior to or during the Mediation. In these circumstances the Mediator will not act (or continue to act) in the Mediation unless all the Parties specifically acknowledge the disclosure and agree, in writing, to the Mediator acting or continuing to act as Mediator.

4. Information of the type which the Mediator should disclose includes:
   - having acted in any capacity for any of the Parties (other than as Mediator in other ADR procedures);
   - the Mediator's firm (if applicable) having acted in any capacity for any of the Parties;
   - having any financial or other interest (whether direct or indirect) in any of the Parties or in the subject matter or outcome of the Mediation; or
   - having any confidential information about any of the Parties or in the subject matter of the Mediation.

5. The Mediator (and any member of the Mediator's firm or company) will not act for any of the Parties individually in connection with the dispute which is the subject of the Mediation white acting as the Mediator or at any time thereafter, without the written consent of alt the other Parties.

Confidentiality

6. Subject to paragraph 8 below, the Mediator will keep confidential and not use for any collateral or ulterior purpose:
   - the fact that a mediation is to take place or has taken place; and
   - all information (whether given orally, in writing or otherwise) arising out of, or in connection with, the Mediation, including the fact of any settlement and its terms.

7. Subject to paragraph 8 below, if the Mediator is given information by any Party which is implicitly confidential or is expressly stated to be confidential (and which is not already public), the Mediator shall maintain the confidentiality of that information from all other Parties, except to the extent that disclosure has been specifically authorised.

8. The duty of confidentiality in paragraphs 6 and 7 above will not apply if, and to the extent that:
    –   all parties consent to disclosure;
    –   the Mediator is required under the general law to make disclosure;
    –   the Mediator reasonably considers that there is serious risk of significant harm to the life or safety of any person if the information in question is not disclosed; or
    –   the Mediator wishes to seek guidance in confidence from any senior officer of CEDR Solve on any ethical or other serious question arising out of the Mediation.

Commitment and availability
9. Before accepting an appointment, the Mediator must be satisfied that he/she has time available to ensure that the Mediation can proceed in an expeditious manner.

Fees
10. CEDR Solve will inform the Parties before the Mediation begins of the fees and expenses which wilt be charged for the Mediation or, if not accurately known at that stage, of the basis of charging and will not make any additional charges other than in exceptional circumstances.

Parties' agreement
11. The Mediator will act in accordance with the agreement (whether written or oral) made between the Parties in relation to the Mediation ('the Mediation Agreement') (except where to do so would cause a breach of this Code) and will use his/her best endeavours to ensure that the Mediation proceeds in accordance with the terms of the Mediation Agreement.

Insurance
12. The Mediator will take out professional indemnity insurance in an adequate amount with a responsible insurer.

Withdrawal of Mediator
13. The Mediator wilt withdraw from the Mediation if he/she:
    –   is requested to do so by any of the Parties (unless the Parties have agreed to a procedure involving binding ADR);
    –   is in breach of this Code; or
    –   is required by the Parties to do something which would be in material breach of this Code.

14. The Mediator may withdraw form the Mediation at his/her own discretion if:
    –   any of the Parties is acting in breach of the Mediation Agreement;

- – any of the Parties is, in the Mediator's opinion, acting in an unconscionable or criminal manner;
- – the Mediator decides that continuing the mediation is unlikely to result in a settlement; or
- – any of the Parties alleges that the Mediator is in material breach of this code.

APPENDIX X
THE SDRP ADVISORY OPINION RULES

The following Rules (amended by the SDRP from time to time) shall govern the giving of an advisory opinion ('the Opinion') and the party or parties shall be taken to have agreed that the Opinion shall be given in accordance with these Rules.

1. The party or parties who wish to submit a request for an Opinion must sign an agreement with the SDRP in relation to costs before the SDRP will consider a request for an Opinion.

2. The request for an Opinion shall be in the SDRP's standard form and shall include:
    (a) the name of the party or parties requesting the Opinion,
    (b) copies of any documents which may be relevant to or have a bearing or the Opinion, and
    (c) a brief statement describing the nature and circumstances and background to the request and why it is requested.

3. The party or parties shall decide how many and which of the Arbitrators shall consider the request and give the Opinion and, if they fail to do so or in the absence of agreement, the Chairman of the SDRP shall so decide and shall notify the party or parties who made the request of his choice.

4. The Arbitrator(s) selected shall have absolute discretion to decide what documents and further information shall be supplied to the Arbitrator(s) and may consult with the party making the request or with any other party or relevant person or body before issuing an Opinion.

5. Any costs relating to the Opinion as agreed with the SDRP, must be paid in full to the SDRP before the Opinion will be issued.

6. The Arbitrator(s) selected to give the Opinion shall have absolute discretion as to the form, length and content of the Opinion.

7. The Opinion shall not constitute a binding arbitral award.

APPENDIX XI
NSDC STANDARD MEDIATION AGREEMENT

MEDIATION AGREEMENT

This Agreement is made the

between:

and

and

(Mediator)

RECITALS

A.   A Dispute has arisen between ... in relation to ... **(Dispute)**.

B.   The parties have requested the Mediator to assist in the resolution of the Dispute.

C.   The Mediator has agreed on the terms and conditions of this Agreement to assist the parties to resolve the Dispute if possible.

OPERATIVE PROVISIONS

1.   The parties appoint the Mediator, and the Mediator accepts the appointment, to mediate the Dispute (**Mediation**) in accordance with the terms of this Agreement.

2.
   2.1. The Mediator will assist the parties to explore options for and, if possible, to achieve a resolution of the Dispute by agreement between them.
   2.2. The Mediator will not make decisions for a party or impose a solution on the parties.

3.   The Mediator will not, unless the parties agree in writing to the contrary, obtain from any independent person advice or an opinion as to any aspect of the Dispute, and if the parties do so agree then only from such personal persons as may be agreed by the party in writing.

4.   The Mediator acknowledges that he has disclosed to the parties to the best of his knowledge any prior dealings he has had with either of them and any interest he has in the Dispute.

5.   The parties must co-operate in good faith with the Mediator and each other during the Mediation.

6.   The Mediator may meet as frequently as the Mediator deems appropriate, with the parties together or with a party alone and in the latter case the Mediator need not disclose the meeting to the other party.

7.   Information, whether oral or written disclosed to the Mediator by a party in the absence of the other party will not be able to be disclosed by the Mediator to the other party unless the party from whom that information was received authorises the Mediator to disclose such information.

8.   The parties and the Mediator agree in relation to all confidential information disclosed to them during the Mediation, including the preliminary steps:
     (a)   To keep that information confidential.
     (b)   Not to disclose that information except to a party or a representative of that party participating in the Mediation unless compelled by law to do so.
     (c)   Not to use that information for a purpose other than the Mediation.

9.

     9.1. The parties and the Mediator agree that the following will be privileged and will not be disclosed in or relied upon or be the subject of a subpoena to give evidence or to produce documents in any arbitral or judicial proceedings in respect of the Dispute or any other:
           (a)   any settlement proposal, whether made by a party or the Mediator;
           (b)   the willingness of a party to consider any such proposal;
           (c)   any admission or concession made by a party;
           (d)   any statement or document made by the Mediator.

     9.2. The parties and the Mediator agree that any statements or comments whether written or oral, made or used by them or their representatives in preparation for or in the course of the Mediation shall not be relied upon to found or maintain any action for deformation, liable, slander or any related complaint and this document may be pleaded as a bar to any such action.

10. The Mediator will not be liable to a party for any act or omission made by him in the performance or purported performance of his obligation in this Agreement.

11. To the extent permitted by law the parties jointly and severally release and discharge the Mediator from all liability of any kind whatsoever arising from the appointment of the Mediator or the conduct of the Mediation and agree to indemnify and keep indemnified the Mediator against all claims except in the case of fraud by the Mediator,

arising from the performance or purported performance of his obligations under this Agreement.

EXECUTED as an Agreement on 2002

Signed for and on behalf of   ....

Signed for and on behalf of   ....

Signed by the Mediator   ....

APPENDIX XII
THE NSDC ACCREDITATION POLICY AND APPLICATION FORM

Accreditation Policy

NSDC is continually updating its list of accredited mediators, arbitrators and tribunal members. It is an aim of NSDC to enable quick and effective ADR solutions by having accredited personnel in each capital city and principal regional centre throughout Australia.

NSDC has adopted the following accreditation policy. Persons who become accredited are required to pay a $50 accreditation fee to NSDC to help meet the administrative costs of the scheme, which is refunded to any accredited person acting in an NSDC matter on a *pro bono* basis. If you would like to be accredited with the NSDC, an application form is attached.

Accredited Mediators

In determining whether to accredit any person as a mediator, the NSDC will base its decision on the overall qualifications and experience of the applicant including, without limitation:

(a) whether the applicant has undertaken a course in mediation of a length and quality approved by the Board or Registrar;
(b) the number of mediations that the applicant has conducted;
(c) references of parties who have used the applicant as a mediator;
(d) the professional experience and qualifications of the applicant;
(e) whether the applicant has a good knowledge and understanding of the Australian Sports Industry; and
(f) whether the applicant currently has, or is prepared to take out, a policy of professional indemnity insurance and keep current whilst the applicant remains accredited.

An applicant does not need to have extensive experience as a mediator to be accredited. For example, a person who has recently completed a mediation course, may be accredited for simpler or smaller disputes. Similarly, it may not be necessary for a person to have undertaken a mediation course if they have had extensive experience as a mediator and provide appropriate references.

Accredited Arbitrators

In determining whether to accredit any person as an arbitrator, the NSDC will base its decision on the overall qualifications and experience of the applicant including, without limitation:

(a) whether the applicant has undertaken a course in arbitration of a length and quality approved by the Board or Registrar;

(b)   the number of arbitrations that the applicant has conducted;
(c)   references of parties who have sat with or used the applicant as an arbitrator;
(d)   the professional experience, specialisation and qualifications of the applicant;
(e)   whether the applicant has a good working knowledge of the rules of natural justice and procedural fairness;
(f)   whether the applicant has a good knowledge and understanding of the Australian Sports Industry; and
(g)   whether the applicant currently has, or is prepared to take out, a policy of professional indemnity insurance and keep current whilst the applicant remains accredited.

An applicant does not need to have extensive experience as an arbitrator to be accredited. For example, a person who has recently completed an arbitration course, may be accredited but may only be nominated for the simpler or smaller disputes.

It may be appropriate to accredit a person as an arbitrator in a particular field – eg., Contract, personal injury, drugs etc.

Accredited Tribunal Members

In determining whether to accredit any person as a Tribunal member, the NSDC will base its decision on the overall qualifications and experience of the applicant including, without limitation:

(a)   whether the applicant has a good working knowledge of the rules of natural justice and procedural fairness;
(b)   the number of Tribunal hearings that the applicant has conducted;
(c)   references of parties who have appeared with or before the applicant sifting as a Tribunal member;
(d)   the professional experience and qualifications of the applicant;
(e)   whether the applicant has a good knowledge and understanding of the Australian Sports Industry; and
(f)   whether the applicant currently has, or is prepared to take out, a policy of professional indemnity insurance and keep current whilst the applicant remains accredited.

An applicant does not have to have extensive experience as a Tribunal member to be accredited. For example, a person who has a good knowledge of the laws of natural justice and an understanding of a particular sport or subject may be accredited to sit as a member of a Tribunal panel.

Any person who is interested in becoming accredited by NSDC should complete the attached form and return it to the National Sports Dispute Centre at 233 Macquarie Street, Sydney 2000.

Accreditation Application Form

Name: _____

Business
Address: _____

_____

Home Address: _____

_____

Phone number: (work)   _____
                       (home)   _____
                       (mobile) _____

Fax number: (work)   _____
                       (home)   _____

Email: _____

Occupation: _____

Qualifications: _____   _____

_____

Application is for accreditation in
(please select from the list below):   **Please tick if you have experience:**

❏ Mediation   ❏ No. of mediations conducted

❏ Arbitration   ❏ No. of arbitrations conducted

❏ Tribunal Member   ❏ No. of tribunals conducted

Specify qualifications in relevant area of accreditation
(please include copies of any certificates etc):

_____
_____
_____
_____

Specify practical experience in relevant area of accreditation: (if not enough room please attach information)

_____
_____
_____
_____

Areas of interest in sports law disputes (please select from list below):

❑   Constitutional disputes   ❑   Contract disputes
❑   Disciplinary proceedings   ❑   Domestic tribunals
❑   Drugs   ❑   Employment disputes
❑   Selection disputes   ❑   Sponsorship disputes
❑   Broadcasting
❑   Other (please specify):

_____

Specify practical experience in relevant areas of interest:

_____
_____
_____
_____

Fees: Are you prepared to provide services on a voluntary basis?

_____
_____
_____

What fees would you otherwise propose to charge?

_____
_____
_____

Please specify two referees:

_____
_____
_____

APPENDIX XIII
NEW ARTICLE 63 OF THE FIFA STATUTES –
THE FIFA FOOTBALL ARBITRATION TRIBUNAL RULES

Creation of an arbitration system
1. The International Court for Football Arbitration (ICFA) is a foundation created by the Congress and is responsible for
    –   establishing and maintaining an Arbitration Tribunal for Football (ATF)
    –   executing arbitration regulations to be observed by ATF
    –   promoting conciliatory options for resolving football disputes.
    The Executive Committee will enact rules for funding ICFA so as to guarantee its independence.

ATF ruling as the sole authority
2. Only ATF is authorised to settle any disputes involving FIFA, the confederations, national associations, leagues, clubs, players, officials and licensed agents for which the value involved in the litigation is the same as or more than a specified value fixed from time to time by the Congress.
    ATF is also responsible for settling disputes arising between a third party and any of the foregoing entities or persons provided they are covered by an arbitration agreement.

ATF ruling as a board of appeal
3. ATF is responsible for dealing with appeals against decisions of the last instance, after all previous stages of appeal provided for at FIFA, confederation, national association, league or club level have been exhausted.
    ATF does not, however, hear appeals on:
    –   violations of the Laws of the Game
    –   suspensions of up to four matches.

Proceedings
4. The ATF proceedings are subject to the provisions of the ATF Regulations.

Funding
5. FIFA, acting as a fund raising agent, will ensure the funding required for ICFA to function properly by levying an amount to be determined by the FIFA Executive Committee on earnings from the marketing of FIFA World CupJ television and marketing rights.

Observance of arbitration Ordinary courts of law
6. The confederations, national associations and leagues shall recognise ATF as the supreme jurisdictional authority. They shall agree to take every precaution to ensure that their members, players and officials observe the ATF procedure for arbitration. The same obligation applies to licensed agents.

Recourse to ordinary courts of law is prohibited, unless specifically provided for in FIFA Regulations.

The national associations shall, in order to give effect to the foregoing, insert a clause in their statutes by which their clubs and members shall not be permitted to take a dispute to courts of law but shall be required to submit any disagreement to the jurisdiction of the association or to ATF.

Compliance with FIFA's decisions

7. The confederations, national associations and leagues shall agree to comply fully with any decisions passed by the authorities responsible at FIFA which according to these Statutes are final and not subject to the right of appeal. They shall agree to take every precaution to ensure that their members, players and officials comply with these decisions. The same obligation applies to licensed agents.

Sanctions

8. Any breach of the aforementioned provisions shall be sanctioned in accordance with the FIFA List of Disciplinary Measures (cf. Art. 44, par. 4). In particular, any club that contravenes the terms outlined above may be sanctioned by being suspended from all international activity (official competitions and friendly matches) in addition to receiving a ban on all international matches (involving national associations and clubs) played in its stadium'.

APPENDIX XIV
THE FIFA REGULATIONS FOR THE STATUS AND TRANSFER OF PLAYERS

Chapter XIV
Dispute resolution, disciplinary and arbitration system

Art. 42

1. Without prejudice to the right of any player or club to seek redress before a civil court in disputes between clubs and players, a dispute resolution and arbitration system shall be established, which shall consist of the following elements:

   (a) Conciliation facilities, through which a low-cost, speedy, confidential and informal resolution of any dispute will be explored with the parties at their request by an independent mediator. Such mediation will not be a precondition to, nor suspend the resolution of the dispute according to formal mechanisms described in (b).

   (b) (i) The triggering elements of the dispute (i.e. whether a contract was breached, with or without just cause, or sporting just cause), will be decided by the Dispute Resolution Chamber of the FIFA Players' Status Committee or, if the parties have expressed a preference in a written agreement, or it is provided for by collective bargain agreement, by a national sports arbitration tribunal composed of members chosen in equal numbers by players and clubs, as well as an independent chairman. This part of the dispute must be decided within 30 days after the date on which the dispute has been submitted to the parties' tribunal of choice.

   (ii) If the decision reached pursuant to (i) is that a contract has been breached without just cause or sporting just cause, the Dispute Resolution Chamber shall decide within 30 days whether the sports sanctions or disciplinary measures which it may impose pursuant to Art. 23 shall be imposed. This decision shall be reasoned, also in respect of the findings made pursuant to (b)(i), and can be appealed against pursuant to (c).

   (iii) Within the period specified in (ii), or in complex cases within 60 days, the Dispute Resolution Chamber shall decide any other issues related to a contractual breach (in particular, financial compensation). This decision shall be reasoned, and can be appealed against pursuant to (c).

   (iv) In addition, the Dispute Resolution Chamber may review disputes concerning training compensation fees and shall have discretion to adjust the training fee if it is clearly disproportionate to the case under review. Furthermore, the Dispute Resolution Chamber can impose disciplinary measures on the basis of Art. 34, par. 4 of the FIFA Statutes where these regulations or the Application Regulations so provide, or pursuant to specific written mandate by the FIFA Players' Status Committee. The Dispute Resolution Chamber shall rule within 60 days after the date on which a case has been submitted to it by one of the parties to the dispute (with the exception of those disciplinary measures referred to in Art. 23, which are covered by (ii). These decisions shall be reasoned, and can be appealed against pursuant to (c).

(v)   The Dispute Resolution Chamber may award financial compensation and/or impose disciplinary measures on the club concerned, if it is established pursuant to (b)(i) that a player terminated his contract with this club with just cause or sporting just cause and the player, as a result of the procedural provisions in these regulations, has been suspended from playing in the national championship of his new club. The Chamber shall rule within 60 days after the date on which a case has been submitted to it by the player concerned. This decision shall be reasoned, and can be appealed against pursuant to (c).

(vi)   All other measures provided for in these regulations will be taken by the FIFA Players' Status Committee, with the exception of those measures which are under the jurisdiction of the Disciplinary Committee.

(vii) All rulings taken pursuant to these regulations shall be published.

c.   Appeals contemplated in (b) will be brought before a chamber of the Arbitration Tribunal for Football (TAF) provided for under Art. 63 of the FIFA Statutes, irrespective of the severity of any sanction or the amount of any financial award. This chamber of the Arbitration Tribunal for Football (TAF) shall be composed of members chosen in equal numbers by players and clubs and with an independent chairman, in compliance with the principles of the New York Convention of 1958. The tribunal must rule within 60 days or, in exceptional and particularly complex cases, within 90 days, after the date on which a case decided by the Dispute Resolution Chamber pursuant to (b) has been submitted to it. These appeals shall not have a suspensive effect. The tribunal's rulings shall be published.

2.   The conciliation facilities envisaged under 1(a) above shall be supplied by FIFA. The Dispute Resolution Chamber provided for under 1 (b) above shall be instituted in the FIFA Players' Status Committee. The rules of procedure of the Dispute Resolution Chamber are set out in the Application Regulations and may be reviewed from time to time by the FIFA Players' Status Committee.

3.   Before reaching its decision on the matters covered under l(b) above, the Dispute Resolution Chamber shall ask the national association which held the player's registration before the dispute arose to give its opinion.

Art. 43

The dispute resolution system and arbitration system shall take account of all relevant arrangements, laws and/or collective bargaining agreements, which exist at national level, as welt as the specificity of sport.

Art. 44

The FIFA Players' Status Committee shall not address any dispute under these regulations if more than two years have elapsed since the facts reading to the dispute arose.

REGULATIONS GOVERNING THE APPLICATION OF THE REGULATIONS FOR THE STATUS AND TRANSFER OF PLAYERS

Chapter VII
Rules and procedures for dispute resolution

Art. 15 – Composition of the Dispute Resolution Chamber
1. The Chairman of the Player's Status Committee shall chair the Dispute Resolution Chamber.
2. The Dispute Resolution Chamber shall be composed of representatives of players and clubs in equal number.
3. The members of the Dispute Resolution Chamber shall be designated by the Executive Committee at the proposal of the President of FIFA based upon nominations from representative players' associations and clubs and/or leagues.

Art. 16 – Procedure before the Dispute Resolution Chamber
1. The Dispute Resolution Chamber of the FIFA Players' Status Committee shall review disputes coming under its jurisdiction pursuant to Art. 42 of the FIFA Regulations for the Status and Transfer of Players at the request of one of the parties to the dispute. Failure by one of the parties to appear before the Dispute Resolution Chamber does not impact on the jurisdiction of the Chamber, which shall adjudicate on the dispute based on all the facts known to it.
2. In order to submit a dispute to the Dispute Resolution Chamber, a party shall file a written request with the FIFA general secretariat. Such a request must contain the following elements:
    (a) the complainant's name and other relevant details,
    (b) if the complainant is not a natural person, a copy of its statutes and relevant certificates of incorporation as well as proof that the person filing the request on behalf of the complainant is entitled to represent it in legal proceedings,
    (c) the name and other relevant details of the legal representative assisting the complainant, if any,
    (d) the name and other relevant details of other clubs and/or players involved in the dispute, including e.g. the club accused of having induced a breach of contract.
    (e) a summary presentation of the relevant factual, legal and regulatory considerations.
    (f) ruling of any national arbitration tribunal or national court regarding this dispute.
    In addition, the request shall be accompanied by a copy of all the relevant documents pertaining to the dispute.
3. The FIFA Players' Status Committee shall issue detailed internal rules of procedure for the Dispute Resolution Chamber. These rules of procedure shall ensure that the following principles be observed:
    (a) The Dispute Resolution Chamber shall afford the parties the opportunity to make their views known in full knowledge of the relevant facts of the case.
    (b) Parties shall have the opportunity to make written observations and their oral explanations may be heard, if deemed necessary by the Dispute Resolution Chamber.

(c) Parties shall be given enough time to prepare their defence, having due regard to the need for a speedy resolution within the deadlines provided for in Art. 42 of the FIFA Regulations for the Status and Transfer of Players.

(d) Parties will be able to rely on professional legal assistance.

(e) Hearings before the Dispute Resolution Chamber shall not be open to the public.

(f) Decisions by the Dispute Resolution Chamber shall be published promptly, in extract or in full.

4. The Dispute Resolution Chamber shall send a copy of all the relevant documents pertaining to the dispute to the national association which held the registration of the player involved in the dispute when the dispute arose and set a deadline within which the association may send its written observations on the dispute. A copy of these observations shall be forwarded to the parties to the dispute.

Art. 17 – Mediation

1. At the request of a party to a dispute, the FIFA general secretariat shall appoint an independent mediator which shall contact the parties to attempt mediation.

2. Mediation attempts shall not suspend the procedure before the Dispute Resolution Chamber, unless all the parties to the dispute agree to such suspension.

APPENDIX XV
AMERICAN ARBITRATION ASSOCIATION
INTERNATIONAL ARBITRATION AND MEDIATION RULES

Commercial Dispute Resolution Procedures (Including Mediation and Arbitration Rules)
As Amended and Effective on September 1, 2000

Commercial Mediation Rules
M-1 Agreement of Parties
Whenever, by stipulation or in their contract, the parties have provided for mediation or conciliation of existing or future disputes under the auspices of the American Arbitration Association (AAA) or under these rules, they shall be deemed to have made these rules, as amended and in effect as of the date of the submission of the dispute, a part of their agreement.

M-2 Initiation of Mediation
Any party or parties to a dispute may initiate mediation by filing with the AAA a submission to mediation or a written request for mediation pursuant to these rules, together with the appropriate Filing Fee (page 10). Where there is no submission to mediation or contract providing for mediation, a party may request the AAA to invite another party to join in a submission to mediation. Upon receipt of such a request, the AAA will contact the other parties involved in the dispute and attempt to obtain a submission to mediation.

M-3 Requests for Mediation
A request for mediation shall contain a brief statement of the nature of the dispute and the names, addresses, and telephone numbers of all parties to the dispute and those who will represent them, if any, in the mediation. The initiating party shall simultaneously file two copies of the request with the AAA and one copy with every other party to the dispute.

M-4 Appointment of the Mediator
Upon receipt of a request for mediation, the AAA will appoint a qualified mediator to serve. Normally, a single mediator will be appointed unless the parties agree otherwise or the AAA determines otherwise. If the agreement of the parties names a mediator or specifies a method of appointing a mediator, that designation or method shall be followed.

M-5 Qualifications of the Mediator
No person shall serve as a mediator in any dispute in which that person has any financial or personal interest in the result of the mediation, except by the written consent of all parties. Prior to accepting an appointment, the prospective mediator shall disclose any circumstance likely to create a presumption of bias or prevent a prompt meeting with the parties. Upon receipt of such information, the AAA shall either replace the mediator or immediately communicate the information to the parties for their comments. In the event that the parties disagree as to whether the mediator shall serve, the AAA will appoint another mediator. The

AAA is authorized to appoint another mediator if the appointed mediator is unable to serve promptly.

M-6 Vacancies
If any mediator shall become unwilling or unable to serve, the AAA will appoint another mediator, unless the parties agree otherwise.

M-7 Representation
Any party may be represented by persons of the party's choice. The names and addresses of such persons shall be communicated in writing to all parties and to the AAA.

M-8 Date, Time, and Place of Mediation
The mediator shall fix the date and the time of each mediation session. The mediation shall be held at the appropriate regional office of the AAA, or at any other convenient location agreeable to the mediator and the parties, as the mediator shall determine.

M-9 Identification of Matters in Dispute
At least ten days prior to the first scheduled mediation session, each party shall provide the mediator with a brief memorandum setting forth its position with regard to the issues that need to be resolved. At the discretion of the mediator, such memoranda may be mutually exchanged by the parties.

At the first session, the parties will be expected to produce all information reasonably required for the mediator to understand the issues presented.

The mediator may require any party to supplement such information.

M-10 Authority of the Mediator
The mediator does not have the authority to impose a settlement on the parties but will attempt to help them reach a satisfactory resolution of their dispute. The mediator is authorized to conduct joint and separate meetings with the parties and to make oral and written recommendations for settlement. Whenever necessary, the mediator may also obtain expert advice concerning technical aspects of the dispute, provided that the parties agree and assume the expenses of obtaining such advice. Arrangements for obtaining such advice shall be made by the mediator or the parties, as the mediator shall determine.

The mediator is authorized to end the mediation whenever, in the judgment of the mediator, further efforts at mediation would not contribute to a resolution of the dispute between the parties.

M-11 Privacy
Mediation sessions are private. The parties and their representatives may attend mediation sessions. Other persons may attend only with the permission of the parties and with the consent of the mediator.

M-12 Confidentiality
Confidential information disclosed to a mediator by the parties or by witnesses in the course of the mediation shall not be divulged by the mediator. All records, reports, or other documents received by a mediator while serving in that capacity shall be confidential. The

mediator shall not be compelled to divulge such records or to testify in regard to the mediation in any adversary proceeding or judicial forum.

The parties shall maintain the confidentiality of the mediation and shall not rely on, or introduce as evidence in any arbitral, judicial, or other proceeding:

a. views expressed or suggestions made by another party with respect to a possible settlement of the dispute;

b. admissions made by another party in the course of the mediation proceedings;

c. proposals made or views expressed by the mediator; or

d. the fact that another party had or had not indicated willingness to accept a proposal for settlement made by the mediator.

M-13 No Stenographic Record
There shall be no stenographic record of the mediation process.

M-14 Termination of Mediation
The mediation shall be terminated:

a. by the execution of a settlement agreement by the parties;

b. by a written declaration of the mediator to the effect that further efforts at mediation are no longer worthwhile; or

c. by a written declaration of a party or parties to the effect that the mediation proceedings are terminated.

M-15 Exclusion of Liability
Neither the AAA nor any mediator is a necessary party in judicial proceedings relating to the mediation.

Neither the AAA nor any mediator shall be liable to any party for any act or omission in connection with any mediation conducted under these rules.

M-16 Interpretation and Application of Rules
The mediator shall interpret and apply these rules insofar as they relate to the mediator's duties and responsibilities. All other rules shall be interpreted and applied by the AAA.

M-17 Expenses
The expenses of witnesses for either side shall be paid by the party producing such witnesses. All other expenses of the mediation, including required travelling and other expenses of the mediator and representatives of the AAA, and the expenses of any witness and the cost of any proofs or expert advice produced at the direct request of the mediator, shall be borne equally by the parties unless they agree otherwise.

Administrative Fees

The nonrefundable case set-up fee is $150 per party. An AAA administrative fee of $75 per hour of conference time spent by the mediator is also charged. The $150 case set-up fees will be applied toward the AAA administrative fee. In addition, the parties are responsible for compensating the mediator at his or her published rate, for conference and study time (hourly or per diem).

All expenses are generally borne equally by the parties. The parties may adjust this arrangement by agreement.

Before the commencement of the mediation, the AAA shall estimate anticipated total expenses. Each party shall pay its portion of that amount as per the agreed upon arrangement. When the mediation has terminated, the AAA shall render an accounting and return any unexpended balance to the parties.

COMMERCIAL ARBITRATION RULES

R-1 Agreement of Parties*

The parties shall be deemed to have made these rules a part of their arbitration agreement whenever they have provided for arbitration by the American Arbitration Association (hereinafter AAA) under its Commercial Arbitration Rules or for arbitration by the AAA of a domestic commercial dispute without specifying particular rules. These rules and any amendment of them shall apply in the form in effect at the time the demand for arbitration or submission agreement is received by the AAA. The parties, by written agreement, may vary the procedures set forth in these rules.

*A dispute arising out of a contract, agreement or plan between a consumer and a business will be administered in accordance with the AAA's Supplementary Procedures for Consumer-Related Disputes, unless the parties agree otherwise after the commencement of the arbitration. Consumers are not prohibited from seeking relief in a small claims court for disputes or claims within the scope of its jurisdiction, even in consumer arbitration cases filed by the business.

R-2 AAA and Delegation of Duties

When parties agree to arbitrate under these rules, or when they provide for arbitration by the AAA and an arbitration is initiated under these rules, they thereby authorize the AAA to administer the arbitration. The authority and duties of the AAA are prescribed in the agreement of the parties and in these rules, and may be carried out through such of the AAA's representatives as it may direct. The AAA may, in its discretion, assign the administration of an arbitration to any of its offices.

R-3 National Panel of Arbitrators

The AAA shall establish and maintain a National Panel of Commercial Arbitrators and shall appoint arbitrators as provided in these rules. The term 'arbitrator' in these rules refers to the arbitration panel, whether composed of one or more arbitrators and whether the arbitrators are neutral or party-appointed.

R-4 Initiation under an Arbitration Provision in a Contract

(a) Arbitration under an arbitration provision in a contract shall be initiated in the following manner:

i. The initiating party (the 'claimant') shall, within the time period, if any, specified in the contract(s), give to the other party (the 'respondent') written notice of its intention to arbitrate (the 'demand'), which demand shall contain a statement setting forth the nature of the dispute, the names and addresses of all other parties, the amount involved, if any, the remedy sought, and the hearing locale requested.

ii. The claimant shall file at any office of the AAA two copies of the demand and two copies of the arbitration provisions of the contract, together with the appropriate filing fee as provided in the schedule included with these rules.

iii. The AAA shall confirm notice of such filing to the parties.

(b) A respondent may file an answering statement in duplicate with the AAA within 15 days after confirmation of notice of filing of the demand is sent by the AAA. The respondent shall, at the time of any such filing, send a copy of the answering statement to the claimant. If a counterclaim is asserted, it shall contain a statement setting forth the nature of the counterclaim, the amount involved, if any, and the remedy sought. If a counterclaim is made, the party making the counterclaim shall forward to the AAA with the answering statement the appropriate fee provided in the schedule included with these rules.

(c) If no answering statement is filed within the stated time, respondent will be deemed to deny the claim. Failure to file an answering statement shall not operate to delay the arbitration.

(d) When filing any statement pursuant to this section, the parties are encouraged to provide descriptions of their claims in sufficient detail to make the circumstances of the dispute clear to the arbitrator.

R-5 Initiation under a Submission

Parties to any existing dispute may commence an arbitration under these rules by filing at any office of the AAA two copies of a written submission to arbitrate under these rules, signed by the parties. It shall contain a statement of the nature of the dispute, the names and addresses of all parties, any claims and counterclaims, the amount involved, if any, the remedy sought, and the hearing locale requested, together with the appropriate filing fee as provided in the schedule included with these rules. Unless the parties state otherwise in the submission, all claims and counterclaims will be deemed to be denied by the other party.

R-6 Changes of Claim

After filing of a claim, if either party desires to make any new or different claim or counterclaim, it shall be made in writing and filed with the AAA. The party asserting such a claim or counterclaim shall provide a copy to the other party, who shall have 15 days from the date of such transmission within which to file an answering statement with the AAA. After the arbitrator is appointed, however, no new or different claim may be submitted except with the arbitrator's consent.

R-7 Applicable Procedures

Unless the parties or the AAA in its discretion determines otherwise, the Expedited Procedures shall be applied in any case where no disclosed claim or counterclaim exceeds $75,000, exclusive of interest and arbitration costs. Parties may also agree to use the Expedited Procedures in cases involving claims in excess of $75,000. The Expedited Procedures shall be applied as described in Sections E-1 through E-10 of these rules, in addition to any other portion of these rules that is not in conflict with the Expedited Procedures. All other cases shall be administered in accordance with Sections R-1 through R-56 of these rules.

R-8 Jurisdiction

(a) The arbitrator shall have the power to rule on his or her own jurisdiction, including any objections with respect to the existence, scope or validity of the arbitration agreement.

(b) The arbitrator shall have the power to determine the existence or validity of a contract of which an arbitration clause forms a part. Such an arbitration clause shall be treated as an agreement independent of the other terms of the contract. A decision by the arbitrator that the contract is null and void shall not for that reason alone render invalid the arbitration clause.

(c) A party must object to the jurisdiction of the arbitrator or to the arbitrability of a claim or counterclaim no later than the filing of the answering statement to the claim or counterclaim that gives rise to the objection. The arbitrator may rule on such objections as a preliminary matter or as part of the final award.

R-9 Mediation

At any stage of the proceedings, the parties may agree to conduct a mediation conference under the Commercial Mediation Rules in order to facilitate settlement. The mediator shall not be an arbitrator appointed to the case. Where the parties to a pending arbitration agree to mediate under the AAA's rules, no additional administrative fee is required to initiate the mediation.

R-10 Administrative Conference

At the request of any party or upon the AAA's own initiative, the AAA may conduct an administrative conference, in person or by telephone, with the parties and/or their representatives. The conference may address such issues as arbitrator selection, potential mediation of the dispute, potential exchange of information, a timetable for hearings and any other administrative matters. There is no administrative fee for this service.

R-11 Fixing of Locale

The parties may mutually agree on the locale where the arbitration is to be held. If any party requests that the hearing be held in a specific locale and the other party files no objection thereto within 15 days after notice of the request has been sent to it by the AAA, the locale shall be the one requested. If a party objects to the locale requested by the other party, the AAA shall have the power to determine the locale, and its decision shall be final and binding.

R-12 Qualifications of an Arbitrator

(a) Any neutral arbitrator appointed pursuant to Section R-13, R-14, R-15, or E-5, or selected by mutual choice of the parties or their appointees, shall be subject to disqualification for the reasons specified in Section R-19. If the parties specifically so agree in writing, the arbitrator shall not be subject to disqualification for those reasons.

(b) Unless the parties agree otherwise, an arbitrator selected unilaterally by one party is a party-appointed arbitrator and is not subject to disqualification pursuant to Section R-19.

R-13 Appointment from Panel

If the parties have not appointed an arbitrator and have not provided any other method of appointment, the arbitrator shall be appointed in the following manner:

(a) Immediately after the filing of the submission or the answering statement or the expiration of the time within which the answering statement is to be filed, the AAA shall send simultaneously to each party to the dispute an identical list of names of persons chosen from the panel. The parties are encouraged to agree to an arbitrator from the submitted list and to advise the AAA of their agreement.

(b) If the parties are unable to agree upon an arbitrator, each party to the dispute shall have 15 days from the transmittal date in which to strike names objected to, number the remaining names in order of preference, and return the list to the AAA. If a party does not return the list within the time specified, all persons named therein shall be deemed acceptable. From among the persons who have been approved on both lists, and in accordance with the designated order of mutual preference, the AAA shall invite the acceptance of an arbitrator to serve. If the parties fail to agree on any of the persons named, or if acceptable arbitrators are unable to act, or if for any other reason the appointment cannot be made from the submitted lists, the AAA shall have the power to make the appointment from among other members of the panel without the submission of additional lists.

(c) Unless the parties have agreed otherwise no later than 15 days after the commencement of an arbitration, if the notice of arbitration names two or more claimants or two or more respondents, the AAA shall appoint all the arbitrators.

R-14 Direct Appointment by a Party

(a) If the agreement of the parties names an arbitrator or specifies a method of appointing an arbitrator, that designation or method shall be followed. The notice of appointment, with the name and address of the arbitrator, shall be filed with the AAA by the appointing party. Upon the request of any appointing party, the AAA shall submit a list of members of the panel from which the party may, if it so desires, make the appointment.

(b) If the agreement specifies a period of time within which an arbitrator shall be appointed and any party fails to make the appointment within that period, the AAA shall make the appointment.

(c) If no period of time is specified in the agreement, the AAA shall notify the party to make the appointment. If within 15 days after such notice has been sent, an arbitrator has not been appointed by a party, the AAA shall make the appointment.

R-15 Appointment of Neutral Arbitrator by Party-Appointed Arbitrators or Parties

(a) If the parties have selected party-appointed arbitrators, or if such arbitrators have been appointed as provided in Section R-14, and the parties have authorized them to appoint a neutral arbitrator within a specified time and no appointment is made within that time or any agreed extension, the AAA may appoint a neutral arbitrator, who shall act as chairperson.

(b) If no period of time is specified for appointment of the neutral arbitrator and the party-appointed arbitrators or the parties do not make the appointment within 15 days from the date of the appointment of the last party-appointed arbitrator, the AAA may appoint the neutral arbitrator, who shall act as chairperson.

(c) If the parties have agreed that their party-appointed arbitrators shall appoint the neutral arbitrator from the panel, the AAA shall furnish to the party-appointed arbitrators, in the manner provided in Section R-13, a list selected from the panel, and the appointment of the neutral arbitrator shall be made as provided in that section.

R-16 Nationality of Arbitrator

Where the parties are nationals or residents of different countries, the AAA, at the request of any party or on its own initiative, may appoint as a neutral arbitrator a national of a country other than that of any of the parties. The request must be made prior to the time set for the appointment of the arbitrator as agreed by the parties or set by these rules.

R-17 Number of Arbitrators

If the arbitration agreement does not specify the number of arbitrators, the dispute shall be heard and determined by one arbitrator, unless the AAA, in its discretion, directs that three arbitrators be appointed. The parties may request three arbitrators in their demand or answer, which request the AAA will consider in exercising its discretion regarding the number of arbitrators appointed to the dispute.

R-18 Notice to Arbitrator of Appointment

Notice of the appointment of the neutral arbitrator, whether appointed mutually by the parties or by the AAA, shall be sent to the arbitrator by the AAA, together with a copy of these rules, and the signed acceptance of the arbitrator shall be filed with the AAA prior to the opening of the first hearing.

R-19 Disclosure and Challenge Procedure

(a) Any person appointed as a neutral arbitrator shall disclose to the AAA any circumstance likely to affect impartiality or independence, including any bias or any financial or personal interest in the result of the arbitration or any past or present relationship with the parties or their representatives. Upon receipt of such information from the arbitrator or another source, the AAA shall communicate the information to the parties and, if it deems it appropriate to do so, to the arbitrator and others.

(b) Upon objection of a party to the continued service of a neutral arbitrator, the AAA shall determine whether the arbitrator should be disqualified and shall inform the parties of its decision, which shall be conclusive.

R-20 Communication with Arbitrator

(a) No party and no one acting on behalf of any party shall communicate unilaterally concerning the arbitration with a neutral arbitrator or a candidate for neutral arbitrator. Unless the parties agree otherwise or the arbitrator so directs, any communication from the parties to a neutral arbitrator shall be sent to the AAA for transmittal to the arbitrator.

(b) The parties or the arbitrators may also agree that once the panel has been constituted, no party and no one acting on behalf of any party shall communicate unilaterally concerning the arbitration with any party-appointed arbitrator.

R-21 Vacancies

(a) If for any reason an arbitrator is unable to perform the duties of the office, the AAA may, on proof satisfactory to it, declare the office vacant. Vacancies shall be filled in accordance with the applicable provisions of these rules.

(b) In the event of a vacancy in a panel of neutral arbitrators after the hearings have commenced, the remaining arbitrator or arbitrators may continue with the hearing and determination of the controversy, unless the parties agree otherwise.

(c) In the event of the appointment of a substitute arbitrator, the panel of arbitrators shall determine in its sole discretion whether it is necessary to repeat all or part of any prior hearings.

R-22 Preliminary Hearing

(a) At the request of any party or at the discretion of the arbitrator or the AAA, the arbitrator may schedule as soon as practicable a preliminary hearing with the parties and/or their representatives. The preliminary hearing may be conducted by telephone at the arbitrator's discretion. There is no case service fee for the first preliminary hearing.

(b) During the preliminary hearing, the parties and the arbitrator should discuss the future conduct of the case, including clarification of the issues and claims, a schedule for the hearings and any other preliminary matters.

R-23 Exchange of Information

(a) At the request of any party or at the discretion of the arbitrator, consistent with the expedited nature of arbitration, the arbitrator may direct (i) the production of documents and other information, and (ii) the identification of any witnesses to be called.

(b) At least five (5) business days prior to the hearing, the parties shall exchange copies of all exhibits they intend to submit at the hearing.

(c) The arbitrator is authorized to resolve any disputes concerning the exchange of information.

R-24 Date, Time, and Place of Hearing

The arbitrator shall set the date, time, and place for each hearing. The parties shall respond to requests for hearing dates in a timely manner, be cooperative in scheduling the earliest practicable date, and adhere to the established hearing schedule. The AAA shall send a notice of hearing to the parties at least 10 days in advance of the hearing date, unless otherwise agreed by the parties.

R-25 Attendance at Hearings

The arbitrator and the AAA shall maintain the privacy of the hearings unless the law provides to the contrary. Any person having a direct interest in the arbitration is entitled to attend hearings. The arbitrator shall otherwise have the power to require the exclusion of any witness, other than a party or other essential person, during the testimony of any other witness. It shall be discretionary with the arbitrator to determine the propriety of the attendance of any other person other than a party and its representatives.

R-26 Representation

Any party may be represented by counsel or other authorized representative. A party intending to be so represented shall notify the other party and the AAA of the name and address of the representative at least three days prior to the date set for the hearing at which that person is first to appear. When such a representative initiates an arbitration or responds for a party, notice is deemed to have been given.

R-27 Oaths

Before proceeding with the first hearing, each arbitrator may take an oath of office and, if required by law, shall do so. The arbitrator may require witnesses to testify under oath administered by any duly qualified person and, if it is required by law or requested by any party, shall do so.

R-28 Stenographic Record
Any party desiring a stenographic record shall make arrangements directly with a stenographer and shall notify the other parties of these arrangements at least three days in advance of the hearing. The requesting party or parties shall pay the cost of the record. If the transcript is agreed by the parties, or determined by the arbitrator to be the official record of the proceeding, it must be provided to the arbitrator and made available to the other parties for inspection, at a date, time, and place determined by the arbitrator.

R-29 Interpreters
Any party wishing an interpreter shall make all arrangements directly with the interpreter and shall assume the costs of the service.

R-30 Postponements
The arbitrator may postpone any hearing upon agreement of the parties, upon request of a party for good cause shown, or upon the arbitrator's own initiative.

R-31 Arbitration in the Absence of a Party or Representative
Unless the law provides to the contrary, the arbitration may proceed in the absence of any party or representative who, after due notice, fails to be present or fails to obtain a postponement. An award shall not be made solely on the default of a party. The arbitrator shall require the party who is present to submit such evidence as the arbitrator may require for the making of an award.

R-32 Conduct of Proceedings
(a) The claimant shall present evidence to support its claim. The respondent shall then present evidence to support its defense. Witnesses for each party shall also submit to questions from the arbitrator and the adverse party. The arbitrator has the discretion to vary this procedure, provided that the parties are treated with equality and that each party has the right to be heard and is given a fair opportunity to present its case.
(b) The arbitrator, exercising his or her discretion, shall conduct the proceedings with a view to expediting the resolution of the dispute and may direct the order of proof, bifurcate proceedings and direct the parties to focus their presentations on issues the decision of which could dispose of all or part of the case.
(c) The parties may agree to waive oral hearings in any case.

R-33 Evidence
(a) The parties may offer such evidence as is relevant and material to the dispute and shall produce such evidence as the arbitrator may deem necessary to an understanding and determination of the dispute. Conformity to legal rules of evidence shall not be necessary. All evidence shall be taken in the presence of all of the arbitrators and all of the parties, except where any of the parties is absent, in default or has waived the right to be present.

(b) The arbitrator shall determine the admissibility, relevance, and materiality of the evidence offered and may exclude evidence deemed by the arbitrator to be cumulative or irrelevant.

(c) The arbitrator shall take into account applicable principles of legal privilege, such as those involving the confidentiality of communications between a lawyer and client.

(d) An arbitrator or other person authorized by law to subpoena witnesses or documents may do so upon the request of any party or independently.

R-34 Evidence by Affidavit and Posthearing Filing of Documents or Other Evidence

(a) The arbitrator may receive and consider the evidence of witnesses by declaration or affidavit, but shall give it only such weight as the arbitrator deems it entitled to after consideration of any objection made to its admission.

(b) If the parties agree or the arbitrator directs that documents or other evidence be submitted to the arbitrator after the hearing, the documents or other evidence shall be filed with the AAA for transmission to the arbitrator. All parties shall be afforded an opportunity to examine and respond to such documents or other evidence.

R-35 Inspection or Investigation

An arbitrator finding it necessary to make an inspection or investigation in connection with the arbitration shall direct the AAA to so advise the parties. The arbitrator shall set the date and time and the AAA shall notify the parties. Any party who so desires may be present at such an inspection or investigation. In the event that one or all parties are not present at the inspection or investigation, the arbitrator shall make an oral or written report to the parties and afford them an opportunity to comment.

R-36 Interim Measures**

(a) The arbitrator may take whatever interim measures he or she deems necessary, including injunctive relief and measures for the protection or conservation of property and disposition of perishable goods.

(b) Such interim measures may take the form of an interim award, and the arbitrator may require security for the costs of such measures.

(c) A request for interim measures addressed by a party to a judicial authority shall not be deemed incompatible with the agreement to arbitrate or a waiver of the right to arbitrate.

**The Optional Rules may be found at pages 43 of this pamphlet.

R-37 Closing of Hearing

The arbitrator shall specifically inquire of all parties whether they have any further proofs to offer or witnesses to be heard. Upon receiving negative replies or if satisfied that the record is complete, the arbitrator shall declare the hearing closed.

If briefs are to be filed, the hearing shall be declared closed as of the final date set by the arbitrator for the receipt of briefs. If documents are to be filed as provided in Section R-34 and the date set for their receipt is later than that set for the receipt of briefs, the later date shall be the closing date of the hearing. The time limit within which the arbitrator is required to make the award shall commence, in the absence of other agreements by the parties, upon the closing of the hearing.

R-38 Reopening of Hearing

The hearing may be reopened on the arbitrator's initiative, or upon application of a party, at any time before the award is made. If reopening the hearing would prevent the making of the award within the specific time agreed on by the parties in the contract(s) out of which the controversy has arisen, the matter may not be reopened unless the parties agree on an extension of time. When no specific date is fixed in the contract, the arbitrator may reopen the hearing and shall have 30 days from the closing of the reopened hearing within which to make an award.

R-39 Waiver of Rules

Any party who proceeds with the arbitration after knowledge that any provision or requirement of these rules has not been complied with and who fails to state an objection in writing shall be deemed to have waived the right to object.

R-40 Extensions of Time

The parties may modify any period of time by mutual agreement. The AAA or the arbitrator may for good cause extend any period of time established by these rules, except the time for making the award. The AAA shall notify the parties of any extension.

R-41 Serving of Notice

(a) Any papers, notices, or process necessary or proper for the initiation or continuation of an arbitration under these rules, for any court action in connection therewith, or for the entry of judgment on any award made under these rules may be served on a party by mail addressed to the party, or its representative at the last known address or by personal service, in or outside the state where the arbitration is to be held, provided that reasonable opportunity to be heard with regard to the dispute is or has been granted to the party.

(b) The AAA, the arbitrator and the parties may also use overnight delivery or electronic facsimile transmission (fax), to give the notices required by these rules. Where all parties and the arbitrator agree, notices may be transmitted by electronic mail (E-mail), or other methods of communication.

(c) Unless otherwise instructed by the AAA or by the arbitrator, any documents submitted by any party to the AAA or to the arbitrator shall simultaneously be provided to the other party or parties to the arbitration.

R-42 Majority Decision

When the panel consists of more than one arbitrator, unless required by law or by the arbitration agreement, a majority of the arbitrators must make all decisions.

R-43 Time of Award

The award shall be made promptly by the arbitrator and, unless otherwise agreed by the parties or specified by law, no later than 30 days from the date of closing the hearing, or, if oral hearings have been waived, from the date of the AAA's transmittal of the final statements and proofs to the arbitrator.

R-44 Form of Award

(a) Any award shall be in writing and signed by a majority of the arbitrators. It shall be executed in the manner required by law.

(b) The arbitrator need not render a reasoned award unless the parties request such an award in writing prior to appointment of the arbitrator or unless the arbitrator determines that a reasoned award is appropriate.

R-45 Scope of Award

(a) The arbitrator may grant any remedy or relief that the arbitrator deems just and equitable and within the scope of the agreement of the parties, including, but not limited to, specific performance of a contract.

(b) In addition to a final award, the arbitrator may make other decisions, including interim, interlocutory, or partial rulings, orders, and awards. In any interim, interlocutory, or partial award, the arbitrator may assess and apportion the fees, expenses, and compensation related to such award as the arbitrator determines is appropriate.

(c) In the final award, the arbitrator shall assess the fees, expenses, and compensation provided in Sections R-51, R-52, and R-53. The arbitrator may apportion such fees, expenses, and compensation among the parties in such amounts as the arbitrator determines is appropriate.

(d) The award of the arbitrator(s) may include: (a) interest at such rate and from such date as the arbitrator(s) may deem appropriate; and (b) an award of attorneys' fees if all parties have requested such an award or it is authorized by law or their arbitration agreement.

R-46 Award upon Settlement

If the parties settle their dispute during the course of the arbitration and if the parties so request, the arbitrator may set forth the terms of the settlement in a "consent award."

R-47 Delivery of Award to Parties

Parties shall accept as notice and delivery of the award the placing of the award or a true copy thereof in the mail addressed to the parties or their representatives at the last known addresses, personal or electronic service of the award, or the filing of the award in any other manner that is permitted by law.

R-48 Modification of Award

Within 20 days after the transmittal of an award, any party, upon notice to the other parties, may request the arbitrator, through the AAA, to correct any clerical, typographical, or computational errors in the award. The arbitrator is not empowered to redetermine the merits of any claim already decided. The other parties shall be given 10 days to respond to the request. The arbitrator shall dispose of the request within 20 days after transmittal by the AAA to the arbitrator of the request and any response thereto.

R-49 Release of Documents for Judicial Proceedings

The AAA shall, upon the written request of a party, furnish to the party, at the party's expense, certified copies of any papers in the AAA's possession that may be required in judicial proceedings relating to the arbitration.

R-50 Applications to Court and Exclusion of Liability

(a) No judicial proceeding by a party relating to the subject matter of the arbitration shall be deemed a waiver of the party's right to arbitrate.

(b) Neither the AAA nor any arbitrator in a proceeding under these rules is a necessary party in judicial proceedings relating to the arbitration.

(c) Parties to an arbitration under these rules shall be deemed to have consented that judgment upon the arbitration award may be entered in any federal or state court having jurisdiction thereof.

(d) Neither the AAA nor any arbitrator shall be liable to any party for any act or omission in connection with any arbitration conducted under these rules.

R-51 Administrative Fees

As a not-for-profit organization, the AAA shall prescribe an initial filing fee and a case service fee to compensate it for the cost of providing administrative services. The fees in effect when the fee or charge is incurred shall be applicable.

The filing fee shall be advanced by the party or parties making a claim or counterclaim, subject to final apportionment by the arbitrator in the award.

The AAA may, in the event of extreme hardship on the part of any party, defer or reduce the administrative fees.

R-52 Expenses

The expenses of witnesses for either side shall be paid by the party producing such witnesses. All other expenses of the arbitration, including required travel and other expenses of the arbitrator, AAA representatives, and any witness and the cost of any proof produced at the direct request of the arbitrator, shall be borne equally by the parties, unless they agree otherwise or unless the arbitrator in the award assesses such expenses or any part thereof against any specified party or parties.

R-53 Neutral Arbitrator's Compensation

(a) Unless the parties agree otherwise, members of the National Panel of Commercial Arbitrators appointed as neutrals on cases administered under the Expedited Procedures with claims not exceeding $10,000, will customarily serve without compensation for the first day of service. Thereafter, arbitrators shall receive compensation as set forth herein.

(b) Arbitrators shall be compensated at a rate consistent with the arbitrator's stated rate of compensation, beginning with the first day of hearing in all cases with claims exceeding $10,000.

(c) If there is disagreement concerning the terms of compensation, an appropriate rate shall be established with the arbitrator by the AAA and confirmed to the parties.

(d) Any arrangement for the compensation of a neutral arbitrator shall be made through the AAA and not directly between the parties and the arbitrator.

R-54 Deposits

The AAA may require the parties to deposit in advance of any hearings such sums of money as it deems necessary to cover the expense of the arbitration, including the arbitrator's fee, if any, and shall render an accounting to the parties and return any unexpended balance at the conclusion of the case.

R-55 Interpretation and Application of Rules

The arbitrator shall interpret and apply these rules insofar as they relate to the arbitrator's powers and duties. When there is more than one arbitrator and a difference arises among them concerning the meaning or application of these rules, it shall be decided by a majority vote. If that is not possible, either an arbitrator or a party may refer the question to the AAA for final decision. All other rules shall be interpreted and applied by the AAA.

R-56 Suspension for Nonpayment

If arbitrator compensation or administrative charges have not been paid in full, the AAA may so inform the parties in order that one of them may advance the required payment. If such payments are not made, the arbitrator may order the suspension or termination of the proceedings. If no arbitrator has yet been appointed, the AAA may suspend the proceedings.

APPENDIX XVI
ADR RULES OF THE INTERNATIONAL CHAMBER OF COMMERCE

FOREWORD

ICC has almost eight decades of experience in devising rules to govern and facilitate the conduct of international business. These include those designed to resolve the conflicts that inevitably arise in trading relations. The present ADR Rules represent ICC's most recent initiative in this field.

The ICC-ADR Rules are the result of discussions between dispute resolution experts and representatives of the business community from 75 countries. Their purpose is to offer business partners a means of resolving disputes amicably, in the way best suited to their needs. A distinctive feature of the Rules is the freedom the parties are given to choose the technique they consider most conducive to settlement. Failing agreement on the method to be adopted, the fallback shall be mediation.

As an amicable method of dispute resolution, ICC ADR should be distinguished from ICC arbitration. They are two alternative means of resolving disputes, although in certain circumstances they may be complementary. For instance, it is possible for parties to provide for ICC arbitration in the event of failure to reach an amicable settlement. Similarly, parties engaged in an arbitration may turn to ICC ADR if their dispute seems to warrant a different, more consensual approach. The two services remain distinct, however, each administered by a separate secretariat based at ICC headquarters in Paris.

The ICC ADR Rules replace the 1988 ICC Rules of Optional Conciliation and join the Rules of Arbitration, the Rules for Expertise and the Docdex Rules as an important component in ICC's range of dispute resolution services.

The ICC ADR Rules, which are effective as of 1 July 2001, may be used in domestic as well as international contexts.

June 2001

SUGGESTED ICC ADR CLAUSES

OPTIONAL ADR

'The parties may at any time, without prejudice to any other proceedings, seek to settle any dispute arising out of or in connection with the present contract in accordance with the ICC-ADR Rules.'

OBLIGATION TO CONSIDER ADR

'In the event of any dispute arising out of or in connection with the present contract, the parties agree in the first instance to discuss and consider submitting the matter to settlement proceedings under the ICC ADR Rules.'

OBLIGATION TO SUBMIT DISPUTE TO ADR
WITH AN AUTOMATIC EXPIRATION MECHANISM

'In the event of any dispute arising out of or in connection with the present contract, the parties agree to submit the matter to settlement proceedings under the ICC ADR Rules. If the dispute has not been settled pursuant to the said Rules within 45 days following the filing of a Request for ADR or within such other period as the parties may agree in writing, the parties shall have no further obligations under this paragraph.'

OBLIGATION TO SUBMIT DISPUTE TO ADR,
FOLLOWED BY ICC ARBITRATION AS REQUIRED

'In the event of any dispute arising out of or in connection with the present contract, the parties agree to submit the matter to settlement proceedings under the ICC ADR Rules. If the dispute has not been settled pursuant to the said Rules within 45 days following the filing of a Request for ADR or within such other period as the parties may agree in writing, such dispute shall be finally settled under the Rules of Arbitration of the international Chamber of Commerce by one or more arbitrators appointed in accordance with the said Rules of Arbitration.'

ADR RULES OF THE INTERNATIONAL CHAMBER OF COMMERCE

Preamble
Amiable settlement is a desirable solution for business disputes and differences. It can occur before or during the litigation or arbitration of a dispute and can often be facilitated through the aid of a third party (the 'Neutral') acting in accordance with simple rules. The parties can agree to submit to such rules in their underlying contract or at any other time.
The International Chamber of Commerce ('ICC') sets out these amicable dispute resolution rules, en titled the ICC ADR Rules (the 'Rules'), which permit the parties to agree upon whatever settlement technique they believe to be appropriate to help them settle their dispute. In the absence of an agreement of the parties on a settlement technique, mediation shall be the settlement technique used under the Rules. The Guide to ICC ADR, which does not form part of the Rules, provides an explanation of the Rules and of various settlement techniques which can be used pursuant to the Rules.

Article 1
Scope of the ICC ADR Rules
All business disputes, whether or not of an international character, may be referred to ADR proceedings pursuant to these Rules. The provisions of these Rules may be modified by agreement of all of the parties, subject to the approval of ICC.

Article 2
Commencement of the ADR Proceedings
A. Where there is an agreement to refer to the Rules

1

Where there is an agreement between the parties to refer their dispute to the ICC ADR Rules, any party or parties wishing to commence ADR proceedings pursuant to the Rules shall send to ICC a written Request for ADP, which shall include:

a) the names, addresses, telephone and facsimile numbers and e-mail addresses of the parties to the dispute and their authorized representatives, if any;

b) a description of the dispute including, if possible, an assessment of its value;

c) any joint designation by all of the parties of a Neutral or any agreement of all of the parties upon the qualifications of a Neutral to be appointed by ICC where no joint designation has been made;

d) a copy of any written agreement under which the Request for ADR is made; and

e) the registration fee of the ADR proceedings, as set out in the Appendix hereto.

2

Where the Request for ADR is not filed jointly by all of the parties, the party or parties filing the Request shall simultaneously send the Request to the other party or parties. Such Request may include any proposal regarding the qualifications of a Neutral or any proposal of one or more Neutrals to be designated by all of the parties. Thereafter, all of the parties may jointly designate a Neutral or may agree upon the qualifications of a Neutral to be appointed by ICC. In either case, the parties shall promptly notify ICC thereof

3

ICC shall promptly acknowledge receipt of the Request for ADR in writing to the parties.

B. Where there is no agreement to refer to the Rules

1

Where there is no agreement between the parties to refer their dispute to the ICC ADR Rules, any party or parties wishing to commence ADR proceedings pursuant to the Rules shall send to ICC a written Request for ADP, which shall include:

a) the names, addresses, telephone and facsimile numbers and e-mail addresses of the parties to the dispute and their authorized representatives, if any;

b) a description of the dispute including, if possible, an assessment of its value; and

c) the registration fee of the ADR proceedings, as set out in the Appendix hereto.

The Request for ADR may also include any proposal regarding the qualifications of a Neutral or any proposal of one or more Neutrals to be designated by all of the parties.

2

ICC shall promptly inform the other party or parties in writing of the Request for ADR. Such party or parties shall be asked to inform ICC in writing, within 15 days of receipt of the Request for ADR, as to whether they agree or decline to participate in the ADR proceedings. In the former case, they may provide any proposal regarding the qualifications of a Neutral and may propose one or more Neutrals to be designated by the parties. Thereafter, all of the parties may jointly designate a Neutral or may agree upon the qualifications of a Neutral to be appointed by ICC. In either case, the parties shall promptly notify ICC thereof.

In the absence of any reply within such 15-day period, or in the case of a negative reply, the Request for ADR shall be deemed to have been declined and ADR proceedings shall not be commenced. ICC shall promptly so inform in writing the party or parties which filed the Request for ADR.

Article 3
Selection of the Neutral

1

Where all of the parties have jointly designated a Neutral, ICC shall take note of that designation, and such person, upon notifying ICC of his or her agreement to serve, shall act as the Neutral in the ADR proceedings. Where a Neutral has not been designated by all of the parties, or where the designated Neutral does not agree to serve, ICC shall promptly appoint a Neutral, either through an ICC National Committee or otherwise, and notify the parties thereof. ICC shall make all reasonable efforts to appoint a Neutral having the qualifications, if any, which have been agreed upon by all of the parties.

2

Every prospective Neutral shall promptly provide ICC with a *curriculum vitae* and a statement of independence, both duly signed and dated. The prospective Neutral shall disclose to ICC in the statement of independence any facts or circumstances which might be of such nature as to call into question his or her independence in the eyes of the parties. ICC shall provide such information to the parties in writing.

3

If any party objects to the Neutral appointed by ICC and notifies ICC and the other party or parties thereof in writing, stating the reasons for such objection, within 15 days of receipt of notification of the appointment, ICC shall promptly appoint another Neutral.

4

Upon agreement of all of the parties, the parties may designate more than one Neutral or request ICC to appoint more than one Neutral, in accordance with the provisions of these Rules. In appropriate circumstances, ICC may propose the appointment of more than one Neutral to the parties.

Article 4
Fees and Costs

1

The party or parties filing a Request for ADR shall include with the Request a non-refundable registration fee, as set out in the Appendix hereto. No Request for ADR shall be processed unless accompanied by the requisite payment.

2

Following the receipt of a Request for ADR, ICC shall request the parties to pay a deposit in an amount likely to cover the administrative expenses of ICC and the fees and expenses of the Neutral for the ADR proceedings, as set out in the Appendix hereto. The ADR proceedings shall not go forward until payment of such deposit has been received by ICC.

3

In any case where ICC considers that the deposit is not likely to cover the total costs of the ADR proceedings, the amount of such deposit may be subject to readjustment. ICC may stay the ADR proceedings until the corresponding payments are made by the parties.

4

Upon termination of the ADR proceedings, ICC shall settle the total costs of the proceedings and shall, as the case may be, reimburse the parties for any excess payment or bill the parties for any balance required pursuant to these Rules.

5

All above deposits and costs shall be borne in equal shares by the parties, unless they agree otherwise in writing. However, any party shall be free to pay the unpaid balance of such deposits and costs should another party fail to pay its share.

6

A party's other expenditure shall remain the responsibility of that party.

Article 5
Conduct of the ADR Procedure

1

The Neutral and the parties shall promptly discuss, and seek to reach agreement upon, the settlement technique to be used, and shall discuss the specific ADR procedure to be followed.

2

In the absence of an agreement of the parties on the settlement technique to be used, mediation shall be used.

3

The Neutral shall conduct the procedure in such manner as the Neutral sees fit. In all cases the Neutral shall be guided by the principles of fairness and impartiality and by the wishes of the parties.

4

In the absence of an agreement of the parties, the Neutral shall determine the language or languages of the proceedings and the place of any meetings to be held.

5

Each party shall cooperate in good faith with the Neutral.

Article 6
Termination of the ADR Proceedings
1
ADR proceedings which have been commenced pursuant to these Rules shall terminate upon the earlier of:
a)   the signing by the parties of a settlement agreement;
b)   the notification in writing to the Neutral by one or more parties, at any time after the discussion referred to in Article 5(1) has occurred, of a decision no longer to pursue the ADR proceedings;
c)   the completion of the procedure established pursuant to Article 5 and the notification in writing thereof by the Neutral to the parties;
d)   the notification in writing by the Neutral to the parties that the ADR proceedings will not, in the Neutral's opinion, resolve the dispute between the parties;
c)   the expiration of any time limit set for the ADR proceedings, if not extended by all of the parties, such expiration to be notified in writing by the Neutral to the parties;
f)   the notification in writing by ICC to the parties and the Neutral, not less than 15 days after the due date for any payment by one or more parties pursuant to these Rules, stating that such payment has not been made; or
g)   the notification in writing by ICC to the parties stating, in the judgment of ICC, that there has been a failure to designate a Neutral or that it has not been reasonably possible to appoint a Neutral.

2
The Neutral, upon any termination of the ADR proceedings pursuant to Article 6(1), (a)-(c), shall promptly notify ICC of the termination of the ADR proceedings and shall provide ICC with a copy of any notification referred to in Article 6(1), (b)-(c). In all cases ICC shall confirm in writing the termination of the ADR proceedings to the parties and the Neutral, if a Neutral has already been designated or appointed.

Article 7
General Provisions
1
In the absence of any agreement of the parties to the contrary and unless prohibited by applicable law, the ADR proceedings, including their outcome, are private and confidential. Any settlement agreement between the parties shall similarly be kept confidential except that a party shall have the right to disclose it to the extent that such disclosure is required by applicable law or necessary for purposes of its implementation or enforcement.

2
Unless required to do so by applicable law and in the absence of any agreement of the parties to the contrary, a party shall not in any manner produce as evidence in any judicial, arbitration or similar proceedings:
a)   any documents, statements or communications which are submitted by another party or by the Neutral in the ADR proceedings, unless they can be obtained independently by the party seeking to produce them in the judicial, arbitration or similar proceedings;

b)   any views expressed or suggestions made by any party within the ADR proceedings
      with regard to the possible settlement of the dispute;
c)   any admissions made by another party within the ADR proceedings;
d)   any views or proposals put forward by the Neutral; or
e)   the fact that any party had indicated within the ADR proceedings that it was ready to
      accept a proposal for a settlement.

3

Unless all of the parties agree otherwise in writing, a Neutral shall not act nor shall have
acted in any judicial, arbitration or similar proceedings relating to the dispute which is or
was the subject of the ADR proceedings, whether as a judge, as an arbitrator, as an expert or
as a representative or advisor of a party.

4

The Neutral, unless required by applicable law or unless all of the parties agree otherwise in
writing, shall not give testimony in any judicial, arbitration or similar proceedings
concerning any aspect of the ADR proceedings.

5

Neither the Neutral, nor ICC and its employees, nor the ICC National Committees shall be
liable to any person for any act or omission in connection with the ADR proceedings.

APPENDIX
SCHEDULE OF ADR COSTS

A

The party or parties filing a Request for ADR shall include with the Request a non-refundable registration fee of US$ 1,500 to cover the costs of processing the Request for ADR. No
Request for ADR shall be processed unless accompanied by the requisite payment.

B

The administrative expenses of ICC for the ADR proceedings shall be fixed at ICC's discretion depending en the tasks carried out by ICC. Such administrative expenses shall not
exceed the maximum sum of US$ 10,000.

C

The fees of the Neutral shall be calculated en the basis of the time reasonably spent by the
Neutral in the ADR proceedings, at an hourly rate fixed for such proceedings by ICC in
consultation with the Neutral and the parties. Such hourly rate shall be reasonable in amount
and shall be determined in light of the complexity of the dispute and any other relevant
circumstances. The amount of reasonable expenses of the Neutral shall be fixed by ICC.

D

Amounts paid to the Neutral do not include any possible value added taxes (VAT) or other
taxes or charges and imposts applicable to the Neutral's fees. Parties are required to pay any

such taxes or charges; however, the recovery of any such taxes or charges is a matter solely between the Neutral and the parties.

APPENDIX XVII
INTERNATIONAL PARALYMPIC COMMITTEE PROTEST RULES

HANDBOOK PART I
SECTION II – GENERAL REGULATIONS

CHAPTER 5 – CLASSIFICATION

9. Classification (Protests)

Protests, although in and of themselves a right of athletes and classifiers, should not be used in a manner that would unfairly affect the outcome of the competition. 'Tactical protests' are a breach of the principles of fair play.

9.1 The SAEC's[*] are responsible for the selection of Sports Classification Juries.

9.2 A member of the Sports Classification Jury should normally be exempted from dealing with a protest concerning a classification that he/she bas been involved with him/herself.

9.3 The decision of the Sports Classification Jury is final and without appeal.

9.4 Classification Protest Procedure
The following regulations for classification protests shall apply:

9.4.1 All protests must be made on the official IPC Protest Form and handed to the respective Chairman of the Sports Classification Jury. The protest must be accompanied by a protest fee which will be refunded if the protest is upheld, otherwise it remains with the SAEC.
In accordance with 7.4 the Classification Committee may protest a competitors classification following observation during competition. Such a protest shall be without fee.

9.4.2 Protest on own classification
Such protests must be handed in not later than six (6) hours after classification.

9.4.3 Protest on another competitor
Only the Chef de Mission (or his/her representative) or relevant classification committee can make such protests.

9.4.4 Protest in Team Sports
Only the Head of Delegation (or his/her representative) or relevant classification committee can make such protests.

9.4.5 Classification protests shall be dealt with as soon as possible after the protest has been received. The head of classification shall decide the time of the hearing.

9.4.6 At re-classification tests the competitor may be accompanied by a person of his/her choice.

---

[*] SAEC: Sports Assembly Executive Committee.

9.4.7 If a competitor refuses to attend a protest re-classification test he/she will be banned from further participation.

9.4.8 The final decision will be written on the official form. The original will be kept by the SAEC concerned and copies will be distributed to the athlete concerned, his/her NSO and the Organising Committee.

9.4.9 Following any re-classification the implementation of the change shall be according to the rules of the SAEC'S.

9.4.10 Any records set by an athlete who was reclassified will not be ratified.

9.4.11 If it can be shown that the IPC Code of Ethics for Classification has not been followed during a classification, the competitor shall be reclassified by a different classification panel.

CHAPTER 6 – REGULATIONS FOR OFFICIAL AND SANCTIONED IPC COMPETITIONS

11. Protests

11.1 Classification Protests
See Section II – Chapter 5.

11.2 Sports Technical Protests
Protest concerning the conduct of competition shall follow the procedures of the specific sports rules (see Sections III and IV).

11.3 General Protests

11.3.1 All protests dealing with IPC General Regulations and By Laws including matters of discipline must be made in writing and handed over to the Chairperson of the Protest Jury of three (3) persons appointed by the IPC Executive Committee for each official competition.
The Protest must be accompanied by a protest fee of 100 USD. The fee will be refunded if the protest is upheld, if not it remains with IPC.

11.3.2 The Protest Jury shall deal with the protest without delay.

11.3.3 A person, a committee or a team accused must be given the opportunity to be heard.

11.3.4 Protest Jury decisions shall be in writing and handed over to the protesting party.

11.3.5 The Protest Jury may invoke penalties in the form of:
– Disqualification
– Suspension
– Rebuke

ooo

HANDBOOK PART II
SECTION IV – SUMMER SPORTS

CHAPTER 2 – ATHLETICS

APPENDIX V – CLASSIFICATION PROTEST RULES

It is the policy of IPC Athletics to allow classification protests during the Games, under specific circumstances. It is the aim of IPC Athletics that all classification issues will be settled before the Games commence but it is also recognised that in certain circumstances, this is not possible. The following are the classification and classification protest rules.

IPC Athletic Classification

(...)

8. The protest system is clearly defined and takes into account the designation of the athlete, i.e., whether the classification is permanent (P), review (R), or new (N). It also takes into account who can protest and when the protest has to be made.
    There are four (4) categories:

Category A
Protests on athletes who have a permanent classification (P) must be made by the Team Manager or Chef de Mission of a country at the Games. These protests can be made up to 72 hours before the first competition event of the Games.
Athletes with a permanent classification (P) cannot change or have their classification changed during the Games.
If, in the view of the Classification Committee, a permanent athlete's class needs to be reviewed as a result of performances during the Games, that review can only take place after the individual athlete's last competition event at the Games.

Category B
Athletes who have a review (R) classification are usually athletes who are on the borderline of two classes. Their classification is being reviewed because the classification committee is concerned. The classification committee can make this decision up to 72 hours before the first competition event of the Games.
The classification procedure of a review athlete includes a medical examination, functional assessment prior to the Games and review during the athlete's first event at the Games. The final decision must be made within 30 minutes of the announcement of the official results of that event.

Category C
Athletes who are new (N), have never been classified at an international Games. After the performance of their first event, the classification of a new (N) athlete may be protested by the chef de mission or team manager or the chief athletic coach of a country. This protest must be made within 30 minutes of the announcement of the official results of the event.
The classification procedure for a new athlete includes a medical examination, func-

tional assessment prior to the Games and review during the athlete's first event at the Games. The final decision must be made within 30 minutes of the announcement of the official results of the event.

Category D
If a review (R) athlete or a new (N) athlete is subsequently observed, during the Games, to show more function than they did at the time of the initial assessment during the Games, then the only people allowed to make a classification protest are members of the classification committee. The basis of the protest will be that the athlete has cheated during the classification process.
If the athlete is found to have cheated after the appropriate assessment has been undertaken, then the penalty will be disqualification from the Games. Any medals that have been won, will be returned.
NOTE:
If the Classification Committee believes that the athlete was co-operative at the times of assessment, and that the classification is an error on their behalf, then the initial classification (the classification confirmed after the first competition event) will stand for the particular Games. At the end of the Games, the classification Committee may review the athlete's classification and either allocate the category (P) or (R) for future competitions.

9. The Chairman of the IPC Athletic Classification Committee will appoint a protest panel where necessary. This protest panel should not include (where possible) people who were involved in the initial assessment.
    Prior to the Games commencing, any protest should be heard as soon as practicable for the people involved, including the athlete.
    A protest during the Games requires an immediate hearing because the results of the event will be held up, pending the result of the protest (if the particular athlete is involved in the results).

10. The athletic program will, as far as is possible, be organised such that if an athlete shifts from a more disabled class to a less disabled class, then the athlete will not miss out on his or her competition. It has been our experience, after 8 international Games that 90% of changes involve an athlete going from a more disabled class to a less disabled class. Those athletes that do the reverse, obviously will miss out on the particular event. If an athlete's classification is changed after assessing their performance during their first event, they are not entitled to medals that their performance may have merited in that event or in any other events, i.e., the result cannot be transferred to another event.

11. A fee will be charged for a protest made by the chef de mission or the team manager or the team athletic coach. The classification committee do not have to pay a fee to make a protest. The actual fee will be determined by the IPC Athletic Executive and may very from Games to Games. If the protest is successful, i.e., the decision is in favour of those people making the protest, then the fee will be refunded in full. The classification committee will have the right to dismiss any protest it considers frivolous without

holding a review of the athlete's classification. In these circumstance, the fee tended with the protest will be kept by IPC Athletics.

CHAPTER 3 – BOCCIA

14. Clarification and Protest
14.1 During a match a side may feel that the referee has overlooked an event or made an incorrect decision which effects the result of the match. At that time, the side may draw the referee's attention to this situation and seek clarification.

14.2 During the match a player/captain may request a ruling from the Head Referee, whose decision is final.

14.3 If a side feels that the referee has not acted in accordance with the rules then they must not sign the referee's result sheet. Within 30 minutes, a written protest must be presented to the Competition Secretariat for consideration and action. If no written protest is received then the result stands. (ref-17.)

19. The Captain's Responsibility
19.1 In Team and Pairs Division, each side is led by a captain. The captain should be clearly identified to the referee. The referee will act as the executive of the team and assume the following responsibilities:
(...)
–   Submitting a protest.

CHAPTER 8 – LAWN BOWLS

12. Protest procedure
12.1 When a game is in progress the Umpires decision shall be final.

12.2 All other protests come under the jurisdiction of the Sports Technical Committee who shall adhere to the WBB and the IPC rules.

CHAPTER 9 – POWERLIFTING

Powerlifting Classification Rules

5. Sport Classification Juries (Protest Committees).
1.   Sports Classification Juries shall comprise at least 2 medical persons (at least one Medical Doctor) and one technical person.

2.   The medical Officer shall in cooperation with the Powerlifting Classifier appoint a Classification Jury Chairperson.

3.   Whenever possible, a member of the Powerlifting Classification Juries should be exempted from dealing with a protest concerning a classification that he/she has been involved with him/herself. In such cases the Chief Classifier shall appoint a temporary substitute for the jury.

4.   The decision of the Sports Classification Jury is final and without appeal.

5.   The Sports Section shall keep alt protest forms filed.

6. Classification protest

1. Protest on own classification:

    Such protest must be made in writing on the official protest form and handed to the chairman of the Sports Classification Jury, not later than 6 hours after classification. The protest must be accompanied by a protest fee of $ US 100 which will be refunded, if the protest is upheld. If it is not, the protest fee remains with the Powerlifting Committee.

    Reclassification wilt take place as soon as practicable.

    The athlete shall present him/herself to the protest committee with the classification form.

2. Protest on another competitor:

    Such protest must be made in writing on the official protest form and handed to the Chairman of the Powerlifting Classification Jury and accompanied by a protest fee of $ US 100. This fee will be returned if the protest is upheld, otherwise it remains with the Powerlifting Committee. Only the chief of delegation (or his/her representative) or chairman of any of the Sports Sections can make such protests. Reclassification will take place immediately.

CHAPTER 11 – SHOOTING

1. General Rules Shooting

1.1. Basic Rules

The U.I.T. rules shall be enforced in al cases except where they are modified by these rules of the International Shooting Committee for the Disabled (hereafter called ISCD). The U.I.T. Rules are re-enforced and not inserted or restated here and the rules in this book must be read in conjunction with the U.I.T Rules.

The International Paralympic Committee (hereafter called the IPC) Rules are not inserted or restated here and the Rules in the ISCD Shooting Rulebook must be read in conjunction with the IPC Rules if applicable.

(...)

1.1.7 All protests, appeals inclusive, regarding technical matters must be handled as per U.I.T. Rules (General Technical Rules, chapter 13), however the protest fees are set in the rulebook of the ISCO. Protest fee (US $50) must be delivered by hand to the Organising Committee. Appeals must be accompanied by a fee of US $100. If the protest is upheld, the protest fee must be returned by the Organising Committee. If the protest is denied the protest fee will be retained by the ISCD. The decision of the Jury d'Appeal is final. (Model of protest form appendix G).

(...)

4. Functional classification

4.1 Basic rules

(...)

4.1.8 Protests, regarding the functional classification, must be made to the functional classification panel of the ISCD. The classification protest fee ($US 100) must be paid to the head of the protest jury of the functional classification panel. Protest fee must be returned if the protest is upheld and will be retained by the ISCD if the protest is denied.

4.1.9 A protest, made by the competitor against his/her classification, must be lodged within 30 minutes after classification.

4.1.10 A protest, made by others, which is lodged 24 hours prior to the start of the competition which results in re-classification, then the new class will be applied in that competition. When re-classification takes place during competition, the new class will be applied in the next competition.

4.1.11 The decision of the classification panel that handles the protest is final.

CHAPTER 13 – SWIMMING

SAEC-SW SWIMMING RULES
Section 2 GN General Rules

GN 4   Disqualification

(...)

GN 4.2   If a competitor does not attend a classification protest when requested they may be disqualified from further competition.

GN 7   Paralympic Games, World Championships, SAEC-SW Championships and General Rules for SAEC-SW

(...)

GN 7.4   Protests

    GN 7.4.1   Protests are possible

        (...)

        e.   against decisions of the referee; however, no protest shall be allowed against decisions of fact.

    GN 7.4.2   Protests must be submitted

        a.   to the referee for technical protests or to the head of classification for classification protests

        b.   in writing on the SAEC-SW official forms [Appendix V]. These forms wilt be made available, on site, by the Organising Committee.

        c.   by the responsible team leader only

        d.   together with a deposit of one hundred US dollars [$100] or the fee agreed upon by the SAEC-SW and the Organising Committee.

        e.   within thirty [30] minutes following the conclusion of the respective event,

        f.   in case of a classification protest prior to the first day of competition the protest shall be submitted six [6] hours after the completion of the classification of all swimmers. If this time expires between 2200 and 0800 hours, the classification protest wilt be delivered by 0800 hours on the following day.

    If conditions causing a potential protest are noted prior to the competition, a protest must be lodged before the signal to start is given,

    GN 7.4.3   All protests shall be considered by the referee and/or the head of classification. lf they reject the protest, they must state the reasons for their decision. The team leader may appeal the rejection to the Jury of Appeal whose decision shall be final. The final decision shall be in writing on the SAEC-SW official form [Appendix V]. A copy for the team leader concerned shall be distributed.

GN 7.4.4 A FCS classification protest panel at IPC competition will consist of three [3] authorised classifiers appointed by the head of classification. The protest panel must consist of at least one medical and one technical classifier who has not previously classified the swimmer within a two [2] year period.

GN 7.4.5 If a technical or classification protest is rejected, the fee shall be forfeited to SAEC-SW. If the protest is upheld the deposit shall be returned.

GN 7.4.6 For FCS classification and reclassification procedures refer to the classification manual.

GN 7.5   Jury of Appeal

GN 7.5.1 The decision of the Jury is final.

GN 7.5.2 A technical Jury will consist of the technical delegate/assistant technical delegate, technical adviser, referee and head of classification.

GN 7.5.3 A classification Jury for the FCS wilt consist of the technical delegate, head of classification and at least two authorised classifiers appointed by the head of classification. The Jury must consist of at least one medical and one technical classifier.

GN 7.5.4 A classification Jury for the visually impaired will be appointed by the Chief IBSA Ophthalmologist.

GN 7.5.5 A classification Jury for swimmers with mental handicap/intellectual disability will be conducted according to the INAS-FMH ruling.

GN 7.6   Organising Committee

(...)

GN 7.6.3 The Organising Committee, in conjunction with the appointed technical delegate and the assistant technical delegate, shall be responsible for the entire management of the contest, including the arrangement of the programme of events, arrangement for the classification of swimmers, all technical equipment and installation prior to and during competition, appointment of officials and adjudication of protests.

CHAPTER 14 – TABLE TENNIS

3. Regulations for international championships

(...)

3.13 The draw and playing system in the team and class events

(...)

Protests

All protests must be made through the Referee with the appropriate fee, set by the Organising Committee.

–   The Referee will resolve the matter on subjects within his jurisdiction.

–   The Referee will refer all matters not within his jurisdiction to the international Jury selected by the International Table Tennis Committee.

–   The protest fee will only be refunded if the protest is upheld.

- A classifier may re-classify a competitor at any time during a championships.
- If a player is re-classified after a protest or by a classifier during a championships he/she will transfer to the new class in the next event and the draw will be altered.

  Example: if a player during the team event is re-classified from class 6 to class 7 he will for the individual event be transferred to class 7 and the draw for class 7 will be altered.

- If it is deemed that a player has deliberately misled the classifiers he shall be immediately disqualified at the discretion of the Referee.

ooo

HANDBOOK PART III
SECTION IV – SUMMER SPORTS

CHAPTER 1 – WINTER SPORTS CLASSIFICATION

1. Generalities

(...)

1.4 Protests

For classification protest rules see IPC Handbook, Section 11 – Chapter 5. Special regulations:

(...)

CHAPTER 5-5.1 – RULES COMMON TO CROSS COUNTRY EVENTS

903 The jury and its duties

903.3 The Jury must ensure that the competition is organized and carried out according to the FIS and IPC rules.

903.3.1 The Jury must clarify and decide:

(...)

- whether protests should be accepted and disqualifications announced.

(...)

904 The FIS and IPC Technical Delegates (TD) and their duties

(...)

904.4 Duties after the Competition

(...)

- Subsequently they meet with the Jury and deal with any infractions and protests,

(...)

931 Disqualification, protests and appeals

(...)

933 Protests

    933.1 A protest shall be considered by a Jury or higher tribunal provided that:

        933.1.1 The protest has been delivered within the time limit specified.

        933.1.2 The protest has not been deliberately delayed to obtain an advantage.

        933.1.3 The protest is accompanied by 100 Swiss Francs, or an equivalent value.

    933.2 Protests against the admission of a competitor must be delivered in writing to the Competition Secretary before the competition begins.

    933.3 Protests against the conduct of another competitor or of an official must be delivered in writing to the Competition Secretary within one hour after the publication of the unofficial rest list.

    933.4 Protest concerning timekeeping must be delivered in writing to the Competition Secretary within one hour after the publication of the unofficial result list.

    933.5 Protests concerning erroneous and clerical errors, or contraventions of the IPC Rules only established after the competition, will be considered if sent by registered post through the competitor's National Association to the IPC Nordic SAEC (through its Chairperson) within one month of the competition. These protests must be dealt with within a month.

    933.6 If an error is proved, the corrected results must be published and the prizes redistributed.

CHAPTER 5-5.2 – PARTICULAR RULES OF RELAY COMPETITIONS

957 Protests

For protests, art. 933.

APPENDIX XVIII
SPORTS LAW OF THE PEOPLE'S REPUBLIC OF CHINA OF 29 AUGUST 1995

Law of the People's Republic of China on Physical Culture and Sports

(Adopted at the 15th Meeting of the Standing Committee of the Eighth National People's Congress on 29 August 1995, promulgated by Order No. 55 of the President of the People's Republic of China on 29 August 1995 and effective as of 1 October 1995)

Chapter I
General Provisions

Article 1

This Law is formulated in accordance with the Constitution for the purpose of developing undertakings of physical culture and sports, building up the people's physique, raising sports performance level and promoting the socialist material, ideological and cultural development.

Article 2

The State promotes development of undertakings of physical culture and sports and carries out mass sports activities to improve physical fitness of the whole nation. The work of physical culture and sports shall adhere to the principle of combining popularization with the raising of standards based on the unfolding of the national fitness campaign so as to promote coordinated development of various sports.

Article 3

The State adheres to the principle that physical culture and sports should serve economic, construction, national defense and social development. Undertakings of physical culture and sports shall be incorporated into the plan for national economy and social development.
The State promotes reform in the sports administration system. The State encourages enterprises, institutions, public organizations and citizens to run and support undertakings of physical culture and sports.

Article 4

The administrative department for physical culture and sports under the State Council shall be in charge of the work of physical culture and sports throughout the country. Other relevant departments under the State Council shall administer the work of physical culture and sports within their respective functions and powers.
The administrative departments for physical culture and sports of the local people's governments at or above the county level or the organs authorized by the people's governments at the corresponding levels shall be in charge of the work of physical culture and sports within their administrative areas.

Article 5
The State provides special guarantee to physical activities of children, juveniles and young people to improve their physical and mental health.

Article 6
The State helps ethnic minority areas develop undertakings of physical culture and sports and cultivates sport talents of ethnic minorities.

Article 7
The State promotes education and scientific research in physical culture and sports, popularizes advanced and practical achievements in sports science and technology, and develops undertakings of physical culture and sports by relying on science and technology.

Article 8
The State awards the organizations and individuals that have made contributions to the cause of physical culture and sports.

Article 9
The State encourages international exchanges in sports. In conducting international exchanges in sports, the principles of independence, equality, mutual benefit and mutual respect shall be adhered to, the State sovereignty and dignity defended and the international treaties the People's Republic of China has concluded or acceded to shall be observed.

Chapter II
Social Sports

Article 10
The State advocates citizens' participation in social sports activities so as to improve their physical and mental health. Social sports activities shall be carried out in spare time and en a voluntary, small-scale and diversified basis, following the principle of suiting such activities to the local conditions and conducting them in a scientific and civilized way.

Article 11
The State implements the National Fitness Program, carries out the Physical Training Qualification Standards and conducts monitoring of the people's physique.
The State practices a skill-grading system for social sports instructors, who shall guide social sports activities.

Article 12
The local people's governments at various levels shall create necessary conditions for citizens' participation in social sports activities, support and help the development of mass sports activities.
In urban areas the role of the residents' committees and other community organizations at the grass-roots level shall be brought into play in organizing residents to carry out sports activities.

In rural areas the role of the villagers' committees and cultural and sports organizations at the grass-roots level shall be brought into play in carrying out sports activities suitable to rural conditions.

Article 13
State organs, enterprises and institutions shall carry out various kinds of sports activities and organize athletic competitions of mass character.

Article 14
Trade unions and other public organizations shall organize sports activities in light of their own characteristics.

Article 15
The State encourages and supports the exploration, consolidation and improvement of national and folk traditional sports.

Article 16
The whole society should be concerned about and support the aged and disabled people to participate in physical activities. People's governments at various levels shall take measures to provide conditions for the aged and disabled people to participate in physical activities.

Chapter III
School Sports

Article 17
Departments of education administration and schools shall take physical culture and sports as a component part of school education and cultivate talents with all-round development in moral, intellectual and physical qualities.

Article 18
Schools must offer Physical Education and make it a subject for assessing students' academic performance.
Schools shall create conditions for organizing sports activities suitable to the special features of students who are in poor health or disabled.

Article 19
Schools must implement the National Physical Training Qualification Standards and ensure that the students have time for sports activities every day at school.

Article 20
Schools shall organize various kinds of after-class sports activities, carry out after-class athletic training and competitions, and in light of specific conditions hold a school-wide sports meet every school year.

Article 21
Schools shall, according to relevant regulations of the State, have qualified physical

education teachers and ensure that they enjoy the privileges commensurate with the nature of their work.

Article 22

Schools shall, according to the criteria set by the department of education administration under the State Council, have sports fields, sports installations and facilities and sports apparatus.
Sports fields in schools must be used for sports activities and may not be used for any other purposes.

Article 23

Schools shall institute a system of medical examination for students. The administrative departments for education, physical culture and sports and public health shall strengthen the monitoring of students' physique.

Chapter IV
Competitive Sports

Article 24

The State promotes the development of competitive sports, encourages athletes to raise their athletic performance level and achieve excellent results in sports competitions so as to win honors for the country.

Article 25

The State encourages and supports spare time athletic training to foster reserve sports talents.

Article 26

Athletes and teams that participate in major national and international sports competitions shall be selected and formed on the principle of fairness and according to qualifications Specific measures shall be formulated by the administrative department for physical culture and sports under the State Council.

Article 27

In nurturing athletes, training and management must be carried out in a strict, scientific and civilized way. Athletes shall be educated in patriotism, collectivism and socialism as well as in morality and discipline.

Article 28

The State grants preferential treatment to outstanding athletes in their employment and enrollment for schools.

Article 29

The national sports association of an individual sport shall manage the registration of athletes of such sport. A registered athlete may, in accordance with the regulations of the administrative department for physical culture and sports under the State Council, participate in relevant sports competitions and flow from one team to another.

Article 30
The State practices a skill-grading system for athletes and referees, and a grading system of professional and technical titles for coaches.

Article 31
The State practices classified administration of sports competitions at different levels. Comprehensive national games shall be administered by the administrative department for physical culture and sports under the State Council or by the administrative department for physical culture and sports under the State Council in conjunction with other relevant organizations.
National competition of an individual sport shall be administered by the national association of the said sport.
Measures for the administration of local comprehensive sports games and local individual sport competitions shall be formulated by the local people's governments.

Article 32
The State practices an examination and approval system for national sports records. National sports records shall be confirmed by the administrative department for physical culture and sports under the State Council.

Article 33
Disputes arising in competitive sports activities shall be mediated and arbitrated by sports arbitration institutions. Measures for the establishment of sports arbitration institutions and the scope of arbitration shall be prescribed separately by the State Council.

Article 34
The principle of fair competition shall be followed in sports competitions. Organizers of competitions, athletes, coaches and referees shall abide by sportsmanship, and may not practice fraud or engage in malpractice for selfish ends.
Use of banned drugs and methods is strictly prohibited in sports activities. Institutions in charge of testing banned drugs shall conduct strict examination of the banned drugs and methods. It is strictly forbidden for any organization or individual to engage in gambling activities through sports competitions.

Article 35
Symbols such as titles, emblems, flags and mascots of major sports competitions to be held within the territory of the People's Republic of China shall be protected in accordance with the relevant regulations of the State.

Chapter V
Public Sports Organizations

Article 36
The State encourages and supports public sports organizations to organize and conduct sports activities in accordance with their articles of association to promote the development of undertakings of, physical culture and sports.

Article 37
Sports federations at various levels are mass sports organizations that link and rally athletes and sports personnel and shall fully play their roles in the development of undertakings of physical culture and sports.

Article 38
The Chinese Olympic Committee, as a sports organization whose chief task is to develop and promote the Olympic movement. shall represent China to participate in international Olympic affairs.

Article 39
Public organizations of sports science are academic mass organizations of personnel engaged in sports science and technology, which shall fully play their roles in promoting the development of sports science and technology.

Article 40
The national sports association of an individual sport shall be in charge of the popularization and enhancement of such sport, and shall represent China in the corresponding international sports organization.

Chapter VI
Conditions of Guarantee

Article 41
The people's governments at or above the county level shall include sports expenditure and funds for sports capital construction in financial budgets and plans for capital construction investment at the corresponding levels and along with the development of national economy gradually increase their input to undertakings of physical culture and sports.

Article 42
The State encourages enterprises, institutions and public organizations to raise funds on their own for the development of undertakings of physical culture and sports and encourages organizations and individuals to donate to and sponsor. undertakings of physical culture and sports.

Article 43
Relevant departments of the State shall strengthen the management of sports funds. No organization or individual may misappropriate or intercept sports funds.

Article 44
The administrative departments for physical culture and sports of the local people's governments at or above the county level shall, in accordance with the relevant regulations of the State, strengthen the management of and supervision over business operations in sports activities such as body-building and competitive sports.

Article 45
The local people's governments at or above the county level shall. In accordance with the regulations of the State governing land allotment for public sports installations and facilities in urban areas, incorporate the construction of public sports installations and facilities into urban construction plans and general plans for land utilization so as to achieve rational distribution and overall arrangement.
In planning the layout of enterprises, schools, streets and residential quarters, sports installations and facilities shall be incorporated into the construction plan.
Townships, nationality townships and towns shall build and improve sports installations and facilities along with the economic development.

Article 46
Public sports installations and facilities shall be open to the public and be easily accessible to them for sports activities. Students, the aged and disabled people shall be given preferential treatment in this regard, and sports installations and facilities shall be fully utilized.
No organization or individual may seize or damage public sports installations and facilities. Where temporary occupation of sports installations and facilities is necessitated by special circumstances, it shall be subject to the approval of the administrative department for physical culture and sports and the department of construction planning and such installations and facilities shall be returned without delay. If any sports field is to be used for other purposes according to urban planning, new sports field shall, in accordance with the relevant regulations of the State, be constructed beforehand for replacement.

Article 47
Sports equipment and apparatus to be used for national and international sports competitions must be subjected to examination and approval of institutions designated by the administrative department for physical culture and sports under the State Council.

Article 48
The State promotes physical culture and sports education, establishes various types of colleges, schools, departments and specialities of physical culture and sports to nurture professional personnel in such fields as sports, training and coaching, Physical Education teaching, scientific research, management and mass sports.
The State encourages enterprises, institutions, public organizations and citizens to operate professional institutions for physical culture and sports education in accordance with law.

Chapter VII
Legal Liability

Article 49
Whoever commits fraud or other acts violating the discipline or sports rules in competitive sports shall be punished by the relevant public sports organization in accordance with the provisions of its articles of association- State functionaries who are held directly responsible shall be subject to administrative sanctions in accordance with law.

Article 50
Whoever resorts to banned drugs or methods in sports activities shall be punished by the relevant public sports organization in accordance with the provisions of its articles of association; State functionaries who are held directly responsible shall be subject to administrative sanctions in accordance with law.

Article 51
Whoever engages in gambling activities through competitive sports shall be ordered to stop the illegal practice by the public security organ in conjunction with the administrative department for physical culture and sports and shall be punished by the public security organ in accordance with the provisions of the Regulations on Administrative Penalties for Public Security. Whoever commits bribery, fraud, or the organizing of gambling shall, if the case constitutes a crime, be investigated for criminal responsibility in accordance with law.

Article 52
Whoever seizes or damages public sports installations or facilities shall be ordered by the administrative department for physical culture and sports to make corrections within a time limit and shall bear civil liability according to law. Whoever commits any of the acts specified in the preceding paragraph and violates the administration of public security shall be punished by the public security organ in accordance with the relevant provisions of the Regulations on Administrative Penalties for Public Security; if the case constitutes a crime, the offender shall be investigated for criminal responsibility according to law.

Article 53
Whoever creates disturbances or disturbs public order in sports activities shall be criticized and educated and such act shall be stopped; if the case violates the administration of public security, the offender shall be punished by the public security organ in accordance with the provisions of the Regulations on Administrative Penalties for Public Security; if the case constitutes a crime, the offender shall be investigated for criminal responsibility according to law.

Article 54
Whoever, in violation of the State financial or accounting rules, misappropriates or intercepts sports funds shall be ordered by the authorities at higher levels to return the misappropriated or intercepted funds within a time limit; the responsible persons directly in charge and other persons directly responsible for the offense shall be subject to administrative

sanctions in accordance with law; if the case constitutes a crime. The offender shall be investigated for criminal responsibility in accordance with law.

Chapter VIII
Supplementary Provisions

Article 55
Specific measures for the administration of sports activities in the Army shall be formulated by the Central Military Commission in accordance with this Law.

Article 56
This Law shall be effective from 1October 1995.

SELECT BIBLIOGRAPHY

Acland, A.F., A Sudden Outbreak of Common Sense: *Managing Conflict Through Mediation* (1990), London: Hutchinson Business

Beloff, M., Kerr, T. & Demetriou, M., *Sports Law* (1999), Oxford: Hart

Carroll, E. and Mackie, K., *International Mediation – The Art of Business Diplomacy* (1999), London: Kluwer

Cloke, K., Mediating Dangerously: *The Frontiers of Conflict Resolution* (2001), San Francisco: Jossey-Bass

Deutsch, M., & Coleman, P.T., *The Handbook of Conflict Resolution* (2000), San Francisco: Jossey-Bass

Gardiner, S., James, M., O'Leary, J., Welch, R., Blackshaw, I., Boyes, S. & Caiger, A., *Sports Law* (2001), 2nd edn, London: Cavendish Publishing

Griffith-Jones, D., *Law and the Business of Sport* (1997), London: Butterworths

Katsh, E. & Rifkin, J., *Online Dispute Resolution: Resolving Conflicts in Cyberspace* (2001), London: Jossey-Bass

Lowenheim, P., M*ediate, Don't Litigate: Resolve Disputes Quickly, Privately* (1989), New York: McGraw Hill

Mackie, K., *Commercial Dispute Resolution – An ADR Practice Guide* (2000), 2nd edn, London: Butterworths

Siekmann, R.C.R., & Soek, J., *Basic Documents of International Sports Organisations* (1998), The Hague: Kluwer Law International

Siekmann, R.C.R., Soek, J., & Bellani, A., *Doping Rules of International Sports Organisations* (1999), The Hague: TMC Asser Press

Siekmann, R.C.R., & Soek, J., *Arbitral and Disciplinary Rules of International Sports Organisations* (2001), The Hague: TMC Asser Press

TABLE OF CASES

Advisory opinion CAS 2000/C/267, Australian Olympic Committee (AOC) 'Full Body Swimsuits', 1 May 2000, Recueil des Sentences du TAS/Digest of CAS Awards 1998-2000 (Matthieu Reeb, ed., The Hague/London/New York 2002), p. 725 et seq.

Donoghue v. Stevenson [1932] AC 562.

Elmar Gundel v. FEI/CAS I Civil Court Swiss Fed Trib, 15 March 1993.

Enderby Town Football Club Ltd v. Football Association Ltd [1971] 1 All ER 215.

Greig v. Insole [1978] 3 All ER 449.

Harding v. United States Figure Skating Association [1994] 851 FSupp 1476 741 F.2d 155, at p. 159 (7th Circ. 1994).

ISL Marketing AG and The Federation Internationale de Football Association v. J.Y.Chung, Case no: D2000-0034, 3 April 2000.

Jordan Grand Prix Ltd. v. Sweeney, Case no: D2000-0233, 11 May 2000.

Lennox Lewis v. The World Boxing Council and Frank Bruno [1995] High Court (unreported).

McCaig v. Canadian Yachting Ass'n & Canadian Olympic Ass'n. Case 90-01-96624 [1996] (QB Winnipeg Centre).

McInnes v. Onslow-Fane [1978] 3 All ER 211.

Michels v. United States Olympic Committee, 16 August 1984, Seventh Circuit 741 F.2d 155; 1984 U.S. App. LEXIS 19507.

Modahl v. British Athletic Federation [2001] All ER (D) 181 (Oct).

N. v. Federation Equestre Internationale (FEI) I Civil Division Swiss Fed Trib, 31 October 1996.

NIKE Inc. v. Granger & Associates, Case no: D2000-0108, 2 May 2000.

Raducan v. International Olympic Committee II Civil Court Swiss Fed Trib, 4 December 2000.

Revie v. Football Association [1979] The Times, 19 December 1979.

Scott v. Avery [1856] 5 HL Cas 811.

UCI v. J. 7 NCB, CAS 97/176 Award of 28 August 1998, p 14.

Union des Associations Europeennes de Football v. Alliance International Media, Case no: D2000-0153, 25 April 2000.

Union Royale Belge des Societies de Football ASBL v. Bosman [1995] ECR I-4921 Case C-415/93.

INDEX

ABOUT THE AUTHOR

Ian Stewart Blackshaw is an English Solicitor of the Supreme Court and an International Sports Lawyer. A former Vice President Legal Affairs of the ISL Sports Marketing Group, Switzerland, he gained a Master's Degree in International Sports Law at the Sports Law Centre of Anglia Polytechnic University, Chelmsford, England. He is Visiting Professor at the FIFA International Sports Studies Centre at Neuchatel University, Switzerland, where he lectures on Intellectual Property, Licensing and Merchandising and also European Competition Law and Sport. He is also a member of the Arbitration and Mediation Panels of the UK Sports Dispute Resolution Panel and has recently been appointed an arbitrator at the Court of Arbitration for Sports in Lausanne, Switzerland. He has written and contributed to a number of books, including the Second Edition (2001) of '*Sports Law*' by Simon Gardiner, et al. He writes regularly on topical sports legal issues for several Journals, including the *New Law Journal, Solicitors Journal, Sports Law Bulletin* and *The International Sports Law Journal* (ISLJ) of whose Advisory Board he is a member. He is also a regular contributor to '*The Times*' of London and BBC Sport Radio programmes. He is a regular speaker at International Sports Law Conferences in the UK and abroad and also on the International Sports Law Master's Programme at the T.M.C. Asser Instituut.

Previous publications by or in cooperation with the

Asser International Sports Law Centre
T.M.C. Asser Instituut - The Hague - The Netherlands

Basic Documents of International Sports Organisations, R.C.R. Siekmann and J.W. Soek, eds. (The Hague/Boston/London, Kluwer Law International 1998)

Doping Rules of International Sports Organisations, R.C.R. Siekmann, J.W. Soek and A. Bellani, eds. (The Hague, T.M.C.Asser press 1999)

Arbitral and Disciplinary Rules of International Sports Organisations, R.C.R. Siekmann and J.W. Soek, eds. (The Hague, T.M.C.Asser press 2001)

Professional Sport in the European Union: Regulation and Re-regulation, A. Caiger and S. Gardiner, eds. (The Hague, T.M.C.Asser press 2001)